DARK COMMERCE

Dark Commerce

How a New Illicit Economy Is Threatening Our Future

Louise I. Shelley

PRINCETON UNIVERSITY PRESS

PRINCETON AND OXFORD

Copyright © 2018 by Princeton University Press

Published by Princeton University Press
41 William Street, Princeton, New Jersey 08540
6 Oxford Street, Woodstock, Oxfordshire OX20 1TR

press.princeton.edu

All Rights Reserved

Library of Congress Control Number 2018938103
ISBN 978-0-691-17018-3

British Library Cataloging-in-Publication Data is available

Editorial: Eric Crahan and Pamela Weidman
Production Editorial: Jill Harris
Jacket art and design by Will Brown
Production: Jacqueline Poirier
Copyeditor: Cynthia Buck

This book has been composed in Adobe Text Pro

Printed on acid-free paper. ∞

Printed in the United States of America

10 9 8 7 6 5 4 3 2 1

To all the TraCCCsters past and present who have done so much to combat illicit trade and to the many others around the world who do so with much courage

CONTENTS

ACKNOWLEDGMENTS

To write this book, I have been enormously helped by scholars, practitioners, businesspeople, and members of civil society. Fortunately, an increasing number of forums and conferences held in the last few years, both on illicit trade generally and on specific elements of it, have helped me understand this complex topic better.

For this research, my reading has gone beyond my usual fare in the social sciences, business and economics, history, and international relations to include a diverse literature in many fields new to me—science and public health, environmental studies, and cybercrime. I needed to expand my reading in these new fields because the scientific, public health, and environmental communities have all begun to focus on the consequences of illicit trade. Unlike the social science community, these communities do not emphasize these problems as consequences of globalization, more open borders, and the rise of international trade. Nor do they question whether the problems are getting worse as a result of regulation. They see illicit commerce through scientific analyses that measure the extinction of species and provide data on the decline of bird, animal, and fish populations, the destruction of forests and other habitats, and diverse public health indicators.[1] They observe the growth of illicit online marketplaces, such as Silk Road, through data mining and advanced analytics. All these indicators reveal that the growth of illicit activity may be having irreversible impacts on the planet and deleterious effects on human health. Their analyses were invaluable to the development of my understanding of illicit trade.

This reading was essential to my understanding of business trends, in both online marketplaces and the expanding and diverse markets for counterfeits.[2] All this reading complemented my analysis of the extensive and rich literature on black markets and the illicit global economy. The readings cited here have been essential for my analysis.[3]

A rich and important literature exists about the different components of illicit trade, starting with the pioneering work *Illicit*, by Moisés Naím, which focuses on the diverse elements of illicit trade such as drug, human, and counterfeit trafficking.[4] Numerous fine works I read focus specifically on a component of the problem—cybercrime,[5] human and drug trafficking, illicit trade in environmental products, or the economics of illicit trade.[6] Others focus on the networks responsible for illicit trade.[7] Some fascinating analyses I read for this book are even more specialized, including examinations of the drug trade in Latin America, human trafficking in China, and Nigerian organized crime.[8] Still other studies have a specific historical focus, analyzing illicit trade in pre-revolutionary France, smuggling along the US-Mexican border, and the opium trade in nineteenth-century China.[9] Many multilateral organizations, such as the United Nations, Europol, and Interpol, and research-oriented NGOs have published informative studies based on valuable on-the-ground experience.

Many insights have been obtained from fellow academics, but especially from practitioners who confront the realities of illicit trade on a daily basis. I have been fortunate that practitioners on many different continents have helped me understand the corruption, the illicit networks, and the routes that facilitate illicit trade. Many of them I have met through my six-year participation in the Global Agenda Councils of the World Economic Forum on organized crime and illicit trade, my membership in the Global Initiative against Transnational Organized Crime, and my participation in the illicit trade group of the OECD. Practitioners have pointed me to cases or directed me toward online searches of very specific terms that guided me to unusual insights. For example, with this kind of help, I gained knowledge I had lacked about law enforcers who go to the dark side in the cyberworld. Because some of the actual sources of these insights and new information need to stay anonymous, in the notes I often cite news accounts as the source.

The research for the book has taken me to distant locales. In 2015, I spent a quarter of the year on different trips to the Middle East and Asia (China, India, Malaysia, and Taiwan) made possible by my selection as an initial Andrew Carnegie Fellow by the Carnegie Corporation. This fellowship provided me with valuable time for research and writing and was extended to a full two years through the generosity of the president of George Mason University, Angel Cabrera, and the dean of the Schar School of Policy and Government, Mark Rozell. My thinking and writing evolved significantly at the Bellagio Residence of the Rockefeller Foundation, where I was in residence the month before the 2016 elections.

Traveling to the diverse regions discussed here was crucial to my analysis of illicit trade, as many of these regions are key trade hubs, for both the licit and illicit economies. I have traveled to South Africa twice to observe the rhino in its locale and hold discussions with practitioners and researchers trying to save this special, ancient creature. Moreover, I have visited hot spots of illicit trade and money laundering in France, Italy, Panama, Turkey, and the United States, where it is possible to see illicit products sold in plain view. I have also drawn on my past travels to the former Soviet Union and Latin America.

In preparation for writing, I attended many meetings addressing different aspects of illicit trade and sponsored by multilateral bodies in Europe, the United States, and the Middle East, such as the Organization for Security and Cooperation in Europe (OSCE), the Organization for Economic Cooperation and Development (OECD), the United Nations, the World Bank, the Global Agenda Council meetings of the World Economic Forum (WEF), the Global Initiative against Transnational Organized Crime, the *Financial Times*, the International Institute for Strategic Studies (IISS), NATO, Siracusa International Institute for Human Rights and Criminal Justice, and the Munich Security Forum, as well as international anti-corruption conferences in Malaysia and Panama. At many of these meetings, I have met policymakers, corporate officials specializing in countering illicit trade, and NGO officials often focused on the victims of illicit trade.

I thank the key people who have made many of these groups function well, such as David Luna and the illicit trade group of the OECD; and Adam Blackwell and Christina Bain, with whom I worked particularly closely in recent years on illicit trade within the World Economic Forum. I received invaluable and current information from the listservs and groups in which I participate, including the FININT listserv, the regular publications of the Global Initiative against Transnational Organized Crime, and the Organized Crime and Corruption Reporting Project (OCCRP). Furthermore, the members of both the Association of Certified Anti-Money Laundering Specialists (ACAMS) and the Anti-Corruption Advocacy Group have helped me understand so many different complex financial issues connected to illicit trade, corruption, and money laundering.

I have many people to thank more specifically for reading portions of the manuscript, including Robert Rotberg and Laurence Cockcroft, who helped me improve my writing on corruption and illicit trade. John M. Sellar, Frances Beinecke, and Raisa Scriabine read and helped me improve my thinking and writing on the book's environmental analysis; John had the perseverance to work through the whole manuscript, and Raisa read much of it. Solvej Krause read and provided fine suggestions for the introduction. Michael Loughnane helped me with the business side of illicit trade and operations in the cyberworld. Guadalupe Correa-Cabrera and my long-serving and invaluable graduate assistant, Camilo Pardo, were especially helpful in improving my Latin American perspective. Chris Corpora read parts on the development of illicit trade. Kasey Kinnard of TraCCC was invaluable in improving the analysis of the rhino horn trade. Dipanwita Das, my daughter-in-law, provided me with valuable insights on the history of trade in India. My partner, Richard Isaacson, read and reread my analysis, helping me to improve my logic and my writing. He has been with me every step of the way!

All the members of the Terrorism, Transnational Crime, and Corruption Center (TraCCC), which I direct, have been invaluable in helping me in so many areas. We have traveled together around the world, and the seminars we have held have not only enriched my thinking but provided a warm and supportive environment in which to learn about so many aspects of illicit trade. I want to thank all who have been recent members of this community at George Mason University, and especially Judy Deane, the deputy director.

I thank my extremely helpful editor, Eric Crahan, who has been with me since the start of the process, encouraging me to make this a fine work. Cynthia Buck did an excellent job of copyediting the manuscript. I also want to thank two anonymous reviewers of the final manuscript who helped me improve the final product.

DARK COMMERCE

Introduction

THE FUNDAMENTAL TRANSFORMATION OF ILLICIT TRADE

Since ancient times in the Middle East, traders—both licit and illicit—have sold tangible goods. Currencies and contracts developed with commerce, as traders needed to pay for goods.[1] Traders had personal relationships with their fellow merchants. Grave robbers of antiquity knew to whom to take their ill-gotten gains, just as did the thieves who disposed of stolen personal property through fences in ancient Mesopotamia.

Yet after four thousand years, technology changed the fundamentals of trade, in both the legitimate and illegal economies, with the global spread of the internet, cell phones, and the digitization of economies. Most observers focus on the transformation of legal trade as people shop online, pay bills, and use credit cards through their computers and cell phones. This new phenomenon has displaced local markets in many parts of the world. No longer are markets, downtowns, or malls functioning as visible centers of daily life—they are being replaced by the impersonal online marketplaces of the new technology. The impact on the economy, on employment, and on all our lives has been profound. But meanwhile, highly significant changes have come to illicit commerce as well.

In the last three decades, the most advanced forms of illicit trade have broken with all historical precedents. Old forms of illicit trade persist, but the newest forms of illicit trade, tied to computers and social media, operate as if on steroids. Illicit trade is developing rapidly in all sectors. No area of this trade has diminished in its volume or its geographic reach, because many profit from this dark commerce, not just those associated with traditional crime groups.

In the past, illicit traders produced and benefited from counterfeit currency; now they depend on illicit financial flows, illegally earned or transferred money, and cryptocurrencies, easily acquired through online purchases.[2]

In this new world of illicit commerce, trade is impersonal and anonymized, and vast profits are made in relatively short periods, with limited accountability to sellers, intermediaries, and purchasers. Billions use the internet and communicate through encrypted software; WhatsApp alone had 1.5 billion active users monthly at the end of 2017.[3] New technology, communications, and globalization fuel the exponential growth of many of the most dangerous forms of illegal trade—the massive sales of narcotics and child pornography online, the escalation of sex trafficking through web and social media–based advertisements, and the sale of endangered species, for which revenues now total in the hundreds of millions of dollars.[4]

In the cyberworld—particularly in its most hidden part, the Dark Web (entered only through special anonymizing software such as Tor)—payments are no longer made in state-backed currencies. Instead, customers pay for their purchases in a plethora of new anonymized cryptocurrencies, of which Bitcoin is the best known. Moreover, in this illicit world, the very commodities have changed, and many can no longer be touched or exchanged by human hands. Rather, many of the most pernicious illicit traders buy commodities based only on algorithms, such as malware, Trojans, botnets, ransomware (which denies users access to their data), and spam, marketed by malicious suppliers in both the developing and developed worlds.[5] Franchises and rentals of these products are also available in the Dark Net, a computer network with restricted access that is used chiefly for illegal peer-to-peer file sharing.[6]

These virtual products have greatly harmed ordinary citizens, stealing their identities, passwords, and money out of their bank accounts. The losses tied to these intangible goods now total vast sums. Estimated losses to ransomware alone were estimated to total $5 billion in 2017, and $15.4 billion was lost to identity theft in 2014 as individuals and, especially, businesses and institutions paid large sums to recover access to crippled computer systems in private homes, hospitals, and other critical locales.[7]

The changes in crime wrought by new technology are most evident in the G-7 countries, the largest economies in the world, but they are by no means confined to these seven countries: investigations of computer-facilitated crime have identified their impact in the vast preponderance of the world's countries. In one recent online ransom attack, victims were identified in 189 countries.[8] The United States has been particularly hard hit as online trade via the new technology has contributed to the exponential growth in opioid-related deaths, the theft of inventions and new products needed to drive economic growth, and the extensive distribution of malware that undermines computer systems.

This transformation in technology was unanticipated. No one predicted the reach of the World Wide Web, the billions of users of social media and encrypted telecommunications, the rise of alternative payment systems, or the massive exploitation of the Dark Web (the part of the World Wide Web that is only accessible by means of special software, allowing users and website operators to remain anonymous or untraceable).

The spread of the internet was originally interpreted almost entirely as a force for good. The assumption that greater connectivity and greater access to information would lead to more prosperity and greater intercultural understanding was rarely questioned and is still implicit in the way we continue to think about digital transformations. Not enough serious attention is given to the dark sides of the globalized digital economy, one part of which is analyzed in this book.

The centrality of the internet to crime commission was not considered nearly two decades ago when the UN General Assembly, in 2000, adopted the United Nations Convention against Transnational

Organized Crime.[9] The policymakers did not prepare for the massive changes in illicit activity that would accompany the new technological revolution. Nor did the architects of the framework against global international crime anticipate the increasing power and wealth of nonstate actors, criminals, terrorists, and even multinational technology corporations, all of whom would challenge the power of the states that developed and endorsed this convention.[10] Neither did they foresee the increasing globalization of corruption, facilitated by vast illicit financial flows, offshore owners, and the anonymous shell companies to which illicit trade is intimately tied.[11]

In just a few years, this threatening new world has grown significantly, and its trajectory is only upward.[12] Since the Dark Web and encryption have increased anonymity and technology companies control access to their own databases, it is hard to identify the malicious actors behind the diverse forms of dark commerce. Perpetrators often operate out of countries, such as Ukraine, that have little law enforcement capability to pursue the online criminals who invade the accounts of individuals around the world and commit financial crime on a global scale.[13] Multinational law enforcement operations to disrupt these networks often do not successfully remove all the key nodes. A key person in a massive criminal network dubbed "Avalanche" (discussed in chapter 5) was arrested in Poltava, in central Ukraine, but was shortly released from confinement by an official in Ukraine's highly corrupt legal system and has not been seen since.[14]

In this new world of technologically facilitated crime, such cases reflect the hard reality that even lengthy and expensive law enforcement operations often have only short-term success in taking down cybercriminals trading in illicit goods. And when the criminals are removed, the pernicious websites or platforms are shortly replaced by even more powerful criminal networks. The Dark Web site Silk Road (discussed in chapter 3) processed $1.2 billion in transactions in a little over two years, netting its owner $80 million.[15] Taken down in 2013 after an intensive US law enforcement effort, it was rapidly supplanted by Silk Road 2.0 and its successors, which have engaged in even larger-scale illegal trade.

The greatest rates of growth in illicit trade, outside of the cyber arena, are in environmental crime.[16] A growing global population is increasingly seeking the world's limited resources. Enhanced demand results in increased prices and shortages, which often contribute to the growth of illegal and black markets that deplete the planet's wild-life, timber, and fish. The illicit rhino trade (discussed in chapter 4) is just one example of an iconic species that is rapidly being driven to extinction through the nefarious human hand. Rhino poaching can be quantified and is highly publicized, but many other species are being exterminated without much notice. In fact, the illicit trade in diverse species is contributing significantly to the world's sixth great extinction. We now face *dysfunctional selection,* a term I coined to explain the non-evolutionary change that results in the survival of the less fit. Instead of the process described by Darwin that has guided the evolution of human life for past six million years, the natural selection of the strongest members of a species, we are seeing the survival of the less robust, like the tuskless elephant. This elephant—an evolutionary response to a species subject to excessive poaching to obtain ivory—is a less desirable mate for female elephants.[17]

At present, the global community is regulating the sale not only of flora and fauna but fishing, timber logging, carbon emissions from automobiles, and even carbon markets. Criminals have always profited by getting involved in time-sensitive sectors. The Japanese *Yakuza* controlled ports where fish were unloaded, the Mafia in New York controlled the Fulton Fish Market, and La Cosa Nostra in Italy, like their counterparts in New York, ran garbage collection.[18] These criminal enterprises are able to maximize profits because perishable products need to be transported to market expeditiously and garbage needs to be removed before it smells and rats arrive. But now, with the ever-expanding global population—it has nearly doubled since 1970, to approximately 7.4 billion—we are living on a *time-sensitive planet.*[19] Therefore, trade in the commodities needed for human survival—protected trees, fish, and wildlife—is the fastest-growing form of illicit trade.[20]

Future generations will live on a planet with not only less biodiversity but also fewer of the protein sources needed for human life. Moreover, the destruction of once-great rainforests and other protected woodlands has a significant impact on global warming. Therefore, these forms of illicit trade are resulting in a planet that will be less sustainable in the future.

Growing illicit trade is linked to many other elements needed for human survival. The absence of adequate water supplies in many developing countries, particularly in megacities, is leading to the rise of illicit entrepreneurs, known as *water mafias*, who exploit the need for water for survival.[21] The impacts of illicit trade in water rights can be even more pernicious than water mafias, as happened in Syria before the Arab Spring, discussed in chapter 3. The impact of climate change and extreme drought, exacerbated by the illicit trade in riparian rights, drove a massive rural-to-urban migration. The resulting instability contributed to the Arab Spring. Other regions of the world will face many more *climate refugees* in the future. Therefore, climate change has a domino effect in that it sets off many of the other forms of dark commerce discussed in this book.

Poorly regulated carbon markets, created in Europe to trade carbon emission allowances to encourage countries and companies to limit their carbon dioxide (CO_2) emissions, provided a windfall for a diverse group of illicit perpetrators, including bankers, traders, organized criminals, and terrorists, and led to losses of 5 billion euros for the European Union—the costliest crime its leading members had ever suffered. Consequently, the illicit traders of the world now quickly detect and exploit the constantly shifting financial opportunities arising from our resource-challenged planet, whereas those who are responsible for governance often fail to consider the need to crime-proof the new innovative mechanisms they have designed to counter the threats to the planet created by climate change.[22] In some contexts, corrupt officials intentionally fail to regulate the activities of water mafias because they receive payoffs from those providing illegal services.

For the average consumer, it is often difficult to accurately evaluate whether a product has been sourced ethically, as supply chain transparency in many sectors is still lacking. But by prioritizing affordable products that can be delivered in only a few days over products with known ethical provenance, consumers become willful participants in the most harmful elements of the illicit economy. Ignorance, willful blindness, and/or corruption go far in explaining the current accelerating assault on the environment by illicit actors. Failing to anticipate and counter such threats makes the planet less inhabitable and undermines the future viability of life on earth.

Defining the Problem

What is *illicit trade*? It is a new term that the international community is now trying to define, since not knowing what it is has been exacerbating our efforts to combat the problem.

Illegal trade, which is clearly defined, is not the same as illicit trade, which is broader. Criminal or illegal trade is addressed by the UN Convention against Transnational Organized Crime and refers to criminalized acts, such as drug, human, and arms trafficking. Law enforcement is ready to allocate resources to address these threats to the community, but much less ready to respond to less clearly harmful and legally defined forms of illicit trade. A police commander tasked with investigating human or drug trafficking or combating terrorism is hesitant to allocate resources to proactively seek intelligence about sellers of counterfeit Guccis and Rolexes or cigarette smugglers and bring them to justice. Moreover, policing illicit trade is often more complicated, since its illegal nature is not readily apparent. A recently unearthed and smuggled ancient coin, for instance, is part of illicit trade. But if a similar coin entered the system of international commerce before 1970, then its sale is legal.[23] With such gray areas of commerce, it is hardly surprising that many possible cases of illicit trade are not enforcement priorities, as enforcers and prosecutors far too often see things as being either black or white. The effects of illicit trade—the way in which its tentacles reach throughout society and government, bringing corruption, violence, and exploitation—are often underappreciated or unseen by the very people who are best placed to respond.

Yet the elements of illicit trade are all around us. We encounter them on our computers connected to the internet, or as inhabitants of rural communities who are offered counterfeits, often harmful ones, at the local markets where we shop. To date there is no commonly accepted definition of the phenomenon, but in international policy circles and in the media the term "illicit trade" is being used with increasing frequency. The *Financial Times* and *The Economist* convened meetings on illicit trade, *The Economist* runs the Illicit Trade Environment Index and the Organization for Economic Cooperation and Development (OECD) has a task force on the topic. Since 2012, the World Customs Organization (WCO) has been publishing its *Illicit Trade Report*, which it describes as a new paradigm, as it never previously publicized its efforts to fight cross-border crime.[24]

How do we define the phenomenon of illicit trade in a way that adequately explains the diverse trade in many prohibited items in very different environments? Illicit trade was initially, but inadequately, defined almost two decades ago as "a cross-border commercial activity for the provision of goods and services that violates the laws of the exporting and/or importing country."[25] Yet not all illicit trade crosses borders. The United Nations Protocol to Prevent, Suppress, and Punish Trafficking in Persons Especially Women and Children specifically states that individuals do not need to be brought across borders to be victims of this crime. Such a definition is needed because the majority of sexually exploited girls in the United States are American citizens, and the same holds true of trafficking victims in India, the majority of whom are citizens. Apart from its limitations, this dry and restrictive definition does not capture a phenomenon that is having such major impacts across the planet.

Therefore, the OECD in 2016 provided a more ample definition based on the consequences of illicit commerce: "Illicit trade involves goods & services that are deemed illegal as they threaten communities and society as a whole. Illicit trade has a negative impact on economic stability, social welfare, public health, public safety & our environment."[26] Illicit trade can be conducted in the real world, in the virtual world, or in a hybrid of the two where stolen property is marketed on websites such as Amazon and eBay.

Within this very broad framework are diverse categories of trade in goods and services whose sale is often facilitated by corruption.

Corruption is most often associated with the criminalized drug trade, yet corruption is the grease used to make all forms of illicit trade operate smoothly, even in cyberspace, as we will see in chapter 3. Illicit trade could not be carried out without both high-level and lower-level forms of corruption, and transnational corruption has facilitated its global growth.

There are different submarkets of illicit trade, ranging from the most illegal—where states invest most of their law enforcement resources—to the ancient crime of trade in stolen goods, which often commands insufficient attention.[27] One researcher suggests that there are two additional marketplaces. One is the "irregular sale of regulated commodities, such as antiquities, or fauna and flora, goods that infringe upon intellectual property rights, and goods that do not conform to applicable local standards."[28] As we discuss in chapters 2 and 3, trade regulation in these goods emerged as a result of scientific evidence and concerns over the survival of cultural heritage and of the planet's diverse species. This marketplace, in which natural resources such as timber, minerals, and gold are traded illicitly, is very correlated with high-level corruption.

The other marketplace is the one in which states tax items of mass consumption.[29] Illicit trade in these consumer items is costly for states, as smugglers' evasion of local excise taxes costs nations billions in needed tax revenue.[30] The smuggling of cigarettes, tobacco, and alcohol has been at the heart of contraband smuggling for several centuries, as we see in chapter 1.

The book discusses all types of illicit marketplaces operating in the real and virtual worlds and expands significantly on the regulated commodities to include the trade in a vast range of products, from counterfeit sneakers to pharmaceuticals and pesticides, that undermines the sustainability of life and the planet and causes much greater harm than just financial losses to the holders of patents or copyrights.[31]

Illicit traders are not specialized; they seize targets of opportunity and use existing trade routes to maximum advantage. Many illicit products go through the same pipelines used for legal products and are sold by the same vendors.[32] This is the concept of *convergence*, and it applies in the virtual world as well as the real one: many Dark Net sites sell drugs, arms, and malware on the same platform.[33] Yet the legal response to illicit traders, who are generalists, is often stove-piped as specialized units assigned to combat them focus only on drugs, people, or wildlife, illustrating how bureaucratic structures can hamper the effective fight against illicit trade.

Illicit commerce often intersects with the licit economy. Counterfeit cds and contraband cigarettes are sold in European open-air markets along with fruits and vegetables. Trafficked and smuggled people, counterfeit electronics, cigarettes, and illicit drugs may all travel the same routes. Coming into Europe from the East, they traverse Dubai, the Black Sea, and the Balkans before arriving in Naples, a port controlled by the Camorra, an important Italian organized crime group.[34] Entry of similar commodities into the United States, for instance, often follows trade routes from the South, including those that traverse Central America, Mexico, and the southern US border. The siloed response of many countries and international agencies to each form of illicit trade helps explain the global incapacity to combat illicit trade effectively.

Illicit trade's intersection with the legitimate economy explains why it is not necessarily an element of the *informal economy*. Corporations may be better able to compete in a highly competitive global economy when they engage in or facilitate illicit trade.[35] Therefore, manufacturers, extractive industries, maritime, transport, fishing, and timber companies, as well as banks, real estate companies, and financial institutions, have all participated in illicit trade, as subsequent case studies confirm.

The participation of legitimate companies in the illicit economy ensures that much of illicit trade is not confined to black markets. Some of its products, such as smuggled antiquities, are even sold in high-end stores and auction houses. Nor is illicit trade necessarily part of the shadow economy, defined as "the part of an economy involving goods and services which are paid for in cash, and therefore not declared for tax."[36] Taxes are paid on some illicit goods, such as purchased antiquities, the profits made by banks from laundering drug profits, and the sale of Volkswagens whose emission systems have been deliberately rigged to evade detection.[37] The illicit economy also is not confined to cash but involves many diverse payment systems, such as wire transfers, cryptocurrencies, and prepaid credit cards. Often it is the commodity, rather than the payment, that is illicit.

Trade abuse can help mask kleptocratic theft. Often no trade occurs, or a minimal trade transaction is disguised as a much larger one, to justify the movement of large funds. This phenomenon is referred to as *trade-based money laundering*.[38] The global trading system is often misused to facilitate large-scale corruption as well as criminal misconduct.[39]

Organization of the Book

Illicit trade is a lucrative business, but few analysts have focused on its dynamics and logic. They may provide statistics that estimate its revenues, but far too few examine the mechanics of this complex commerce. Historians of slavery analyze the business of the slave trade, drug specialists focus primarily on the mechanics of drug trafficking, and tech analysts look at the new enterprises of the masterminds of cybercrime. This book suggests that, because so much illicit trade now converges, there are common business practices and challenges of illicit commerce that distinguish it from its legitimate counterpart, as discussed in chapter 5.

The first part of the book provides the historical context to contemporary illicit trade. Chapter 1 traces the history of illicit commerce from its documented origins in antiquity more than four thousand years ago through the Age of Revolutions in the late eighteenth century. Commerce supported the growth of empires, yet even in ancient times officials expressed concern over the smuggling of goods. Piracy evolved over time, and some pirates worked for themselves as well as the state, presaging the cyber-privateers of the contemporary period.

Chapter 2 examines the emerging complexity and diversity of illicit trade after the age of revolutions and through the end of the Cold War period. The major components of contemporary illegal trade—drugs, arms, and trafficked people—became significant only in the last two centuries. Before this time, the most valued trade commodity, textiles, was central to illicit trade.

Chapter 3 analyzes illicit trade in the post–Cold War era, when computing and expanded personal telecommunications enabled the paradigm shift in illicit trade. The rise in conflicts during this period has been a major driver of growth as drugs, people, and natural resources are traded for the arms needed to sustain wars.

Chapter 4 provides a case study of the exponential growth of the illicit rhino horn trade. This analysis is included not just because it concerns a charismatic animal, but also because the dynamics of the trade in its horns can be tracked with some precision, which is not possible for almost any other form of illicit trade.

Chapter 5 analyzes evolving business models of illicit trade in response to technological change. Illicit trade, like licit trade, operates with business logic: it seeks targets of opportunity, strategic alliances, and forms of trade with worthwhile profit margins. Historical and cultural traditions shape trade practices in both legal and illegal commodities.

Chapters 6 and 7 reveal that illicit trade has grown because it has many beneficiaries—there are many winners as well as losers. It takes much more than organized crime to do this much harm to the planet and to human life. Behind this dark commerce are states, powerful politicians, businesspeople, and corrupt officials at all levels of government. Many of its facilitators are employed by the legitimate economy as lawyers, accountants, bankers, chemists, and members of the tech community, all of whom help illicit trade operate on a global scale.

The book concludes by looking at the future of illicit trade. This trade exists for diverse reasons, and thus there is no one solution, and a response based exclusively on law enforcement and legal action is not sufficient. Can we change the present trajectory of illicit trade as it targets the very resources that we need to sustain life on the planet? The vast majority of the countries of the planet signed the Paris Climate Agreement, agreeing to controls that would limit carbon emissions and thereby restrict the extent of climate change.

Is the global community also ready to work together to address illicit trade and the factors that are contributing to its growth?

Such change requires more than modifying regulations on trade: we must also control the world's population and the demands that its inhabitants make on the planet. We must rethink the financial system to provide more transparency, restructure the corporate world to focus on accountability, and implement strong anti-corruption measures to combat the facilitators of illicit trade. We need to find ways to control pernicious nonstate actors who have been major beneficiaries of globalized trade. Are there areas of illicit trade that we should either decriminalize or regulate less in order to concentrate on the most severe threats to the global community?

Much of our new technology has been developed, and is owned and maintained, by the private sector. Therefore, the regulation of cyberspace is not exclusively in the hands of government but often requires the cooperation of the private sector, which is inherently more interested in profit than in governance. This conflict of interest makes it more difficult to reduce illicit trade, unless fruitful public-private partnerships prevail and states can regulate the tech giants. The absence of harmonized policies across states, a consequence of divergent political policies, will limit the ability of governments to control the growth of illicit commerce.

The challenges are great and the windows of opportunity to reverse the planet's present dangerous trajectory are closing. We will explore the possibility that useful technical solutions are available; using some of the same technology that is currently fueling the expansion of illicit trade, these technical fixes could help us address many of the problems identified here. It remains to be seen how much they could help. Will we use such solutions to change our current trajectory in time? Or are we are seeing another harmful force on the planet that makes Stephen Hawking's prediction ever more likely—that the earth's inhabitants must find other worlds to inhabit in the next one hundred years?[40]

1

Illicit Trade

PAST AS PROLOGUE

Commerce developed as human beings began to trade goods for their survival as well as luxury items to enhance their lives. Ancient writing developed to record and regulate commerce.[1] Trade routes developed by land and sea to move valuable cargoes. Societies that assumed a leading role in commerce could amass significant wealth.

Illicit commerce emerged early in human history as trade provided opportunities for criminal as well as legal enrichment. The growth of commerce created new moneymaking opportunities, for both illegitimate and legitimate participants in trade. The new crimes that emerged, such as thievery, smuggling, and fencing, were outlawed nearly four thousand years ago in Mesopotamia.[2] Several centuries later, in the thirteenth century BC, piracy in the Aegean and Mediterranean Seas was reported: the "Sea Peoples" were attacking ships laden with commercial cargo.[3]

The Evolution of Fencing

One of the world's earliest legal documents, the Code of Hammurabi, dates to approximately 1754 BC and was found by French archaeologists over a century ago. The Code is inscribed on a pillar now prominently displayed in a place of honor at the Louvre Museum in Paris and includes the following provision[4]:

> If a free person buys or receives in pawn anything from another free person who is a minor, or from a free person's slave, without a contract signed by witnesses, that person is a fence and shall be executed.[5]

The harsh laws of Hammurabi's Code governed Babylonian life. Much more limited than our legal codices today, this short document of 282 laws had many provisions dealing with property relations. This is hardly surprising, as the emergence of written language in the Middle East was strongly motivated by the need to record trade, preserve contracts, and regulate property relations.

From archaeological excavations of this period, we know that inhabitants of Mesopotamia had valuable household items, jewelry, and other items worth stealing.[6] Therefore, the absolute rulers of the time needed to protect not only their citizens' welfare but also their property.

Fences are not executed today as in ancient Mesopotamia, but this enduring "profession" is still with us. Fast-forward to Western popular culture. The great Bertolt Brecht and Kurt Weill song "Mack the Knife" has become one of the most popular ballads of the twentieth century, popularized by singers in many genres—The Doors, Sting, Louis Armstrong, Ella Fitzgerald, Frank Sinatra, Bobby Darin.[7] Yet most listeners have no idea who the sinister Mack is.

Mack was the protagonist of *The Threepenny Opera*, set in the sordid criminal world of 1920s Germany. Mack, a charismatic professional thief, cavorts with the fences who allow him to capitalize on what he has stolen. Although fences existed in pre–World War II Germany, Brecht, like so many writers before him, had mined history to find inspiration. In his earlier incarnation, Mack was Macheath, the dashing rogue of John Gay's *Beggar's Opera*, set in early-eighteenth-century London, the heyday of the fence at a time when the city was rife with crime.[8] Fencing was an equal employment profession in the early 1700s: Moll, the heroine of the early great novel *Moll Flanders* by the famous author Daniel Defoe, fences the goods she steals to her "Governess." The problem of fencing crops up in many diverse locales and has never disappeared.

Fences are also part of our contemporary life. When I was working on my doctorate in pre-gentrified Philadelphia, one of my fellow graduate students was doing what in social science jargon is called "participant observation." In other words, my late colleague Carl Klockars spent fifteen months associating with the professional fence "Vincent Swaggi," who ran his "business" for thirty years in Philadelphia.[9] Although Vincent had a constant flow of goods, he was never rich because his business could not grow significantly.

But life changed for fences with the advent of e-commerce. The virtual world, as we will repeatedly see, has facilitated the growth of illicit trade to unprecedented levels. It has transformed the world's oldest professions—fencing and prostitution—in ways never seen before. Unfortunately for him, Vincent Swaggi did not live to see the rise of e-fencing (electronic fencing), which enabled sales of stolen property to grow exponentially.

Online commerce started, and almost immediately the alarm bells sounded—the fencing of stolen property had already moved to the internet, where the risk of detection was low and profits were high. By 2007, analyses revealed that "fencers who use the Internet to market their goods can get 70 to 80 cents on the dollar compared to what the merchandise sells for at retail, whereas street sellers tend to receive only 30 cents on the dollar. . . . Additionally, there is no easy way for law enforcement to find the identity of an online seller or follow that person to locate and identify the supplier."[10]

Online fencing was a great benefit to thieves. In the past, many fences were selling property they had stolen from private individuals, like Macheath after his cohorts delivered their catch of the day to London fences, or Vincent Swaggi after receiving goods from local burglars and robbers. But with the ability to expand the selling of stolen goods via the internet, commercial enterprises became even greater targets of professional thieves. In 2016, the US Organized Crime Survey of the National Retail Federation revealed that 58 percent of the surveyed retailers had identified or recovered stolen goods online.[11]

The Smirnovs of Vancouver, Canada, epitomize the transition to online fencing. Ludmilla and Evgeni Smirnov are not colorful figures like Macheath and his associates, nor are they embedded in their community like Vincent Swaggi. The numerous victims of the Smirnovs' thefts illustrate the proliferation of the online fencing of retail goods. To sell on a large scale, they had to acquire on a grand scale. They marketed on eBay what was stolen on their command from major supermarket chains in Vancouver, Portland, Oregon, and other locales along the Pacific Coast of the United States and Canada. Operating on eBay under the names "Crestsmile" and "Vipsmile," they specialized in the teeth whitener trade, but their stolen property also included hair growth treatments, Alli diet pills, and airbags for cars. Their target market was eastern Europe and Russia, where the internet is full of websites lauding the benefits of Crestsmile.[12] Making $70,000 to $140,000 monthly in online sales of stolen goods, they rapidly acquired the attributes of wealth—a Lexus and two properties in Vancouver—all purchased with no declared income. Yet they were leaving a trace on the internet. From "March 2010 to April 2012, the couple conducted 27,750 separate sale transactions," a level of trade that was not possible without the facilitation of computers.[13] This was Macheath and Swaggi on steroids.

The unraveling of this fencing operation, despite its virtual dimension, was the result of old-fashioned police work. When supermarkets, facing significant losses, focused their security operations on large-scale shoplifters of dental products, the Smirnovs in their Lexus were caught in a handoff of these stolen goods.

The end of the Smirnovs' online fencing operation is not unique. In many cases, illicit trade in the virtual world intersects with the real world. This permits the dismantling of criminals' online activities that would otherwise be hard to penetrate because of the anonymity offered by the cyberworld.

The Origins of Illicit Trade in Antiquity

As commerce developed, the disposal of stolen goods was only one of many problems associated with illicit trade. With the rise of counterfeit goods and currency as well as smuggling and attacks on cargo transport, early governments needed to ensure that trade products were authentic, that the currency paying for them was real, and that commerce safely reached its destination.[14]

SMUGGLING

An early mention of smuggling was found in the ninth- to seventh-century BC letters of the archive of a governor of Nippur in the Assyrian Empire. Established in the second millennium BC, this empire stretched from the Levant on the west to the Persian Gulf in the east. The letters in the Nuppur governor's archives reveal that smugglers brought iron from Anatolia outside the state-controlled monopoly.[15] Smugglers were present on the Assyrian border, and special roads were utilized by those moving contraband.[16] These archival records reveal that, almost three thousand years ago, the government of a major empire was seeking to regulate trade and to establish monopolies, pricing, and access to goods, and that states were already monitoring smuggling groups and the routes they used to evade controls.

COUNTERFEITS: GOODS AND CURRENCY

The governments of ancient Greece and Rome faced other serious challenges to legitimate trade. Efforts to authenticate goods by means of trademarks was well established in ancient Rome, as the state needed to certify its products for sale. A 2016 exhibition in the wonderfully preserved Trajan Market in the Imperial Forum in Rome documents the diversity of trademarks used on clay and glass vessels to guarantee their authenticity.[17] They also certified pharmaceuticals to ensure that individuals consumed only drugs that met standards.

Importation of counterfeits dates back at least two millennia. The great naturalist and historian Pliny the Elder, who lived from AD 23 to 79, said, "Such is the audacity of man, that he hath learned to counterfeit Nature, yea, and is so bold as to challenge her in her work."[18] This articulate statement is a comment not just on the increasing craftsmanship of artisans but on an actual problem: the importation of counterfeit minerals and stones from India, including beryl and opals.[19]

The sale of counterfeit products was not just a problem in the Western world. "In the Aztec Empire some dishonest dealers sold counterfeit cacao beans. Honest sellers divided beans into piles according to their origin. But the counterfeiters used artificial coloring to sell inferior beans or even disguised worthless amaranth dough or avocado seeds with cacao hulls."[20]

Counterfeit currency in trade was even more pervasive and widespread than fake goods. Counterfeit coinage has been documented from very early in ancient Greek history, dating back to 550 to 600 BC.[21] Counterfeit coins have been found at shrines of deities and in excavations of markets, and they have been identified in treasury records. Already in the fourth century BC, a significant number of counterfeit silver coins were in circulation in Athens, prompting the government to respond with legislation to address their pervasiveness. Many of these counterfeit silver coins came from Syria, which appears to have been a production center, but illicit coinage also came from a much larger region, some of it originating from Arabia, Palestine, and even Persia.[22] This suggests the broad geography of the international trade of illicit coinage and its impact on the Greek economy. Penalties for engaging in such activity were severe. According to ancient Greek regulations, individuals could be executed for engaging in counterfeiting, and those tasked with properly analyzing and identifying counterfeit coinage could be whipped fifty lashes for failing to detect it.[23]

In 375 BC, the ancient Greeks in Athens developed a novel legal solution to deal with the counterfeit coinage. Seized counterfeits were not destroyed but rather, according to the law, consecrated to the gods and placed under the care of the Mother of the Gods.[24] There they were secured and could not be reused.[25] This was a clever method to get counterfeits out of circulation, but why would a god prefer counterfeits to real coinage?

The experiences of the ancient Greeks with counterfeit currency were far from unique. The early currencies of Chinese civilization—which had coinage for millennia before it developed paper currency—were illegally reproduced by private citizens in different eras; fakes have been documented in copper, iron, and paper. Counterfeit money was so extensive that an entire treatise was written on the subject.[26]

THE INTEGRITY OF TRADE

Scientific advances have contributed to the regulation of trade. The first legendary example dates to ancient Greece. One of the early principles of science was discovered in the third century BC by the great scientist Archimedes, who resided in Syracuse in eastern Sicily. To respond to a royal request to determine whether a crown produced as a tribute to the gods actually consisted of the quantity of gold provided to the craftsman, Archimedes needed to develop an accurate method of measurement to determine if the goldsmith was duplicitous. We cannot be certain whether, as legend has it, he ran around naked shouting, "Eureka, I found it!," but he did discover the principle of buoyancy.[27] According to that principle, any "body completely or partially submerged in a fluid (gas or liquid) at rest is acted upon by an upward, or buoyant, force the magnitude of which is equal to the weight of the fluid displaced by the body."[28] Measuring the amount of water displaced by the crown and comparing it to the amount of gold provided to the craftsman by the king, Archimedes discovered that the king had been cheated. An effort to determine product reliability thus led to one of the world's early great scientific discoveries.

THE SECURITY OF TRANSPORT

For trade, a key element of Mediterranean, Middle Eastern, and Chinese civilizations, to thrive, goods needed to be safely transported from source to destination. This is what we now refer to as the "supply chain." Goods were transported in ancient times by sea and across land. The raiding of caravans and piracy—the attacking of vessels at sea—have been recorded for millennia. The *Odyssey*, thought to have been written between 750 and 700 BC, contains the first recorded literary references to piracy, which that work does not view in neutral terms. Nestor says in the Homeric tale: "O Stranger who are you? . . . Are you traveling for trade or are you just roaming around like pirates."[29] This line, which indicates that piracy was considered the antithesis of trade, is one of many recurring references to piracy in the work of Homer, to whom the element of plunder seems to have been central.[30]

The pirates were taking not only goods but also human beings, then viewed as property. The captives were sold into slavery, generating significant revenues for the pirates. Although slavery was a natural element of life according to Aristotle, not all trading that procured slaves was viewed in a positive light because of its linkages to piracy.[31] As one scholar of Hellenistic slavery wrote, "pirates, after all, are already disapproved of for their piracy, [and] the fact that they deal in slaves just confirms their low status and enhances condemnation of them."[32]

The Greek historian Thucydides suggests that the first effort to counter piracy was made by King Minos of Crete, the great ruler who in the fifth century BC built a navy. Rulers of Corinth, an ancient Greek city-state from 700 to 338 BC, also thought they could improve state revenues by cracking down on piracy. Thus, unauthorized trade, a recurring theme throughout history, was already being combated 2,500 years ago by rulers of different Greek states as they tried to secure their kingdoms' revenues.[33]

Crete and Corinth were dependent on sea trade. Trade by land passage posed other challenges to safe transport, some of which are recorded on cuneiforms from Mesopotamia. Caravans containing many pack animals loaded with valuable goods worth stealing were plundered as they traversed the numerous trade routes that crisscrossed the Middle East.[34] Frankincense and myrrh from the Arabian Gulf—the gifts immortalized in Nativity scenes—traveled to parts of the Roman Empire.[35] Among the other goods plundered in South Arabia and Mesopotamia were precious stones, alabaster, iron, and purple wool, cloth destined for royalty.[36] Because trade and military routes often coincided, the state assumed an important role in protecting these caravans from attacks by nomads. Bedouins, ever since the time of cuneiform sources and up to the nineteenth century, have been named as raiders of caravans. But some of the nomadic attackers, seeing the financial advantages of participation, transitioned into legitimate trade.[37]

Caravan travel in other regions faced similar challenges from tribal attackers. The merchants who used the famous Silk Road, which stretched from China to Constantinople, encountered the fierce tribes of Central Asia. The Han government derived considerable profit from this route, and the Chinese used force, treaties, and heavy reprisals to gain control over the Central Asian tribes that pillaged caravans. Because of security concerns, caravans rarely traveled without armed protection.[38] Yet, because of the value of the diverse cargo, perils remained for millennia for those who navigated the Silk Road. Silk and other textiles, then as now, were a key and valuable good of international trade, as we discuss shortly.

Raiders of caravans and ships often had high status, because they gained strategic assets for the state.[39] Although the lore focuses on the threat to caravans from tribes and nomads, the historical record reveals that the perpetrators of most identified raids in the pre-Islamic Middle East were governors.[40] The same principle applied at sea. Most piracy was state-sponsored, and the existing ancient records identify only a small number of private pirate ships.[41]

Post-antiquity

Approximately a millennium and a half separates the discussion of antiquity from the next stage of our analysis. But during the intervening centuries, there was no fundamental change in the forms of illicit trade or the punishments imposed. The same previously identified activities are documented in different locales. The historical record provides evidence of piracy in fifth-century Southeast Asia, but piracy there probably predates this period. A Buddhist monk in AD 414 recorded examples of piracy in the Malaccan Straits and the South China Sea (the latter a presently hotly contested area). Chinese sailors noted the same phenomenon. From the thirteenth century to the sixteenth, large ships with up to three hundred men raided the coasts of China and Korea.[42] Therefore, diverse regions faced the challenges of piracy, which proved highly lucrative for those who could share its rewards and trade in the illicitly attained goods.

The great social historian Charles Tilly analyzed the importance of bandits and piracy in his seminal article on war-making and state-making. "Full-fledged states often commissioned privateers [and] hired sometime bandits to raid their enemies," he wrote, revealing that governments have used criminals for political purposes for several centuries.[43] Deploying violence on behalf of monarchs, pirates influenced political and economic developments. Piracy continued on a massive scale in the Mediterranean, contributing to the wealth and power of families closely associated with this activity. City-states such as Monaco had their origins in the proceeds of such trade. Lanfranco, a founding member of the ruling Grimaldi family of Monaco, enriched his family through his acts of piracy.[44] He was not alone: the coasts of Italy and France retain the relics of fortified homes built with fortunes gained through piracy. Illicit commerce can contribute to economic growth for some, a recurring insight in analyses of the winners and losers of illicit trade.

Piracy endured for centuries and would not be outlawed until 1856, when the Paris Declaration Respecting Maritime Law forbade the use of force by licensed private actors. The signatories to this agreement included not only maritime powers, such as France and Great Britain, but also states with a weaker naval presence, such as Prussia. The Declaration did not, however, outlaw the activities of ships that were acting under the provision of a sovereign state.[45] This exception would have important implications for the present.

State involvement in piracy and caravan attacks in ancient times is not a relic of the past, as there is a contemporary analogy—cyberattacks. In ancient and more modern times, great wealth was concentrated in the caravans and on the ships that moved large quantities of valuable cargo. Today valuable assets are held in cyberspace—banking information, credit cards, personal data, and new technology. But with the past as prologue, it is hardly surprising that many who carry out the attacks in the cyberworld are acting on behalf of states, which have targeted these new vehicles for storing wealth.

What we could call "cyber-buccaneers" may be the descendants of the sea-based pirates who operated in the Caribbean Sea during the seventeenth century, attacking Spanish ships.[46] For others, the term "cyber-privateer" may seem more fitting: "privateers," originating in the thirteenth century, were private individuals authorized by the state to attack shipping belonging to an enemy, often but not exclusively at times of war.[47] Cyber-privateers take us back to the time of Francis Drake. To the Spanish, Drake was a pirate ("el Draque," the dragon), but to Tudor England he was a prominent explorer who served the Crown. Drake was the second man, after Magellan, to circumnavigate the world, but he had a dual function, as he served the British Crown through his piracy.[48] Adding a religious element to his piracy was Catholic Europe's skeptical view of the Protestant Drake.

Today the target of the raiders has changed, but the sponsors of large-scale cyberattacks, as in the past, are often governments. Hoping to benefit from their ability to attack through proxies and obtain valuable commodities, governments empower cybercriminals to engage in illicit commerce in return for their service to the state. Some of Russia's best cybercriminals, after being arrested, have been offered the equivalent of a "get out of jail free" card in exchange for service to the Russian state. The dual role of today's "pirates" is epitomized by the theft of 500 million Yahoo accounts in 2016, a crime that the US Justice Department charged had been committed by Russian spies and hackers.[49]

Counterfeiting remained an enduring problem in medieval Europe, and brutal punishments were meted out to convicted counterfeiters, such as boiling them alive in oil.[50] In contrast, in China and other parts of Asia, copying was viewed as a form of flattery, and therefore the problem of counterfeits, outside of the sphere of currency, did not share the same opprobrium.

In this historical period, hunting became a pleasure sport for the ruling elite across a vast territory spanning from the British Isles to India.[51] The first efforts to protect animals from poaching were made on behalf of the royal prerogative to hunt, not because of conservation concerns. Even though the royal hunts killed many animals, the need to ensure animals for posterity preserved many species during these hundreds of years of absolute monarchies.[52]

With royal and noble control of massive bodies of land, access to these lands was strictly regulated, and ordinary citizens who entered the forests and preserves of the rulers faced dramatic penalties, and punishments were even harsher if they hunted animals. The legendary Robin Hood, who robbed the rich and gave to the poor, took to Sherwood Forest after poaching a deer in the royal forest, an act of treason punishable by death.[53]

Prior to the Renaissance, much illicit commerce, except for that tied to poaching and piracy, was urban-based, since rural communities were not as well integrated into trade routes as they have been in more recent centuries. Fraudsters might circulate among rural markets, and smugglers would move among cattle farmers, but illicit trade was primarily an urban, riverine, and coastal phenomenon.[54] Today rural areas, even remote ones, have only recently been integrated into illicit trade, in part as a result of new technologies and communications. This spread into rural areas represents a very dramatic shift from the trade locales that prevailed for centuries, even millennia.

1500-1800

The foundations of the modern world were laid in the centuries following the Renaissance in Europe. Human migration had begun on a significant scale in these centuries as a result of the expansion of trade and colonization. Immigrant communities, especially enclaves of minority groups—now often referred to as *diasporas*—were key to facilitating both legitimate and illicit trade.

In this period, we see the emergence of many characteristics of contemporary illicit commerce—its diversity, its violence, its political and economic impact, and the corruption that facilitates it. Counterfeits ascended in importance during these centuries, and illicit financial flows accompanied the illegal transport and sale of goods. Violent punishments against illicit traders were often imposed by authoritarian governments.

After Europeans discovered the New World, the Americas were integrated into global trade, especially after their colonization. Empires expanded in many regions, and trade played a central role in their growth. Empires outside of Europe, such as the Ottoman Empire stretching from North Africa into the Middle East, relied on trade and taxation of commerce to maintain and consolidate control. Smuggling thrived under the Ottomans, despite high penalties, because smugglers paid premium prices.[55] Trading companies, under charters from European governments, expanded throughout Asia. According to the eminent historian of Indian trade K. N. Chaudhuri, the arrival of Spanish and Portuguese traders increased the speed of trade in the Indian Ocean and diminished the "introspectiveness of India and China."[56]

The first wave of globalization was as contentious as it is today. "For the growth of world trade in the eighteenth century did not merely bring together distant markets. It stimulated illicit trade, popular rebellion, and reformist debate."[57] The dominant ideology of *mercantilism* in the most economically advanced countries of Europe during these centuries promoted state regulation of their economies to augment national power. Yet the new rules, the creation of royal monopolies, and the imposition of high taxes contributed to the significant growth of smuggling and contraband as citizens sought goods at more accessible prices.

Long overlooked by many historians was the diversification from the Renaissance through the era of revolutions of illicit trade.[58] Even before the industrial revolution, many Europeans had disposable capital and were ready to buy smuggled goods.[59] In France, a vibrant illicit trade included many products sought by consumers, such as salt, tobacco, wine, wax, silk, leather, and drills for the paper industry.[60]

A significant illicit trade also functioned further west in the Mediterranean. Cadiz and Seville in Spain were "bridgeheads to the Americas" and locales where fraud flourished, according to Fernand Braudel, the great scholar of the Mediterranean world. As he explains, "Everyone in Cadiz knows the *metedores* (smugglers and runners), often gentlemen fallen on hard times who specialized in the fraudulent conveyance of bullion or precious goods, sometimes mere tobacco, from overseas, and who made no secret of their trade."[61] These same locales are key to the massive cigarette smuggling into contemporary France, as discussed later in the book.

In the 1700s, the smuggling of goods into England, then the leading trade power of the world, was so pervasive that John Wesley, the founder of the Methodist Church, delivered sermons against buying illicitly imported goods. He made it clear that salvation was not possible for citizens who continued to participate in smuggling.[62] Wesley's sermons explained that those who participated in illicit trade hurt the state's treasuries and consequently themselves.[63] This argument, without the religious focus, is repeated today in regard to the smuggling of highly taxed items desired by consumers, such as cigarettes and alcohol, and the illicit trade in computers and cell phones in societies that impose high import duties on those products.

COUNTERFEIT MONEY AND ILLICIT FINANCIAL FLOWS

Illicit commerce is often accompanied by fake money. In the eighteenth century in Europe and in Russia after 1769, countries began to rely on paper currency and long-term national debt to pay for their ever-expanding militaries and extensive imperial projects. "Printing banknotes was as cheap and quick for criminals as it was for governments, despite the attention of government spies and policemen and the risk of severe punishments. Archival materials reveal a sprawling web of printers, smugglers, and passers of forged rubles that incorporated persons of all the major ethnic, religious, and social groups that inhabited Russia."[64] These networks, which were integrated into those for legitimate commerce, stretched from Europe into the far reaches of the Czarist Empire.[65]

This pattern of illicit financial flows presages the billions of dollars that have left the post-Soviet states for Europe since the collapse of the Soviet Union, much of it heading to western Europe. The networks for the illicit flows are now also integrated into those for legitimate commerce.

The Political Dimensions of Illicit Trade

Smuggling was targeted not just at utilitarian items for consumption. France, under the ancien régime, was a center of intellectual thought, but one that also censored religious and intellectual ideas. In the sixteenth century, people were burned at the stake for smuggling and selling the books of theologians such as Luther, Calvin, and Erasmus. Subsequently, books of Enlightenment thought were also suppressed. Control of these potent thoughts was rational. "In 1789, ideas from the new Enlightenment 'science' of economics," explains the scholar Caroline Spence, "converged with contraband revolt from below to help topple the old regime."[66]

Smuggling and State-Building

Smuggling can also build states.[67] In the 1500s, there was a two-way trade between the great maritime powers of Venice and the Ottoman Empire in the items needed for war—iron, horses, and weapons— even though both powers had outlawed transnational trade in these commodities.[68] These critical goods could only be moved illegally with the complicity of officials who received payoffs to facilitate or ignore such commerce, which nonetheless helped these states retain their competitive advantage in their region.

Peter Andreas has also shown the importance of illicit trade for state-building. In *Smuggler Nation*, he states that the United States, since the colonial period, has been built on contraband trade in different commodities, including military goods, consumer products, and slaves.[69] Smuggling during the Revolutionary War helped the American colonists sustain their war effort against the British, and smuggling from the Caribbean of munitions and gunpowder that the British had banned for export to the colonies was decisive in the American victory in that war.[70]

Smuggling and Resistance

Smuggling prior to the Revolution was also a form of resistance by the American colonists against British rule, especially the tax policies imposed by the Crown.[71] The Massachusetts governor estimated that after the passage of the Revenue Act in 1767—which raised taxes on imported consumer goods to provide funds to maintain British troops—83 percent of tea in Boston and 90 percent in New York and Philadelphia was illegally imported.[72]

Individuals of high social status participated. John Hancock, the most visible signer of the Declaration of Independence, was raised by his wealthy uncle Thomas Hancock, who made his fortune from smuggling. Accusations were also made in court that John Hancock was involved in smuggling wine. He was defended by the future president John Adams, and his culpability was not proven. In verdicts reflecting colonial resistance, jurors often freed smugglers, as in this case.

Even before the famous Tea Party in Boston, when massive amounts of tea were thrown into the harbor off of a docked ship, visibly challenging British rule, less overt signs of resistance had been evident. The extent of illicit trade in the colonies was high by any standard—historical or contemporary. More than tea came illegally into the colonies on ships arriving from the French, Dutch, and Spanish West Indies. This trade in illicit goods was facilitated by corruption, as British customs officials augmented their modest salaries from the Crown with bribes from colonial shippers. British crackdowns on "smuggling in the years leading up to the revolution provoked riots, protests and tar-and-feathering of customs agents and informants."[73] The British government estimated that over £700,000 per year—then a very significant sum and not trivial today—was brought into the American colonies illegally.[74]

Colonial resistance and profiteering from smuggling in Spanish and Portuguese colonies in South America was also recorded. Smuggling in gold continued with little successful intervention by the colonial powers. This contraband trade was facilitated both by former employees of the royal mint and by slaves at the other end of the economic and social spectrum.[75] Fleets from Brazil were involved in smuggling tobacco on a grand scale: illegal exports of tobacco from the New World were estimated to be two to three times the size of legitimate exports.[76] Farther south, in the seventeenth and eighteenth centuries, the port near Buenos Aires was already a major smuggling center for imported goods entering the colonies.[77] Gold continues today to be smuggled on a large scale from Colombia and Peru. A 2017 federal case resulted in conviction of a Peruvian smuggler who moved looted gold worth hundreds of millions of dollars from Peru to the United States.[78] Brazil is now a key exit point for illicit "white cigarettes," which are cigarettes legally produced at the point of production—in this case in Paraguay—with the intent of being smuggled.

Participation in illicit commerce as a form of dissent increased in the nineteenth century as resentment against colonial rule grew in Asia as well.[79] Citizens strove to deprive the state of needed tax revenues and to circumvent regulations as a means of opposing the authority of colonial rulers. Opposition to state power through smuggling became even more overt when individuals imported military-related equipment. But even in the absence of military and war-making imports, smuggling reduced revenues for the state and thus served larger political objectives.

Large-scale smuggling preceded the French Revolution and involved much of the French population, who resisted the oppressive taxes of the authoritarian monarchy.[80] This smuggling was brutally repressed, however, when an estimated thirty thousand traffickers were brought before the French courts between 1730 and 1789 and given very harsh sentences.[81] Therefore, the economic control of trade by the monarchy was the first symbol of French authoritarian power to be attacked. Indeed, one historian cogently argues that the French Revolution began, not with the storming of the Bastille to liberate political prisoners, "but with the burning of Paris customs gates two days earlier."[82]

State-Based and Private Violence Accompanying Illicit Trade

The violence accompanying illicit trade, which was both private and state-imposed, was not a new phenomenon. Perpetrators used force on both sea and land to carry out their illicit commerce.[83] Yet the level of violence by the state against perpetrators in this period is less well known.

One historian has described the violence accompanying the illicit tobacco trade in pre-revolutionary France as the historical predecessor of the drug lords of present-day Mexico. Like the *narcocorridos* (songs glorifying drug lords) of today, in France songs were sung to Louis Mandrin, who violated the king's monopoly on tobacco trade. When smuggling violated the prerogatives of kings, smugglers were hunted like drug traffickers today. Those appalled by President Rodrigo Duterte's massive killing of drug traffickers in today's Philippines should look to the period in French history when the king had a monopoly on another addictive substance—tobacco. A sample of approximately 900 sentences meted out between 1733 and 1771 in just one jurisdiction in southeastern France reveals the severity of the state response: "162 men, roughly a fifth of the sentences, were sentenced to death, sixty-five of them to be broken on the wheel and ninety-seven to be hanged."[84]

The violence associated with illicit trade was not restricted to the West. In the middle of the sixteenth century, a significant illicit trade developed between China and Japan and also between China and Southeast Asia. Asian traders as well as Portuguese were involved in these violent trade hubs, and the Chinese attempted to curb both the violence and the illicit trade by appointing a "grand coordinator" to curb the smuggling.[85] The Chinese state exerted authority in a similar way three hundred years later, in regard to the opium trade, a topic discussed in the following chapter.

Diasporas

The period of mercantilism was accompanied by an increased number of people who migrated to foster commerce. These moves could be difficult: many of those who migrated were minorities in their new locale, and often they were not welcomed by the communities where they settled.[86]

Much attention is given now to the role of diaspora communities as facilitators of contemporary illicit trade.[87] The transport of elephant ivory links Pakistani diaspora communities in Africa, dating to the colonial era, to trade networks operating in the Indian subcontinent and beyond to Southeast Asia.[88] African diaspora communities in Europe facilitate the human smuggling and trafficking between these two regions.[89] But trade diasporas are nothing new; such communities have existed since ancient times, when merchants moved within the Middle East to sell their goods.[90]

The international linkages of diaspora communities to both licit and illicit trade grew more significant in the eighteenth and nineteenth centuries as a result of the population movements associated with colonialism and increasing international trade.[91] Many of the settlers favored their own interests over those of the colonial rulers. In the seventeenth century, Jewish merchants used "extensive family networks that spanned the Dutch Republic, England, and the British Caribbean," and Dutch settlers in the British colonies used their contacts in the Netherlands to avoid payment of taxes by using circuitous routes to hide the ultimate destination of their cargoes.[92] The mis-invoicing of trade was a key element of illicit trade in the past, as it is today.

Textile Trade: A Historical Case Study

A historical survey of illicit commerce in textiles, one of the most lucrative trade commodities, illustrates many of the concepts discussed in this chapter. The legendary theft of Chinese silkworms by monks under the Byzantine emperor Justinian in the sixth century foreshadowed the current theft of intellectual property. The subsequent European cultivation of silkworms destroyed the Chinese monopoly and weakened the economic power of Central Asia and China.[93] Further undermining the trade were the bandits who attacked caravans and stole the valuable cloths shipped along Asia's Silk Road.

Illicit traders also sought to break monopolies linked to the textile trade. The discovery of the New World led to the export of many valuable commodities from the colonies to Europe. Gold flowed to Spain and Portugal, as well as many foods that are now staples of the European diet. But the most valuable export of this period was something that you have probably never heard of—cochineal. Cochineal is a dye based on insects that live on cactus and yield a brilliant red color.[94] Sent to Spain in 1520, cochineal traveled east as well as west. Within six decades of its discovery in Mexico, cochineal was already being used in the dyes of the legendary carpets of Central Asia that are often dubbed "Bukharan rugs."[95]

The English in the late sixteenth century sent dozens of raiding parties to the Caribbean to seek the cochineal dye.[96] The pirate Francis Drake mentioned earlier was the son of a cloth-maker; he raided ships not only for gold but also for this widely sought and valuable textile dye that existed only in the New World. The Spanish held a monopoly on cochineal and imposed restrictions on its export.[97] Despite the thefts by Drake and others, cochineal remained a Spanish-controlled monopoly for 250 years and was not disrupted until the cactus and the insect were smuggled into Haiti at the end of the eighteenth century.[98] Smuggling was a valuable tool in breaking state monopolies.

At the end of the fourteenth century and the beginning of the fifteenth, English manufacturers used counterfeits to compete against the Venetians, who dominated in textile production. After 1570, according to Fernand Braudel, the great scholar of the Mediterranean world, northern ships and merchants sent large shipments of counterfeits to the Mediterranean, flooding the area with clever imitations of the excellent southern textiles and even marking them with the universally reputed Venetian seals in order to sell them under that "label" on the usual Venetian markets.[99] This account reads very much like a contemporary Italian report on the economic losses and discrediting of Italian brands as counterfeit goods flow from China into modern Italy.[100] Brazenly labeling these high-level counterfeits "Made in Venice" presages the chutzpah of many contemporary counterfeiters, who deliberately mislabel the origin of the goods they produce. Italy first faced challenges to its fine textile tradition from counterfeiters almost five hundred years ago, with severe economic and political consequences, and its experience illustrates two important themes of this chapter— the growth of counterfeiting and the centrality of smuggling to the political welfare of states.[101]

Illicit trade in cotton, cloth, embroidered materials, and dyes continued on a significant scale between 1500 and 1800, with dramatic consequences. The English successfully challenged the Venetians but subsequently faced their own problems with imports. In September 2017, I visited an exhibition on South Asian art at the Victoria and Albert Museum, the prominent museum of fine arts in London. Displayed there were the diverse and beautiful chintzes (elaborately painted textiles imported from India) that were used in stylish clothing and housewares in the seventeenth and eighteenth centuries.[102] The signage for the exhibition stated that these textiles were extensively smuggled into England to satisfy consumer demand.

France's textile challenge also came from the East. In this new era of greater ease of global trade, calico prints (expensive luxury printed cotton from India used for house furnishings and clothing) became all the rage among the fashion-conscious in France. As a consequence, the French monarchy, in need of large revenues to maintain its courts and palaces, imposed high taxes on almost all commodities sought by citizens, including this desired textile. Restrictions on calico prints were also motivated in part by the desire to safeguard local industry. Initiated in 1683 and continuing for seventy-three years, the French ban on the importation of printed cotton fabrics was not successful, as there was high demand and the country was replete with smugglers willing to risk the severe sanctions for smuggling calico.[103] In eighteenth-century France, sixteen thousand calico smugglers were either executed or shot by government agents![104] As Michael Kwass, one of the new wave of fine historians focusing on illicit trade, wrote on France during this period, the sale of tobacco and calico cloth, two highly regulated products, "generated cycles of repression and revolt that disrupted public order, destabilized border provinces, and, combined with other forms of collective action, shook the monarchy well before the French Revolution."[105]

Smuggling into and out of the American colonies was routine. Silk and other luxury goods were imported into the American colonies directly from Europe, violating the British requirement that the colonists import all manufactured goods from England.[106]

This chapter's analysis ends in 1800, but the following century saw continued smuggling in the components for textiles, a trade of strategic importance. Andreas's *Smuggler Nation* devotes a chapter to "blood cotton and blockade runners," analyzing the attempts by the North during the Civil War to blockade the Southern ports to prevent cotton export, a key product for the British textile industry and a key revenue source for the Confederacy. The Confederacy also counted on cotton "as a political and economic weapon."[107] The smuggling of cotton helped sustain the war effort in the nineteenth century, just as the illicit trade in drugs, arms, oil, and antiquities functions as an essential source of funding in conflicts today.[108]

With the past as prologue, illicit trade persists in the trafficking of people in all phases of textile production today. Labor is trafficked at every stage of the supply chain, from the labor of the children, in countries such as Uzbekistan, who harvest the cotton crop to that of those engaged in the sewing, assembling, and pressing elements of clothing production.[109] The problem is global: from the United States to hotspots in Europe, such as Italy; to the Indian subcontinent, especially Bangladesh; to the free-trade zone of Jordan; to China and South Asia.[110] Labor trafficking is even more pervasive in the production of counterfeit brands, where there is even less control over supply chains. One form of illicit trade accompanies another.

Conclusion

The history of illicit trade is also a history of the rise of rulers and states that have attempted to regulate commerce. In the past, as today, the nature of trade and its regulation were key concerns, because economies depended on commerce for their wealth and rulers and governments derived revenue from taxing imported and exported goods. Therefore, stolen, counterfeit, and smuggled products were all harmful to the state, and engaging in these acts was punishable by serious penalties. Our historical analysis reveals that the penalty of death was imposed on those engaging in illicit trade from the time of Hammurabi through the end of the eighteenth century, and extrajudicial killings were common in the past as they are today.

With the rise of the Enlightenment and moral philosophy, the issue of trade became a concern. The famous Scottish economist and moral philosopher Adam Smith, born in the eighteenth century to a customs officer, addressed the question: What is the state's right to establish monopolies and regulate trade? Even though Smith came from the British "rule of law" tradition and could not approve of smugglers who violated the laws of their country, he emphasized the culpability of the state rather than the citizen in illicit commerce. Smith wrote that the smuggler would have been "in every respect an excellent citizen had not the laws of his country made that a crime which nature never meant to be so." British law conformed to this perspective, imposing only civil, not criminal, penalties on those caught trafficking illegal goods.[111] But as we have seen from this historical analysis, the French monarchy in this period took a very different perspective and did not view the smuggler as an excellent citizen: that state's regulations made him a criminal.

The central tension between these two perspectives remains today. Is illicit trade, and those who engage in it, penalized merely because certain state policy has been established, or are there even more profound issues at stake? Should the state invest large resources in pursuing some of those who engage in the most serious forms of illicit trade and impose heavy penalties on them?

Contemporary illicit trade and smuggling take very different forms from that known in this historical period, and among the most pervasive are drugs, people, wildlife, and natural resources. Today's illicit trade could undermine the sustainability of life and the inhabitability of the planet. Are we now facing challenges of such gravity that we must alter the foundations of our moral philosophy on trade? The enormous tensions that now permeate global trade and its regulation suggest that important elements of our intellectual framework of the last few hundred years are now being challenged by our new reality.

2

The Making of Modern Illicit Trade

FROM 1800 TO THE END OF THE COLD WAR

Modern illicit trade dates only from the conclusion of the French and American Revolutions. In the century prior to the age of revolutions, illicit commerce had often facilitated political resistance against autocratic rulers. Illicit trade's political role persisted in the two centuries after the era of revolutions as colonial conflicts multiplied, two world wars were fought, and Communist revolutions affected many regions.

Illicit commodities changed after 1800. As one specialist on contraband has observed, people smuggle distinct products in different periods.[1] Eighteenth-century Enlightenment ideas affected attitudes toward governance, but also toward humanity. Without the writings of some Enlightenment and religious thinkers, the slave trade might have remained a key form of legitimate commerce. Illegal trade in human beings persists today despite prohibitions. But this trade, now referred to as *human trafficking*, affects a much smaller share of the world's population than in previous centuries and millennia. Drugs became a significant illicit commodity only in the mid-nineteenth century, when the illegal drug trade motivated the Opium Wars fought in China. The key commodities associated with contemporary illicit trade—drugs and humans—became significant components of prohibited commerce only within the last two hundred years.

This period laid the groundwork for contemporary illicit commerce, which is now thriving in the cyberworld. Without the extraordinary scientific and technological developments of the last two centuries—ushered in by Enlightenment thinkers' emphasis on the rationality of science—the global community would not be facing the dramatic change in commerce as both its licit and illicit versions transition to online marketplaces.[2] This era of great technological advances and scientific development included the Industrial Revolution, Darwin's research on the evolution of species, the great physics revolutions in the early twentieth century, and subsequently the invention of the computing and communications technologies that transformed contemporary life. Out of this innovation in science and technology came new regulations that safeguarded commerce in many items but also greatly expanded the number of products whose trade became illicit. Protections for intellectual property and antiquities; legal frameworks to safeguard air, land, water, and the species that inhabit the planet; frameworks to protect against trade in conventional weapons as well as weapons of mass destruction—all these measures were introduced. These developments resulted from the need to sustain life and the planet while simultaneously fostering innovation.

The locus of illicit trade shifted over the centuries. At the start of this historical chapter, England's role as a great maritime power and its naval supremacy made it a key arbiter of both licit and illegal commerce across the globe. As American economic power grew, it became an ever more important force in both legitimate and illicit commerce. The geographic focus of illicit trade shifted again by the end of this era as Asian countries, especially China, became the world's major exporters of both licit and illicit products. Asian countries, enriched by their trade, now provide significant markets for diverse illegal goods.

The Nineteenth Century in Perspective

European colonial domination of large swaths of the globe in the nineteenth century contributed to the proliferation of illicit commerce, as colonized populations viewed resistance to established trade as a form of protest against external rule. Colonial rulers compounded the growth of illicit trade through their efforts to divide and conquer their expansive territories. The tools of exploration and discovery allowed European powers to map their territories. The artificial boundaries set up by colonial powers to facilitate their rule often divided communities, to the benefit of the rulers rather than the ruled. This was certainly clear in the actions of colonial powers in India, Africa, and the former Ottoman Empire at the end of the First World War. Local inhabitants had no respect for these artificial boundaries, which cut off their traditional trade paths.[3] These borders, legacies of colonialism, remain key locales of illicit trade today in Southeast Asia, on the Indian subcontinent, and in East Africa, Latin America, and the Caribbean. Illicit trade routes established in the nineteenth century are now used to move precious metals, drugs, contraband, and people.[4]

Addictive products, such as opium in China, alcohol in Africa, and cigarettes in the Caribbean, provided imperial powers with the locally generated resources needed to build colonial-era administrations. Trade in addictive substances not only perpetuated dominance by colonial rulers but shifted trade from traditional goods to products harmful to human life.[5]

European powers were not the only colonial rulers. The declining Ottoman Empire governed a vast territory that extended from North Africa to Iraq. In its final decades, the long extant problem of smuggling became ever more prominent as the central state bureaucracy lost control over its far-flung territories.[6] The illicit commerce of this period laid the groundwork for the very current problem of smuggling across the Mediterranean and between the Middle East and Europe. The Balkan states, formerly part of the Ottoman Empire, are now used to smuggle drugs, weapons, and people from Turkey into Europe.[7] Guns smuggled from the Balkans were allegedly used in a Paris terrorist attack.[8] Ottoman routes from North Africa to the southern Mediterranean coast of Europe have been recommissioned to move drugs, people, and cigarettes.

As the Ottoman Empire weakened over several centuries, European powers took antiquities from Egypt and Greece, their appropriation of these countries' pasts foreshadowing the current illicit trade in cultural property. Napoleon, after his conquest of Egypt, hauled off large quantities of antiquities that now fill the exhibition halls and vaults of the Louvre in Paris. Lord Elgin, in the early nineteenth century, bribed the Ottoman rulers of Athens in order to remove the great marble friezes from the Parthenon and transfer them to Britain, where they are now displayed at the British Museum in London as "the Elgin marbles." They figure in the *Time* magazine list of the top ten examples of "ill-gotten goods," but their removal from Greece was not then illegal.[9] Not until 1970, with the adoption of the UNESCO Convention on the Means of Prohibiting and Preventing the Illicit Import, Export, and Transfer of Ownership of Cultural Property, was illicit trade in antiquities first prohibited.[10]

The lands of the Middle East are now pockmarked with the debris left in the wake of antique treasure hunters' renewed search for buried statues, coins, rings, insignia, and the like, which can be smuggled to antiques dealers or sold online or through auction houses. The UNESCO Convention, backed up by inadequate law enforcement, has been ineffective in stemming the looting that provides funding for corrupt officials and for criminal and terrorist networks.[11]

European domination of colonial territory included not only its cultural property but also its wildlife. European administrators criminalized hunting by African communities, who hunted primarily for survival. They fined, imprisoned, and even shot to death some African hunters, yet at the same time protected the rights of "European sport hunters." This is one reason why some African communities continue to engage in extralegal forms of hunting, resisting the ways in which governments or private landowners try to safeguard wildlife.[12] It is their turn now, having regained control over their traditional territory, to exploit the land.

The End of the Legal Trade in Human Beings: A Momentous Change

As we can see from the depictions of slaves in paintings and sculptures in Egyptian pharaonic tombs, references to slavery in Hammurabi's Code, and cuneiform sales contracts of slaves surviving since ancient Babylon (500 BCE), slavery dates back millennia. The essence of this illicit trade changed profoundly in 1807, when the British for the first time in recorded history initiated a global effort to ban the slave trade.

The ideas of the Enlightenment and the French revolutionary ideals of "Liberty, Equality and Fraternity" had an enormous impact on European thought and led in the nineteenth century to the end of the legal commerce in slaves. When Britain outlawed the slave trade early in that century, it was rejecting the Aristotelian concept of "natural slavery," and even the ideas of its own great Enlightenment thinker John Locke, who justified the perpetuation of slavery.[13] Britain then deployed its superior naval power, at great national expense, to force other countries to follow suit.[14]

Prior to this period, the slave trade was legal in many locales and often state-sanctioned. Moreover, slavery was so accepted and acceptable that slave traders often operated with licenses from the Crown.[15] Slaves were obtained from diverse sources—bought on location in Africa, captured during war, and enslaved by pirates who captured ships and their crews. Humans were traded in many regions of the world and sent to North and South America and the Middle East as a high-value commodity.[16]

The ideas of the European Enlightenment changed perceptions of slavery. By 1780 in Britain, slavery had been frequently and "systematically denounced as contrary to reason, liberty, natural law, morality, and, perhaps most important, both the Christian faith and national virtue."[17] The influential religious leader John Wesley, the founder of Methodism, stated that every slaveholder, slaver, merchant, and investor in slave property was stained with guilt.[18] Abolition was not achieved through a slave rebellion but as a result of non-enslaved masses mobilizing for the first time in history to eliminate slavery.[19]

Key to this movement was the aristocrat William Wilberforce, who, following a religious conversion, made his life's mission the passage of an antislavery law. The great economist Adam Smith, taking a long view of history, thought that it was unlikely that slavery would ever be abolished. Yet Smith's view of the future of slavery was misplaced, because he overestimated the impact of economic forces and underestimated the impact of religious and philosophical ideas on human action. Religious faith in Britain was key to the abolition of the slave trade just as faith-based movements are key in the United States today in the struggle against modern forms of slavery.

Britain's outlawing of slavery had an impact that extended far beyond the borders of the island kingdom. At that time Britain not only was a major colonial power with a global empire but also had an influence on many countries because of its dominance of the sea.[20] Therefore, in 1807, the United States, partly in response to British pressure, passed a federal law prohibiting Americans from participating in the African slave trade.[21] Not too many American slavers, who earned much from their trade in people, were fervently committed to obeying this law. Therefore, despite the passage of the antislavery law, the United States remained "both an illicit import market for African slaves and a leading trafficker of slaves to foreign ports."[22] American ships continued to traffic in slaves after Spanish and Portuguese vessels caved in to the pressure from the British Navy as it searched vessels from the Iberian Peninsula.[23] Judges in the courts of New York made it impossible to prosecute slavers, and even though the federal law established the death penalty for this offense, only one slaver was executed. A retired slave trader from Rhode Island went on to serve in Congress, suggesting that participation in this illicit trade did not invite social stigma.[24]

British financial and diplomatic pressure was unrelenting, ensuring that by the Congress of Vienna in 1814–1815, several other countries, including Holland, Sweden, Portugal, and Spain, had all taken steps against the slave trade.[25] But often these legal prohibitions, as in the American case, were more symbolic than actual.

To suppress the global slave trade, Britain used its vast maritime resources, spending an estimated 1.8 percent of national income annually for sixty years after 1807 to curtail the trade.[26] Contemporary development aid provided by developed countries is estimated by the OECD at 0.32 percent of national income.[27] Nineteenth-century British expenditures for antislavery efforts were closer to modern defense expenditures (national average of 2.3 percent in 2013) than to development assistance.[28]

In 1845, one British sea captain who was expected to stop the slave trade off the coast of West Africa wrote of the difficulty of implementing antislavery policy:

> Here we are, on the most miserable station in the wide world . . . attempting an impossibility—the suppression of the Slave Trade. We look upon the whole affair out here as a complete humbug. . . . So long as a slave, worth only a few dollars here, fetches 80*l* or 100*l* in America, men and means will be found to evade the strictest blockade.[29]

The captain's comments are today echoed by many law enforcement personnel trying to block the influx of drugs and people across the US-Mexican border, or by European officials trying to stem the flow of migrants into southern Europe. Then as now, outsized profits provided great incentives to continue the trade in people.

Not even all of British's naval power and financial investment achieved the desired reduction in the slave trade. Three million slaves left Africa after British abolition, an estimated two-thirds moved illegally. In the sixty-year period after 1807, 7,750 ships were captured, 85 percent of them as a result of British orders. To deter detection in West Africa, "native slave traders were compelled to keep their slaves farther from the coast, waiting for messages about some zone of clandestine trade, or hoping that the watching British sloop would weigh anchor and depart."[30]

The British effort to suppress the slave trade started in the Atlantic Ocean, focusing on Africa's western coast. But its suppression efforts later extended to the Arabian Sea and the Indian Oceans and then the Red Sea.[31] Great Britain's abolition of the slave trade in West Africa outlawed that region's key export, as 90 percent of its trade with Europe was in slaves.[32] Observing the dire economic impact of the prohibition of the slave trade on West African elites, "Western European philanthropists talked much of persuading Africans to exchange the slave trade for other commerce." They proposed other trade products such as salt, indigo, rice, coffee, and palm oil. But the profits from these items were minimal when compared to the revenue derived from the slave trade.[33] Their proposals anticipated the twentieth-century concept of crop substitution for contemporary drug producers.

Britain began its effort to ban the slave trade in the Arabian Sea in 1822, negotiating with the sultan of Muscat and Zanzibar for the next few decades to curtail slavery in East Africa. A historian of the region, however, after examining the trade records, concluded that this effort was no more than window dressing, as the slave trade continued in two directions. Child slaves were exported from Hyderabad in India to Tanzania, a trade justified as beneficial for the welfare of the children. "Slaves from East Africa were trafficked East on a significant scale for a quarter of a century, even after the abolition treaties of 1873."[34]

Today a monument remains in Zanzibar commemorating the victims of the slave trade, who were kept in holes belowground before sale and shipment to other parts of Africa and the Arabian Peninsula. A sign at the entrance to this site reads, "Slaves were kept in terrible conditions, so many died of suffocation and starvation. The amount was terrible."[35]

Key to the continuation of the slave trade in Zanzibar, as in many locales, was greed and profit, which surpassed all laws and conventions. The British, despite strident antislavery rhetoric, failed to enforce their antislavery laws in Tanzania and India as they sought to limit discontent with their rule by the local elite, who benefited from the slave trade.[36] Complicity and maintenance of order are recurring and enduring themes we will observe in the diverse forms of illicit trade discussed in this book.

Further legal efforts to limit the African slave trade were made throughout the nineteenth century. By 1839, Britain had signed bilateral conventions with almost all maritime powers allowing for mutual search and seizure on the high seas when there was suspicion that ships might be transporting slaves. Treaties were also negotiated with African states forbidding the slave trade.[37] In 1862, a treaty was signed between the United States and Great Britain agreeing to suppress the African slave trade.[38] Later, in response to public outrage over King Leopold's brutal enslavement of the Congolese population after colonization, an international antislavery conference was convened in Brussels in 1890. Unfortunately, the conference focused less on the trade in slaves than on the endurance of slavery and did little to change the exploitation and decimation of the Congolese population.[39]

The transatlantic slave trade was not the only human trade in the nineteenth century. The trade in "coolies," unskilled laborers from China, was based on deception and force. The coolies exported from southern China to the United States and other locales in the Americas were subject to extreme labor exploitation, although they were not technically enslaved.[40]

The Rise of the Drug Trade—"All Is Fair in the Pursuit of Profits"

Narcotics were used in traditional cultures in both Latin America and Asia for many centuries. Until the mid-nineteenth century, drugs were not a significant element of illicit commerce, but then the Chinese prohibition on drug imports in the face of rising abuse set off wars with the British Empire.

Britain's approach to the opium trade was diametrically opposed to its approach to the slave trade. Whereas the suppression of the trade in humans was a costly policy motivated by a strong religiously based abolitionist movement in Britain, the opium trade with China was promoted to advance Britain's financial interests. Illicit trade in opium became an important revenue generator for the Crown in the nineteenth century because it was a key export of India, Britain's most important colony. Britain sought to expand its markets to offset the high costs of colonial administration in India. The traders benefiting from this commerce provide a clear example of the close relationship of licit business with state-sanctioned criminal activity.[41]

The heralded trilogy of Amitav Ghosh brings to life the state-sponsored opium trade. *Sea of Poppies*, the first volume, focuses on the era when the British used their powerful naval fleet to move the drug. Subsequent volumes look at the battles that were fought as the British tried to retain the right to trade Indian-raised opium in China.[42] In the nineteenth century, the key source of poppies, the plant from which opium is produced, was the shores of the Ganges rather than the fields of Afghanistan.[43] Karachi, Pakistan, then part of British India, was a center of drug smuggling, a distinction it maintains today.[44]

The origins of the illicit drug trade lay in a prohibition regime, the corruption of Chinese officials, the weakness of the Chinese state, and the political and economic interests of the world's great power—Britain.[45] Then as now, the drug trade was more than a criminal activity. Large-scale violence accompanied this trade, and high-level interests encouraged both its ban and its expansion.

Chinese rulers of the Qing dynasty (1644–1911/12), observing the deleterious impact of drug consumption, outlawed the importation of opium in 1839 and appointed a commissioner, Lin Tse-hsu, to end the trade. For the British, opium from India could be exchanged for highly marketable Chinese goods.[46] After the ban, British smuggled opium chests into China by bribing Chinese officials. When silver was smuggled out of China to help pay for the purchased opium, China's financial reserves were depleted.[47] This illicit trade presaged the illicit financial flows linked to the contemporary drug trade. Corruption and other forms of illicit trade accompanied large-scale drug trafficking from its inception.

In 1839, Commissioner Lin Tse-hsu dumped large quantities of opium into the sea in Canton to protest British trade activity, sparking a conflict reminiscent of the tea dumped into Boston Harbor by American revolutionaries in 1773.[48] The twentieth-century "war on drugs" in the United States was foreshadowed by the nineteenth-century Opium Wars, first fought by Britain in 1840 and then again in 1856.[49]

As a young man in 1840, William Gladstone, subsequently a four-time prime minister of Britain, denounced the First Opium War as "unjust and iniquitous," and he maintained his opposition when the Second Opium War began years later.[50] The great historian of China John King Fairbank characterized the opium trade as the most long-lasting and systematic international crime of modern times.[51] Fairbank was prescient, but he did not live to see the drug trade's more modern manifestations in Latin and North America, Africa, Afghanistan-Pakistan, and other locales.

In the Second Opium War (1856–1860), the Americans and the French joined with the British against the Chinese, forcing the legalization of the opium trade and the opening of trade ports in China.[52] One key American participant in the opium trade was President Franklin D. Roosevelt's grandfather, Warren Delano, a senior partner in Russell and Company, a Boston trading company, who deemed that all was "fair in the pursuit of profits."[53] Consequently, Warren Delano's involvement in illicit trade was no impediment to his daughter's entrée into good society as a debutante and her marriage into the prominent Roosevelt family.[54]

Chinese consciousness is still affected by the Opium Wars. On a June 2015 trip to China, I was taken to the Police Museum in Taizhou on China's Pacific coast, several hours south of Hangzhou. Among the many exhibits on crime prevention was a well-developed historical section focusing on the great damage done to China by British drug smuggling. The two Opium Wars were displayed as a period of weakness of the Chinese state, and the commander of the Chinese fleet that fought the British was depicted as a great hero. The lessons for the contemporary Chinese are clear—drugs are a threat not just to individual life but to the political security and stability of the state. It is a lesson many other states have learned in recent decades.

The history of China's opium trade and the great powers behind it presages many aspects of the contemporary drug trade. Apart from its profits and violence, the drug trade, then as now, was accompanied by corruption. The corruption of Chinese officials undermined the ever-weakening governance of the Qing dynasty. Also, the opium trade was not a stand-alone phenomenon. During the Second Opium War, looting from the Forbidden City in Beijing contributed to the presence in Western collections of a great many art treasures that Chinese authorities would like to recover.[55]

In the nineteenth century, the British Empire and other colonial powers provided drugs to economically and politically weaker countries. The political utility of the drug trade to control populations may explain why an international response was so long in coming. Only in 1909, decades after the Opium Wars, was the first international meeting on the opium drug trade held—the Shanghai Opium Commission. The International Opium Convention, passed at a 1912 meeting in The Hague, required that countries that were parties to the convention prevent the export of raw and prepared opium. The prohibitions enacted in this convention terminated a key revenue generator for states and ended most marketing of drugs as a tool of state policy. Further mechanisms were developed with the 1925 International Opium Convention. Only in 1961 did the international community develop a convention to control other narcotic drugs in addition to opium.[56]

Historically, powerful states marketed drugs to the colonies they dominated. Today, by contrast, most cultivated narcotics are produced in the developing world and marketed widely in the most affluent countries of the developed world.[57]

Technological Innovation

Two major forms of contemporary illicit commerce that are top revenue generators, the production and sale of counterfeits and the illegal trade in intellectual property, emerged as major forms of illicit trade only with the industrial revolution.

As innovations in manufacturing, transport, and weaponry accelerated in the latter half of the nineteenth century, the inventors and their companies were eager to safeguard their new marketable products from theft and subsequent commercial exploitation. Their fear of the loss of their intellectual property was justified: valuable inventions often were stolen, and traders prospered through the reproduction and sale of what they had illegally acquired. Peter Andreas points out in *Smuggler Nation* that Americans illegally acquired key inventions—often from Britain, such as the cotton-carding machine—that were key to the growth of the new American economy, just as the stealing of the silkworm in the sixth century under Justinian had significant economic benefits for the Byzantines.[58]

Leisure travel increased in the late nineteenth century, and millions attended world's fairs in England, France, and other industrial centers that showcased advances in manufacturing, science, and technology. Yet with so many participants, these fairs presented a great many opportunities for copying inventions, resulting in significant financial losses to inventors and producers. National financial interests ultimately outweighed each country's desire to impress foreign tourists. Consequently, many governments refused to participate in a planned 1873 international exhibition in Vienna to display recent inventions. To ensure participation and attract exhibitors, a legal framework was developed to protect innovators.

A "special Austrian law secured temporary protection to all foreigners participating in the exhibition for their inventions, trademarks and industrial design." This temporary measure was followed by draft legislation that culminated in the 1883 signing by eleven countries of the Paris Convention for the Protection of Industrial Property. Most of the provisions of this convention have stayed in place for more than a century, although many countries are now signatories to a subsequent law enacted in 1967.[59] In 1886, a companion convention was approved in Berne that provided for the protection of literary and artistic works. It is the oldest legal agreement concerning copyright, and it remains significant today.[60]

The nineteenth-century problem of theft and subsequent production and trade of stolen intellectual property foreshadowed the challenges for inventors and designers today, when more products have become accessible through the web and also through the hacking of computer systems. For this reason, doctoral students seeking patents for the inventions they develop during their doctoral research resist placing their dissertations online.[61] Hackers steal not only existing inventions and technology but also the plans for innovative products yet to be made. This challenge was not anticipated before the rise of the virtual world.[62]

Nineteenth-century technological advances also had important consequences for life on the planet. Ships became faster and weapons technology more advanced, threatening both bird and mammalian life. In the late nineteenth century, over five million colorful birds were slaughtered annually to festoon women's hats with feathers. The first popular movement to protect wildlife, the Audubon Society in the United States, developed in response to these massive killings. Widespread consciousness of the value of species diversity subsequently led to the first legislation on environmental protection in the early twentieth century.[63] By that time, some species, such as the passenger pigeon, once omnipresent in North America, had already been driven to extinction.[64]

The most profitable industry of the nineteenth century, immortalized in Herman Melville's *Moby-Dick*, was whaling. With better ship construction, the whalers soon emptied the oceans of whales, leading to the collapse of this once-lucrative industry.[65] Unlike the public reaction to the killing of birds for ladies' hats, the whales disappeared in the nineteenth century without changing environmental consciousness. It was not until 1946 that the International Convention for the Regulation of Whaling was signed, part of the broader twentieth-century effort to protect the environment.[66]

Arms

The mid-nineteenth century saw the emergence of another important and durable form of illicit trade, one tied to the growth of technology and the industrial revolution. A growing arms trade was facilitated by new manufacturing methods that increased their production and affordability. The greater availability of arms over the course of the nineteenth century, due to both numbers and reduced price, compounded the difficulties for states trying to maintain control over their weapons, and the licit trade in arms was accompanied by the growth of illicit commerce.

Starting in the 1850s, individuals of many religious, ethnic, and geographic backgrounds participated in the clandestine arms trade. As a historian explained, "illicit traffic in small arms gave rise to networks of manufacturers, merchants, smugglers, insurgents and revolutionaries that crossed imperial, nation, and regional boundaries."[67]

Some participants in the arms trade were members of local elites. Texans who sympathized with the Mexican Revolution in the beginning of the 1900s helped equip the fighters with American-produced arms.[68] An especially colorful illustration comes from a Texas border town where smugglers stored weapons in the local county jail before shipping them south of the border.[69] American-produced weapons still cross the southern border, but the recipients now are drug trafficking organizations rather than revolutionaries.

As weapon production dispersed over time from the United States and Europe, Other lethal networks were created.[70] Many of these networks survive to this day. The illegal gun trade that developed in the Arab Middle East led to brigandage, more crime, and bandits and weakened the Turkish and Persian rule resented by the Arabs. Documenting this weapons trade in the early 1900s, a British survey concluded that this commerce might have a far-reaching impact and lead to "incurable disorder"—a prescient observation in light of the current state of much of the Arab Middle East and North Africa.[71]

The Twentieth Century

The twentieth century was particularly violent, marked by two world wars, liberation struggles against colonial powers, numerous regional political conflicts, mass death, purges, and genocide. This violence was accompanied by titanic political changes as colonialism ended, the rise of fascism led to World War II, and communism became a powerful ideology and a system of governance that did not provide for the consumer needs of its citizens. Great advances in medicine, science, and technology extended life expectancy, ushered in a new era of globalization, and revolutionized communication among the inhabitants of the planet, and massive marketing led to an era of widespread global consumerism.

Illicit commerce broadened in the twentieth century as well. Improved transport and communications integrated remote areas into international trade routes, and illicit commerce ceased to be primarily an urban phenomenon and became less reliant on the seas and ports.

Wars and conflicts produce shortages that make consumers as well as combatants participants in illicit commerce. Black markets and contraband trade prevail not only during wars but also in the postwar years, for as long as consumer goods remain unavailable.[72] And of course, illicit trade in weapons equips combatants.

The pillaging of wildlife, as well as trade in oil, minerals, gems, and timber, became central to the funding of armed conflicts in many regions of the world. In fact, resource wars have become increasingly common.[73] This is not a new problem, but the threat has escalated in the post–World War II period.[74] In contrast to previous centuries, illicit commerce in the twentieth century was rarely tied to nation-building.

The rise of multinational bodies such as the League of Nations and subsequently the United Nations has played a key role in the suppression of illicit trade, particularly the trade in women, children, and drugs.[75] The United Nations helped frame a response to transnational crime and illicit trade, beginning with the 1961 Single Convention on Narcotic Drugs.[76] This and subsequent legal frameworks address a broad range of transnational illicit commerce and its perpetrators and facilitators.

NEW FORMS OF ILLICIT TRADE

New forms of illicit commerce were a result of both technological advances and new regulations that prohibited many forms of trade. The new technologies created new commodities such as radioactive material and hazardous waste, as well as the internet, which enabled new and expanded forms of illicit trade. The international community created many new tools to counter the proliferation of illicit commerce, including treaties to address the trade in endangered species (the Convention on International Trade in Endangered Species of Wild Fauna and Flora, or CITES), the trade in chlorofluorocarbons (CFCs) (the Montreal Protocol on Substances That

Deplete the Ozone Layer), and the trade in components for weapons of mass destruction (WMDs).[77] Restrictions on the disposal of toxic waste followed the recognition in the 1980s of the harmful health and environmental effects of toxic dumping in the developing world.[78]

CONFLICTS AND ILLICIT TRADE

World wars, regional conflicts, and civil wars are all conducive to illicit commerce. Smuggling and illicit trade were endemic in World War II. All elements of society participated, including civilians, who did so to survive, and military elites and resistance fighters, who procured weaponry through illicit markets. A recently released World War II manual for British spies provides guidelines on how to smuggle contraband weaponry. For example, large metal drums to hold oil are compartmentalized with oil in one section and arms in the other. Fish barrels were also used as transport vehicles for weapons.[79]

The termination of war ended much of the smuggling and illicit trade as well, but the international community is still seeking to recover the valuable art that was stolen and often traded illegally during World War II. The 2015 movie *Woman in Gold* traced a family's long-term attempt to recover a valuable painting by Gustav Klimt that was stolen in the Nazi era. Following recovery, the painting was sold by the heirs for $135 million.[80] In August 2016, a massive digging operation was undertaken in Poland to locate a suspected trainload of valuables sought by treasure hunters who were certain they would find stolen art and gold that disappeared in World War II.[81]

The decades following World War II were followed by many independence struggles waged against colonial powers. In India, while some followed the path of nonviolent resistance of Gandhi, other opponents to British rule smuggled weapons from the United States.[82] The Indian example is far from unique.

Colonial struggles and postcolonial conflicts in Africa led to massive rhino loss, as slaughter of these animals helped fund fighters and buy arms. Ironically, the South African apartheid government was alleged to have used rhino horn to support military struggles in neighboring countries, as revealed by inquiries after the transition to African National Congress (ANC) rule under Nelson Mandela. The 1994 Kumleben Commission of Inquiry into the Alleged Smuggling of and Illegal Trade in Ivory and Rhinoceros Horn in South Africa found substantial evidence that the South African Defence Force (SADF) might have been involved in the killing and smuggling of rhinos and other animals in the 1970s. And as late as 1986, the SADF may also have been funding UNITA (National Union for the Total Independence of Angola) in Angola and RENAMO (Mozambican National Resistance) in Mozambique, which was battling the FRELIMO (Mozambique Liberation Front), a Marxist political party that supported the ANC (now the ruling party of South Africa).[83]

Resistance to foreign rule also justified illegal activity, giving legitimacy to smuggling and smugglers, as the ends justified the means. Colonialism ended between 1945 and 1960 in Asia and Africa as three dozen countries obtained their independence from European powers.[84] In some countries, it has been three generations since colonial rule, but the smuggling norms of the colonial period still prevail.

Marxist insurgencies, minority groups pressing for autonomy, and peasant rebellions followed the colonial struggles. Many of these groups relied on the trade in illegal drugs and arms to fund themselves. Like Eric Hobsbawm's *Primitive Rebels*, these combatants were often rural and poor. In the postcolonial period, the new bandits, like their historical predecessors engaging in social resistance, often were viewed as heroes by ordinary people.[85] Positive attitudes toward smuggling and contraband trade help explain their pervasiveness in the postcolonial environment.

Conflicts in the second half of the twentieth century have occurred disproportionately in natural resource–rich areas, such as Central and South America, Africa, and Southeast Asia, where abundant plant and animal species and timber can be smuggled for significant profit. This has contributed to the illicit trade undermining the sustainability of life on the planet. A *Conservation Biology* study reported that over 90 percent of the major armed conflicts between 1950 and 2000 were fought within countries containing biodiversity hot spots, and more than 80 percent took place directly within hot-spot areas.[86] The environmental consequences of this have become increasingly apparent as many species have become extinct and others have been placed on the CITES list of endangered species.

The drug trade funded many late-twentieth-century conflicts. Colombia and Peru provide early examples of narcotics sales funding regional conflicts and terrorist groups. In fact, the term "narco-terrorism" was coined by the Peruvian president Fernando Belaúnde Terry in 1983.[87] Subsequently, the connection between the drug trade and conflict funding became only more evident. As the twentieth century advanced, the drug trade helped fund conflicts in Afghanistan, Colombia, and Central America and is increasingly tied to significant urban violence in South Africa.

COMMUNISM AND THE COMMUNIST TRANSITION

The Communist system, with its one-party rule and centrally owned and planned economy, was conducive to the rise of an illicit economy. Communist rule in the post–World War II period stretched from the Pacific Ocean to the eastern border of Europe, encompassing the vast territory of China, Mongolia, the former Soviet Union, and Eastern Europe. But communism was not confined to this vast territory, as countries in Latin America (Cuba), Africa, Southeast Asia (Laos and Vietnam), and North Asia (North Korea) had Communist rulers or Communist officials with major political influence. Subunits of some populous countries were also ruled by Communists. In India, the states of Bengal on the northeast coast and Kerala in South India were under Communist rule for many decades. Many of these states shared patterns of an illicit economy similar to those in Russia and China, with which they were allied.

Under both Mao in the People's Republic of China and Stalin in the Soviet Union, the level of authoritarianism limited economic activities outside of state control. With the death of Stalin in 1953 and Mao in 1976, the authoritarian controls in these two countries and allied Communist states began to weaken. Then the shadow economy and illicit trade blossomed.[88]

Rule evasion became a core feature of Communist societies as citizens sought to obtain consumer goods not produced in adequate quantities and the centrally planned economy focused on military rather than civilian production. Citizens facing chronic shortages of basic consumer items were active participants in black markets and illicit trade as they turned to the markets to purchase food, clothing, and other needed items in constant short supply. Managers of state enterprises often developed mechanisms for obtaining the raw materials they needed to meet the often-unrealistic production targets set by central planners by encompassing illicit trade. Illegal businessmen in the Soviet Union produced goods in underground factories to be illegally traded, despite facing the death penalty for this *illicit entrepreneurship*.[89] The illicit trade in Communist countries was highly correlated with corrosive corruption, a problem that persists today.

Communist states developed not only an illegal and parallel economy but also the mentality associated with it. Many people in China and the Soviet Union prided themselves on their ability to get around the law. The word for "cunning" in Russian, *khitrost'*, had a positive connotation, and people relied on *blat*, their system of personal connections.[90] A culture of illicit exchange endured and was integral to the mainstream culture.[91]

CENTERS OF TRADE

Late in the twentieth century, the locus of trade shifted to Asia as the leading Asian countries assumed an ever-larger proportion of international commerce.[92] China, after transitioning from Mao-style communism, developed into a major industrial producer and participant in international commerce. Industrial growth there started after 1980, and China soon joined Japan and South Korea, whose postwar rise had transformed them into industrial countries and major participants in international trade. And after India opened its economy in 1990, large-scale Indian involvement in international trade ensued as well.

Illicit trade has always accompanied licit commerce. Therefore, while our previous history has focused primarily on illicit trade in

Europe, this later period requires more analysis of its dynamics in Asia. Illicit trade represents only a small proportion of total commerce, but every known form of dark commerce is now present in Asia, much of it integrated into global supply chains. As subsequent discussion of the trade and traders in narcotics, humans, wildlife, fish, and counterfeits makes clear, Asia is now central to illicit trade.

THE SEEDS OF THE NEW TECHNOLOGICAL REVOLUTION

Technological innovation characterized the postwar period in the United States and other developed countries and fostered a new and heightened international connectivity that had never existed previously.

In 1973, the US Defense Advanced Research Projects Agency (DARPA) began a research program to develop methods and techniques to interlink networks of diverse kinds in order to improve remote access and computer-to-computer communications.[93] Later the system was used for robust communications between authorized users (originally military and later scientific) that could survive a nuclear attack; it was not open to the public.[94] Problems arose when this system was subsequently opened up to a large general audience before adequate regulations had been put in place. The technology was quickly adopted by users never anticipated by its developers, who had not constructed the underlying architecture with security as a driver.[95]

Only after 1993, the time period of the next chapter, do we see private firms entering into this arena and building their own networks.[96] The technical community that created computing never imagined that this technological development would scale into a communications method that would reach billions of people throughout the world.[97]

Conclusion

The last two centuries of illicit commerce differ from its historical antecedents. Illicit trade became more diversified, dispersed, and harmful to human life and our fellow species on the planet. In this period, as in the past, illicit trade was never an activity undertaken solely by criminals. Rather, prohibited trade continued because it relied on many sectors of society—businesspeople, government officials, professionals, and consumers. Some government officials who got involved may have been corrupt, but others did so because complicity with illicit trade helped maintain order and the stability of local power elites, such as during the colonial period in East Africa.

Political ideas, as well as state policy, help determine what is illicit trade. This chapter's analysis has shown that the principles of the Enlightenment contributed to the prohibition of slavery. More recently, when Communist ideology, with its commitment to a centrally planned and state-owned economy, criminalized trade outside of state control, massive black markets and second economies arose to satisfy consumer demand for needed and desired commodities that were not available. The legacy of getting around the system endures in the trade patterns of many transitional and post-Communist states.

Already in the nineteenth century, changes in trade policy and the outlawing of certain commodities produced serious disruptions to national and regional economies. The Chinese policy to ban drug importation severely affected India, as opium was one of India's largest crops during colonial rule.[98] Likewise, slaves were a key export of Africa before Britain outlawed the slave trade. The prohibition had dramatic impacts on local economies, particularly in West Africa, and deprived kingdoms of revenues of one of their most lucrative exports. Economic decline was one consequence of this trade ban, even though exports of slaves continued illegally. More recently, drugs have been a key export for many developing countries.

Colonialism defined the nineteenth century and much of the twentieth. During these years, many of the colonized resisted foreign rule by both passive and violent means. Avoiding the taxes paid to distant rulers by smuggling goods became a means of nonviolent resistance, as had been seen in the American colonies prior to the Revolution. The struggles for independence from far-flung colonial rulers also required arms and ammunition, often acquired through illegal trade. Modern illicit trade, like its historical predecessors, served many more functions than the mere acquisition of desired consumer commodities.

During the latter half of the twentieth century, the most lucrative form of illicit trade was the narcotics trade. As the century progressed, diverse types of illegal drugs proliferated and were traded in ever-larger quantities and in ever-more remote parts of the globe. The cultivation of drugs in rural areas marked an important transformation of illicit trade. As described by Braudel, illicit trade was once primarily an urban or maritime phenomenon, but the integration of rural drug-producing regions, such as the Andes in South America and Afghanistan in Asia, into global narcotics supply chains made even remote rural areas part of the illicit global economy.[99]

The narcotics trade and the trade in women and children were not the only forms of international commerce to be increasingly regulated in the twentieth century. The growth of science and technology in the twentieth century, a period of great scientific innovation, had an enormous impact on the forms and definition of illicit commerce—a fact rarely analyzed in the illicit trade literature. Science and technology contributed to the rise of modern commerce, but these developments also fostered the drive for regulatory change.[100]

Twentieth-century science has helped us appreciate the costs of eliminating species, polluting the air, consuming contaminated food, deforesting the land, and overfishing the sea, and that increased knowledge has led to many of the regulations governing the trade in these items. Trade prohibitions expanded as research in conservation and agricultural science, biology, atmospheric physics, medical science, and chemistry enhanced our understanding of sustainability. Early in the twentieth century, some colonists began to advocate for conservation and trade curbs as they came to understand the harm posed to fragile ecological systems through human interventions.[101] Bird advocates, as mentioned earlier, sought to protect avian life after the rapacious demand for feathers to adorn ladies' hats led to the demise of millions of birds.

The private sector in the late twentieth century, seeking to protect its designs and products from counterfeiting, became integral to efforts to control illicit trade. Music and videos were being hijacked and distributed without payments, for instance, and technological innovations were being stolen and copied by competitors.

The expansion of global trade in the nineteenth and twentieth centuries allowed illicit goods to travel along the same routes used by the legitimate economy. The increasing ease of movement of goods, people, and money at the end of the twentieth century merely accentuated trade trends that had been evident for centuries. The end of that century and the beginning of the twenty-first marked an abrupt rupture with millennia of illicit commerce as the technological capacity of traders, trading in many new commodities, expanded exponentially in cyberspace.

3

How Did We Get Here?

DRIVERS OF THE
POST-COLD WAR EXPANSION

Many explain the growth of illicit trade in the post–Cold War period as a consequence of globalization.[1] The term *deviant globalization* has been coined to suggest that illicit commerce grows faster than its legitimate counterpart.[2] Globalization, however, explains only part of the growth of illicit trade, as licit and illicit trade have co-existed for centuries. The illicit economy in recent decades has been fueled by many of the key indicators of the current wave of globalization—increasing global competition, the increasing mobility of goods, money, and people, and the decline of borders, combined with the new technology of the Internet and social media. These features of post–Cold War life have facilitated the rapid rise of both licit and illicit international trade.

The profound political instability and corruption in many locales in the contemporary world undermines legal commerce and makes the rise of illicit trade an ever more pervasive problem. For many of the world's inhabitants today, participation in the illicit economy is a means of survival, and a way out of a precarious situation.[3]

This instability results from the problematic transitions of Communist states; the rise of regional conflicts; the increasing role of nonstate actors, including criminals and terrorists; and the recent displacements of tens of millions of people.[4] The use of economic sanctions for political objectives has also contributed to the rise of illicit trade, as businesses in countries under sanctions engage in smuggling to evade controls.[5] Iran has smuggled oil, and Russia, under sanctions after its invasion of Crimea, has turned Crimea and the Donbas in Ukraine into smugglers' paradises. North Korea has partially financed its nuclear program and its state through state-sponsored smuggling of currency, drugs, wildlife parts, and cigarettes.[6]

The following case studies on Syria and the online marketplace known as Silk Road illustrate some of the major challenges posed by the illicit economy today. Conflict regions and cyberspace are two areas where the problem is most concentrated, but unfortunately, they are far from the only locales where this commerce is operating. The illicit economy is now present on every continent, with participants ranging from the elite of the corporate and financial worlds to the lowest economic levels—the farmers who grow drugs and the trafficked laborers who work in abusive conditions on commercial fishing boats—to the consumers who, both wittingly and unwittingly, participate in dark commerce by purchasing its products.

Syria: The Domino Effect from One Form of Illicit Trade to Many

The deadly crisis in Syria, in which an estimated 475,000 have been killed and 14 million have been wounded or displaced,[7] began with the Arab Spring of 2011, but was not just the rise of a population against an authoritarian leader. Rather, there was another important source of instability: a mass exodus from rural areas as a result of recurring drought and the decline of the famed Fertile Crescent of the Middle East.

In the 1970s, Hafez al-Assad, the father of the current president, Bashar al-Assad, launched an ill-conceived drive to have Syria achieve agricultural self-sufficiency. "No one seemed to consider whether Syria had sufficient groundwater and rainfall to raise those crops," *Scientific American* explained recently. "Farmers made up for water shortages by drilling wells to tap the country's underground reserves."[8] As water became less available, people dug deeper wells in search of even less accessible supplies.

In 2005, to deal with the paucity of water, President Bashar al-Assad made it illegal to dig new wells without a license, which required the payment of a fee.[9] But in a highly corrupt environment, the digging did not stop: those with money for bribes continued to dig deeper. There was an illicit trade in water rights, aggravated by corruption. But the relief was not sustained even with the payment of bribes. The drought in the once-fabled Fertile Crescent continued, and any remaining water was so deep that it was no longer profitable to dig.

Seventy-five percent of Syria's wheat came from drought-affected areas.[10] In the absence of crops, desperation drove individuals living in desert agricultural areas to migrate en masse to the cities. Between 2002 and 2010, shortly after Bashar al-Assad assumed power, Syria urbanized at an incredibly rapid rate. Before the American invasion of Iraq in 2002, there were 8.9 million Syrian city-dwellers; in 2010, there were 13.8 million. Of this rural exodus of almost 5 million people, approximately 1.5 million were fleeing the drought.[11] In a decade, Syria became one of the most urbanized countries in the world.[12] But this population transition occurred in a corrupt and badly governed state that did not show concern for its citizens and their welfare.

Recent migrants to urban areas congregated in the illegal settlements that developed on the periphery of Syrian cities. Neglected by the Assad government, these communities were characterized by a paucity of infrastructure, high crime rates, an absence of services, and unemployment; ultimately, they "became the heart of the developing unrest" during the Arab Spring.[13]

The story of the Syrian drought refugees does not end with the beginning of the Arab Spring. Rather, that uprising was the beginning of a domino effect. The Syrians' departure from rural areas was the first leg of a longer journey that often took a more tragic course, as these rural-to-urban migrants had to then flee civil war and destruction. Many left for Europe via precarious smuggling routes that crossed Turkey, and they also embarked on dangerous boats that traversed the tumultuous waters of the Mediterranean. A whole illicit industry has now arisen to facilitate this movement, or "trade," in people. Individuals sell their remaining valuables to pay the smugglers who can move their families to safety. A few without financial resources will even sell their kidneys to wealthy buyers to pay the fees to get their families to safety.[14] Others pay part of the fee in advance and then, still indebted to the smugglers on arrival, are often forced into work in slavelike conditions in Europe.

The prolonged conflict in Syria has resulted in great human suffering and massive loss of life and infrastructure. Like many others in the world, the Syrian conflict has been partly financed by illicit trade. The smuggling of drugs, humans, oil, and antiquities and the trafficking of cigarettes and other contraband have provided funds to buy weapons and sustain fighters on all sides, from President Bashar al-Assad's government forces to resistance and terrorist groups. Those profiting from the smuggling in Syria include government officials, criminals, and terrorists such as Al-Nusra and ISIS.[15] Illicit trade today, when conducted by nonstate actors or abusive authoritarian leaders like Assad, destroys the state as well as human lives and destabilizes regions. This is the ongoing reality of dark commerce at its worst in the contemporary world.

Key Lessons of the Syria Case

This case is one of the worst examples of the growth of regional conflicts in the post–Cold War period. Illicit trade has funded many of the most important disputes and clashes of recent decades in the Middle East, Africa, Latin America, and Asia and the conflict between Russia and Ukraine.[16] Research indicates that greed, rather than grievance, prolongs these conflicts as the combatants become used to the profits generated by their smuggling and contraband sales.[17]

Conflicts may be started by resource scarcity, but they also have damaging environmental consequences. "Across the Middle East and parts of North Africa, civil war, poaching to buy guns, and refugees' urgent need for food and firewood, are extinguishing relic populations of wildlife and wrecking habitats."[18] The arrival of ISIS in Syria led to not only the looting of antiquities but the killing of the last-known endangered Northern bald ibis.[19]

Resource depletion and climate change lie at the heart of the Syrian conflict and will continue to be key drivers of human displacement in the future. Individuals and families will continue to pay smugglers to move them illegally to unwelcoming lands. To cover their transport costs and ensure their survival en route and at their destination, many will participate in different elements of the illicit economy to survive. Often found at the lowest levels of the illicit economy, these participants bear the brunt of enforcement efforts.[20]

The consequences of climate change are becoming more evident as average global temperatures rise and climate conditions become more erratic. Climate change contributes to droughts, resulting in less available water for agricultural and human consumption; water scarcity, in turn, fuels illegal migration, such as the exodus of Syrians to Europe.[21]

In Africa, large numbers of people are literally marching out of the Sahel. Illegal migration and massive population displacement is also under way in the Bay of Bengal, ground zero for the impact of climate change.[22] There, rising seawater threatens low-lying land, and parts of Bangladesh and other areas in the region are already uninhabitable for parts of the year. As in the Sahel, inhabitants of inundated communities seek the aid of smugglers to move them to locales that can sustain life.

The identified crises in Africa and Asia help explain why displacement is being rapidly exacerbated. In 2018, the United Nations High Commission for Refugees (UNHCR) determined that there were 68.5 million refugees around the world (or 1 out every 113 people), up from 37.5 million a decade ago.[23] With significant growth from the preceding year, the world recorded an all-time high in the number of people displaced by conflict, persecution, and climate change.[24] Many refugees are housed in camps near their homes, where they are vulnerable to diverse forms of exploitation.

Many displaced persons now increasingly live in informal settlements, such as those seen in Syria. Poorly governed cities and megacities expand in the developing world, a consequence of the absence of arable land and potable water. People with no access to the basic elements to sustain life will be increasingly forced to rely on nonstate actors when the state does not deliver needed services. Water mafias that provide water to drink and for daily use have proliferated in Asian and Latin American urban environments, demonstrating that illicit trade arises in the absence of conditions conducive to human survival.[25]

The mass movement of desperate Syrian migrants to adjoining states and Europe has created major political and economic crises in the destination countries, which were not equipped to accept millions of displaced people. In reaction, the receiving states and many other countries in Europe have sought to curtail migrant smuggling, as they do not want to receive any more illegal migrants whose integration will pose serious economic, social, and political challenges. Yet the ongoing illegal migration is a harbinger of the mass population movements in store in the coming decades of the twenty-first century.

Technology and Illicit Trade

At the initiation of illicit trade in cyberspace, it was merely an online version of traditional illicit trade. Yet it shortly added previously unknown products to the repertoire of illicit commerce—intangible goods such as the previously cited malware, ransomware, and botnets, whose value depends only on the ingenuity of illicit entrepreneurs with cyber-skills. The new technologies have allowed illicit traders to communicate in encrypted forms, making it difficult to unravel their networks, learn of their scheduled deliveries, or follow the money.[26] The recent rise of cryptocurrencies has only added to the difficulties in unraveling criminal networks.[27]

Today, with approximately 7 percent of commerce online in the European Union and the United States and online shopping constantly growing, there are ample opportunities for criminals to expand their activities rapidly.[28] Buyers can now purchase opioids, harmful pharmaceuticals and other counterfeits, and sexual services, all through the internet.

Another central hub of illicit trade is the Dark Net, the deepest part of the Internet, accessible only by special software such as Tor.[29] On the Dark Net, vendors seek to evade law enforcement detection and the most dangerous items are sold: narcotics; arms, child pornography; and malicious tools to undermine computer systems that allow users to hack into financial accounts; moreover, parts for nuclear devices and biological weapons are advertised for sale.[30] The harm is not confined to the developed world: the malicious products sold on the Dark Net have affected computers in almost all countries of the world.[31]

Many associate the misconduct in cyberspace with the cyber-criminals of the Soviet successor states. But the ingenuity of the legitimate tech world in North America also has its counterpart in the Dark Net. Silk Road was initiated by an American, and the subsequent successful Dark Net site, AlphaBay, was created by a Canadian.[32]

Silk Road: Anonymous Online Markets and Cryptocurrencies

Key developers of illicit cyber-trade, like the American Ross Ulbricht, aka Dread Pirate Roberts (he took his pseudonym from a fictional character in the novel and film *Princess Bride*) developed the first mega-online market for illicit goods. Online sellers from developed countries often do not have criminal pasts.[33] In fact, Dread Pirate Roberts reached the highest Boy Scout rank of Eagle Scout, an achievement reached by few. Isolated from the world of drug traffickers and addicts, he could not imagine the suffering he was facilitating through Silk Road, his online marketplace for drugs.[34]

The managers and creators of illegal cyber-markets operate outside the constraints of society. Like many innovators in the illicit cyberworld, Ulbricht was a dropout from a physics PhD program who had a high technical capacity but whose capacity for human interactions was less developed.[35] He might have been a failure in legitimate traditional commerce because of his lack of interpersonal skills, but in the anonymous, impersonal cyberworld, he could thrive temporarily.

Ulbricht's goal was to create a market for drugs that would result in their legalization. His libertarian philosophy made him seek to develop a trade model outside state control, avoiding taxation and regulation.[36] Dread Pirate Roberts thought he provided a better marketplace, one where risks were lower, drug quality was higher, and the violence associated with drug trafficking was less prominent. Unfortunately, purchasers died from drugs bought from Silk Road. Ulbricht eventually ordered multiple murders to make his operations profitable (although it is not clear that these killings ever took place), and law enforcement investigating his activities went to the dark side as well.

Large-scale online child pornography developed early in cyberspace, but large online illicit marketplaces, like Silk Road, were not launched for over fifteen years after the founding of Amazon and eBay.[37] Dread Pirate Roberts launched The Silk Road in February 2011, after working for months writing code to establish his site in the Dark Net.[38] With no prior experience in marketing anything, he launched Silk Road with an internet blog post, announcing its existence to drive customers to the Dark Net, where there are no advertisements or search engines.[39] Dread Pirate Roberts watched his business grow exponentially, diversify its drug products, as well as expand into arms sales and software products harmful to financial and computer systems (Trojans, spyware, and malware apps).[40] At the height of Silk Road's operations, 600,000 messages were exchanged monthly between buyers and sellers. Ulbricht received a commission on sales through the Silk Road site. Processing $1.2 billion in transactions in a little over two years through the cryptocurrency Bitcoin, he netted $80 million—unimaginable wealth for a person who had lived at the fringes of society.[41] Regrettably for him, he was never able to enjoy his newly obtained wealth, as Silk Road was taken down in July 2013 after long and laborious effort by law enforcement. Unfortunately, there are risks of large-scale illicit commerce in the cyberworld for criminals who operate in countries with well-functioning law enforcement. Silk Road products were delivered by post and left a trail that could be followed, one element that helped lead to Ulbricht's capture. Dread Pirate Roberts and many of his employees who helped run the site around the world were arrested by police in many different developed countries.[42]

A harsh fate awaited Dread Pirate Roberts. As the sentencing judge explained, he might be a libertarian by philosophy, but his conduct was no different from that of any large drug dealer.[43] She sentenced him to two life sentences, plus forty years without parole, a sentence that has been upheld on appeal.

The judge was correct in characterizing his behavior. Ulbricht did not create a less violent world in which to sell drugs, but he himself became violent in his years as a drug seller. He used Bitcoin to hire multiple hit men in an attempt to kill rivals and people who he thought had stolen cryptocurrency from him.[44]

Moreover, Silk Road did not escape the corruption that accompanies organized crime. Two federal agents from the US Secret Service and the Drug Enforcement Administration (DEA) are now serving seven-year prison sentences. Seeing the intense wealth generated by Silk Road sales and the anonymity of the payment system, one agent stole Bitcoins from Dread Pirate Roberts. This DEA agent provided Ulbricht with inside information on the investigation, helping him evade detection, for which the law enforcer received large Bitcoin payments.[45] This may be the first investigation in the virtual world where federal investigators went to prison for serious acts of corruption. This case affirms that corruption can travel from the real to the virtual world. As humans transfer their modes of conduct into cyberspaces like illegal online marketplaces, corruption will not disappear.

Central Themes

The patterns of criminal behavior associated with the Silk Road site resemble the crime we know in the real world. Cybercrime operates in many familiar ways because it is committed by real-world criminals operating by means of new technology. They simply transfer their criminal and corrupt practices to a new domain.

Silk Road has received much attention because it was the first cyber-supermarket for narcotics, arms, and other illegal commodities, but it has been followed by even larger websites. Going after crime kingpins such as Dread Pirate Roberts does not always eliminate the crime problem. Rather, taking out these major players may provide growth and promotion opportunities for other criminals. Since Silk Road's closure in 2013, transactions for illicit drugs on markets in cyberspace have tripled and revenues have doubled.[46] Once taken down by law enforcement, Silk Road was replaced in about a month by Silk Road 2.0—an indication of the speed at which complex programming can be done when there is a strong financial motivation.[47] Silk Road 3.1 was broken into during the summer of 2017. Each generation of the illicit online marketplace is more active than the past one. AlphaBay, another site that operated from 2014 to its mid-2017 takedown by law enforcement, had 350,000 listings for illegal drugs, goods, and services—more than twenty times greater than the 14,000 listings on Silk Road at the time of its closure.[48] The extraordinary growth of the illicit online marketplace makes its products and services more widely available to consumers around the world.

Cybercriminals, as we will discuss in chapter 5, also sell and rent new products, such as malware, a newly created virtual product that exploits computer systems and harms the accounts of individuals connected to the internet. Cybercriminals are not just traders in information and goods but also creators of a range of new products that can do massive harm. Just as legitimate technology companies are staffed by computer programmers who create new software and products to sell, smart techies in the parallel illicit world, like Dread Pirate Roberts, exploit their advanced knowledge of computers and programming to create harmful new businesses. They are not just traders of goods and information but *illicit entrepreneurs* who start, launch, and run criminal businesses.

As a consequence of illicit entrepreneurship, an estimated 17.6 million Americans in 2014 (or one in six of those age sixteen or older) had their identities stolen. Trade in victims' stolen personal information facilitated lucrative financial crime as their bank accounts were emptied.[49] Another group of cybercriminals operating out of Estonia, a high-tech center, were sentenced in 2016 for infecting four million computers, in one hundred countries, with malware in a multimillion-dollar fraud scheme.[50] These cases reflect the asymmetric harm made possible by technology: a small group of criminals can have a negative impact on millions of lives around the world.

The illicit entrepreneurs of the tech economy—who, like their counterparts in the legitimate economy, are overwhelmingly male and often youthful—represent a new security challenge. During the Cold War era, mature individuals were behind the buttons determining whether there would be a nuclear attack. Today, by contrast, it is often unsupervised and testosterone-driven teenagers or young adults who undermine global security by launching devastating cyberattacks.[51]

Yet not all the illicit traders operating via the new technology are pursuing personal profit. Some states, including Russia and China, are directly employing or engaging criminal actors to engage in cybercrimes that undermine the financial and political health of other countries, their elections, their companies, and their citizens. Hacking into the computer systems of innovative companies to steal intellectual property or personal information is another example of new forms of illicit commerce with important financial implications.[52] An estimated half a billion personal records were stolen in 2015, not only by criminals but also by state-sponsored hackers. This figure may even be understated, as many companies do not want to reveal breaches of their computer systems.[53]

The Drivers of the Growth of Illicit Commerce in the Post-Cold War Period

The two case studies of epicenters of illicit trade in the post–Cold War period—Syria and the online Silk Road—highlight just some of the reasons that illicit commerce has escalated dramatically in the last three decades. Other important changes of the last thirty years, apart from the technological revolution, have also profoundly transformed illicit trade and contributed to its growth: continuing population growth, including the youth bulge; rising income inequality; the enormous expansion of the middle class, particularly in Asia; continuing gender inequality; the transformation of Communist states; and the rise of nonstate actors such as transnational criminals and terrorists.

POPULATION GROWTH

Population growth has been concentrated in the developing world, where corruption is high and the funds needed for development are often stolen and moved offshore. In Africa, Latin America, the Middle East, and South Asia, there is a youth bulge (a large under-thirty population). The large numbers of young people often lack the needed education to obtain the limited legitimate employment. Often they can find jobs only in the illicit economy.[54] Such work may be even more difficult, however, because workers lack job security and benefits and may be exploited. Moreover, because they work outside the legal system, workers face possible punishment from the state. Despite all these negative factors, work within illicit economies for an organized crime group or network is still attractive because it may offer ready cash and a sense of belonging, motivations that also drive youth to join terrorist groups.

INCOME INEQUALITY AND THE RISE OF A MIDDLE CLASS

Income inequality has increased dramatically in recent years, both within and between countries. In many countries since 1980, much of the world's newly generated wealth is concentrated in the hands of the top 1 percent, with even greater concentration in the top 0.1 percent.[55] To put this in more accessible terms, the eight richest people in the world have as much wealth as the world's poorest 50 percent.[56] Since the economic crisis of 2008, the trend toward income inequality has only accelerated. Over half of the 103 countries for which data are available have become less equal in recent years.[57]

This disparity in wealth has political as well as economic consequences. As societies become more polarized, citizens strike back at existing power structures. This was visible in 2016 when the displaced and often struggling middle class in the United States largely voted against the existing political order. Significant protests against corruption have also been seen in Brazil, Russia, and South Africa.[58]

While many of the world's billions live in extreme poverty and insecurity, at the end of 2016 there was a global middle class of 3.2 billion, a figure growing annually by 140 million. Most of this growth is in Asia, primarily India and China.[59] Middle-class consumption enhances demand for many items, including better food, urban homes, and household furnishings. Unfortunately, the scale of this increased demand is putting intense pressure on natural resources—for example, existing fish stocks that should not be depleted to satisfy increased consumption demands, or trees in protected forests that should not be cut down to meet the demand for new housing and furniture.

In the increasingly economically polarized world, a mega-elite often engages in conspicuous consumption, buying up products that were once the possessions only of maharajas, emperors, and kings. In Asia, they want ivory and rhino horns that were once the status symbols of royalty. Asian elites' quest for traditional medicines and other products to improve well-being is driving rhinos, abalone, and wild Appalachian ginseng to extinction.[60] In other regions of the world, the rich want private zoos filled with endangered animals, or the diamonds that may be funding conflicts.[61]

GENDER INEQUALITY AND ILLICIT TRADE

The exclusion of women from positions of power and authority is a problem in the illicit as well as the licit world. Women rarely assume leadership positions in the dark economy: if they play a role, it is a supporting one. They become drug mules, couriers of illicit profits, and front people for money laundering. The only area where women are visible is human trafficking: some women, once trafficked themselves, assume leadership and facilitating roles in the recruitment and exploitation of other women and girls. According to UN data, from 2010 to 2012, 28 percent of convictions for human trafficking were of women, whereas women represented only 10 to 15 percent of those found guilty for other serious offenses.[62]

The increased of trafficking of women from the former Soviet Union brought unprecedented attention to human trafficking in the early 1990s, but the phenomenon is now recognized as a much broader global problem.[63] Women and girls are trafficked not just into sexual exploitation but also into domestic servitude, forced marriage, and labor. In some developing societies, the sale of girls helps families pay for familial needs—food, the education of male children, and medical care needed by family members.[64] The marketing of women and girls through the internet, the Deep Web, the Dark Net, and social media has facilitated the surge in human beings as a trade good.[65]

Women are often exploited in factories, especially in free economic zones, where existing labor protections are absent or ignored.[66] This statement does not begin to capture the misery of the women confined in these facilities. A case in American Samoa—the largest American human trafficking case ever prosecuted—reveals the suffering that these women endure. The textile factory owner, Kil Soo Lee, and his managers used food deprivation, beatings, and threats to increase production at his Daewoosa plant. The owner retaliated against workers who tried to obtain food from the local community by confining them in the fenced compound then ultimately organized a mass beating of the Vietnamese women workers.[67] This criminal conduct resulted in a forty-year prison sentence for Kil Soo Lee.[68]

THE TRANSFORMATION OF COMMUNIST SOCIETIES

Prior to the 1990s, eastern Europe, the Soviet Union, Mongolia, China, parts of Africa, South East and South Asia, and Latin America were governed by Communist parties that maintained one-party rule, centrally planned economies, and limited private property ownership. All shared a common absence of consumer goods. In most of these societies, black markets, rule-breaking, and getting around the system lay at the heart of daily survival. This consciousness remains, even after the collapse of the Communist system in eastern Europe and the Soviet Union.

The troubled transitions from Communist rule have contributed significantly to the extent of and the threat from contemporary illicit trade. The political power vacuum, the pervasive corruption, the absence of border controls in post-Soviet states, and the rise of powerful crime groups were conducive to the proliferation of diverse forms of illicit trade in the 1990s.[69] Of greatest concern has been the trade in WMDs (weapons of mass destruction): the former Soviet Union had a large stockpile of nuclear and radiological materials and biological weapons, and they pose an existential security challenge if they fall into the wrong hands.[70] The theft and trafficking of nuclear materials and radioactive waste improperly safeguarded have remained a recurrent problem in the decades since the collapse of the Soviet Union.[71]

Other forms of disturbing illicit trade originated in Communist states in transition. Today massive quantities of counterfeit goods originate from China, now the factory for the world. In Russia, a new kleptocratic elite lacking an environmental conscience (one consequence of long-term state ownership of land and resources) plunders the great forests of Siberia for profit.[72] Much cybercrime originates from eastern Europe and the former Soviet Union, partly because, with corporate raiding (discussed more in chapter 5) and limited technological entrepreneurship, owners with successful businesses lose them through violence and abuse of the legal system.[73]

Countries in transition from communism are sources not only of illicitly traded goods but also of consumers of these products. Chinese and Vietnamese customers display their new affluence by consuming endangered species and displaying the horn and ivory of the increasingly endangered rhino and elephant.[74]

THE RISE OF NONSTATE ACTORS: CRIMINALS AND TERRORISTS

Transnational Criminals

Transnational criminals and corrupt officials have been among the major beneficiaries of globalization, accelerating the growth of illicit trade internationally. This is not just a phenomenon popularized by the mass media.[75] Organized criminals have entered the political process in many countries not only by bribing government officials and legislators and financing politicians but also by running for office themselves at the state, local, and national levels.[76] In some countries, there is an extra incentive to enter politics, as officials acquire immunity from prosecution.[77]

Traditional organized crime groups, such as the Italian *Mafia* and *Camorra*, the Japanese *Yakuza*, and the Chinese *triads*, have rapidly adapted to the possibilities of the globalized world, moving goods and money transnationally with alacrity and facility. Yet there are also many newer transnational crime groups that have excelled in these skill sets from their inception.[78] Post-Soviet groups have been leaders in deviant global commerce, especially in human trafficking and cyberspace.

The rise of transnational crime in post-Soviet states was rapid. These groups and their corrupt associates accumulated substantial capital with the massive privatization of state resources, which allowed them to acquire government property at bargain prices and embed themselves within the economy.[79] Their ascendency was not unique. Conflicts in recent decades in Afghanistan, the Balkans, and North Africa, to name just a few notable examples, have contributed to the rise of powerful new organized crime groups.[80] Indeed, criminalized power structures have served as enemies of peace.[81] In Afghanistan, a massive drug trade tied to the national leadership made an illicit crop a core element of the economy.[82] At its height, drugs represented approximately 30 percent of Afghanistan's gross national product (GNP).[83]

Crime groups cooperate in ways that licit actors do not. For example, Jamaicans and Turks have collaborated in the narcotics markets of London.[84] Russians have traveled to Colombia to build submarines to help drug lords, establishing and maintaining their relationships there in a strip club near the Miami, Florida, airport.[85] Collaboration among such diverse criminal groups might seem too unrealistic for a Hollywood film, but they prevail in reality.

Terrorists

Since 2000, terrorism has been an increasing global problem. A "new terrorism," unlike its state-supported predecessor, has been responsible for larger-scale attacks with more victims.[86] New terrorists, using false documents and identities to cross borders, rely on illicit commerce to support their organizations.[87] Terrorists equipped with sham papers commit mass murder.[88]

Objects traded far from their point of origin may fund terrorists. Illicitly acquired Syrian antiquities such as coins, cuneiform tablets, rings, and sculptures are subsequently sold in art galleries in Europe, at auction, and online, reflecting the ever-present links between the licit and illicit economies.[89] Heroin sold in Russia, Europe, and elsewhere funds terrorism in Afghanistan.

ISIS and Al-Nusra taxed the transit of commodities and people crossing territory they controlled. According to a retired high-ranking Jordanian military official, these two terrorist groups fought in the morning and then declared afternoon cease-fires to extort money from the human smugglers and refugees departing from the war-torn territory.[90] The extraction of financial resources from vulnerable migrants took precedence over battlefield objectives. According to documents obtained from ISIS, their rate of taxation on goods and services ranged from 10 to 30 percent.[91] Taxed trade goods included counterfeit cigarettes, pharmaceuticals, cell phones, antiquities, and foreign passports obtained from arriving foreign fighters.[92]

In Europe, ISIS recruits funded themselves through small-scale illicit trade and criminal activity.[93] Petty illegal commerce is particularly attractive to terrorists because there is less market saturation, less regulation, reduced competition, and more limited law enforcement than for arms and narcotics trafficking. A high proportion of identified terrorists and members of their networks have criminal records.[94] German analyses revealed that two-thirds of German foreign fighters had prior convictions for property and violent crime, and nearly one-third had been sentenced six or more times, reflecting their serious criminal pasts.[95] In the Netherlands, almost half of identified foreign fighters had prior convictions.[96] Similar patterns have been identified in other European countries.

The Extent and the Impact of Contemporary Illicit Commerce

In 2014, the United Nations Office on Drugs and Crime (UNODC) estimated annual revenues of transnational crime at $1.6 trillion to $2.2 trillion.[97] The total figures were far above estimates from a couple of years earlier, when the global economy was still in recession and cybercrime had not yet escalated to present levels, but its share remains steady. At that time, UN specialists commented, "These immense illicit funds are worth more than six times the amount of official development assistance, and are comparable to 1.5 per cent of global GDP, or 7 per cent of the world's exports of merchandise."[98] These figures may be understated, however, since corruption can undermine the accuracy and extent of reporting: border guards and custom officials who are complicit in the smuggling of goods across frontiers may fail to report the trade. Another reason cybercrime often remains underreported is that companies do not choose to share data on their losses, as such reports would undermine their reputation and could erode their customer base.

The illicit economy is not evenly distributed. It is most pervasive in the developing world, while dark commerce in cyberspace is particularly prominent in the more developed countries. Because the commodities of the illicit economy often converge—following the same trade routes, being transported by the same people, and providing economies of scale for the traders—it can be difficult to differentiate the profits for individual categories of illicit trade.

Examining only the revenues of illicit commerce understates its cost. The transfer of hundreds of billions to criminals, terrorists, insurgents, and corrupt officials enhances the wealth and power of individuals without concern for the welfare of societies, democratic principles, or sustainable economic growth. This trade destabilizes global and regional stability and threatens our future. More concretely, dark commerce operates as an asymmetric threat. It increases corruption and reduces governmental revenues, and corporate losses to dark commerce cut into the funds needed for innovation. Purchases of narcotics and inferior or dangerous pharmaceuticals also have significant health costs, and the planet loses species and biodiversity through the illicit trade in environmental products.

Thus, any such figures must be viewed with some skepticism, as many of those combating illicit commerce have an inherent interest in illustrating the severity of the problem to ensure financial support and attention to their issues. Twenty years ago, the UN estimated global drug revenues at $400 billion (or 8 percent of global trade, larger than the international trade in iron, steel, and motor vehicles).[99] But present-day estimates place revenues at $320 billion, and a much-diminished share of global commerce, despite the fact that an estimated 5 percent of the world's population has tried narcotics in recent years.[100] Both increased competition and better data reporting could explain the revenue decline.[101] It is more likely, however, that the heightening of the menace of the drug threat twenty years ago increased the constituency for the United Nations Convention against Transnational Crime, then under development.

Estimating profits and victimization for the three other highly criminalized forms of illegal trade—human trafficking, smuggling, and the arms trade—is also highly problematic. The International Labour Organization's new index on forced labor suggests that 25 million are victimized. The ILO figures include but do not estimate human trafficking.[102] Revenues for human trafficking are appreciably lower in developing countries in Asia, Africa, and Latin America than in western Europe and the United States, where traffickers achieve the highest profits from sex trafficking.[103] Greater profits in developed countries do not indicate the presence of more victims, but rather the superiority of the proceeds from human exploitation in wealthier societies.

Proceeds from organ trafficking, which is often considered a subset of human trafficking, were estimated at $840 million to $1.7 billion in 2014.[104] These high figures for illegal organ transplants reflect the high cost of the procedure, not the volume of operations.

There are no reliable global estimates of the profits of human smuggling, but at the height of the refugee crisis in 2015, Europol estimated that European smugglers generated between 4.7 billion and 5.7 billion euros, with an estimated 50,000 criminals involved in the trade.[105]

Small arms and light weapons trafficking generates less in profits than other major transnational crime activities: revenues in 2014 were estimated to be $1.7 billion to $3.5 billion, or 10 to 20 percent of the legal arms trade.[106] In a repurposing of the smuggling routes of the Ottoman period, the weapons used in European terrorist attacks travel some of the same Balkan routes as drugs.[107] Estimates suggest that 90 percent of the weapons in the illicit weapon markets in Belgium are of Balkan origin.[108]

Online sales portals also facilitate the weapons trade. Investigations of the terrorists behind French and Belgian attacks from 2014 to 2016 have revealed that some of them purchased their weapons online from Eastern European suppliers.[109] Gun parts sold on the internet in Europe allow criminals and terrorists to reconstruct deactivated weapons.[110]

Underpoliced criminal activity is a major component of illicit trade. Counterfeit goods represent the largest component of illicit commerce. According to the OECD, the global trade of counterfeit and pirated products, often referred to as "fakes," represents up to 2.5 percent of world trade; sales of fakes totaled $461 billion in 2013, a sharp increase from five years previously, when annual global sales were estimated at $200 billion, or 1.9 percent of worldwide imports.[111] In contrast, in Europe, where customs has low rates of corruption and efficient performance, up to 5 percent of 2013 imports—worth as much as 85 billion euros (or $116 billion)—were counterfeits. The OECD estimates may considerably understate the global problem, because they rely on customs data compiled by agencies, many in the developing world, noted for high levels of corruption.[112] Officials in the customs services of many developing countries routinely sell positions for high prices. Employees can then profit from bribes for allowing illicit commodities to enter and exit their countries.

The global smuggling of cigarettes is estimated to cost countries billions of dollars. Not all of this illicit trade is a subset of counterfeiting: some is the trade in diverted cigarette products, and some is the trade in illicit whites (cigarettes legally produced in one country with the intent of being smuggled to another). In Europe alone, the annual turnover in illicit cigarettes is estimated at between 7.8 billion and 10.5 billion euros. Total revenues might be less, but rates of growth for the illicit tobacco trade are higher in the Middle East, Africa, and Australia.[113] New technology facilitates this trade, providing online access to products, and the new social media allows illicit traders to communicate easily on Facebook and Twitter as well as through encrypted social media such as WhatsApp. Even drones have been used, by Ukrainians, to deliver cigarettes.[114]

As competition increases for scarce resources, they become the currency of crime groups that capitalize on that scarcity for their advantage. Therefore, environmental and natural resource crimes are among the fastest-growing forms of illicit trade. The United Nations Environment Program (UNEP) and Interpol (the international police organization) estimate the value of illicit trade in fish, timber, wildlife, minerals, and waste at $91 billion to $258 billion in 2016. These offenses are increasing by 5 to 7 percent annually, or two to three times the rate of the global economy.[115] Destruction by war and the commodification of natural resources to fund conflict have been particularly damaging. "Many of the world's conflicts since World War II have occurred in biological hotspots, defined as regions with at least 1,500 endemic plant species (0.5% of the estimated 300,000 world total), and these valuable locales have lost 70% or more of their original vegetation."[116] The increasing trade in these products is damaging planetary sustainability.[117] It is one of the defining elements of the new illicit economy, and a prime reason why it threatens our future.

Sales of timber and minerals are the most lucrative forms of illicit trade in environmental products. Illegal timber logging, undertaken by corporations, corrupt individuals, and crime groups, generates revenues of between $30 billion and $100 billion annually.[118] The illicit charcoal trade, a funding source for Al-Shabaab (discussed in chapter 7), contributes to soil erosion because trees are removed. The costs of the trade in timber illegally logged in rainforests with great biodiversity are not just the sums generated from the wood, but also the loss of species that cannot survive outside the deforested regions—such as the massive die-off in the last decade of Borneo's orangutans, a species that shares 97 percent of its DNA with humans.[119]

Illegal mining, including the mining of gold, is the next most lucrative category, with revenues estimated in the $12 billion to $48 billion range.[120] Proceeds are so great that before the 2016 peace accords in Colombia, the terrorist group FARC (Revolutionary Armed Forces of Colombia) made more from the illegal gold trade than from narcotics, once its core revenue generator.[121] The United

Nations has reported that gold mined in the Democratic Republic of the Congo (DRC) and routed through Dubai helps fund terrorism.[122]

Diamonds, perhaps the world's best-known precious stones, became known as "blood diamonds" because of their important role in funding conflicts in Angola, Sierra Leone, and the Congo.[123] The Kimberley Process, a combined effort by governments, civil society, and industry to curb the flow of conflict diamonds, was initiated in 2000 in order to provide controls over the supply chains for diamonds and ensure that they do not provide significant funds for rebels.[124] The Process has not achieved the results sought: groups still engaged in conflict have received authorization to export diamonds. Moreover, systems for tracking individual stones remain inadequate.[125]

The abusive working conditions associated with the mining of coltan, a key element in the production of cell phones, has prompted some to ask, "How do I find a smart phone not soaked in blood?"[126] Coltan miners in Colombia have been coerced by FARC into working the mines, and in the DRC children and trafficked laborers are often forced into this work by rebel forces.[127] Having inadequate food, African miners looking for coltan in the forests hunt and kill rare and endangered primates, such as gorillas, to survive.[128] Consequently, illicit mining of one commodity leads to the extinction of another of the earth's irreplaceable resources.

In making an estimated $7 billion to $23 billion annually, illegal wildlife traders contribute to the mass extinction of species presently under way across the planet—the problem I referred to in the introduction as "dysfunctional selection."[129] Illegal, unreported, and unregulated (IUU) fishing is estimated to generate $10 billion to 23 billion annually. Most damage results from the illegal fishing conducted by corporate-owned fishing fleets, or even state-owned fishing companies in China. If present fishing practices continue, 86 percent of global fish stocks are at risk of being overfished, a problem discussed further in chapter 7.[130]

Illegal waste disposal gained notoriety in the early 2000s through the American television show *The Sopranos*, about a US mafia family. Tony Soprano's family, who provide a case study of social mobility, strong-armed their way to upper-middle-class prosperity through the garbage disposal business. Today revenues from illegal, unreported, and unregistered trafficking in toxic waste and e-waste (the waste from unwanted electronic equipment, such as computers and televisions), estimated by the UN at $18.8 billion annually, transcends the scope of even ambitious organized crime families such as the Sopranos.[131] These harmful products are often dumped in the developing world, leading to other pernicious consequences. For example, data left on the computer hard drives dumped in West Africa are exploited by local cybercriminals to perpetrate scams and other online criminal acts.[132] This illustrates the *domino effect* at work: one criminal activity leads to another.

Energy resources are also highly profitable elements of illicit trade and often associated with conflict. At the height of its territorial control, ISIS generated $500 million annually from oil sales by smuggling oil through neighboring states.[133] Efforts since 2015 to counter this trade by bombing ISIS-controlled oil storage facilities, particularly following the Russian entry into the conflict, has caused severe and enduring ecological harm, borne primarily by civilians.[134] Therefore, the costs of this trade should not be measured just in monetary terms.

Other nonstate groups profit from illicit oil sales, often sustaining conflicts.[135] Crime groups working with corrupt officials in the rich and conflict-ridden Niger Delta of Nigeria profit from oil smuggling, and rebels have also caused major ecological damage by tapping into oil pipelines for revenue generations.[136] Militants bombing multiple Agip pipelines in early 2016 "caused thousands of barrels of oil to pollute waterways, farms and fishing grounds in Nigeria's southern Bayelsa state."[137]

Illicit trade in coal from Donbas and in oil and fuel from Russia has played a key role in the conflict following Russia's invasion of Ukraine. Crime groups in the region have exploited the conflict in eastern Ukraine to profit significantly through fraud and illicit energy sales.[138] Los Zetas, a major militarized Mexican crime group, is increasingly linked to oil sales as they siphon off production for sale.[139] Gas smuggling within Libya foments conflict as revenues are used to fund combatants, and illegal oil exports have destabilized Tunisia.[140]

Smuggled gold and precious stones are also funding sources for strife. The conflicts of the Kachin, a Christian minority in mostly Buddhist Myanmar, have been funded by a corrupt and often illicit jade trade flowing to China, controlled by the military junta, drug lords, and companies associated with the military.[141]

Dark commerce harming the environment is most closely connected to conflict and consumer demand. But trade detrimental to the environment can also result from global competition and corporate efforts to increase profits by ignoring regulations to forestall climate change.

For example, Volkswagen is now faced with a criminal case for deliberately toying with the software to control emissions in its cars. Investigations revealed that top corporate officials deliberately concealed high levels of carbon emissions from VW vehicles—almost "40 times the permitted levels of nitrogen oxides"—so that they could sell vehicles in the United States. The former CEO of Volkswagen has been charged by the US Justice Department with fraud.[142] The problem of VW's deliberate sales of defective vehicles was even more pronounced in Europe, where 8.5 million cars of VW's total global sales of 11 million were concentrated. Mortality rates in Europe are likely to increase as a result of these sales.[143] An $18 billion fine was imposed on VW in the United States, and its top leadership was removed.[144] Arrests and a guilty plea followed; this was a more severe penalty for corporate misconduct than is often imposed.[145]

Dark commerce also deprives the earth of its man-made resources and its historical record. The illicit trade in cultural artifacts was identified as a funding source for terrorism by the UN Security Council in 2014.[146] ISIS's involvement in antiquities smuggling has given visibility to the phenomenon, but many others have illegally traded in ancient objects, even within Syria, both before ISIS got involved and now in tandem with the terrorist organization.[147]

The illicit antiquities trade was not pioneered by terrorists. The Mafia has profited from this business, and criminals in Turkey, Greece, South Asia, and Latin America have also benefited. Many stolen and smuggled items have been sold by top dealers in recent decades and have also featured in many legal cases in American and other courts.[148]

The antiquities trade is estimated at $1.2 billion to $1.6 billion annually.[149] Both real and fraudulent antiquities are traded on the internet, making it difficult to accurately value the revenues derived from this sector. Also, such sales are often not investigated because the elite art world is hard for law enforcement to penetrate.[150]

Conclusion

In recent decades, the illicit economy has grown and now represents a notable share of the global economy. Often intersecting with the licit economy, it is less visible and can tap into global distribution networks. This trade has expanded exponentially in cyberspace, which makes the products and services of the illicit economy more widely available. Many participate in this trade because they have no viable economic alternatives. Increasing economic disparity, combined with the absence of legitimate employment, has forced many into the illegal economy. Participants are doing more than smuggling contraband. the illicit economy these days has expanded to a wide range of environmental commodities, the production, transport, and sale of large amounts of counterfeits, and the new malicious products of the cyberworld. Cyber-enabled crimes, the new criminal products of the cyberworld, and the theft of intellectual property by hacking and other cyber-activities—all developments of recent decades—affect citizens, corporations, and the state. These new activities have contributed greatly to the tragic trajectory of illicit trade and will only grow in the future.

The rise in conflicts, mass human displacement, and the globalization of terrorism have all increased human insecurity. For many illicit traders, their profession is not simply a profitable activity, or a form of resistance, as seen in previous historical periods, but rather a means of survival. Consequently, the absence of licit alternative ways to make a living makes it difficult to counter the rise of illicit trade.

Exclusion from the legal economy, which is particularly widespread in the developing world, is also a significant problem in immigrant and marginalized communities in the developed world. Communities with high rates of unemployment and high rates of participation in the illegal economy are prone to urban violence. Elements of the illicit economy in Europe have also contributed to the funding of terrorist attacks in that region in recent years.

The global population is at an all-time high, with many billions inhabiting the planet, placing strain on the Earth's limited resources. With increasing urbanization, people mass in the largest cities of the world, placing ever-greater strains on urban life as they seek potable water to drink and try to eliminate waste in dense urban areas where waste disposal is not readily available. In the absence of effective states, ordinary citizens often have only nonstate actors, or actors linked to corrupt officials, available to deliver costly basic services.

Illicit trade is also a significant problem at the other end of the income scale: some individuals consume large quantities of natural resources illegally obtained from the sea and the land. Corporations aggravate these consumption problems as companies like Volkswagen deliberately circumvent emissions controls and fishing corporations overfish waters. Consumers therefore are not always conscious participants in illicit trade, but their desire for goods helps fuel global illegal commerce.

Illicit trade is a consequence of the most destabilizing conditions in the world, and a key facilitator of their growth. The perpetuation of deadly conflicts, the proliferation of arms and weapons of mass destruction, and the propagation of environmental degradation are some of the most significant developments of illicit trade in recent decades. These developments undermine both weak and strong states and create enormous economic resources for criminal nonstate actors.[151] As the dark economy grows, there are fewer opportunities for a viable licit and inclusive economy. Illicit trade, executed by transnational criminals who no longer need the state or terrorists who seek to destroy the state, is a powerful force in the destruction of the existing order.

4

The Tragic Trajectory
of the Rhino Horn Trade

The rhinoceros has met its ultimate challenge—not habitat depletion or climate change but carnage for a very specific niche market—the demand for illegal rhino horn by wealthy Asian buyers in China and Vietnam. Rhino horn is being supplied to buyers by Asian criminals colluding with South Africans at the source.

This chapter focuses on the illicit trade in rhino horn because it is the most measurable form of illegal commerce. It affects the small number of animals remaining in a relatively limited geographic area. Unlike the trade in elephant ivory, which derives from different locales in Africa, most of the poached rhinos come from one location, southern Africa, and so we are better able to focus on the key actors and the supply chains.

Law enforcement in Africa, Asia, and points in between has failed to disrupt the crime syndicates and transnational networks that are key to the success of the rhino horn trade, as well as the trade in elephant tusks and trade affecting other endangered species. As a high-level South African official, a primary government advocate for the rhino, said to me in a Pretoria meeting in January 2015, "There is not only our corruption but everyone else's along the route."

Apart from the significant and widespread corruption along the entire supply chain, global illicit networks, diaspora communities, and anonymized communications and trade have been key to the exponential growth in the commerce in rhino horn. The threat to this charismatic species illustrates all too clearly the recent targeting of the planet's resources by transnational criminals. In showing how quickly new and devastating forms of illegal activity arise, rhino horn trafficking also provides important lessons for the international law enforcement community. The rhino horn trade is iconic in its growth, as it has become a form of investment and payment in the illicit global economy.[1]

The Tragic Trajectory of the Rhino Trade

Between 2007 and 2014, killings of rhinoceroses grew exponentially, increasing every year. In 2007, 13 rhinos were killed in South Africa alone; in 2014, 1,215 were killed.[2] In 2015, South African authorities reported that 1,175 rhinos were killed, a slight decline from the previous year but still way above the 668 recorded in 2012 (see figure 4.1).[3]

Since then, there has been a slight improvement: official statistics indicate that 529 rhinos were poached in South Africa from January through the end of June 2017, compared with 542 for the same period in 2016.[4]

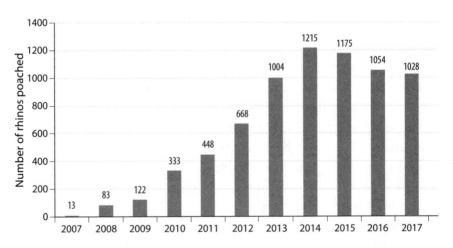

FIGURE 4.1. Recorded Number of Rhinos Poached in South Africa. Source: Save the Rhino, https://www.savetherhino.org/rhino-info/poaching-stats/.

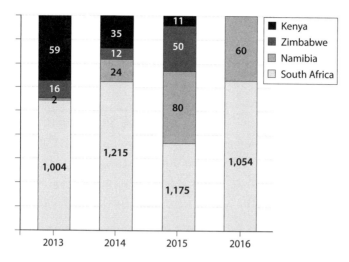

FIGURE 4.2. African Rhino Poaching on the Rise. The worst year in decades for rhino poaching was 2015, although South Africa reported a small decrease. Sources: "TRAFFIC's Engagement on African Rhinoceros Conservation and the Global Trade in Rhinoceros Horn," http://www .traffic.org/rhinos/, accessed May 2, 2018; "Rhino Poaching Statistics," http://www.poachingfacts .com/poaching-statistics/rhino-poaching-statistics/, accessed May 2, 2018; "South Africa Reports Small Decrease in Rhino Poaching, but Africa-wide 2015 the Worst on Record," http://www .traffic.org/home/2016/1/21/south-africa-reports-small-decrease-in-rhino-poaching-but-af.html, accessed May 2, 2018; "South Africa Annual Rhino Poaching Toll Falls for Second Year Running but the Crisis Continues," http://www.traffic.org/home/2017/2/27/south-africa-annual-rhino -poaching-toll-falls-for-second-yea.html, accessed May 2, 2018.

Skeptics suggest that the figures understate the problem: as indicated by the number of orphaned rhinos, actual rhino fatalities
might be a few hundred higher.[5] Even if the decrease in the number
of killings is credible, it is more than offset by the rise of rhino poaching in the rest of southern Africa, notably in neighboring countries,
where there was a marked increase, as evidenced in figure 4.2. Improved policing in South Africa has merely displaced the killing, a
well-known principle of the geography of crime.[6]

The growth of the rhino horn trade has imperiled the sustainability of the species. Today most of the world's remaining rhino
population survives only in some parts of southern Africa, rhinos
having been poached to extinction in the Democratic Republic of
the Congo and Mozambique and several other countries where the
animal was present in large numbers. A century ago, there were
an estimated one million black rhinos of four different subspecies

roaming Africa's savannahs.[7] Now there are only 5,000 black rhinos, almost half of them confined to South Africa, and the remaining white rhinoceros population now numbers only 20,000.[8] The rhinos left in South Africa represent approximately 80 percent of the world's remaining population.[9]

In contrast to many other commodities, growth in the supply of rhino horn did not diminish the price. The United Nations Environment Program valued the rhino horn trade in 2014 at between $64 million and $192 million, with the lowest value being at the source.[10] Others' estimates of the value of the rhino horn in consumer markets are even higher.[11]

The economics of the rhino trade recalls the economics of the drug trade, where the price increases dramatically the further one gets from the farmer and the closer one gets to the consumer.[12] The same rule also operates in the elephant tusk trade, where prices increase 500 percent from bush to market, with the vast profits going to organized crime groups.[13]

Rhino horn has become—and remains—one of the most expensive commodities on earth, surpassing the price of gold, which traded on global markets at $1,300 per ounce in late 2017 ($36,960 to $45,760 per kilogram) and approaching that of cocaine.[14] The current price of rhino horn is estimated to be $60,000 a kilo.[15] Each white rhino horn averages five and a half kilos in weight, and a pair of black horns from Kruger National Park averages one to three kilos. If almost 3,400 rhinos were killed between 2013 and 2015, more than 4,000 tons of illegal rhino horn entered illegal markets in each of those years.[16] The amounts generated through this trade are in the hundreds of millions of dollars, if not more, during this three-year period alone.

In 2008, rhino killings started to escalate. That year was also the beginning of the great global recession in most parts of the world. Sales of luxury goods declined in many regions, but not in Asia, where customers boosted sales of Gucci, Louis Vuitton, and Yves Saint Laurent goods.[17] Fortunately for the traders, the market for rhino horn in Asia operates like a consumer good with continued high demand among the wealthiest citizens of China and Vietnam.

Sales growth in fashion luxury items was in the double digits. But as the growth in rhino horn shows, illicit entrepreneurship in this wildlife part had even higher growth rates, with annual increases often in triple digits. The rhino and elephant trades have scaled faster than the trade for any manufactured luxury good for sale on the Asian market.

Recent data on African exports to China confirm that rhino horn continues to operate as a consumer good rather than a natural commodity.[18] China's recent economic transition to a more service-oriented economy reduced raw materials exports from Africa to China by 40 percent in 2015.[19] Yet the trade in rhino horn did not abate, and high-end-market demand continues in Vietnam and China.

Law enforcement and military strategies in South Africa, particularly in Kruger National Park, may have stemmed the rate of growth in killings in recent years, but they have not stopped the massive slaughter.[20] Those combating the rhino trade in Kruger Park face an increasing number of poachers. Yet poachers' success rates are lower than in the past, evidence that the vast investment in military strategies and law enforcement is having a positive impact.[21] Round-the-clock monitoring of hot spots for the trade, the integration of intelligence gathering and personnel deployment, and the vetting of specialized units have contributed to these improved statistics. But the prospect for the survival of the rhino remains dismal. At current rates of killing, there will soon be insufficient genetic diversity to ensure the viability of the black rhino. The white rhino is expected to decline in Kruger National Park by 2018.[22]

Modus Operandi of the Rhino Horn Trade

Few rhino killers act on their own initiative; there is very little speculative rhino killing. This crime is not like the drug trade of the Colombian cartels, where the criminal organization refined the drugs and then looked for consumers farther north to purchase their commodity. Rhinos are usually only killed on order: those running the poaching in South Africa and Mozambique receive a specific request and funds from Asians at higher levels of the criminal hierarchy.

This different business model is understandable. Most rhino poachers are so poor that they have to be provided with everything to go out and kill the animals—transport, guns, and cell and satellite phones.[23] Therefore, the increased killing of rhinos is not a sign of entrepreneurship in difficult market conditions. The poachers are found among those who frequent local taverns (*shebeens*) in the community. South African researchers have learned that poachers, having once worked together in the mines or served together in prison, travel to Kruger Park from major cities to slaughter the rhinos.[24] In other words, local criminal networks are tapped into for the lowest-level criminal work.

Most poachers—as many as 80 percent, as estimated at one time—venture from the underdeveloped region of Mozambique bordering South Africa across the Olifants River.[25] More recently, there has been a shift to more South African participation.[26] Some Mozambican middlemen have enriched themselves through the rhino trade, as evidenced in their palatial homes, and can now finance these expeditions.[27] Similar, though more limited, participation from middlemen has also been observed in South Africa.[28]

The Supply Chain

Illicit entrepreneurship in the rhino horn trade was able to grow so rapidly because there was demand and money in the markets of Asia, rhinoceroses in southern Africa, antique horn in collections in Europe, and developed criminal networks along the entire supply chain.

THE AFRICAN SOURCE

Many of the slaughtered rhinos inhabited Kruger Park in South Africa, a vast national park of 7,500 square miles and one of Africa's largest game reserves. It is the size of entire countries, such as Israel. The eastern end of the park lies on the border with Mozambique, a country that has not yet recovered from its sixteen-year civil war that ended in 1992. Mozambique remains one of Africa's poorest countries: more than half the population lives below the poverty line.[29] The civil war's legacy of arms and violence endures.

Kruger was first established as a game reserve before the start of the twentieth century by the country's white leadership. This vast, diversified, and magnificent landscape is home to many varieties of mammals and birds. The park was long the treasured playground of the white minority, and during apartheid no blacks were admitted as tourists. It was not until 1993 that the first black visitors could stay overnight in this park, which requires days to see only a section. No wonder an African activist in the late 1990s referred to Kruger Park as "the last paradise of apartheid."[30] Even today there are few black tourists in the park.

An estimated one to two million people live in communities surrounding the park in South Africa and Mozambique. Black communities were displaced to make the park—an example of Rosaleen Duffy's suggestion that the imperatives of Western conservation cause local people to suffer.[31] Environmental conservation and sustainability are consequently values not shared by the majority of Africans living close to national parks. Not enough has been done to stigmatize the poachers residing in local communities. Nor have the South African authorities done enough, to use the old cliché, to win the hearts and minds of residents around the park. Park leaders in other African countries who have focused more on the welfare and employment of surrounding communities have had greater success in reducing poaching.[32]

Education of all kinds in rural South Africa is poor, and that on environmental conservation is limited. Confirming this was a survey of the residents of communities around the South African national parks with the largest rhino populations. Among those surveyed, only 40 percent wanted the animals to survive so that their children or grandchildren could see them.[33]

The presence of wildlife at Kruger brings local inhabitants limited rewards and does little to address their economic situation. The South African communities adjoining the park have an especially high average rate of unemployment, far exceeding the national norm of over 25 percent, because there are few legitimate employment opportunities.[34] The end of apartheid did not end the economic inequality that characterized the period of white rule. Most land is still owned by whites, and many black farm laborers, fortunate to find work, toil for minimal wages on the same lands where their ancestors worked.[35]

Readily available arms, familiarity with violence, and habituation to the precariousness of existence characterize life among many of the poor in southern Africa. The especially elevated rates of violence in the communities around Kruger Park are partly a legacy of apartheid-era policies, which affected the geography of crime. South Africa, like the Soviet Union, had the unusual distinction of having elevated rates of crime and violence in rural areas because of internal passport controls that limited mobility and kept criminals away from cities.[36]

Targeting wildlife, particularly the rhino, is the only possible way to quickly make significant cash.[37] A few killers manage to capitalize on their killing and use the money generated for economic advancement. But for most of the poor young black men in their twenties and thirties who participate in the slaughter, the payment is as dysfunctional as the killing of the rhino. As a young poacher in Mozambique said, "You'll get rich, but you'll die young."[38] The payment for killing a rhino can be $5,000 or even higher, according to South African investigators.[39] Conspicuous consumption is common among those who fatalistically assume that death is imminent. Much of the money gained from the killings is often quickly dissipated on flashy clothes and alcohol.[40]

THE EUROPEAN SOURCE

Rhino horns are also procured by criminal networks operating outside of Africa. In 2013, 500,000 euros' worth of rhino heads and horn were stolen from a warehouse outside of Dublin that was leased by the National Museum of Ireland. Museum officials had mistakenly thought the horn would be safer in storage than on display. The perpetrators of the theft are suspected to be the Rathkeale Rovers, an Irish organized crime group operating transnationally who profit from rhino horn theft in Europe by targeting museums, private collections, churches, and auction houses containing rhino horn.[41] The Rathkeale Rovers sometimes connect with the Vietnamese diaspora networks that operate out of the Czech Republic (as discussed later) and supply rhino horn to Asia.[42]

In one Irish break-in of a manor house, the police found that the only thing missing was the antique rhino horn. Auction houses have seen sky-high prices for objects containing rhino horn, indicating that the objects are being bought to be destroyed or to be displayed as status symbols in Vietnam and China. One Irish auction house has already stopped selling rhino horn items and "declined rhino horn consignments valued at up to €250,000."[43] The illicit rhino trade is causing the kind of distortions in the art market that had previously been associated with antiquities smuggling, not with the illicit wildlife trade.

DEMAND IN ASIA

Rhino horn was never as central to Asian culture as ivory, so why are rhinos so sought after in Asia? Living rhinoceroses were given as gifts in Asia and hunted in India, and their horns were valued in different parts of the continent as an aphrodisiac and as an antidote to poison.[44] Rhino horns were made into libation cups for rulers because they could indicate the presence of poisons, a constant concern of monarchs.[45]

The Chinese have valued rhino horns as a rare commodity since antiquity. The trade of rhino horn has been traced back to 2600 BC.[46] Within Chinese society, there was great demand for rhino horn for medicinal use in treating fevers, strokes, and liver ailments. It was also prized as a status symbol. Rhino horn was a highly valued gift, and it figured in the rank badges of imperial Chinese officials as one of the eight treasures.[47] By the Tang dynasty (starting in the early seventh century AD), the rhinoceros had largely disappeared from Chinese territory because of overhunting, and imports became the source of most rhino horn in China. But the horn was so precious that in the seventh to tenth centuries, it was used exclusively by the imperial household—only the emperor and the crown prince could fix their crowns with rhino horn. Most rhino horn vessels in China and Taiwan today date from the Ming dynasty (1368–1644), though these were always of limited quantity because the horn was already so rare, despite the presence of imports, in the sixteenth century.[48]

Many aspects of traditional Asian society have disappeared with urbanization, industrialization, and increasing international trade. But the belief in the power of animal parts to impart strength, cure disease, and ensure well-being has remained strong in many parts of Asia, fueling this market.

Important changes in Asia in the mid-2000s would have important impacts on the growth of the rhino horn trade. Japan, South Korea, and Taiwan by then had largely eschewed the rhino horn trade, as they observed international legal norms governing wildlife trade. China and Vietnam developed a new class of wealthy individuals as they transitioned away from totally Communist state-owned economies.[49] Wealth more than poverty appears to be a driver of this element of the illicit wildlife trade.[50]

As the international community observed in the post-Communist transition of the Soviet Union, a new elite emerged with neither a social nor an environmental conscience. The same tendency has been observed in both Vietnam and China.[51] One of the greatest honors you can give a guest at a Vietnamese dinner party is a meal made of an endangered species.[52] Efforts to educate citizens in Vietnam about not purchasing rhino horn have had some success by focusing on the damage done to the country's reputation, a potent force in Asian society.[53]

Rhino horn is now used in limited areas: in the treatment of cancer, in traditional medicine, and as a "rave drug," a potent status symbol among the wealthy seeking excitement. Rhino horns are also given as valuable gifts.[54] In the sphere of traditional medicine, practitioners engaged in the illicit kidney trade are also involved in offering rhino horn.[55]

A new wealthy class developed in Vietnam, but not the infrastructure to satisfy its medical needs. In the mid-2000s, Vietnamese health officials proclaimed that rhino horn could cure cancer, halting its progression or shrinking existing tumors. Some have suggested that corrupt health officials, bribed by transnational criminals, became advocates for rhino horn consumption. But these pronouncements had a dual purpose—radiation and chemo treatments are not always available, and endorsing rhino horn as a traditional medical treatment for cancer offered patients hope.[56] Today some cancer patients take rhino horn alongside chemotherapy.[57]

The Environmental Investigative Agency (EIA) has identified almost 700 kilograms of rhino horn trade linked to China.[58] Analysts believe that the purchase of rhino horn in China is increasingly an investment by wealthy Chinese who believe that the coming extinction of the rhino will raise the price of existing stock. In the Chinese media for a decade, 75 percent of sources refer to rhino horn as an investment or collectible. But despite extensive purchases, research suggests that it has not proven to be a good investment, although some of the prices achieved for antique horn seem to contradict this conclusion.[59]

Dynamics of the Rhino Horn Trade: The Perfect Storm

The rhino horn trade expanded exponentially when a perfect storm occurred. All the necessary conditions were present: an unending supply of individuals willing to poach for money, a culture of tolerance for rhino killing, an absence of respect for legal norms, high levels of corruption, and well-developed illicit networks in South Africa that could facilitate the trade to Asia. Some of these facilitating conditions are unique to the history and culture of southern Africa, but unfortunately, many of them are more universal and characterize the vast swaths of Africa that are now a major source of exports of endangered wildlife.

The illicit rhino horn trade began its rapid growth because traffickers tapped into existing trade routes for licit and illicit goods and the smuggling of people. Fortunately for the traffickers, the demand for rhino horn is in Asia, the prime export arena for South African goods in the post-apartheid area; the illicit rhino horn trade accompanies the vast licit movement of raw materials that flows from Africa to Asia.[60] Rhino horn, like elephant tusks and pangolin scales, is also used to pay for consumer goods produced in Asia and sought by African consumers. China remains South Africa's largest trade partner.[61]

CONVERGENCE

The rhino horn trade converges with many other criminal activities—such as drugs, arms, cigarette smuggling, and human trafficking, both locally and along the long and convoluted trade routes linking South Africa with Asia.[62] Long, hollowed-out trucks move rhino horn along with smuggled cigarettes in South Africa. The trucks pass unimpeded because the cigarette trade was under the patronage of President Jacob Zuma's son.[63] The illicit rhino horn trade also converges with other forms of illicit wildlife trade. Seizures reveal the convergence of the illegal abalone trade and the illicit rhino horn trade—by as much as 90 percent at some stages of the supply chain, according to anti-poaching specialists.[64] Protected abalone is often exchanged for methamphetamines, suggesting another point of convergence between the rhino horn and drug trades.[65] The trade intersects at the higher levels of the trafficking organizations in South Africa, although not necessarily at the procurement stage.[66]

The convergence also occurs along the supply chain because of the facilitators. Czech criminal facilitators became the subjects of "Operation Rhino" in 2013 after Czech customs officials, acting on a tip from those investigating cigarette smuggling, found rhino horn at Ruzyně Airport in a package addressed to a fictitious person in Vietnam. The horns were skillfully embedded in resin and asphalt to avoid X-ray detection and then hidden in a big coil of copper wire.[67]

The Czech Republic is not the only trans-shipment point for rhino horn. According to Julian Rademeyer, who has investigated this trade extensively, "Airlines including Kenya Airways, Ethiopian Airlines and Qatar Airways were regularly used by rhino horn syndicates to smuggle their contraband from Maputo airport to Nairobi, Addis Ababa, Thailand, Hong Kong and Vietnam."[68]

Rhino smugglers along the supply chain have carefully identified and recruited corrupt officials, both local and international. Often these officials do more than turn a blind eye; they may serve as key personnel in the conspiracies to move the horn. The rhino horn is hidden, not only with other illicit commodities, but also with less valuable licit goods, such as copper wire, that pass unnoticed through customs and across numerous borders. The sellers of rhino horn receive payment both in cash and through trade-based money laundering, a complex system that allows imports from China, such as clothing and electronics, to pay for the purchase of the rhino horn.[69] Mislabeling of trade products allows transfer payments to be made for the horn under the pretense that the payer is making payments for a legitimate commodity.

The growth trajectory of the rhino horn trade, like that of elephant ivory, merely reflects the capacity of the traffickers to adapt and to obtain, move, and market their product to affluent populations. Unlike the illicit drug trade, with which the rhino horn and elephant ivory trade often converge, the purchasers are not part of a criminal community but are often affluent and high-status individuals from Asia's legitimate economy.

ATTITUDES TOWARD THE RHINO TRADE

Corruption is a key facilitator, but it is not the only explanation for the limited success of efforts to combat the illicit rhino horn trade.[70] Many who trade in rhino horn along the Africa-to-Asia supply chain do not accept the trade ban. Hundreds of smugglers, buyers, and poachers interviewed by a South African researcher revealed that they did not recognize their activity as illegal.

"It starts with the poachers who are individuals that have lost their ancestral lands and the associated hunting rights as a result either of colonial expropriation or of the establishment of protected areas and transfrontier conservation parks."[71] The white Afrikaner farmers who breed rhinoceroses believe that it is their right to extract maximum profit from this enterprise. Many buying the horn in Asia are unconcerned that the trade is illegal and consider their purchases just an investment or a disposable commodity.[72]

Traders in rhino horn share a great deal with other traders in illicit commodities such as drugs, people, and harmful counterfeits. They think of themselves as entrepreneurs rather than as criminals.[73] With this failure to acknowledge the harm they cause, it is hardly surprising that the trade in rhino horn grows without successful deterrence.

The Participants in the Illicit Rhino Horn Trade

Diverse networks are active in the rhino horn trade. Whereas some of this trade includes traffickers with strong ties to the legitimate southern African economy who specialize in illicit wildlife trade, the criminal networks responsible for the poaching in South African parks are transnational: based in Asia, they have high-level facilitators in Africa. The rhino deaths reported in the official South African statistics are only related to the second group of traffickers.

PSEUDO-HUNTERS

Before there was massive slaughter of rhinos in South Africa's parks, pseudo-hunts were used to procure horn for Asian customers. Those behind the pseudo-hunts—networks of farmers who raised significant numbers of rhinos, safari organizers, and taxidermists— exploited a loophole in the protection of rhinos: a limited number of white rhinos can be hunted legally in South Africa.[74] Therefore, the rhino farmers advertised and organized "hunts" in which customers could kill rhinos, and then the farmers separated the horns from the animals and shipped them to Asian customers after preservation by the taxidermists with whom they were colluding.

The main customers for these legal hunts—who paid at least $30,000 apiece to secure their trophies—were initially Americans and Europeans.[75] Yet with growing Asian demand for rhino horn, there was a change in clientele. The first recorded Vietnamese rhino hunters arrived in 2003. Soon there were increasingly large numbers of Asian "hunters" who shared none of the characteristics of big game hunters. As one of South Africa's top rhino specialists explained, "It has been noted that these hunters were generally unskilled and inexperienced and prepared to shoot even young female rhinos as long as they came away with a horn."[76]

These hunts, which continued for years, masked a large illegal trade in rhino horn to Asia.[77] By 2010, Vietnamese hunters had killed 329 rhinos, almost equal to the number poached. The so-called hunters "legally" exported their horns from hunts that cost them $20 million. With the help of specialists who falsified the documents needed to export horn from South Africa, they secured a product that would retail in Vietnam for $200 million to $300 million.[78]

The pseudo-hunters of the Laos-based Vixay Keosavang network masqueraded trafficked South Asian women as hunters to obtain rhino horn, conveniently without relying on poachers. These slight young women who had never held a rifle posed for photographs as "hunters" beside the corpses of killed rhinos—the pseudo-hunt network's documentation of the "legal" killing.[79] These women were subject to double abuse—not only were they victims of sex trafficking, but their identities were used for rhino horn smuggling, as they were named as the owners of the trophies shipped out of South Africa to Southeast Asia.

The most notorious South African orchestrator of fake hunts is the rhino game farmer Dawie Groenewald, the alleged ringleader of the so-called Groenewald Gang. He has a criminal record for illicit wildlife trade; rhino killing is only one of many animals subject to his abuse. Charged and convicted in the United States in 2010 for illegally importing a leopard, a 2014 US federal indictment accused Groenewald of again violating the Lacey Act, which provides for the protection of endangered species.[80] Operating a safari business out of Alabama, he duped American hunters into believing they were legally hunting rhinos, but the horns of the animals they killed were sent through the black market to Asian buyers.[81] The US Department of Justice indictment of Groenewald documents eleven illegal hunts, many committed with great brutality. In one hunt, the rhino had to be shot and killed after being repeatedly wounded by a bow, and in another Groenewald used a chainsaw to remove the horn from a sedated rhino that had been hunted with a tranquilizer gun.[82]

The presence of the large Vietnamese diaspora in the Czech Republic, a country with a long history of hunting, led Groenewald to move his pseudo-hunt business there. His customers, according to Czech research, represented approximately 90 percent of all the southern white rhinoceros "hunted" by Czechs in South Africa.[83] The other 10 percent of Czech hunters went to the safari ranch of a former Czech official who moved to South Africa and allegedly returned with more assets than when he departed his homeland.[84] Hunts for white rhinos were offered on his farm's website until recently.[85] The human–rhino horn trafficking convergence also operated in this business model: some of the Czech visitors were allegedly provided with trafficked women brought from the Czech Republic.

CRIMINAL NETWORKS

The majority of reported killings of rhinos by poachers in South Africa are tied to four Asian-based criminal networks. The first is a triad-based network linked to the Chinese diaspora community that settled in South Africa in the 1990s, which moves rhino horn to Southeast Asia and Hong Kong.[86] The second network involves the Laos-based Vixay Keosavang and Vannasang networks, which maintain close ties to Thailand, Cambodia, and Vietnam, through which countries much rhino horn transits.[87] Both of these networks are known to trade with the Bach brothers, who operate the smuggling route between Thailand and Vietnam via Laos.[88] Keosavang, Vannasang, the Bachs, and others in their network operate registered businesses around wildlife farming, hospitality, or gold trading. This criminal network has diversified criminal businesses trading in narcotics, smuggling cars, and trafficking humans.[89]

The third is a Mozambique-based narcotics syndicate that also smuggles guns, ivory, and rhino horn and has links to other narcotics and wildlife traffickers in Tanzania, Zanzibar, and Kenya. Although this is a multiethnic network, its leaders are of South Asian ethnicity and have ties to designated Pakistani narcotics trafficking networks.[90]

There is also a Chinese network based in Shuidong that operates in Mozambique, Zanzibar, and Tanzania, deals in various forms of sea products and ivory, and has traded rhino horn in the past.[91]

NETWORKS AND FACILITATORS

High, mid- and low-level corruption facilitates the rhino horn trade at the source. Corruption at lower levels facilitates the killing as corrupt park rangers and guards and employees of national and private reserves in Mozambique and South Africa provide information to poaching syndicates about the rhinos' location. On occasion, line personnel provide cover for poaching teams as they approach and then travel within protected areas.[92] Some corrupt park employees run their own poaching rings, and others, according to intelligence sources, pass information to poachers on social media, using coded signals and photos.[93] This illustrates the crucial role of new technology in the exponential growth of the rhino horn trade.

Midlevel facilitators include those involved in registering and falsifying the records of pseudo-hunts. Officials can also issue fraudulent CITES permits authorizing exports of rhino horn that should not be permitted to leave the country.[94] In addition, rhino traffickers have facilitators in the private sector who help mislabel and transport goods, establish front companies, and arrange legal representation to defend them if they are arrested.

High-level officials are also key to the rhino horn trade. A team of investigative journalists revealed the personal relationship of the South African minister of security with a Chinese organized crime figure who ran massage parlors frequented by the minister. The investigators alleged that this corrupt relationship helped facilitate the illicit rhino horn trade.[95] The minister's promotion coincided with members of the security apparatus blocking planned measures to combat the rhino horn trade.[96]

Foreign officials stationed in South Africa are also complicit in the trade.[97] Senior Vietnamese diplomatic staff working in South Africa—including the first secretary, the economic attaché, and the political counselor of the embassy—have been directly implicated in the illegal rhino horn trade.[98] In late 2015, a North Korean diplomat was found to be trafficking in rhino horn from South Africa.[99] This is hardly surprising, as North Korea has used revenues from illicit trade in wildlife to fund its overseas operations and possibly its nuclear program since at least the early 2000s.[100]

Response to the Poaching

Many well-known people try to save wildlife, hoping to stem rhino poaching. President Barack Obama issued a presidential executive order authorizing funds to counter illicit wildlife trade.[101] The United Kingdom's Prince Charles and Prince William hosted an international conference in 2014 to combat illegal wildlife trade.[102] Desmond Tutu, retired South African archbishop, led a prayer for lions and other wildlife in 2014.[103] Unfortunately, these measures have done little to slow the killing machine fueled by illicit commerce.

Fly into Johannesburg Airport and you will see very large posters condemning rhino slaughter throughout the terminal. Many local and international NGOs (non-governmental organizations) work in South Africa to protect endangered rhino, and millions of dollars pour into South Africa from rich individuals, national governments, and multilateral organizations to save the rhino from extinction.[104] With over 150 organizations in South Africa attempting to stop rhino poaching, there is often duplication of effort and an absence of coordination.[105] NGOs also work in Asia, countering the trade through media campaigns and law enforcement support.

South Africa and the international community have used diverse strategies to curtail rhino poaching.[106] These include the militarization of security at Kruger National Park, deployment of advanced technology, the dehorning of rhinos, public education and media awareness campaigns to stem demand, and enhanced law enforcement. South African rhino farmers, eager to profit from their animals and their stockpiles of rhino horns, have pressed for legalization of sales. Unfortunately, though these measures have curtailed the growth trajectory of the rhino killings, they have not curtailed the slaughter.

Enforcement efforts have been prioritized over development assistance and job development in local communities.[107] As one of South Africa's leading experts on the rhino horn trade has pointed out, there needs to be investment in land rights and in "schools and hospitals as a reward for village communities that support the fight against poaching."[108] Unfortunately, the communities around the park remain poor and criminogenic. Many perceive that white farmers get rich from the trade and only the low-level black poachers are sent to prison.

The military control center for rhino protection is housed at Sku-kuza in Kruger National Park. When I visited, it was apparent that the investment and commitment of those charged with the protection mission is significant. They are using new technology, such as drones, to support their enforcement and analytic efforts.[109]

Militarized protection of the park is controversial and expensive. For many, it is hard to accept that a natural preserve is protected by heavily armed units. For others, it recalls the repressive forces of apartheid-era South Africa. Approximately fifty poachers were killed in 2014 in the park. Those killed are often members of adjoining communities whose deaths leave their family members in desperate straits.[110]

Work as a park ranger is demanding, high-risk, and stressful, often requiring lengthy separations from family members. Rangers who shoot suspected poachers can be brought to court for pulling the trigger too fast.[111] Yet self-protection is needed, as park rangers are killed and wounded across Africa, and inadequate support is provided to the families of murdered and injured guardians.[112] Many Africans perceive that more attention is paid to the dead rhinos and other wildlife than to the rangers who die in their defense or the killed poachers.

Efforts to suppress supply from South Africa include more than enforcement strategies. To save rhinos, some of these animals have had their horns removed, under sedation, to eliminate their attractiveness to poachers. Other rhino guardians have proposed poisoning the horns to undermine their value and cause harm to the purchasers.[113]

Efforts to reduce demand accompany those aimed at reducing supply. Public education campaigns in Vietnam and China, often implemented with the help of celebrities, explain that the animals are killed to obtain the horns and that the horn has no magical power, as it is made of the same material as fingernails.[114]

Significant efforts are being made to end the impunity of those behind the pseudo-hunts and the transnational criminal networks that procure and sell the rhino horns. Privately funded investigations complement state efforts in Africa and Southeast Asia, and they are yielding some results. All too often, however, it is the low-level poacher rather than the higher-level member of the criminal network who is prosecuted.

In Africa and Southeast Asia, where pervasive corruption in police and judicial bodies has reduced accountability, ending impunity is key. The king of pseudo-hunters, Groenewald, has now been charged with multiple crimes on two continents (in the United States and South Africa).[115] The South African authorities failed to honor an extradition request from the United States for three years, and when detained in 2017, Groenewald was shortly released on bail. His 2010 case in South Africa has been stalled for years as the challenges to the legal trade in rhino horn proceed through South African courts, and corruption may yet influence the proceedings.[116]

The South African government prosecuted and convicted the local representative of the Thai-Laotian network, Chumlong Lemtongthai, in 2012.[117] The Czechs have pursued and prosecuted organizers of pseudo-hunts and smugglers.[118] Couriers have been arrested in Asia, but major networks like the Chinese network based in Shuidong have functioned for an extended period with impunity.[119]

Malaysia, Hong Kong, and Thailand in 2017 and 2018 made notable arrests of wildlife smugglers moving rhino horn. In December 2017, Thai customs officials' seizure of 12.5 kilograms of rhino horn from South Africa led to the arrest of a key figure in the previously mentioned Bach crime syndicate. Shortly after that, Thai authorities closed in on Bach himself, arresting him on the northeast border near Laos.[120] Illustrating the impact of privately funded efforts, the case investigation was supported by the US-based Elephant Action League and the Freeland Foundation, two organizations that pursue wildlife crime.

Future Trends

The boom business in rhino horn may go on for a time. South African farmers have stockpiled rhino horns, and in May 2017 they success-fully persuaded the South African courts, after a lengthy legal battle, to legalize the domestic trade.[121] Powerful South African financial interests coincide with those of affluent purchasers in Asia. Inter-national sale is not authorized under CITES, and it may never be, as CITES permits are required for the export of certain rhino horns.[122] But the presence of significant transnational criminal networks in South Africa continues to make it possible for the legitimate internal rhino trade to intersect quickly with the illegitimate global trade. It can also lead to an increase in medical tourism as Asian tourists come to South Africa to consume rhino horn.[123]

It also remains possible that old carved rhino horns of high quality stolen from museums and private collections will be laundered in the art and antiques markets. The potential profits from such crimes are significant. One antique rhino horn libation cup (presumably genuine) sold in Hong Kong in 2011 at a Sotheby's auction for almost $2.4 million.[124] The US Fish and Wildlife Service's anti-poaching operation, Operation Crash, and a rhino-related investigation un-dertaken by the US Justice Department found that the trade is linked with the arts market.[125]

Failing to Save the Rhino

Despite the priority given to saving rhinos, the killing continues, not only because of greed and globalization but also as a consequence of some of the most intractable problems of the international com-munity and South Africa. Rhino poaching in South Africa results, in part, from an economy that has redistributed few resources to the black majority, embedded corruption at the highest levels of government, and promoted agricultural policies leading to declining yields. High unemployment levels, elevated rates of intrapersonal violence, and a land restitution program that is a long way behind schedule—all contribute to the problem of poaching, as there are few opportunities for legitimate earnings.[126] Transnational criminals take advantage of South Africa's efficient communications and transport systems, which facilitate the illegal movement of horns, along with the high volume of air and sea traffic between South Africa and Asia. Rhino horn is easily concealed in larger shipments of legal goods, a familiar problem of the convergence of the licit and illicit.

The exponential growth of the illicit rhino horn trade makes it one of the best examples of successful illicit entrepreneurship. Overall profits from the drug trade far surpass those in rhino horn trade, yet it does not grow as rapidly.[127] Rhino horn trade has scaled at a pace resembling that of a supercharged cyber-business, though its growth has occurred largely without the web and the availability of counterfeit rhino horn online is thought to have driven demand.[128]

Unfortunately for the traffickers, this growth is not sustainable. The supply of rhino is finite. This "living fossil," one of the planet's largest surviving mammals, has inhabited the earth for an estimated 55 million years since the Eocene period but may not survive in the wild another few decades.[129]

Charles Darwin conceptualized natural selection as "evolutionary change [that] occurs through variation between individuals; some variants give the individual an extra survival probability."[130] According to Darwin's theory of evolution, "One general law [leads] to the advancement of all organic beings, namely, multiply, vary, let the strongest live and the weakest die."[131] Yet with massive poaching, Darwin's ideas no longer apply: often the strongest die and the weakest live.[132] Rather, we are seeing "dysfunctional selection," which I define as non-evolutionary change that results in the survival of the less fit. According to dysfunctional selection, no attributes of the species or those of any specific members of the species, such as intelligence or problem-solving, will give it any preferential chance of survival.

The rhinos' destruction is also dysfunctional because it harms the environment in which they live. Rhinoceroses are a key part of the ecosystem of the savannah. Their grazing is "really important for maintaining diversity, as well as the coexistence of trees and grasses, by creating a shifting patch mosaic on the landscape."[133]

Therefore, it is the fittest for the past environment that are most targeted for elimination—the rhinos with the longest horns or the elephants with the largest tusks. Their slaughter has undermined the gene pool of the species. Illustrative of this is the increasing prevalence of the tuskless elephant, a less desirable mate for female elephants but an evolutionary response to a species subject to excessive poaching.[134]

According to Darwin's theory of natural selection, the rhino should be one of the most successful creatures to have inhabited this planet. It has survived enormous changes in climate through millions of years. Ice ages, droughts, continental drifts—rhinoceroses have seen it all. But they are facing extinction. Dysfunctional selection is clearly at work.

Conclusion

As I was completing this chapter, the discovery of gravity waves by the Laser Interferometer Gravitational-Wave Observatory (LIGO) collaboration, proving the last element of Einstein's theory of relativity, received the Nobel Prize. The discovery was the culmination of forty years of intense work. At its initiation, some doubted its feasibility. Over time, however, international collaboration in science and technology and continued investments in research led to the technical capacity to measure something both small and distant.

Many of the elements of what brought success to LIGO are present in the efforts to save the rhino. Well-funded, large, multidisciplinary international teams of environmentalists, scientists, and law enforcement try to stem the killing. Rhinos, as an endangered species, are now protected by international treaties and agreements. Despite all this collaboration, we are not seeing incremental progress toward a powerful solution. Instead, we are watching a Greek tragedy unfold before our eyes—the inexorable march to destruction of the remaining long-surviving rhino, the victim of complex forces of human nature, history, economics, culture, and the growth of transnational crime and corruption.

Saving the rhino is unfortunately not a problem of science, where advances in technology can provide the magic solution. Instead, we are looking at the rationality of markets. If there is supply and demand, entrepreneurial actors will find ways to connect these two. Laws, treaties, and law enforcement are just constraints that increase the costs of doing business. Consequently, we are seeing the ongoing destruction of a great and historic species to satisfy man's immediate desires. The rapid elimination of the remaining white and black rhinos provides important lessons for those trying to sustain the planet. The fastest-growing forms of illicit commerce are those targeting our fellow species, threatening the future of human life on earth.

5

Business Models

HISTORICAL TRANSFORMATION OF ILLICIT ENTREPRENEURSHIP AND TRADE

A great transformation of commerce is presently under way. More and more commerce is moving online, and trade is increasingly conducted through personal communication devices. As the location of trade shifts into the cyberworld, we are not facing an entirely alien phenomenon. Rather, the new illicit traders, like their predecessors and their counterparts in the legitimate economy, seek sales and profits to sustain their businesses. To operate successfully, they search for targets of opportunity, strategic alliances, and forms of trade with worthwhile profit markets. To grow, participants in illicit commerce must find capital for their businesses, as well as develop a market niche and a marketing strategy for their goods. As illicit traders grow their businesses, they are confronted with new challenges—recruiting and retaining employees, experts, and contractors; mitigating risk while retaining good profit margins; managing competition; and incorporating new technology into their sales and marketing models. If they are successful, they must choose whether to withdraw profits, reinvest their profits in existing trade products, or diversify. Sometimes illicit traders may move their profits into the legitimate economy, either partially or entirely.

The Stages of Illicit Trade

Three large-scale criminal cases illustrated in table 5.1 reveal how illicit trade, entrepreneurship, and financial flows have changed dramatically with the development of the new technology of the internet, cell and smart phones, the Dark Web (the part of the web accessible by Tor and similar software that hides your location and identity), credit cards, and cryptocurrencies.[1] The cases will also be used to illustrate fundamental principles of the dynamics of illicit business.

Table 5.1 outlines the primary transformation of illicit trade. The first stage, which existed for at least 3,750 years, involved concrete objects traded by known individuals, using currency and tangible financial instruments, often backed by states, and items of value such as gold and silver. This form of trade, which has been with us since the dawn of written legal history, is still with us today, as we will see in the first case of a long-lasting American car theft ring.

Stage 2, illustrated by the Pharmaleaks case, represents the transitional form of illicit trade that has arisen as the new medium of the internet has allowed illicit sellers to rapidly grow their businesses and expand their customer base. Just as we saw the Smirnovs in chapter 1 scaling the age-old profession of fencing to its online version, the transitional phase is not unique to computers or to computer crime. Throughout much of history, technological innovation has merely extended existing modus operandi into a new medium.[2] In the Pharmaleaks case, Russian online criminals sold large quantities of counterfeit pharmaceuticals to American, western European, and Australian customers. In the impersonal world of stage 2, there are no longer personal connections between buyer and seller. In contrast to stage 1, stage 2 introduces the new tools of the global financial system—credit cards and wire transfers. This is cyber-assisted crime.[3]

The third stage, represented by the Avalanche case, includes not just illicit trade but illicit entrepreneurship. The sellers produce and market virtual and intangible products to sabotage computers and

TABLE 5.1. THE STAGES OF ILLICIT TRADE

Time Frame	Products	Financial Payments
Stage 1: Hammurabi to the mid-1990s—trade in stolen goods and tangible items	People dealing in tangible property (e.g., Operation Dual Identity)	Cash, trade-based money laundering, barter, Western Union and other wire transfer businesses
Stage 2: Mid-1990s to the present—computer-facilitated crime	People dealing in tangible property but selling on-line, usually through the web (e.g., Pharmaleaks, counterfeits, antiquities, wildlife parts)	Payment systems tied to the global financial economy (credit cards, prepaid credit cards, wire transfers, trade-based money laundering);efforts made to hide identity of buyers and sellers
Stage 3: Late 1990s to the present—crime linked solely to computers	People dealing in intangible property through the web and the Dark Web (e.g., Avalanche) in crimes such as malware, Trojans, spam, botnets, phishing tools, fake antiviral software, hacking tools, ransomware, denial-of-service attacks, and other malicious computer products; theft of identities, credit card numbers, and intellectual property such as songs, videos, and products in development; and employing people to deploy pernicious cyber-tools	Payment systems tied to the global economy and to cryptocurrencies (e.g., Bitcoin, Liberty Reserve); online gaming used to launder money; transactions often anonymized

computer systems, such as botnets, malware, and Trojans, and services such as denial-of-service attacks. Seller-buyer relationships and payments are intentionally anonymized in the Dark Web, as encryption is used to hide the identities of sellers and purchasers.[4] Some of the currency has gone virtual and is not tied to any currency or metal of value.

The evolution from stage 1 to stage 2 took almost four millennia. Yet the evolution from stage 2 to stage 3 was extremely rapid—only a few years. This illustrates the transformative property of the new technology. Unfortunately for the global community, all three stages of illicit trade now coexist.

Stage 1: Operation Dual Identity—Illicit Trade in Tangible Goods and Currency

In Tampa, Florida, a few cars had been stolen from a local car dealership, and local detectives needed help. An FBI agent who assisted them was directed by his superiors to devote his efforts to more substantial cases. But he kept on investigating the car theft part-time, convinced that he was on to something bigger. His perseverance paid off: a couple of years later, fifty law enforcement agencies across the United States were investigating car thefts in Florida, Texas, and Illinois committed by a group of Cuban American thieves.

Operation Dual Identity, as the criminal operation was subsequently named, revealed one of the largest car theft rings in the United States, operating for over twenty years, during which time more than a hundred people stole a thousand expensive cars. A potential buyer would ask one of the ring members to obtain a specific type of high-end vehicle. The criminal would satisfy the request by either drawing on stock or committing vehicle thefts on order in other states. Key to the deal was obtaining a legitimate vehicle identification number (VIN) from a car of the desired brand. Mexican criminals served as service providers producing counterfeit VIN plates and labels, as well as phony title documents that would facilitate resales.[5] The cars were marketed through underground networks throughout the United States, especially in Chicago and Texas, for cash or its equivalent.[6] As the criminal operation evolved and more criminal activity was conducted in online marketplaces, the car thieves evolved and, consistent with activity in stage 2, sold some vehicles through eBay and Craigslist.[7]

Press releases on Operation Dual Identity reported only on the disruption of the $25 million car theft ring. None reported on what the investigators found when they followed the money.[8] The investigators did not find an offshore bank account, but rather investments of the criminals' proceeds in another illegal activity—marijuana farms. Running a marijuana facility is a tough business. Lights are on all night, and the plants must be monitored twenty-four hours a day to produce good yields. Not many people perform this work voluntarily for a minimum wage. But working on a marijuana farm was then illegal and remains so today in most states. Undocumented migrants would not labor in such farms voluntarily, as doing so would enhance their risk of deportation. Legal workers would avoid such difficult jobs that paid little and might lead to their arrest.

To secure workers, the Spanish-speaking leaders of the car theft ring pursued a logical business strategy—they imported hundreds of smuggled Spanish-speaking workers from Mexico. Forcing smuggled Mexicans to work in illegal employment for long hours, the marijuana farm operators then transitioned from smuggling to trafficking individuals. Operation Dual Identity may be the best example of convergence between the drug trade and human trafficking in the United States, but it is far from unique.

Similar patterns are observed in the marijuana farms of Great Britain. The exploited there are Vietnamese, often children, as illegal marijuana cultivation is controlled by members of the Vietnamese diaspora community. Similarly inhumane conditions are recorded there, as the laborers work long hours under glaring lights without any protective glasses.[9]

Stage 2: Pharmaleaks—Tangible Property Sold on the Web through the Global Financial System

The Pharmaleaks case, representing stage 2, illustrates many of the defining aspects of the illicit online marketplace.[10] Unlike the long-existing car theft business representative of stage 1, which delivered good profits over an extended period, the cyber-pharmaceutical business scaled rapidly and delivered an excellent rate of return for the three-year period in which it functioned. Analysis of the cyber-criminals' financial transactions reveals that they netted more than $25 million over this period—about the same revenues collected by the Operation Dual Identity criminals over twenty years. The cybercriminals behind Pharmaleaks, however, earned far less than Dread Pirate Roberts (discussed in chapter 3), who sold narcotic drugs on the Dark Net market Silk Road. Nevertheless, the criminals of Pharmaleaks enjoyed a very significant rate of return for a limited investment.

The Pharmaleaks investigation unmasked three online black market pharmaceutical sites—GlavMed, SpamIt, and RXPromotion—each of which operated out of Russia on the World Wide Web between 2007 and 2010, generating $185 million in sales of Viagra as well as unregulated or counterfeit medicines for heart disease, infections, obesity, pain, and mental health.[11] Fortunately for the purchasers of Pharmaleaks products, when tested, some of these counterfeit medicines, sold without requisite prescriptions, did have the appropriate active ingredients in the correct proportions.[12] But other purchasers of some online pharmaceuticals were not as fortunate, as we will see in chapter 6.[13]

Pharmaleaks's financial data could be analyzed because rival online illicit pharmaceutical companies hacked into their competitor's business records and then distributed these leaked documents "very broadly on under-ground forums and file-sharing sites, and other times distributing to a variety of journalists, e-crime researchers, law enforcement agencies as well as a broad range of underground actors." These methods mimicked the exposures of WikiLeaks—hence the name Pharmaleaks.[14] In contrast to WikiLeaks, Pharmaleaks also issued physical threats, undermining the presumption that the criminal trade in the cyberworld is devoid of the violence of street-level commerce.

Viagra was a product of choice for the cybercriminals because of its high profit margins. A decade earlier, the street value of Viagra had already created a distinct financial advantage for traffickers over trading narcotics. Heroin could be marked up 66 percent, cocaine 4,600 percent, and opium 27,400. Yet the markup figure for Viagra was an astonishing 166,700 percent.[15] The comparative profit advantage of the counterfeit pharmaceutical trade helps explain its explosive growth. Interpol evaluates the annual turnover from pharmaceutical crime at $75 billion.[16]

Surprisingly, the masterminds behind Glavit and Spamit, Igor Gusev and Pavel Vrublevsky, did not fully capitalize on the price advantage of counterfeit Viagra for two reasons—high advertising budgets and costly corruption that limited their profits to approximately 16 percent.[17]

Legitimate online sellers such as Amazon use independent contractors called "affiliates" to drive customers to their websites. In the parallel world of affiliates for criminal traders and sellers of pirated digital content, diverse techniques are used, such as spam, chat forums, blogs, social media, and SMS messages.[18] The cost of advertising in the criminal online world is much higher than in legitimate commerce because of the risks and the high cost charged to develop and disseminate spam. Highly competent affiliates working for criminals can make $5,000 daily, or $300,000 monthly.[19]

The managers of Pharmaleaks paid commissions to affiliates of 25 to 60 percent, depending on the service provided.[20] In return, the spammers working for Gusev and Vrublevsky blanketed people's email in many countries, becoming some of the largest propagators of spam on the internet. Spam may be costly for the company but highly profitable for the spammer. As a New Scotland Yard specialist explained in 2012, "A spammer only needs a 0.0001 percent response rate to be in profit."[21] The companies behind Pharmaleaks at their height were responsible for almost half of the spam sent in the world; therefore, they drew many customers, but payments to spammers reduced their profit margins significantly.[22]

The Pharmaleaks companies also paid corrupt bank insiders to secure access to payment systems that linked them to global banking, permitting purchasers to charge the drugs they ordered through credit cards. Credit card charges for Pharmaleaks were processed through a few key banking hubs known for their facilitation of money laundering, such as Azerbaijan and Latvia. The banking relationship was the key for the online pharmaceutical business model in the days before cryptocurrencies. Once these bogus pharmaceuticals sellers were cut off by Western law enforcement from the financial institutions that facilitated their credit card payments, the businesses went into a nosedive. The online criminals cursed the credit card companies, writing in Russian, "The . . . Visa is burning us with napalm."[23] But with the sales drop, the level of spam on the internet also declined dramatically.[24]

Pavel Vrublevsky was eventually sentenced to two and a half years in a Russian prison for his computer crimes when he crossed the wrong people. But after a short period of detention, he took the Russian government equivalent of an offer "you cannot refuse": work for the Russian government and "get out of jail now." Released, he was appointed the head of the Russian government's national payment system.[25] Vrublevsky's appointment may have been owed not only to his high-level computer skills but to his vast contacts with the managers of botnets whose tools are used to produce spam and propagate false news.[26] Through management of the Russia's state payment system, Vrublevsky was perfectly placed to hide irregular payments among the mass of normal payments and to pay the rogue IT community responsible for the cyber-campaigns of the Russian state.[27]

Vrublevsky personifies the cyber-buccaneer or cyber-privateer—the criminal who preys off others for profit, but simultaneously serves his government in cyberspace.[28] The Russian criminal world provides fertile recruitment for state-sponsored hackers, especially when foreign investigations point the way to the most talented criminals.

Stage 3: Avalanche: Virtual Products Sold through the Global Financial System and Cryptocurrencies

The Avalanche case, resulting from the cooperation of many police forces around the world, addressed one of the world's largest and most costly criminal enterprises operating in the Dark Web. At the time of its takedown, the network had infected computers in 189 countries, with as many as 500,000 computers affected daily.[29] The network, operated by Ukrainian and Bulgarian master criminals for almost a decade, met little challenge from law enforcement in their home countries.[30]

In 2016, a key figure in the network, Krasimir Nikolov, was arrested after Western investigators, following payments from victims of ransomware attacks, were led to Bulgarian accounts associated with Nikolov.[31] Shortly afterwards, in December 2016, the police in Poltava, a central Ukrainian city, arrested Gennady Kapkanov, another key figure behind Avalanche, after a violent struggle with a commando squad that came to arrest him. Unfortunately, his detention was short-lived. After Kapkanov was released by a judge, the police soon lost track of him, reflecting either the corruption or incompetence of regional Ukrainian law enforcement.[32]

The Avalanche network caused global harm because it "hosted more than two dozen of the world's most pernicious forms of malicious software" sold to customers worldwide.[33] Customers have no equivalent to a Google search engine in the Dark Web. Therefore, the cybercriminals behind Avalanche found customers by advertising their products and their locales on postings on exclusive underground online criminal forums that operate in the Dark Net.

Malware sold by the criminals of Avalanche infected the computers of both individuals and companies and could be used as weapons in cyberspace. The superstar of the malware world, GozNym, was sold on the Avalanche platform and used to target twenty-two financial institutions in the United States. In Germany alone, the criminals caused damage estimated at 6 million euros (approximately $7.5 million) to just the online German banking system.[34] They also sold Corebot, a Trojan used to steal banking and credential information in order to access online bank accounts.[35]

Ransomware sold to criminals resulted in victims' losses in the hundreds of millions of dollars.[36] Those purchasing the Nymaim malware were able to encrypt the computer files of their victims, blocking access to the contents of their computer systems. Victims would pay significant sums to their ransomware attackers to obtain a key that would allow them to decrypt their files. Many online heists via ransomware generated tens of millions of dollars. The criminals also used malware to seek revenge on law enforcement. Ransomware bought from the Avalanche network facilitated an attack on the Allegheny County District Attorney's Office in Western Pennsylvania, which admitted paying the equivalent of $1,400 in Bitcoins to recover access to its computer files, affirming the role of cryptocurrency in Avalanche payment systems.[37]

The Three Stages of Illicit Trade and the Business Dynamics of Illicit Trade

Illicit commerce has changed profoundly in the past three decades. Yet analysis of the Operation Dual Identity, Pharmaleaks, and Avalanche cases shows that despite the rapid evolution of illicit trade, such enterprises still function as businesses. Table 5.2 outlines the key differences between licit and illicit entrepreneurs and traders. Both types of traders operate with a business logic: they need to find customers, effectively market their products, manage supply chains, and use technology to the best advantage. They also need to vet their employees. Where illicit merchants diverge most significantly from their licit counterparts is that they engage in subterfuge to hide their products and supply routes, systematically engage in corruption, consistently exploit workers, pay little or minimal attention to quality control, and increasingly rely on the Dark Net rather than the internet for their activities.[38] Rather than looking for integrity, illicit traders need to ensure that employees and contractors have the appropriate bone fides of past criminal activity and cyber-skills useful to computer attackers.[39]

Like the legitimate economy, the cyberworld specializes and outsources. For instance, the masterminds of Pharmaleaks did not attempt to run their spam in-house to reach potential customers; instead, they hired large numbers of spammers with specialized capabilities to push advertising over the internet, paying them on commission and on the basis of referrals.

Other criminal tools have not, however, lose their value: violence and intimidation remain tools of illicit business in both the real and the virtual worlds.[40] Violence, as discussed in the introduction, was attempted by the Silk Road creator and operator Dread Pirate Roberts, who hired hit men to defend his financial interests. The criminals of Pharmaleaks threatened violence in the virtual world, and Kapkanov fought off the police commandos with a Kalashnikov rifle.[41]

Criminals' illicit activity intersects with the legitimate economy through their use of banks, credit cards, mail services, and legitimate transporters. The perpetrators of Pharmaleaks received payments

TABLE 5.2. ENTREPRENEURSHIP AND TRADE

	Licit Entrepreneurship and Trade	Illicit Entrepreneurship and Trade
Business logic?	Yes	Yes, but often shorter time perspective, especially in cyber-related businesses
Consumers	Seek desired products, at fair prices, that are legally available both in brick-and-mortar stores and online	Seek products that are not legally available and cheaper sources of supply; often not aware of origin
Access to capital	Easier access to capital from many legal sources, banks, crowdsourcing, stock markets, venture capital funds	Extortion, crowdsourcing; low-profit crimes may provide venture capital for more profitable ones; corrupt officials may use natural resources under their control
Personnel	Wide range of personnel to choose from, especially individuals with high skill and education levels; expected to adhere to labor standards and law; training provided; diaspora communities are important	Exploit migrants and the vulnerable, especially those without access to legitimate employment; coercion often used; web used to find personnel; training often provided; diaspora communities are important
Marketing strategies	Advertising, affiliates drive individuals to online web sites; access to sophisticated marketing and advertising companies	Online media used for marketing; criminal affiliates drive purchasers through spam to websites; Dark Net; advertising through private chat groups and forums
Growth strategies	Diversification, franchises, strategic alliances	Diversification, franchises, strategic alliances, corruption
Product development	Licit entrepreneurs need budgets for research and development; attention to quality control	Theft of new product designs and intellectual property; investment in development of malicious tools for computer; quality control not a concern
Dealing with competition	Legal means—improve pricing, emphasize competitive advantage in marketing	Use extralegal means, including violence, corporate raiding (Russia)
Transport and supply chain logistics	Seek most efficient routes to move goods; transparency of supply chains	Use traditional trade routes for illicit goods; use secondary ports and FTZs to transfer illicit goods; use subterfuge and nondirect routes to disguise commodities; merge illicit trade with licit trade

from American credit cards, and Nikolov of Avalanche used known Bulgarian banks. It is this intersection of the illicit and licit worlds that makes criminal organizations most vulnerable, however, and it helped bring down several of these criminal operations.

Business Dynamics in the Illicit and Licit Worlds

BUSINESS LOGIC

Stages 1, 2, and 3 of illicit business all operate with a business logic, although only Operation Dual Identity was long-lasting. Illicit traders often have shorter time frames than their counterparts in the legitimate world, as they do not anticipate long-term survival. The masterminds of all three cases more closely resembled entrepreneurs than mere smugglers seeking to evade taxation or regulations. They all established integrated transnational criminal businesses. The participants in Operation Dual Identity imported laborers from abroad to exploit on their farms. The Russian entrepreneurs of Pharmaleaks established numerous websites to enable their cross-border trade, and the criminals of Avalanche provided global support services to ensure effective deployment of the criminal tools they sold.

ILLICIT TRADE REFLECTS CULTURE AND HISTORY

Illicit traders, like their counterparts in the licit economy, reflect the history and culture of trade in their country or region. The traders of Operation Dual Identity continued a centuries-long tradition of illicit flows and routes across the US-Mexican border. However, the commodities involved have evolved. Highly taxed consumer products such as alcohol and cigarettes have been supplanted by people, drugs, and weapons.[42]

The Pharmaleaks case reflects Russia's history as an exporter of raw materials rather than a producer or trader of manufactured goods. There were no Russian domestic pharmaceutical products to sell. Therefore, the Russians who marketed pharmaceuticals online, needing to acquire the medicines abroad, purchased prescription drugs directly from India and China. The Pharmaleaks businesses, while highly profitable, generated less in revenues than a vertically integrated business, where the supply chain from production through sale is controlled by the same entity. The sale of Chinese counterfeits online, for example, is a vertically integrated business.

The Russian competitive advantage, as seen in this case, is the high level of math and science education in the Soviet and post-Soviet systems; this level of knowledge among the population allows cyber-crime to flourish. Unfortunately, the absence of significant legitimate cyber-companies in the Soviet successor states limits the possibilities for licit employment for those with advanced cyber-skills.

Immigration to support trade has created diaspora communities.[43] These communities, as discussed in the historical chapters, aided illicit trade in the past and continue to do so today. For example, members of the Lebanese diaspora in West Africa have played critical roles in the illicit trade that funds Hezbollah.[44] Individuals within Turkish diaspora communities in western Europe have played key roles in the distribution of heroin smuggled through the Balkan route.[45]

CONSUMERS AND MARKETS

All traders need to find purchasers. The criminals of Operation Dual Identity used their personal networks to find customers, thereby limiting their customer base. The most recent stages of illicit trade reveal significant online outreach to find purchasers of illicit goods on an international scale. An important asymmetry exists: a few illicit merchants operating from a few countries may sell to large numbers of buyers around the world.[46]

Illicit entrepreneurs and traders exploit the fact that the global marketplace is now highly competitive as to price, and that consumers are naive about the threats to their personal health and to society from counterfeit and online purchases. Fortunately, the products shipped by Pharmaleaks were generally reliable. In other cases, online purchasers were not so fortunate and were hospitalized or even died from poor-quality pharmaceuticals.

ACCESS TO CAPITAL

To start a business, traders in both the licit and illicit worlds need access to capital. Early-stage capital is hard for all businesses to acquire, and gaining access to capital is even hard for some illicit entrepreneurs and traders, who often originate from marginalized communities. Therefore, they often start small, using one form of illicit activity to generate money for another.

In contrast, well-placed officials often do not need start-up capital. Health, forestry, and labor officials in many countries have leveraged their government positions to illegally market the natural resources under their control. Access to capital is not a challenge for the residents of contested border areas where smugglers have operated for generations. Familial continuity in illicit trade alleviates the need for start-up capital. Successful smugglers pass their skills and their routes from generation to generation, whether on the US-Mexican border, at the port of Marseille, or on the borders of the Ottoman Empire, in the Balkans on the western boundary and in the Kurdish mountain areas in the east.[47]

Illicit traders generate funds through petty illicit commerce, extortion, auctions, stock shares, and more recently, new techniques are used in the online world. Often illicit traders generate capital by exploiting the most vulnerable. Criminals can coerce children to be beggars or compel women and girls to be prostitutes. Traffickers repatriate the profits from this exploitation to build large homes and invest in other businesses.[48]

Two kinds of large-scale petty crime—cigarettes and counterfeits—have been used as *venture capital* for larger-scale illicit activity. For example, Italian investigators revealed that the Camorra, the Neapolitan-based organized crime group, obtained significant profits from sales of pirated DVDs and then reinvested the profits in drugs, the arms trade, and usury.[49]

In the Czech Republic, members of the Vietnamese diaspora community generated venture capital through the low-level illicit cigarette trade. With this initial capital, they were able to become key conduits for imported counterfeit goods from Asia to western

Europe. Capital and connections allowed Vietnamese criminals to advance to the extremely profitable illicit rhino horn trade.[50]

Somalia provides an intriguing example of how working capital can be generated for illicit activity. Pirates there financed their maritime ventures through "investments" from local communities and members of the Somali diaspora community. Once capital was raised, a stock market was established in Haradheere, once a small fishing village, 250 miles from Mogadishu, to finance different pirate expeditions.[51] Auctions were also held to allocate shares in future pirate ventures. This was a far cry from Adam Smith's image of capitalism, although the illicit actors relied on known methods of the legitimate economy.

In the new digital economy, illicit entrepreneurs also generate capital through trade, crowdfunding, and crowdsourcing, as illustrated by the colorful case of a Ukrainian hacker who was eager to revenge himself on a blogger who had unmasked his identity.[52] He crowdsourced Bitcoins from his fellow fraudsters in the Dark Net to buy high-grade heroin off the Silk Road website. Then he had the purchased drugs delivered to the US-based blogger after alerting law enforcement about the drug delivery.[53] Fortunately, the hacker was revealed, and he, rather than the blogger, faced criminal charges.

PERSONNEL RECRUITMENT AND PERSONNEL POLICIES

Illicit businesses need to hire and retain personnel who can perform needed tasks. Foot soldiers for illicit trade are often displaced and smuggled people, as well as youth in areas with high unemployment rates. Employees can serve as couriers of goods and money and as sellers of drugs, counterfeits, and illicit wildlife products.

Organized criminals profile and target individuals and agencies, often investing significant time and even expense to recruit them. To achieve these results, criminal traders need psychological insight, an ability to assess vulnerability, and a willingness to utilize blackmail.[54]

Naive housewives, students, and the long-term unemployed answer online ads and become "money mules" for illicit traders shifting money between bank accounts and countries. Their pay and benefits are negotiated through web portals. Their success in this activity is usually short-lived, since many are identified and subject to criminal sanctions, as occurred in the Avalanche case.[55]

The training of the low-level personnel of the illicit economy is immortalized in Charles Dickens's *Oliver Twist* in the character of the Artful Dodger, who trains the boys under his command as pickpockets and lowly criminals. On-the-job training has not disappeared. Trafficked young girls are often trained by their traffickers in how to satisfy customers.[56] Drug couriers are taught how to conceal the commodities they transport, and wildlife smugglers are instructed how to disguise the parts they are transporting.

Online training is also provided in launching a successful malware infection campaign. Recruits to cybercrime organizations are taught how to anonymize their identities, ensure security for the operation, and deploy cryptocurrencies successfully.[57]

Illicit entrepreneurs, unlike legitimate companies and traders, do not need to pay attention to labor conditions and worker safety. Major international companies such as Nestlé and other big chocolate companies have been accused of using cocoa from farms with child laborers.[58] Apple was criticized following multiple suicides by workers at the Chinese Foxconn factories that produce its products.[59] Walmart, Gap, and other clothing importers have bought apparel from factories in Bangladesh that failed to ensure worker safety.[60]

By contrast, illicit entrepreneurs can force workers to toil long hours in unsafe conditions without hazard pay. They can compel miners to work without protective equipment. Such labor practices, as discussed in reference to marijuana farms, cut costs and increase the competitiveness of the traders' products. These practices contravene the norms of international law, but in the world of illicit trade there is no expectation of any kind of fair labor treatment and few mechanisms by which workers can object to mistreatment. Moreover, the labor abuses of illicit entrepreneurs who produce counterfeits, mine coltan, or sell illicit timber are rarely confronted by civil society activists seeking better labor conditions for workers. The anonymity of the producers and the absence of transparency in supply chains preclude accountability.

DEVELOPING NEW MARKETS AND FINDING CUSTOMERS

Illicit entrepreneurs pursue many of the same business objectives as their legitimate counterparts—growth, desirable products, and effective marketing. There are important differences, however, in their clients and their products. Illicit entrepreneurs often market items that cannot be sold in legitimate markets, such as sex with minors, child pornography, drugs, banned substances like endangered species, and illegal computer products such as malware, spam, and botnets. Moreover, illicit traders often market in ways forbidden in legitimate markets—by generating spam, coercing buyers, or creating addictions.[61]

Drug dealers may generate customers by offering small quantities that "hook" some customers; newly addicted, they then become loyal clients. At higher levels of the drug trade, major drug traffickers develop new markets and risk mitigation strategies and deploy violence and corruption for maximum effect.[62]

Illicit traders may not have access to Madison Avenue or public relations firms, but they develop marketing strategies suitable to their customer base. Human traffickers find victims and customers through a variety of techniques. Human traffickers in the Northeast of the United States distributed business cards in locales frequented by migrant workers from Mexico and Central America, using coded symbols for sex, with telephone numbers to call.[63] Like their licit counterparts in the upper Midwest, where Hispanic customers are not online, they relied on traditional promotion through handouts.[64]

Pimps in the United States, however, find potential victims not only in malls and at bus stops but increasingly through social media. They display their material success on Facebook, Instagram, and Snapchat in images that specially target young girls, the recruitment pool sought by the traffickers.[65]

Different strategies are used to find customers for sexual services through the internet. Websites such as Craigslist and Backpage have been used in the United States to market trafficking victims and their images. After the state attorneys general cracked down on the sexual service ads of Craigslist, the ads migrated to Backpage.[66] But

Backpage was not the innocent consolidator of ads that it had falsely claimed to be.

Backpage's misrepresentation was revealed quite by accident. Like many companies, Backpage outsourced its computer services to a developing country where tech services could be hired more cheaply. By hiring a Philippine-based company called Avion to handle its sexual advertisements, Backpage could claim that it did not control sex-related ads. Backpage officials falsely believed that the location of Avion's computer system outside of the United States gave it security from scrutiny.[67]

This profit-making strategy was revealed when Filipino investigators in a totally unrelated case involving irregularities in real estate sales, seized Avion's computers. Those computers were sent for forensic analysis to the United States, where the investigators for the real estate case discovered files related to the sex trafficking of minors that connected Avion's files to Backpage.

The computer files revealed that Backpage had Avion "lure advertisers—and customers seeking sex—from sites run by its competitors."[68] Avion, while under contract to Backpage, helped create new advertisements, sometimes editing the content to hide the minor age of the girls offering sexual services and thereby disguising the criminal element of the ad.

The sexual advertisements placed on Backpage generated good profits for the pimps but massive profits for the corporate owners of Backpage.[69] Growth was at a rapid rate possible only in the tech world. Backpage revenues from its prostitution ads were $5.8 million in 2008, and that grew to $135 million in gross revenue in 2014, with 82 percent profitability. Continued growth is anticipated.[70] Prior to the arrest of Backpage's CEO in late 2016, the attorney general of California reported that Backpage's internal reports showed that from January 2013 to March 2015, 99 percent of its income was "directly attributable" to its adult advertising and more than $51 million of its revenue was derived from California in that period. Backpage's founders were each rewarded for that profitability with a $10 million bonus in 2014.[71] In early April 2018, the combined efforts of different federal law enforcement agencies resulted in the

seizure of backpage.com by the government.[72] Shortly after the seizure, seven top officials of Backpage were arrested after a ninety-
three-count indictment was issued by a Phoenix grand jury, alleging
conspiracy, facilitating prostitution, and money laundering. The
indictment alleged that Backpage had laundered $500 million in
prostitution-related revenue since 2004 and that several young girls
who responded to Backpage ads were murdered.[73]

GROWTH STRATEGIES

Many start-ups fail in the legitimate economy. To survive in ever-
changing markets, both licit and illicit businesses must be responsive
to a challenge for sellers in both worlds—consumer demand. Counterfeiters trading in outdated or unappealing fashion can lose significantly, just as happens to legitimate retailers when their products do
not appeal to purchasers. Traders in both the licit and illicit sectors can
grow fast if they create a monopoly or achieve market dominance.[74]

To achieve growth online criminals must run streamlined, often
lean and automated operations. Whereas trade for millennia has
been based on interpersonal relations, in cyberspace criminal
traders rarely, if ever, meet in person.[75] Their contacts are often
established and maintained through the forums and communications of the Dark Web.

Corruption is a tool that can facilitate growth. Illicit entrepreneurs and traders avoid regulations and taxes and use corrupt officials to ensure that their commodities are purchased. Moreover,
corrupt officials can help eliminate the competitors of illicit traders
by selectively applying regulations. Corruption can also ensure that
particular illicit businesses are not investigated.

In the online world, as in the tangible world, providers must satisfy customers to grow. In the Dark Net, as on legitimate sites such
as Amazon, there are rating systems for purchases. Customers can
evaluate their sellers and leave comments to advise other buyers.
"The administrators take a 5–10% cut of each sale and set broad
policy. . . . They pay moderators in Bitcoin to run customer forums
and handle complaints." But in this illicit world, there are those

seeking to game the system. Vendors such as Mr420 offer to provide fake reviews.[76]

DIVERSIFICATION

Many businesses, in both the legitimate and illegitimate worlds, seek to diversify to ensure that they are not dependent on sales of one particular commodity. Illicit actors shift between several forms of illicit trade to optimize profits and reduce risk. Economies of scale are gained by working in diverse sectors simultaneously, achieving what is referred to as "convergence": multiple forms of crime being committed by the same groups.[77] The criminals use the skill sets they obtained in one area to enter new types of illicit trade that will prove profitable, deploying a strategy well known to the legitimate business community.

Diversification can occur rapidly because those engaging in illicit trade are more flexible and adaptable than the bureaucratic structures that oppose them. Nonstate actors can seize on market opportunities as they find them, and they can shift quickly to new income sources when revenue streams are curtailed. Mexican crime groups, for instance, have diversified from the drug trade into human smuggling and the sale of energy products.[78]

Europol has also noted increasing diversification among many European-based criminals who have recently expanded into human smuggling. They estimate that approximately five thousand international organized crime groups operate in the European Union, and that over one thousand of these are so-called poly-crime groups deriving their profits from multiple criminal activities.[79]

The criminals behind Operation Dual Identity also diversified by engaging in multiple criminal offenses, including human smuggling, identity theft, marijuana production, drug trafficking, home invasions, and even murder.[80]

Terrorist groups have also diversified the illicit commodities they trade. The Colombian terrorist organization FARC, known for its drug trafficking, acquired a new illegal funding source before the peace talks with the Colombian government—gold. Gold extraction combines less risk with higher profits, helping to explain why over 80 percent of the gold extracted in Colombia is now mined illegally.[81] FARC's recent revenues from the illegal gold trade exceeded its revenues from the drug market. Yet FARC's business practices were transferred to this new commodity. In gold mining, as in the drug trade, intimidation, violence, extortion, and exploitation of indigenous populations are the general operating principles. Furthermore, both products harm the environment: the drug trade causes soil depletion and destruction through the use of toxic chemicals, and the illicit gold trade puts dangerous chemicals in the water and the process of extraction is harmful to human life.[82]

The terrorist group ISIS (Islamic State) sold oil but also profited from kidnapping, extortion, and the sale of contraband and antiquities.[83] Diversification has benefits beyond the financial. Pernicious nonstate actors can confound law enforcement by shifting commodities and locales, thereby reducing risk.

Criminals trading in natural resources, as we saw with the rhino horn trade, have been able to expand their businesses rapidly because they are not new to illicit commerce. Many environmental criminals were previously engaged in corruption, counterfeiting, and drug, arms, and human trafficking, as well as cyber and financial crime.[84]

Online criminals, as mentioned previously, may market different commodities in succession, as did the criminals behind Pharmaleaks. Before they entered the illicit pharmaceutical business, they had traded in child pornography. Once they lost the ability to charge for their medicines, they moved into selling fraudulent antiviral software.[85]

Online criminal markets in the Dark Net also diversify. The same site may sell drugs, weapons, malicious computer software, and tech support to deploy the pernicious tools they market. Assassins for hire are also offered on the Dark Web.[86]

STRUCTURE AND DECISION-MAKING

Italian hierarchical crime groups, such as the Cosa Nostra, Camorra, and 'Ndrangheta, are among the most studied criminal organizations in the world.[87] To survive over an extended time they have focused on internal codes of ethics (being men of honor), respect for the chain of command, effective deployment of violence, and their reputations. As Diego Gambetta has written in *The Sicilian Mafia*, the roots of that organization lie in its certification of horses traded in the nineteenth century in an environment of distrust.[88]

Newer criminal organizations are less hierarchical than the Mafia, and illicit traders often operate with network structures. They therefore have greater flexibility than many legitimate companies, which are more bureaucratic and have more formalized decision-making. This structure enables new illicit traders to respond rapidly to emerging opportunities. This is why criminal traders, once they have depleted the natural world of plants or wildlife in one locale through over-exploitation, simply take illicit trade to another locale. The poaching of elephants, for instance, is being moved to ever more remote and conflict-ridden regions of Africa as the elephants are killed off.[89]

Different structures are found among online illicit traders such as Avalanche, which was "structured much like an IT company, with programmers, web designers, system administrators, and other roles found in legitimate enterprises." The Avalanche network survived as a business, despite increasing law enforcement scrutiny over time, because it had good leadership, successful advertising, innovative products, and good customer support.[90]

To develop, illicit businesses need strategic plans or visions for growth. Research done by cyberspecialists who have penetrated on-line criminal communities often reveals the transmission of strategies from the real into the virtual world. Therefore, it is hardly surprising that their plans include product development, improved logistics, development and maintenance of supply chains, and incorporation of new technology.

STRATEGIC ALLIANCES

Strategic alliances often facilitate growth in the illicit as in the licit world. Alliances in the illicit world often link highly diverse groups that transcend significant ethnic divides, geographical borders, and even political conflicts. For example, Armenians and Azeris, sworn enemies, together extorted markets in Russia. Israelis collaborated with Bedouin human smugglers.[91] Taiwanese and mainland Chinese cybercriminals operate out of Indonesia to target Chinese speakers.[92]

Legitimate multinational trading companies establish offices and franchises globally, providing broad geographic reach, but illicit alliances, outside the cyberworld, are not often as global and are more task-focused. For example, British investigators reported on the cooperation of Jamaican and Turkish drug traffickers in the United Kingdom.

In the Dark Web, where Tor or other software allows one to enter anonymously, traders may not know the country of residence of their business associates.[93] Compounding this anonymity are digital currencies, which further obscure the identity and nationality of sellers and purchasers. In a 2014 malware case successfully prosecuted by the US Justice Department, through cooperation with foreign law enforcement, the diverse online traders were Algerian, Bulgarian, and Russian, and some resided in the United Kingdom.[94]

PRODUCT DEVELOPMENT

Legitimate companies must invest in product development if they are to grow. But this is not the case with illicit traders who prey on the products of others, whether it be fashion design, pharmaceuticals, or electronic parts.[95]

Innovations in science and technology are targeted by illicit traders at the conception stage but are particularly vulnerable to expropriation when they reach a certain economic threshold. The loss of future products is especially costly to legitimate businesses, and particularly valuable to illicit traders, as they can exploit the new technologies they acquire at minimal cost. This problem has been identified in diverse Western countries, and some of the thieves of these products are believed to be state-supported criminals.

American law enforcement has identified product theft as a key concern, particularly in such tech havens as California. Starting in 2010, Sweden also initiated a number of internet-related cases for copyright infringement through file-sharing and crimes against industrial property rights with the help of the internet.[96] Sometimes thieves copyright stolen product designs in China, precluding their future sale in the large Chinese markets.

The dynamism and ingenuity of the synthetic drug market is revealed in the official statistics of the United Nations Office on Drugs and Crime. Between 2009 and 2016, 106 countries and territories reported the emergence of 739 new psychoactive substances.[97] The rise of the synthetic drug trade is an excellent example of illicit entrepreneurship. Synthetic drugs have seen massive growth in recent decades, reflective of the importance of technology to the growth of illicit trade. Growth has been seen in ecstasy, amphetamines, methamphetamines, and other synthetically produced drugs such as fentanyl. The trade in synthetic drugs, often referred to as "designer drugs," also reflects the trend in licit trade of premium prices being paid for fashionable consumer items.[98] In markets, lower prices are paid for items derived from agricultural labor, and this is true whether one is consuming food or drugs derived from poppies, opium, or marijuana plants.

Synthetic drugs have the additional advantage of enabling traffickers to move production closer to consumers, thereby decreasing transport costs and reducing the possibility of detection along long supply chains. Shortening the distance from production to distribution also reduces the costs of corruption, as there are fewer people to bribe before the product enters the market. Synthetic drugs such as ecstasy and crystal meth are now available in almost all markets, but striking growth rates have been recorded in Asia, Australia, and the Middle East. Captagon (a psychostimulant) is king in Saudi Arabia.[99]

Beginning in the mid-2000s, synthetic drugs began to be produced in the poorer, traditional drug cultivation countries, such as Myanmar. One synthetic drug seizure there in 2015 yielded 27 million pills.[100]

New products that target computers, such as malware, botnets, and Trojans, are among the areas of greatest growth in illicit markets.[101] They are one area in which criminals actually invest their own resources to develop new products for sale, franchising, and leasing.

QUALITY CONTROL

Many legitimate corporations, especially in markets where citizens have rights, devote significant attention to quality control in order to prevent harm to brand reputation or to prevent damaging lawsuits and fines. Television and online ads in the United States alert accident victims that they too can sue Toyota for accidents relating to defective car seat belts or seek damages from pharmaceutical companies for harmful drugs that have been placed on the market prematurely.[102]

Quality control is not a significant concern of many illicit entrepreneurs or traders who sell counterfeits, as they do not depend on brand reputation or repeat business. Moreover, if consumers take action for personal injury, the copyright holder rather than the counterfeiter will often be sued for inferior products.

Many illicit entrepreneurs do not care if they manufacture or sell defective infant formula, pesticides, medicines, and even baby toys manufactured with harmful ingredients or under very unsanitary conditions.[103] Many of the most harmful products are destined for markets with few legal regulations on product safety, such as the states of the former Soviet Union or the countries of Africa. In Soviet successor states, sales of toys produced with toxic components, disguised and sometimes sold under the labels of major corporations, are marketed to unwitting customers.[104]

ADDRESSING COMPETITION

Illicit traders have certain advantages in dealing with competitors, as they can more readily use extralegal means such as corruption, collusion, and price-fixing. These advantages help them limit competition, achieve market dominance, and fix prices.[105]

Illicit actors often threaten or use violence to ensure compliance by their suppliers, sellers, or middlemen. Violence is particularly pronounced in the drug trade, where groups battle over control of territory and routes. Drug traffickers routinely use threats and actual brutality to ensure that customers pay in a timely fashion.

Human trafficking is accompanied by violence as pimps try to take over rivals' girls. Despite the idea that online marketplaces reduce violence, the online world is not violence-free, and force is used or threatened against competitors or those who fail to make payments or produce goods.[106]

In Russia and many other post-Soviet states, a practice known as *corporate raiding* has developed to eliminate competitors; it operates very differently from the Western concept of the same name. Competitors may be targeted through corrupt and violent means, and organized crime, complicit legal officials, and fraudulent documents are deployed to deprive owners of their assets.[107]

LOGISTICS

Logistics experts are needed by both licit and illicit traders. For those in the licit world, logistics considerations include the security of supply chains and the costs and efficiency of delivery. Amazon has rapidly grown to be the eighth-largest retailer in the world because it combines online accessibility with attention to prompt and accurate delivery.[108]

Illicit traders share some of these business tenets of the legitimate world, but not all. They need to ensure delivery of their product to market. But they do not want transparency of trade or cargoes that can be tracked and traced. They seek locales where they can evade detection, bribe officials, and avoid taxes and regulations. They often rely on fake documents such as passports, driver's licenses, and ID cards to help facilitate deliveries. A whole service industry of facilitators has developed to produce these illegal documents that support illicit trade.

Like the sellers of licit goods from the internet, the illicit traders rely on numerous small packages to distribute their goods. Deliveries of counterfeit electronics, medicines, and drug packets arrive at recipients' homes by post and specialized delivery services. The postal service is particularly favored because local law enforcement in the United States does not have jurisdiction over its deliveries. Breaking down shipments into small, discrete packages makes it much more difficult for law enforcement to detect the illicit trade.[109] Yet it also requires that illicit traders make many individual sales to achieve a profit. It is an Amazon approach to the illicit economy.

TRANSPORT

Illicit commerce travels in many different ways—by land, sea, and air. It moves with legitimate shipping and trucking companies, or its shippers operate in the world of dark commerce, ready to serve customers without asking questions. Smuggled products are even moved into highly regulated ports when criminal shippers and recipients use ingenuity and technology to aid their logistics. Corruption is key to many illicit deliveries.

Many historic trade routes have been repurposed to serve illicit traders. The ancient Silk Road now serves the northern route for the heroin trade out of Afghanistan.[110] The route that Marco Polo helped initiate between Italy and China has been repurposed to accommodate a massive counterfeit trade into Italy.[111] The slave trade route between West Africa and Brazil is now employed by the drug traffickers of Latin America and Brazil to move cocaine into Europe. The historic trade passage between East Africa, Yemen, and the Indian subcontinent is now the locale for a converging drug, wildlife, and counterfeit trade.[112]

Illicit trade need not travel along obscure or complex routes. Significant illicit shipments can still be moved into major ports through subterfuge and by hacking into the computer system of the port authority, revealing the innovativeness of some smugglers. A Suriname-based group smuggled containers' worth of drugs into Dutch and Belgian ports. The drug-filled containers were dropped at the port and then stolen before inspection. After the containers were emptied, they were returned. The drug smugglers could achieve this feat by retaining sophisticated computer security specialists who hacked into the ports' computers.[113]

The flexibility of crime networks and their absolute ruthlessness in pursuing profits are responsible for human smugglers packing many people into boats that are often not capable of staying afloat.

This practice explains the high mortality rate of contemporary human smuggling.

Legitimate shipping companies and postal services can be both witting and unwitting shippers of illicit goods. Online sales have fueled the opioid epidemic in the United States as customers buy through both the World Wide Web and the Dark Web. The ordered drugs are often delivered by American and foreign postal carriers. Finding illicit items is difficult under existing legislation, which fails to require foreign shippers to provide advanced electronic data concerning their contents and intended recipients.[114]

Legitimate global trade in tangible goods thrives where there is first-class infrastructure, communications, and commercial systems. Illicit trade often passes through many locales that are of secondary importance to global traders, such as Naples in Italy, Vladivostok in Russia, Karachi in Pakistan, Dubai in the United Arab Emirates, Cape Town in South Africa, and Miami, Florida. These are noted ports, but they are not on the "A" list of global commerce.

Poor countries, with limited enforcement capacity and high levels of corruption, have very low scores on the Illicit Trade Environment Index. These locales are key to illicit trade. It is hardly surprising that the illicit wildlife and timber trade flows through Laos, Myanmar, Vietnam, Cambodia, and Indonesia, countries with the poorest scores in Asia.[115]

Illicit trade hubs share certain attributes. They are often close to centers of organized crime, and they have high levels of corruption and limited regulatory authority. In addition to these hubs, free-trade zones (FTZs) have become critical to the movement of illicit trade, as they lack effective regulation.[116] In these murky environments, it is possible to hide the illicit in the licit. Shippers and officials surreptitiously change shipping invoices to disguise the movement of illegal commodities and avoid taxation. According to the International Chamber of Commerce:

FTZs have provided a mechanism for counterfeiters to move illegal fake products around the world. Increasingly, counterfeiters use transit or transshipment of goods, through multiple, geographically diverse FTZs for no other purpose than to disguise the illicit nature of the products.[117]

The Jebel Ali free-trade zone in the UAE is a major hub of the illicit trade in cigarette and counterfeits, including pharmaceuticals.[118] Through this zone move billions of illicit "white" cigarettes destined for European markets.[119] Yet not all FTZs are located in countries that rate poorly on Transparency International's Corruption Perception Index. For example, Singapore is rated number six in the world for its low level of corruption, yet it has a different standard for its FTZ because of its eagerness to facilitate trade.[120] In its FTZ, as the *Economist* Intelligence Unit reports, "Neither Singapore Customs nor any other government authority is a consistent presence."[121]

THE ROLE OF SUBTERFUGE: ABSENCE OF TRANSPARENCY

Much human ingenuity goes into devising the disguises used to hide the contents of illegal packages. Shipments of cocaine are packed inside fish fillets heading to New York and inside pineapples headed to Spain.[122] Oriental rugs are interwoven with opium and smuggled into the Manchester airport in the United Kingdom.[123] In Zimbabwe, officials found more than 15 million cigarettes hidden within four train cars allegedly shipping full loads of timber.[124]

Illicit shipments often travel circuitous routes. For example, counterfeited goods shipped from Bangladesh and China into Europe "passed through the ports of Antwerp and Hamburg, where, thanks to the collaboration of Customs officers, the goods were unloaded and temporarily stored in warehouses. The goods were then redirected to Italy," a distribution hub for counterfeits. Transfers from the port of entry were made by Air China cargo flights headed for Milan, Brescia, and Rome.[125] This case reveals the centrality of corruption to illicit trade, even in western Europe.

Bulk shipments of drugs, timber, or elephant tusks require obfuscation. These products are often taken, with minimal oversight, through multiple trans-shipment points, particularly free-trade zones, and locales with high degrees of corruption. For example, when shippers of an illicit cargo of ivory tusks directed the shipment through airports in West Africa, the Middle East, and then several in Asia before reaching its final destination in Thailand, they made it very difficult for law enforcement to identify them as its senders.[126]

Combining licit and illicit goods often facilitates delivery. Such combinations can be as small-scale as landscaping companies taking ferns and rocks from Shenandoah National Park to plant in clients' gardens along with plants legally obtained from nurseries. Traders of Civil War relics combine legally sourced items with those dug up illegally from government-preserved battleground sites.[127] Ivory horn travels in a shipment with legitimate trade items such as seaweed, cashew nuts, and seashells.[128]

Iranians' efforts to circumvent sanctions for their nuclear weapons program led to massive subterfuge. A German and Turkish investigation conducted between 2010 and 2012 identified nine hundred shipments of smuggled cooling devices and other apparatuses directed to five separate shell companies established by Iranians in Istanbul. Eight hundred of these shipments originated from India, and an additional one hundred came from Germany. The Istanbul-based front companies misidentified the cooling devices as valves and plumbing fixtures when they reexported them to Iran, thereby hiding the ultimate purchaser of the goods—Iran's nuclear program.[129] North Koreans have engaged in similar subterfuge for decades to build their nuclear program.[130]

The Use of Technology: The Web, the Deep Web, or the Dark Web

Traders must incorporate new technologies to stay competitive. Pernicious nonstate actors have been among the earliest and most successful adapters of new online technology. They use the searchable World Wide Web, the Deep Web (the part not accessible to conventional search engines), and the Dark Web, and some function in all three elements. The Dark Web, at five hundred times the size of the surface World Wide Web, provides a vast territory in which massive amounts of information can be stored and made available only to a select group of users.[131] This is very conducive to its criminal abuse.

Online platforms and social media are also abused to allow individuals to buy opioids, counterfeit pharmaceuticals, and illicit wildlife products.[132] The new technology is a force multiplier for the growth of illicit trade, as seen in all three stages of illicit trade. According to a 2015 *New York Times* report:

> Ordering illegal drugs from China is as easy as typing on a keyboard. On guidechem.com, more than 150 Chinese companies sell alpha-PVP, also known as flakka, a dangerous stimulant that is illegal in the United States but not in China, and was blamed for 18 recent deaths in one Florida county.[133]

Just as false news can be disseminated through Facebook because it lacks appropriate filters to weed out erroneous communications, neither can Facebook control the posts that facilitate illicit trade. Social media has enabled arms sales to conflict-ridden areas where terrorists operate, such as Libya, Iraq, Syria, and Yemen. An analysis of Libyan Facebook accounts between September 2014 and April 2016 "documented 97 attempts at unregulated transfers of missiles, heavy machine guns, grenade launchers, rockets and anti-matériel rifles, used to disable military equipment." Facebook is hosting a virtual weapons bazaar, as are other social media platforms. Some of the weapons offered are those provided by the United States to Syrian rebels.[134]

Cybercriminals choose to operate through the World Wide Web, the Deep Web, or the Dark Web based on the visibility they want for their products, the volume of sales they seek to generate, and the level of criminality associated with their products. Therefore, products that command much more attention from law enforcement, such as narcotic drugs, child pornography, and malware, are more likely to be sold in the Dark Web. Counterfeits, even including such items as medicines, are more likely to be sold on the World Wide Web.

Affirming the criminal intent of purchasers in the Dark Web is research conducted in 2014 that determined that "four out of five Tor hidden services site visits were to online destinations with pedophilia materials." Too many have viewed the Dark Web as a haven for privacy without understanding the extensive criminal abuse present there.[135]

In all online environments, profits can be high and products can be sold with a range of prices. In the World Wide Web and the Deep Web, illicit sellers seek an image of legitimacy and often provide options such as credit card payment processors and related payment alternatives such as debit cards, wire transfers, and digital currencies. All these traditional measures reassure customers.[136]

Sales volumes and profit margins can be significant in both the Web and the Dark Web; therefore, it is neither the price nor the number of consumers that is decisive in determining traffickers' marketing strategy. If businesses want customers to make speedy decisions, they use the Web rather than the Dark Web. They may even use spam to direct buyers to their website.

Sales in the Dark Web are based on trust, and building trust takes time.[137] Dark Web purchasers necessarily operate more slowly than those on the Web, since purchasers must obtain the appropriate certifications to acquire entry into the closed communities where the illicit trade occurs. To do this they must learn the required lingo of those who belong to these criminalized networks.[138] It is only logical, if you're buying quantities of synthetic drugs or searching for a kidney, that you would not make a quick decision because you want to be sure you trust the seller. Likewise, the sellers do not want to be entrapped by law enforcement, as happened to Dread Pirate Roberts and other large-scale illicit sellers in the Dark Web.

Corporate Social Responsibility

Corporations in the legitimate world have adopted policies to address the well-being of communities and the environment. This broad concept can include support for nonprofit social, community, and artistic groups as well as concerns about the sourcing of their products to minimize harm to the environment.[139]

Nonstate actors do not show respect for the environment; more-over, many are at the forefront of its destruction. Yet many of non-state organizations are also at the forefront of service provision where the state is absent. They use proceeds from their criminal activity to ensure their future impunity by persuading citizens not to see them just as a negative force in the community. The *Yakuza* (members of transnational criminal organizations in Japan), after the 1995 Kobe earthquake, provided aid in the absence of state assistance. Drug traffickers offer services to those living in Brazil's *favelas*.[140] FARC, at its height, was a major provider of benefits in Colombia, includ-ing schools, medical clinics, and infrastructure support. Terrorist groups in other regions of the world also provide services to their communities, enhancing their legitimacy.[141]

Laundering Profits and Illicit Financial Flows

In a 2013 study of fifty-five developing countries by Global Financial Integrity (GFI), economists estimated that illicit financial outflows—most in the form of misinvoicing of trade—amounted to $947 billion in 2011, representing some 3.7 percent of these countries' combined GDP. Abuse of the trade system is at the heart of the asset-stripping of some of the world's poorest countries.[142]

Multinational institutions and private banks have facilitated this wealth transfer. Loans provided for national development have been siphoned off by corrupt leaders—kleptocrats—because lenders have provided inadequate oversight of the funds. Massive sums have been stolen from Nigeria in the decades since independence. Over $1 bil-lion was allegedly stolen from the Malaysian national treasury by Prime Minister Najib Razak, who deposited much of this money in international banks around the globe, triggering investigations in many countries.[143]

The citizens of Equatorial Guinea, Turkmenistan, and Ukraine have remained impoverished while their national assets are found in the bank accounts of their leaders in many financial centers around the world.[144] The revelations of the Panama Papers and the

Paradise Papers disclose the pervasiveness of this practice among global elites.[145]

The hundreds of billions of dollars gained through the global illicit trade in drugs, humans, weapons, and other activities often enter the legitimate economy. The money is laundered through banks, wire transfer businesses, trade-based money laundering systems, currency exchange businesses, *hawala* traders (the system of underground banking based on trust), and, most recently, cryptocurrencies (currencies that exist only in the cyberworld and are not backed by any government).[146] Money from illicit trade is invested in land, expensive homes, cars, and other businesses, some of them legitimate. Real estate has been purchased with laundered funds in many locales on all continents.[147] One lucrative Turkish-run human trafficking network in the Netherlands used its victims as couriers returning the profits of the Dutch-based trade to build nightclubs in Turkey.[148] In the United States, in six jurisdictions with suspected high rates of money laundering, the financial intelligence unit of the United States, the Financial Crimes Enforcement Network (FinCEN), found that about 30 percent of real estate purchases involve a beneficial owner or representative who had previously been the subject of a suspicious activity report.[149] Profits from the fentanyl trade are laundered into Vancouver real estate by Chinese gangs.[150]

Well-established banks have moved billions in drug profits through their institutions, some of it to offshore locales.[151] Legitimate financial institutions transferred funds from illicit commerce particularly after the 2008 financial crisis, a period when banking standards declined and financial institutions were in survival mode. The multimillion-dollar penalties imposed on Citibank, HSBC, Wachovia, and Deutsche Bank indicate the key role that some bankers have assumed in facilitating illicit commerce.[152] Illustrating a recurring theme of this work—the convergence of the licit and illicit economies—this kind of cooperation is true not just of banks but also of legitimate companies.

In 2000, a group of top American companies, including Hewlett-Packard, Ford, and Whirlpool, were informed by the US Justice Department that they were implicated in a money-laundering scheme called the "Black Market Peso Exchange."[153] Washing machines and cars were bought with drug profits without the knowledge of the sellers and then shipped to Colombia for resale. Purchasers would pay using pesos, thereby completing the cycle of converting the dollar currency proceeds earned by drug traffickers into usable assets.[154]

Financial havens, such as in Panama, have accepted funds from known traffickers aided by professionals. As the game on the website of the Panama Papers states, "Welcome to the secret world of offshore. Your goal is to navigate this parallel universe and hide your cash away. Don't worry! Lawyers, wealth managers and bankers are there to help you."[155] The documents of the Panama Papers revealed that drug traffickers and political leaders used the same law firm to hide their assets.[156]

Wire transfer businesses have moved the profits from both drug and human trafficking. In France, the leading French counter-trafficking official in 2001 implicated Western Union in the movement of money to eastern Europe by sex traffickers.[157] Arizona, a key border state for the illicit movement of drugs and people, took action against Western Union. Arizona's former state attorney general testified, "Western Union is by far the largest provider of illicit money-movement services." In 2010, Western Union entered into an agreement with the state of Arizona, paid a $94 million fine, and was placed under monitors.[158] But the problem did not end. In 2017, Western Union paid a $586 million fine in the United States for moving money resulting from fraud, drug sales, and human trafficking.[159] The large fines have sometimes been perceived as just "the cost of doing business." The problem has been transferred to the cyber-world. In Europe, intercepted email of criminals operating online revealed that they exchanged virtual currency into state-backed currencies by means of Western Union.[160]

Investigations by the tax authorities of Colombia revealed that significant drug profits were moved offshore to Panama by means of trade-based money laundering. These transfers were facilitated by significant corruption in the Colombian customs service: drug cartel members had infiltrated regional offices that allowed the certification of exports to Panama. The products might be coffee or some other commodity for which an exaggerated value was attached to the invoice.[161] Payment would then be made for the amount in the overvalued invoice, justifying the transfer of significant sums overseas. "Over-invoicing" is a key element of trade-based money laundering, as it allows the movement of funds far in excess of what is needed to pay for what has actually been moved. Corruption at the receiving end, as seen in the Panama Papers, affirms that trade-based money laundering often requires corruption in both the source and recipient countries. Trade-based money laundering reveals the centrality of trade abuse to the movement of funds out of the developing world and the laundering of ill-gotten gains of criminals and terrorists.[162]

In the cyberworld, money is increasingly laundered through cryptocurrencies. Intercepted communications of criminals in the Netherlands have revealed that many financial companies are used by crime groups to launder their money. Although some criminals still rely on payments in traditional currencies such as PayPal and MoneyGram, others are linked to cryptocurrencies such as FBTC Exchange, WebMoney, Bitonic, and xmlgold.eu. WebMoney, founded in Russia in the late 1990s but now in use globally, works in traditional currencies as well as gold and Bitcoin by means of an e-wallet (a digital mechanism to secure one or more currency purses). Prepaid cards and vouchers are also widely employed by online criminals as well as in underground banking.[163]

Criminals are holding their money in cryptocurrencies such as Bitcoin, a sensible decision with Bitcoin rising in value. When he was arrested, Alexander Cazes, the alleged creator of the Dark Web site AlphaBay, according to his indictment had "over $5 million in Bitcoin, $1.8 million in Ethereum, and $760,000 in Zcash, in addition to conventional bank accounts, valuable cars and expensive real estate properties."[164]

Revealing the scale of the money laundering through cryptocurrency was the 2017 arrest of Alexander Vinnik, a thirty-seven-year-old Russian, in Greece on an American arrest warrant for having laundered $4 billion through his Bitcoin exchange.[165]

Conclusion

Illicit business organizations often flourish in countries where the rule of law is weak and corruption is high. Yet countries with greater adherence to the rule of law and effective law enforcement are not exempt from the challenges posed by illicit businesses. Many associate "offers you can't refuse" only with the drug trade or with developing countries, but illicit traders and entrepreneurs also operate successfully in the G-7, the most affluent countries of the world. In developed countries, however, illicit commerce is less central to the national economy and represents less of the country's GDP than in the developing world.

The licit and the illicit are not distinct, and they intersect more often than many realize. This is true in both the real world and the virtual world. Legal and illegal products traverse the same supply routes and are often sold in the same marketplaces in the real world and in the cyberworld. In the cyberworld, more than six hundred cloud repositories, including those of Amazon, Google, and Groupon, have hosted malware and other malicious computer products. As many as 10 percent of these repositories have been tainted by malicious and illicit products.[166]

The rapid escalation of illicit trade and money laundering in the virtual world is assured, made all the more so by the rise of cryptocurrencies, many of them created with the deliberate intention of supporting criminal activity.[167] There is little to stem the growth of illicit cyber marketplaces at present. Many legitimate sales platforms facilitate the sale of illicit goods and people, and the private sector, which controls this technology, all too often prioritizes profits over human life and the sustainability of the planet.

Traders move rapidly in the cyberworld, whereas efforts to disrupt their activities move more slowly, often hindered by state-based laws crafted for an era of tangible commodities. Therefore, in the coming years we will face an even more asymmetric threat as harmful cyber-trade escalates and state and transnational capacity to counter it remains far behind.

The historical transformation of illicit trade, however, also provides new opportunities, because dark commerce operates through private companies and leaves its traces in the data of financial institutions. Large-scale data analytics, when done well, reveal patterns of criminal activity in cyberspace and expose illicit networks, making it possible for law enforcement to pursue cases without invading privacy or violating individual rights. As long as the malicious use of the Dark Web and cryptocurrencies does not prevail, new ways may be found to contain illicit commerce in the future.

6

Destroyers of Human Life

Illicit commerce employs millions of people worldwide on both a full- and part-time basis. This chapter addresses not only the foot soldiers of the illicit economy—the drug mules, the petty sellers, and the dock personnel who unload the items of dark commerce—but the diverse range of actors who make this vast trade function. The multibillion-dollar commerce harming human life involves many more players than just the organized criminals and terrorists closely associated with the drug trade. Many perpetrators are part of these diverse and dispersed networks.

As our historical analysis revealed, governments and their top officials have been major participants in this illicit commerce. This vast trade intersects with and is facilitated by legitimate businesses in many different countries and relies on professionals from many specialties. In some cases, the facilitation is unwitting, but the profits are so high that some transport, tech companies, and bankers deliberately participate, some stopping only after being named, shamed, and penalized.

Unfortunately, these illicit actors are all around us; their global supply chains connect the most diverse regions of the world. The illicit traders are not only trafficking human beings and causing others to become addicted, but also marketing counterfeit medicines and agricultural products, smuggled cigarettes, and the water people need to survive. Through their sales they are undermining food security and health.

The Vulnerable Illicit Trader

Meet a foot soldier of the illicit economy. At the Museum of Immigration in Paris, headsets are available to visitors so they can listen to immigrants recount their life stories. One especially moving story is told by an illegal North African migrant who lives in southern France on the margins of society. His voyage out of Africa started on a precarious boat that crossed the Mediterranean several years before the mass transports of today. He arrived in impoverished southern Italy, where he found no work. He made his way farther north in Italy, still finding no employment. Then he crossed into France and made his way to Paris. There, he explains, he found no better prospects to make money. He moved south, this time settling in Marseille. He ends his tale by reporting that he found a way to survive—selling cigarettes.

What the immigrant does not mention is that most street cigarette vendors in Marseille, a city with some of the poorest neighborhoods in Europe, are selling illicit cigarettes.[1] One form of illegality lies within another—irregular migrants, lacking the right to work, sell smuggled cigarettes. Like many recent illegal immigrants in different regions of the world, this man is vulnerable to exploitation and arrest and has no legal way to participate in the legitimate economy.

DRUG AND HUMAN TRAFFICKERS

In our historical survey of chapter 2, the diverse range of participants in the trade in drugs and humans were identified. They included states, trading companies, high- and low-level officials, and facilitators from shipping companies to dockworkers. All these actors still participate in this illicit trade today. The global criminalization of the narcotics trade and the trade in people has added to the mix new categories of participants—criminal groups, insurgents, and terrorists. Human smuggling and drug trafficking function as businesses in the sense that not only do the criminals operate according to business models, but legitimate commerce gains from this trade. Technology companies have become as critical to contemporary trafficking in people as the East India Company was to the slave and drug trades.

DRUG TRAFFICKERS

Drug trafficking, a multibillion-dollar transnational crime business, has diverse perpetrators involved in different segments of the market. As in the past, some countries engage in the drug trade to benefit the state. A key contemporary example is North Korea. Under sanctions, North Korea earns much-needed hard currency through the state production of methamphetamines, which its diplomats, often exploiting their diplomatic immunity, distribute overseas.[2]

Diverse facilitators from both the private and public sectors, such as transporters, bankers, and mail services, as well as their employees, participate both wittingly and unwittingly. Illustrative of this is the stewardess whose carry-on bag contained seventy pounds of cocaine—a more educated mule of the drug economy.[3]

CORRUPTION

Corruption facilitates every sector of the drug trade, from the movement of the product to the laundering of the proceeds. In many countries, individuals pay significantly to obtain positions in law enforcement, customs agencies, and the military that allow them to profit from the drug trade.[4] Drug traffickers infiltrate not only state administrative institutions but also the political process, where they influence or block the passage of legislation and undermine the implementation of counter–money laundering policies.[5]

Officials' facilitation of the drug trade may also be coerced. The Latin American expression *plata o plomo* ("silver or lead," meaning money or a bullet) refers to a method for compelling obedience, not just from community members but even from national leaders in the Caribbean and high-level officials in Mexico, Central America, and South America.[6]

THE TOP OF THE CHAIN

The drug trade has enriched heads of state, their families, and top officials. President Manuel Noriega of Panama was tried and imprisoned for his role in narcotics trafficking.[7] Ahmed Karzai, the brother of President Hamid Karzai of Afghanistan, was a major heroin dealer, and the Afghan president, according to a leaked US government cable, actively intervened on behalf of drug traffickers.[8] The Organized Crime and Corruption Reporting Project (OCCRP), an amalgamation of some of the top investigative journalists in the world, decided to create an award that is a dark take-off on *Time* magazine's Person of the Year Award. The OCCRP Person of Year Award, given annually to the political figure who has done the most to facilitate organized crime and corruption, was presented to Venezuelan president Nicolás Maduro in 2016 for his role in facilitating and profiting from drug trafficking. His nephews were indicted in American courts for trying to use the presidential hangar at an airport to smuggle eight hundred kilos of cocaine into the United States.[9]

Top officials in Guinea-Bissau have allowed large amounts of cocaine to pass through their territory for a facilitation fee.[10] The high-level corruption in this West African country provides Latin American drug traffickers with an important transit route to European markets.

In Myanmar, a broader elite benefits rather than just a single individual and his family.[11] The Burmese army still runs the highly profitable drug trade, as it did two decades ago, hosting jungle labs for syndicates to refine drugs and, more recently, protecting producers of synthetic drugs.[12]

Nonstate Actors in the Drug Trade

CRIMINALS AND TERRORISTS

No one criminal, terrorist, or insurgent group monopolizes the narcotics trade. But these groups are key to this thriving trade in every region of the world. Asian groups, such as the Chinese triads and the Japanese *Yakuza*, were involved in narcotics before it became such a global phenomenon, and these groups only grew as the trade expanded.[13]

In Latin America, the Cali and Medellín cartels developed and expanded on the basis of the drug trade.[14] Subsequently, Mexican crime organizations exploited their strategic geographic location—between the cocaine production of Colombia and the markets of the United States—to become large and powerful enough to challenge the authority of the Mexican state.[15] Often glorified by some citizens for their exploits and the services they provide, drug traffickers are the subject of a popular new musical genre—*narcocorridos* (ballads), which are sung to honor them.

The charismatic and ruthless Pablo Escobar, an early leader in the Colombian cocaine economy, viewed himself as an entrepreneur and drew analogies between himself and Henry Ford, the founder of the modern automobile industry. Working with skillful teams of logistic and transport specialists and money launderers, he and other successful Colombia drug traffickers were able to make the business grow enormously in a short period.[16] Colombian crime and terrorist groups forced the Colombian state into retreat, but in a dramatic reversal since the early 2000s, the state has reasserted authority over much of its territory and dramatically reduced the level of violence.

Unfortunately, Mexican crime groups benefited and exploited the decline of Colombian transnational crime. Building on the long years of smuggling across the US-Mexican border, crime groups in Mexico took advantage of the availability of arms in the United States, which contributed to the lethality of these criminal organizations.[17] Fifteen million weapons are in circulation in Mexico, of which 85 percent were estimated in 2012 to be illegal. Approximately 250,000 are purchased annually in the United States, for illegal transport to Mexico, providing significant revenues to gun sellers in the United States.[18] American sellers do not face the inconvenient truth about their buyers because the weapons sales help their bottom line.[19]

Mexican drug dealers have diversified for long-term survival. Now no longer as reliant on drugs, they engage in extortion, stealing oil, smuggling migrants, and extracting and selling coal.[20] Organized crime has transformed the Mexican political system and made daily life more precarious. Unfortunately, this phenomenon is not confined to Mexico.[21] Drug traffickers' increasing economic power and influence over politics has had a very corrosive impact on governance, the rule of law, and the quality of human life in many countries and regions of the world.[22]

In Italy, the Mafia had traditionally eschewed participation in the drug trade, but in the competitive post–World War II environment, they became more significant in European and global drug markets, along with other increasingly important crime groups in southern Italy.[23] Nigerian crime groups that emerged after the country's civil war became the most important drug traffickers on the African continent, effectively developing international links with criminal organizations on other continents.[24]

Turkish drug trafficking organizations, building on historic smuggling routes, worked with crime groups in the Balkans to move heroin to Europe.[25] Russian-speaking organized crime groups, which initially profited from the privatization of state economies, moved significantly into the drug trade as a northern route developed to ship heroin out of Afghanistan.[26] Pakistani-based groups, such as D-company (whose origins lie in India), expanded Karachi's historic role as a drug trans-shipment point and built a powerful transnational crime organization, in part, out of drug proceeds.[27] D-company, like the Mexican drug organization, has diversified and now traffics weapons and counterfeit DVDs and provides financial services through its extensive system of *hawala* operators (a system of underground banking present in South Asia and the Middle East).[28]

Leaders of some of the most successful drug organizations have become very rich.[29] In 1987, *Fortune* included several Colombian cocaine tycoons in its first list of the world's billionaires. Included were Pablo Escobar and the Ochoa brothers—Jorge Luis Ochoa Vasquez and his brothers Fabio and Juan David.[30]

Terrorists are the other important category of nonstate actors who benefit from drug trafficking. The term *narco-terrorism* was coined in Peru in the early 1980s in reference to the Peruvian group Sendero Luminoso, a Maoist terrorist organization that was significantly funded by drugs and sought to overthrow the Peruvian government.[31]

The UN Security Council has repeatedly recognized the relationship between drugs and terrorism.[32] In 2008, the chief of operations at the US Drug Enforcement Agency, Michael Braun, indicated that of forty-three designated terrorist groups, nineteen profited from the drug trade.[33] The US Department of Justice reported in fiscal year 2010 that twenty-nine of the top sixty-three international drug syndicates were associated with terrorist groups.[34] Almost all of these designated terrorist organizations are based in the developing world. Among the terrorist groups involved in the global drug trade are FARC, the Taliban, Hezbollah, and the PKK (Kurdistan Workers' Party).[35] Many other terrorist groups are active in the drug trade at regional levels, such as ISIS affiliates, Al-Qaeda in the Arabian Peninsula (AQAP) in Yemen, and Al-Qaeda in the Islamic Maghreb (AQIM) in North Africa.[36] ISIS itself has been involved in the narcotics trade, particularly the trade in the psychostimulant Captagon.[37]

Drug sales in the cyberworld have earned successful marketers significant revenues in a short time period. Organized, but rarely members of organized crime, the online drug seller has a different profile. One Chinese manufacturer, Zhang Lei—named a "drug kingpin" by the United States and arrested by the Chinese government—sent thousands of kilos of synthetic drugs to the United States and other countries, including Australia, Austria, France, Germany, the Netherlands, and Italy. Profits from US sales for his company CEC Limited, which produced the products that he sold online, were estimated at over $30 million.[38]

The cyberworld has also facilitated the entry of formerly lawabiding citizens, like Ross Ulbricht of Silk Road (discussed in chapter 3), into the heights of the narcotics trade.[39] The absence of real-life interactions in the cyberworld facilitates heinous acts that individuals like Ulbricht might not commit outside the virtual world. Ulbricht is a harbinger of the drug traders of the future.

CORPORATIONS

Since 1979, the exponential rise in deaths from the American opioid epidemic has been a consequence, in part, of the marketing strategies of a few pharmaceutical companies. The most notorious of these is

Purdue Pharma. In 2007, Purdue, a privately held company that produces oxycontin, the drug at the heart of the epidemic, paid $635 million in fines after pleading guilty to false marketing charges brought by the US Department of Justice. Top-level corporate officials were criminally charged and convicted.[40] In September 2017, forty-one state attorney generals in the United States launched investigations into Purdue Pharma, as well as several lesser manufacturers of opioids, as the epidemic raged and the deaths continued to escalate.[41]

PROFESSIONALS AND FACILITATORS

Professionals also play a key role in the drug trade. Doctors have contributed to the US opioid epidemic by too freely prescribing painkillers, and accountants, lawyers, and financial institutions have collaborated with drug trafficking organizations.[42] Banks such as Wachovia, HSBC, and Citibank paid billions in fines for laundering money for Mexican drug cartels. HSBC alone paid $1.9 billion.[43] Public prosecutions may have made the role of banks in money laundering more widely known, but even religious groups have been sanctioned for their efforts to fund their institutions through the laundering of drug proceeds.[44]

The postal service and delivery companies are also important facilitators of illegal drug shipments. The large volume of packages sent through mail and delivery services makes it hard to detect those containing drugs and other illicit commodities, which are often sent to customers in small packages, frequently from India and China.[45] A yearlong investigation in the United States revealed that 500 drug purchases, with a total value of $766 million, were shipped through the mails, with some resulting in the death of the purchasers.[46]

Human Traffickers and Smugglers

Human traffickers and smugglers differ from their counterparts in the drug trade. Outside of Asia, fewer are connected to large criminal organizations; instead, smaller networks of traffickers and smugglers rely on personal relations to recruit people. In the absence of kingpins, profits are more dispersed, and often the facilitators of this illicit trade are less professional than those associated with the drug trade.

Human trafficking is one of the top revenue generators for illicit traders. Many associate this crime only with criminals, but as in the past, government officials and companies are deeply implicated in this illegal activity. When there was a legal slave trade, officials served the powerful trading companies that often ran the slave trade with government licenses. Today many officials continue to facilitate human smuggling and trafficking, but primarily for personal gain rather than in the interests of the state. The great growth in human trafficking and its increasing profitability have been fueled by corporations that facilitate advertisements and payment systems for the sale of sex trafficking victims and the online distribution of child pornography. The rise of the internet, the Dark Web, and social media has fundamentally changed human trafficking as these platforms have also transformed the accessibility and anonymity of drug markets.

Human trafficking includes more than sexual exploitation; labor exploitation, forced marriage, and illegal organ transplantation are all considered elements of this crime. All involve elements of coercion, fraud, and deception but do not require movement, as individuals can be trafficked for marriage or sex within their immediate community. In contrast, smuggled individuals also agree to be transported across borders.[47] In human trafficking, the individual is the victim, whereas smuggling victimizes the state by violating its borders and sovereignty.

OFFICIALS AND TRAFFICKING

Both human smugglers and traffickers need corrupt officials, including border guards, law enforcement, judicial personnel, military, customs officials, consular officers, and other diplomatic personnel.[48]

In Mexico, officials extort bribes and sexual services from child sex trafficking victims to facilitate cross-border movement, and they fail to pursue cases against traffickers.[49] Particularly serious misconduct has been identified in Veracruz and San Fernando in the state of Tamaulipas, where mass graves of suspected trafficking victims were discovered.[50] Similar patterns have been identified in Asia and Africa. In Thailand, mass graves were discovered of many Rohingya, Muslims who fled repression in Myanmar after paying smugglers to expedite their passage. Many of the deceased had been held for ransom before their death to extract more money en route, a pattern also observed with Mexican smuggling. In the summer of 2017, many Thai officials went on trial for facilitating these deaths, and a Thai general and twenty-one other government officials were sentenced.[51]

Trafficking, like the drug trade, benefits both states and high-level officials. North Korea traffics its citizens into labor exploitation overseas—for example, in the Russian Far East.[52] Government officials in Thailand, according to the US State Department's *Trafficking in Persons Report 2016*, "profit from bribes and direct involvement in the extortion of migrants and their sale to brokers. . . . Credible reports indicate some corrupt officials protect brothels and other commercial sex venues from raids and inspections and collude with traffickers."[53] Thailand is not alone. In nearby Vietnam, according to the same report, local officials facilitate trafficking, exploit victims by accepting bribes from traffickers, and profit from reuniting victims with their families.[54] In Uzbekistan, in a labor-trafficking tradition that has endured from the Soviet era, adults are forced to labor during the annual cotton harvest.[55]

CRIMINAL AND TERRORIST SMUGGLERS AND TRAFFICKERS

In Asia, the triads in China and the *Yakuza* in Japan have long been deeply involved in human smuggling, and the *Yakuza* are also active in the sex trafficking industry, which is tied into the bars and nightclubs they control.[56] Outside of Asia, large criminal organizations are not deeply engaged in human trafficking and smuggling. Nigerian and Balkan groups have trafficked people along with drugs.[57] Until recently, Latin American drug organizations were not active in human trafficking and smuggling, but as previously mentioned, with diversification, they as well as Central American gangs profit from this business.[58]

Much of human trafficking is not tied to larger criminal networks but is carried out by smaller groups, often family and friends of the victim. Compounding the psychological harm to the victim in these cases is the violation of a trust relationship.[59]

Europol data on human trafficking suggest the presence of numerous networks rather than larger, consolidated criminal organizations. In 2013–2014, Europol received reports on six thousand organized groups involved in human trafficking. The vast majority, 90 percent, were involved in sexual exploitation; 5.6 percent were cases of labor exploitation, 1.9 percent were for forced sham marriages, and 0.3 percent concerned forced criminality and begging. These data may represent citizen concerns more than they reflect the actual distribution of victims.[60] About 70 percent of European citizens suspected to be involved in human trafficking are citizens of the Balkans. Non-European networks often have participants of Chinese or Nigerian origin. The Chinese are known to be proficient in the production of fake documents, and the Nigerians specialize in the black market for stolen identifications.[61]

In recent years, human smuggling in Europe has escalated faster than the drug trade. Ninety percent of those smuggled are helped by professional facilitators. Millions have attempted to reach Europe from North Africa, the Middle East, Pakistan, Afghanistan, and East Asia. Those behind this smuggling are community members, not just members of criminal organizations.[62] Chinese spent $600 million on smugglers to reach Europe, and the comparable figure for Vietnamese is $300 million.[63] This is hardly surprising, as human smuggling has been a longtime activity of Chinese organized crime groups and professional networks.[64] The sums derived from Far East Asian smuggling are dwarfed by the multibillion-dollar business precipitated by the Syrian conflict, the chaos in North Africa, and the drought in the Sahel, all of which have made many people desperate to reach Europe.

Social media and cell phones are more responsible for the growth in smuggling than the internet. Individuals learn of smuggling services through social media such as Facebook, where connections are made and smugglers' services are retained.[65] With marketing available through the new technology, the number of smugglers has increased rapidly. Europol has identified participants in human smuggling from over one hundred countries, with an estimated fifty thousand criminals involved. Therefore, these networks are more diverse than for human trafficking. Smugglers originate from eastern Europe and the Balkans, as well as from North Africa (Egypt, Tunisia, Libya), the Middle East (Turkey and Syria), and Pakistan.[66]

In contrast with trafficking, many more participants in smuggling networks are non-Europeans: 44 percent of the networks comprise non-EU nationals, and 26 percent include both Europeans and non-EU citizens. Fewer than one-third are composed solely of Europeans. This reveals the transnational nature of smuggling.[67] Network analysis reveals multinational collaborations.[68] Criminal groups—especially Chinese, Nigerian, and Romanian groups—work with diaspora communities overseas to limit detection. Balkan trafficking routes of the Ottoman era have been revived, often staffed by smugglers from extended family networks.[69]

Smugglers, selling their transport services, give little thought to the survival of those with whom they contract, as future business is not dependent on previous customers. High fatality rates have resulted. In 2016, the director of the International Organization for Migration wrote that, for recent years, "we have calculated 18,501 deaths and migrants missing, most of them drowned in the Mediterranean and other deadly spots."[70] The Mediterranean situation is not unique. Between 2014 and 2016, approximately 17 men, women, and children perished every day en route to a new country, for a total of 7,500 people. On average, there were more than 20 fatalities daily in 2016.[71]

Smuggling on the US-Mexican border was long dominated by so-called coyotes, who knew where it was easiest to move people.[72] Enhanced controls on the US-Mexican border have made smugglers more professional and reinforced their links to the drug organizations that built and maintain the tunnels on that border. Mexican drug organizations extort smugglers moving migrants across territory they control. Typically, transnational smuggling networks may build safe houses only with the permission of the criminal organizations that control key segments of the US-Mexican border.[73]

Human smuggling is also very present between Central and North America, where violent gangs, particularly from Honduras and El Salvador, move people into Mexico and then on to the United States. Increasing numbers try only to reach the relative safety of Mexico. In transit, those smuggled are robbed, kidnapped, and subject to sexual violence by members of crime groups and law enforcement officials who use pellet guns and electric shock devices against the migrants.[74] Smugglers threaten those they move in order to extort money from family members who are paying for their relatives' movement north.[75]

As I discussed in my earlier book *Human Trafficking: A Global Perspective*, human traffickers from different regions of the world operate differently. Their trafficking business models reflect historical patterns of trade and commerce. Therefore, Russian human trafficking is not an integrated business like that of the Chinese, who have been traders for centuries. Russia sells off women like a natural resource, whereas the Chinese model sees human trafficking and smuggling as yet another form of trade that generates revenues.[76]

Women are more active in human trafficking than other areas of transnational crime.[77] Trafficked women recruit other women to gain their freedom or to progress up the occupational hierarchy and become traffickers and brothel managers themselves. Women have assumed an important role in human smuggling networks in Asia. One of the most famous, Sister Ping, had a highly successful smuggling business until a ship transporting 286 of her clients ran aground off the coast of New York. Ten people drowned trying to get to shore, and Sister Ping was subsequently prosecuted by the US government.[78]

Terrorists related to the Al-Qaeda network are involved in human trafficking less as a revenue source and more as a form of intimidation and retaliation. The trafficking of Yazidi women by ISIS, as well as women and girls by Boko Haram, the West African affiliate, has been heavily publicized.[79] But there are historical precedents: the

PKK in Turkey has profited from human trafficking and smuggling, and children in Africa have been trafficked by terrorist groups, such as Al-Shabaab, to serve as child soldiers.[80]

Terrorist groups such as Al-Nusra are involved in the kidney trade today.[81] Purchasers enter chat rooms on the Dark Net to find suppliers of kidneys and doctors ready to perform the necessary surgery.[82] Wealthy buyers travel to access kidneys "sold" by desperate individuals in the Middle East, including refugees. Buyers may pay up to $80,000 to secure a kidney outside the legitimate market, a demand that is filled by purchasing or coercing the most vulnerable, for very limited compensation, to surrender a kidney.[83] In the absence of decent postoperative medical care, this sale may place the seller's life in jeopardy, but the proceeds of a kidney sale may pay the smuggling fees to Europe for family members.[84]

CORPORATIONS

The increasing prominence of human trafficking and smuggling within illicit trade is due in large part to the asymmetric advantage afforded these illicit actors by the anonymity of the internet and by encrypted social media such as WhatsApp (used by over one billion people in 180 countries), WeChat (a Chinese-based service with almost one billion users monthly), and Viber. Traffickers can communicate in complete privacy using these free communications technologies, and the companies offering them do not have to maintain records of calls or text content. Apple and Google have engineered their smartphones to block law enforcement access to this information even with a court order. Communications concerning trade in people can proceed with impunity.[85]

Unfortunately, the internet and the numerous platforms it provides for online sales have also contributed to the phenomenal growth in human sexual exploitation internationally. Between 2010 and 2015, the National Missing and Exploited Children Center reported an 846 percent rise in reports of suspected child sex trafficking—an increase found to be "directly correlated to the increased use of the Internet to sell children for sex."[86] The adult advertisements on Craigslist and

Backpage, as previously discussed, reveal the large financial gains made in the licit economy from human exploitation.

When DARPA, the agency that developed the internet, analyzed the temporary sexual advertisements and peer-to-peer connections within the Deep Web, it found that "over a two-year time frame traffickers spent about $250 million to post more than 60 million advertisements." This large advertising budget suggests the large number of victims and the high profits to be made to justify the extensive advertising budget. Although the research was conducted in the United States, this analysis revealed the global expanse of the traffickers.[87] The DARPA analysis recalls the high profit margins of slavers in past centuries, but now the money is made in cyberspace rather than on the high seas and the auction blocks.

Many nontech corporations profit from or facilitate human trafficking and smuggling. Some corporations unwittingly—but in some cases deliberately—hire trafficked individuals to increase profits and obtain more docile employees. Men may be trafficked into dangerous work on fishing boats and at logging, mining, and construction sites, as discussed further in the next chapter. Hotels as well as apparel factories may retain trafficked women. Supporting such exploitation are many professional facilitators, including recruiters, transporters, and travel agencies. Financial institutions rarely intentionally benefit from human trafficking—as they do from the massive proceeds of the drug trade—but not enough has been done to detect the proceeds of human trafficking within their financial transactions.[88]

The Illicit Cigarette Trade

The trade in counterfeit, diverted, and illicit white cigarettes resembles the trade in drugs and humans, with which it often intersects. Ignored by many law enforcers, this trade provides an ideal funding source for states, corrupt officials, criminals, and terrorists. Its foot soldiers, as we saw in Marseille, are often from the most vulnerable populations. Many leaders of illicit trade are rich and powerful politicians who escape sanctions, whereas the street sellers—usually immigrants, displaced peoples, and refugees—are the ones targeted by law enforcement, and they suffer disproportionately. But the huge profits from this trade benefit more powerful and often malicious actors.

STATES AND HIGH-LEVEL OFFICIALS

North Korea once again figures as a country profiteering from this lucrative form of illicit commerce as an exporter of its counterfeit cigarettes.[89] North Korean diplomats distribute this product internationally, just as they do with drugs. Following the trail of the illicit cigarette trade led US investigators to many diverse and extremely serious forms of illicit trade, including illicit ivory trade and WMD financing.[90]

State leaders also benefit from this trade. The highly competitive OCCRP Man of the Year Award was presented in 2015—the year before it was awarded to President Maduro—to Milo Djukanović, the continuously serving president or prime minister of Montenegro from 1991 to 2016, elected president again in 2018.[91] Among the many cited crimes that merited this distinction was his major role in cigarette smuggling, for which he was particularly singled out in the award statement. The distinguished OCCRP jury concluded:

> Djukanovic and his close associates engaged in extensive cigarette smuggling with the Italian Sacra Corona Unita and Camorra crime families. He was indicted in Bari and freely admitted the trade, but said his country needed money. He invoked diplomatic immunity to get the charges dropped.

According to OCCRP, his smuggling did not stop with the indictment but continued through a surrogate, Djukanović's head of security, "who was three times indicted but never convicted of cigarette smuggling related activities."[92]

The forensic evidence for this award was strong—the Italian courts presented wiretap-derived evidence and hundreds of thousands of documents to show that Djukanović and the Montenegrin government were making $700 million annually from this illicit trade in the 1990s. Their collaborators, Italian organized crime groups, laundered $1 billion from this trade through Swiss banks based in Lugano.[93]

Turning from Europe, in Paraguay the head of state helped facilitate another form of illicit cigarette trade—the trade in illicit whites. In 2016, President Horacio Cartes spoke at New York University in a talk entitled "Introducing Paraguay: A Land of Opportunity." His remarks were preceded by a warm welcome by the university president, who described President Cartes as "a remarkable man." "I love the diversity of your business acumen . . . ranging from beverages to tobacco to soccer."[94] This introduction reminds us of the tolerance that Western countries too often show for the misdeeds of corrupt foreign leaders, and even for behavior harmful to human life.

Examining President Cartes's family tobacco production (of which he is a key shareholder) raises multiple red flags. Paraguay, with a small domestic consumer market, produces a significant share of the world's illicit whites—an estimated 65 billion cigarettes annually—and is responsible for 11 percent of the world's contraband cigarettes.[95] The prime target of Paraguay's smuggled cigarettes is Brazil, where one-third of all purchased cigarettes are illegal, costing the government an estimated tax loss of $1.2 billion annually.[96] This large-scale smuggling funds powerful crime groups in Latin America, such as Los Zetas and the Sinaloa cartel, by helping them launder their money.[97] These cigarettes are also sold in France and elsewhere in Europe.[98]

CRIMINAL AND TERRORIST INVOLVEMENT

Criminal involvement in the tobacco trade, as our historical discussions illustrate, has persisted for centuries. Our analysis has revealed that the illicit cigarette trade is not confined to any single region but intersects with the rhino trade in South Africa and the Czech Republic, flourishes on Native American reservations in New York, and thrives in France, which is the "European champion of illicit cigarette sales."[99] This is a hard-won distinction, as the leading Italian organized crime groups also participate in this trade.[100] One-third of France's contraband cigarettes are smuggled from Algeria, and one-quarter arrive from Spain, where tax rates are lower.[101] Barcelona is a key transit hub where the *trabendo*, or smugglers, operating out of Algeria link with the Spaniards who have been involved for many years in the contraband trade.[102]

Marseille is the French hot spot for illicit cigarette sales—approximately 40 percent of all sales are of illegal imports.[103] This port city has long been a center of illicit trade. Think of *The French Connection*, a film in which drugs arrive from Turkey to be shipped to the United States via Canada.[104] The police in Marseille allocate few resources against petty cigarette traders. This inattention is not a result of corruption, as the sellers lack the funds and the contacts to corrupt French officials.[105]

Avoiding taxation, sellers of smuggled cigarettes can offer them in open-air markets at substantially lower prices than legitimate retail products. In France, cigarettes on the street sell for about five euros a pack for diverted products, and illicit whites or counterfeited products can be found at four euros. In the shops, the prices for legitimate products, at around seven euros, are much higher. The difference in price results in massive tax losses to the state—approximately 4 billion euros annually for the French economy.[106] Moreover, the state may subsequently incur greater health costs: unregulated cigarettes are often produced under unregulated conditions and contain components that are more carcinogenic.

Illicit cigarette trade has been particularly attractive to terrorist groups because it is low-risk and high-profit. One of the two Kouachi brothers who killed the *Charlie Hebdo* cartoonists in Paris in 2015 made money by selling cigarettes.[107] Higher levels of the illicit cigarette chain support terrorism in more significant ways. AQIM, a branch of Al-Qaeda in North Africa, and other jihadists in the region have relied on this trade.[108]

Other terrorist groups also profit from this trade. Hezbollah and Hamas have been identified in multiple cigarette cases.[109] ISIS manipulated the cigarette trade for its benefit on territory it controlled in Iraq and Syria, even though cigarettes are banned under the strict version of Islam propagated by ISIS. Reports out of Mosul reveal that "Daesh made an agreement with oil truck drivers and allowed them to smuggle 50 cartons in a compartment inside the truck in return for intelligence about the petty and main sellers." Then ISIS would arrest and flog the sellers and make significant profits for ISIS.[110]

The triborder area of Paraguay, Brazil, and Argentina remains a major center of threat finance. "Illicit whites" produced in Paraguay are a major currency of terrorist funding not only in that country but in Colombia, where the trade provides funds for FARC.[111]

Older terrorist groups, like the IRA (Irish Republican Army), also profited from the illegal cigarette trade over an extended period.[112] A major illicit cigarette smuggling operation was revealed under most unusual circumstances. In 2013, after Al-Qaeda operatives successfully launched two rockets at a container passing through the Suez Canal in Egypt in transit to Ireland, the subsequent investigation of the damaged ship revealed a $55 million shipment of smuggled cigarettes destined for a well-known Irishman with long-standing ties to the IRA.[113]

FACILITATORS

The sale of almost nine billion illegal cigarettes in France annually points to a large group of facilitators between the source and the street markets.[114] This movement of product is not done by "ants" carrying a few cartons of cigarettes at a time. It requires the complicity of factory workers, shippers, and vendors in Algeria, as well as high-level officials and workers at French and Spanish ports. Individuals must load the trucks from the ships.

Drivers, both knowingly and unknowingly, move large quantities of illicit cigarettes overland from Spain to France. Many claim innocence in regard to their clandestine cargo, but an examination of social media provides evidence of a different reality. Despite complaints to Facebook by those trying to arrest this illicit trade, posts on this social medium continue to advise truck drivers and distributors where to pick up contraband cigarette shipments.[115] The problem has been identified in France, but the trade there is just the tip of the iceberg.[116] In the United Kingdom, Imperial Tobacco has targeted Facebook as a key facilitator of the illicit trade in cigarettes.[117] The new media, as we see throughout this book, is a force multiplier for the growth of illicit trade, as it lies largely outside of regulation.

Truckers can collude with companies to help move large quantities of goods, thereby evading taxes. For example, United Parcel Service (UPS) in the United States was fined $247 million by a federal court in the spring of 2017 for shipping cigarettes without payment of taxes from smoke shops on a New York Indian reservation where cigarettes are allowed to be sold to tribal members only. A similar case is now under way against Federal Express. The judge in the UPS case found that since 2010 more than 683,000 cartons of untaxed "contraband" cigarettes were shipped to unlicensed wholesalers, retailers, and residences. According to the court, UPS was cognizant of its participation and showed a consistent unwillingness to acknowledge its facilitating role.[118]

Illicit Trade in Food and Beverages That Undermine Life

As the first chapter of our historical survey showed, counterfeit food products have been with us since ancient times. Today counterfeit food and beverages sales are a multibillion-dollar business, growing with the increasing value of desired food products and drink and the expanding middle class, particularly in Asia. Illicit trade in food and drink functions on such an industrial scale that its perpetrators can only be companies or significant transnational crime groups, as our analyses of China and Italy will show. Yet the perpetrators of these crimes rarely receive the punishments or the social stigma accorded others who severely harm human life. Therefore, this form of illicit commerce can be expected to grow in the future.

Many sicken and die annually from the lack of food and alcohol security, a result not just of poor hygiene or inadequate refrigeration but of harmful ingredients in food and drink.[119] Food grown in areas where the soil has been contaminated by dangerous pesticides or the disposal of hazardous waste also is harmful to consumers.

The problem is of a scale not often known by consumers, but it has commanded much law enforcement attention. In the three months between November 2015 and February 2016, more than

10,000 metric tons (or over 22 million pounds) and one million liters (over 264,000 gallons) of fake food and drink were confiscated in a coordinated law enforcement operation in fifty-seven countries. British authorities seized enough illicit alcohol to fill 12,000 bathtubs. In other locales, counterfeit non-alcoholic beverages intended for export to children in Africa were found and removed from circulation.[120] Authorities in Italy detected and withdrew from markets at least 85 tons of olives painted with copper sulphate—a potentially toxic substance whose ingestion may result in vomiting—to enhance their color. Monkey meat was seized in Belgium, peanuts repackaged and disguised as pine nuts were confiscated by police in Australia, and in Togo 24 tons of tilapia unfit for consumption was located before going on sale. This dispersion of fake and dangerous comestibles clearly illustrates the callous and despicable indifference shown by producers toward the health and well-being of consumers. Instead, the traders' concern is exclusively profit.[121]

The environment is also harmed by the illicit trade in mezcal, a potent alcohol produced in Mexico. Over time this trade is eliminating the slow-growing cactus plants from which the drink is derived. Farmers lose their future livelihoods, while large profits accrue to middlemen who export mezcal without permission, thereby avoiding taxes, and then sell it for high prices in bars and restaurants in the United States. These middlemen cover their misdeeds by suggesting that they are assisting a "poor farmer."[122]

Even in two cultures that pride themselves on their cuisines, Chinese and Italian, devotion to food and a willingness to spend to enjoy it do not ensure the security of food supplies. Both China and Italy have repeatedly been the focus of massive food scandals involving counterfeit food that placed consumers' lives in jeopardy both at home and even abroad, as the two countries are major food exporters.[123] In Italy, this particular form of criminality even has a name, *agromafie* (agricultural mafia).[124] Careful research by Italian think tanks experienced in calculating the economic impact of organized crime estimated that illicit food trade totaled 16 billion euros in Italy in 2015, as illicit production has expanded beyond the traditional Mafia stronghold of the South.[125] The roots of the Mafia in

Sicily and of 'Ndrangheta in Campania are in rural areas; therefore, the involvement of crime groups in agricultural production is hardly surprising.

The business-savvy Camorra counterfeit mozzarella and the very pricey ham of the northern city of Parma to profit from the desire for these fine food items, which are regulated by the government for quality and provenance.[126] In southern Italy, the home of the Camorra, some food is poisoned with heavy metals as a result of being cultivated at the site of toxic waste dumps in the rural areas around Naples.[127] Despite controls, foods cultivated there are sometimes sold.

Organized crime groups from southern Italy have invested heavily in land in North Africa. Tomatoes and other produce grown there at lower costs and outside European Union market controls are subsequently brought to Italy and then purposely mislabeled as "produced in Europe."[128] Online food sales of products that are not vetted compound the problem.[129]

In Myanmar, counterfeit baby formula, produced without adequate protein, prevents babies from developing. In a Myanmar hospital, a Johns Hopkins public health professor observed a one-year-old child who had been fed counterfeit milk and was the size of a guinea pig.[130]

In China in 2008, 300,000 babies became ill after drinking baby formula adulterated with a toxic industrial compound called melamine, and six died.[131] In the investigation that followed, the Sanlu dairy company, one of the largest Chinese food companies, was held responsible. Other companies were also implicated after an American manufacturer alerted Chinese authorities. A dozen people were tried in the spring of 2017 for selling counterfeit baby formula.[132]

Those who jeopardize human life by placing profits over infant health do this for personal gain but also on behalf of the companies where they are employed.[133] In another Chinese case, rat meat was disguised and sold widely to the public in 2013 as coveted lamb.[134] In the same year, over 1,700 workshops were closed down in China owing to their illicit food production.[135] In 2015, Chinese customs officials seized 100,000 metric tons of frozen chicken, beef, and pork, valued at $483 million. Some of the meat smuggled by the fourteen gangs was over forty years old. Because the smugglers used non-refrigerated trucks to reduce transport costs, the meat had been frozen and refrozen during transit. Consequently, there were serious health risks associated with the product.[136]

In Russia, illicitly produced alcohol has resulted in many deaths. According to official statistics, 14,250 people died in 2015 alone. A case of "illicit entrepreneurship" in late 2016 in the Siberian city of Irkutsk resulted in the death of 72 people. Criminal entrepreneurs deliberately mislabeled the "bath lotion" they produced in their atelier, stating that it contained 94 percent ethyl alcohol when instead it was made with poisonous methyl alcohol. In parts of Russia, surrogate products such as the misrepresented bath lotion intersect with the legitimate supply chain where they can be found for sale in vending machines.[137]

"Water mafias" are suppliers of needed but overpriced water to urban dwellers in Bangladesh, India, and Pakistan and in Central and South America.[138] But providers are not only traditional organized crime figures but individuals from different sectors of society, including city officials, farmers, and real estate agents. One report from Delhi declared:

> Everything about this business is illegal: the boreholes dug without permission, the trucks operating without permits, the water sold without testing or treatment. . . . Bosses arrange buyers, labor fills tankers, the police look the other way, and the muscle makes sure that no one says nothing to nobody.[139]

The water mafia, in relying on corruption, organized crime, and the complicity of ordinary citizens, is a business so dispersed that it cannot be eliminated by arresting a few top criminals.

Doctors and Pharmacists: When the Patient Must Be Vigilant

Unfortunately, the business of substandard, spurious, falsely labeled, falsified, and counterfeit (SSFFC) medicine and vaccines, as well as diverted medicine, is now a significant problem in both the developed and the developing world, as part of this trade includes the importation of pharmaceuticals that are a danger to public health.[140] The scale of this trade is large: Interpol estimates that in 2010 profits from diverted and substandard pharmaceuticals as well as parallel trade reached $75 billion globally, having grown 90 percent between 2005 and 2010.[141]

The suppliers range from "small-scale criminal entrepreneurs to large-scale manufacturers."[142] Distributors in the United Kingdom and the United States, often affluent and educated individuals, have played a key role in the expansion of this criminal activity as counterfeits are sold online and even penetrate legal supply chains. In the United States, the total number of reported incidents grew over 50 percent in the five years from 2011 to 2016, reaching 3,147.[143]

This growth is explained in part by the monopolies of pharmaceutical companies, which keep prices high, combined with citizens' lack of insurance. As a result, a large number of patients are driven into unregulated and illicit markets to purchase treatments. Much of this growth is occurring in the market for expensive antiretrovirals to treat HIV/AIDS, anti-cancer medications, and diabetes treatments. Often these drugs lack the ingredients or the potency they should have. Counterfeits and harmful products bought by American buyers have had life-threatening effects that require visits to emergency rooms.[144]

In Europe, it is estimated that over 9 percent of consumed drugs are counterfeit.[145] With more universal medical coverage than in the United States, the majority of counterfeited pharmaceuticals are lifestyle drugs, such as treatments for erectile dysfunction, slimming pills, and arthritis medication.[146]

The problem of counterfeit drugs is worse in regions with poor control over supply chains.[147] The World Health Organization estimates that as much as 30 percent of the medicine sold in parts of Asia, Africa, and Latin America is counterfeit.[148]

Doctors and pharmacists facilitating illicit pharmaceutical trade in Africa is a problem so widespread that it is even portrayed in popular contemporary fiction. Alexander McCall Smith's famous Botswana woman detective investigates a doctor who overcharges for drugs by substituting a generic for the branded product.[149] This practice is hardly unusual.

Illustrating the scale of the problem is a 2015 Interpol operation attacking production of counterfeit medicine in seven countries in southern Africa—Angola, Malawi, South Africa, Swaziland, Tanzania, Zambia, and Zimbabwe. Investigators arrested 550 people and shut down three illicit manufacturing facilities that produced counterfeit antibiotics, painkillers, erectile dysfunction medicines, contraceptives, and antimalarial medication. A broad network distributed the illicit pharmaceutical products. Overall, 2,100 police, customs officials, and health regulatory officers confiscated more than 150 tons of counterfeit and illicit medicines at markets, shops, warehouses, pharmacies, clinics, and ports in more than fifty cities.[150]

In Tanzania in East Africa, a leading health official received large shipments of donated malaria drugs to redistribute to needy Africans on the continent; instead, he appropriated them for private sale to benefit him and his subordinates.[151] Once diverted, the drugs were not kept under needed temperature controls before consumption and therefore lost potency. Use of this compromised drug contributed to the development of microbial-resistant malaria and prevented the elimination of the disease—the original intent of the costly and massive drug distribution.

In Russia, failure to control the quality of medicine contributes to the poor health of the population and the declining life expectancy of Russians.[152] False medicines enter Russia from China and India as a result of improper customs controls. Russian authorities devote little effort to investigating the distribution of counterfeit medicines, contributing to its growth as a crime of choice for criminals. Of the fifty cases detected and investigated annually, only fifteen to twenty are submitted to a court.[153] This caseload represents the tip of the iceberg: a diverse array of perpetrators remain unprosecuted, including criminal suppliers, distributors, pharmacists, and corrupt customs officials.

The problem of illicit trade in pharmaceuticals is not confined to the developing and transitional world. In Italy, many medicines are stolen from hospitals and subsequently marketed to eastern

Europe.[154] Approximately 10 percent of Italian hospitals are victimized annually, each theft worth about 250,000 euros, with a total loss of 22 million euros. For drugs that need to be kept under controlled temperatures, this stolen medicine may not cure purchasers and may even prove harmful.

Because platforms fail to vet their sellers, online pharmaceuticals sites can sell substandard medicines that harm purchasers or deny them the remedial effects of the drugs they seek.[155] For example, a 2009 US case against online seller Kevin Xu, a Chinese citizen, was initiated after he sold counterfeit medicines that included contaminants and lacked the requisite doses for such serious illnesses as cancer, mental illness, and blood clots. Because these counterfeits were produced in state-owned Chinese facilities, the defendant, fearing for his family, was not cooperative with investigators.[156]

Preventing online sales is hard, as large numbers of small shipments arrive through the mail, making it difficult for the US Postal Service and private delivery companies such as UPS and FedEx to identify problematic packages. Thus, the latter are unwilling facilitators of this trade.[157] Another facilitator is Twitter. Analysis of communications on this social media platform reveals that a small percentage of tweets facilitate the illegal sale of prescription opioids.[158]

Xu's arrest set off a chain of linked investigations in both the United States and the United Kingdom that saved lives. Peter Gillespie, a high-living British chartered accountant and pharmaceutical distributor who imported 72,000 packets of counterfeit medicines—in other words, more than two million doses—was arrested after bringing counterfeit prostate cancer medicine into the United Kingdom that contained only 70 percent of the components needed to treat the disease.[159] Fortunately, the medicine was seized just before entering into the National Health Service (NHS).[160] Gillespie was fully conscious of his deceptive practices: he not only imported drugs but employed equipment to print misleading labels as to the provenance of the medicine.[161] Gillespie's four-year prison sentence was only a temporary deterrent. When he emerged from confinement, he obtained a license to import medicine, as there are limited EU controls on distributors.

Gillespie is unfortunately not a unique example. UK investigators tipped off US law enforcement, who found an unapproved oncology drug sent from a Pakistani company to San Diego. Other frauds with cancer drugs were identified in southern California, Pittsburgh, Iowa, and New York.[162] The importers buying these unapproved and misbranded oncology drugs sold them to doctors in the United States at substantially discounted prices.[163] These cases reveal the different types of actors complicit in dangerous pharmaceutical crime. Many commercial producers in China, India, Pakistan, and Turkey are more concerned with profits than with health.[164] They ship drugs to the United States, where they are not authorized to sell their commodities. Professionals are also complicit, as highlighted by an oncology treatment center in southern California that bought bargain-priced anticancer drugs fully aware that they were not approved by the FDA for distribution, and then injected them into patients.[165]

Doctors are also active participants in the illicit kidney trade, soliciting customers and, at times, interacting with criminal organizations and terrorist groups who seek their slice of this profitable trade. The highly popular Italian detective series *Inspector Montalbano* has an episode devoted to a Sicilian doctor who prospers by performing unauthorized kidney transplants, an operation that can be conducted only with the cooperation of the Mafia.[166] Researchers analyzing this phenomenon have interviewed kidney transplant doctors who confirm their unsavory relationships.[167]

Conclusion

The threats against mankind from illicit trade are grave, and the present state of the response seems dismal. But the human situation must be examined in historical perspective. For millennia, human beings have enslaved other humans. As chapter 2 revealed, only in the last two hundred years have there been laws to end the cross-national slave trade, reflecting a major change in human and legal consciousness. Today incomplete and flawed data suggest that 40 million people may still be enslaved.[168] The number is high, but on a percentage basis, many more human beings today are free than at any time in history. This is the good news.

Human slavery assumed an important economic role throughout history, and abuse of human life continues in other ways today because it brings important financial benefits to those involved. But unlike in the past, this abuse is not officially supported by the state, and when states or government officials engage in labor trafficking, the drug trade, or the selling of illicit cigarettes, they may be subject to opprobrium and, at times, even criminal sanctions.

Those who destroy human life are not just officials who engage in this trade but also professionals, companies and their employees, and pernicious nonstate actors, particularly organized criminals and terrorists. Professionals such as doctors and pharmacists help facilitate the dispersion of harmful pharmaceuticals by prescribing excessive quantities, illegally procuring medicines outside established supply chains—often through the internet—and selling counterfeit or diverted medicines that are not kept under proper temperature controls.

Technology has transformed and expanded the possible ways to harm human life. Online service providers such as Craigslist and Backpage have fostered human trafficking, a high-value revenue stream, through their advertisements. After law enforcement intervention against Craigslist, the problem merely migrated to Backpage, and actions against Backpage have moved payment to less reputable financial processors. Social media enables illicit deliveries, as highly profitable corporations fail to spend the resources needed to curb harmful content.

Global and state resources are disproportionately focused on traffickers in narcotics and only more recently on human trafficking and smuggling. In contrast, insufficient attention is focused on the widespread trade in counterfeit medicines, foods, and alcohol, which has escalated, in part, as a result of sales on the internet and through social media.[169] This activity is more often identified as a violation of intellectual property than as behavior that can kill people.

The combined trade in such harmful commodities as drugs, cigarettes, people, and counterfeit products for consumption transfers hundreds of billions of dollars to corrupt officials, companies, and nonstate actors. This transfer of wealth simultaneously undermines state capacity, both through revenue losses to the state and through the corruption and complicity of the officials who are essential to this trade. Therefore, the destruction of human life hurts not only individuals but also human security and the state.

7

Destroyers of the Planet

Except for the long-standing garbage mafias of Italy and the United States, the perpetrators of environmental crimes are not traditional organized crime groups but rather high-status individuals. While it is true that "it takes a village" to make the world a better place, it takes more than just the world's criminal organizations to harm all elements of the planet's resources—air, sea, land, and water.

Many focus on industrial harm to the environment—factory pollution destroying rivers and aquifers, wholesale clearing of the Amazon to make room for ranches, and pollution of the air by many types of industrial producers. Others focus on unregulated and illegal mining that puts harmful particles into the air, such as asbestos, and unauthorized gold mining that leads to mercury poisoning and adds some 650 to 1,000 tons of toxic mercury to the ecosystem each year.[1]

The phenomena examined in this chapter are a little different. The perpetrators sell our futures by illicitly trading the earth's resources—denuding the world's forests and selling fish from the increasingly depopulated oceans.[2] Through their illicit commerce, they also abuse the strategies we have developed to mitigate climate change. These traders are numerous, and the culprits multiply as lawyers, accountants, travel agents, shippers, and many other facilitators make this global trade possible. Corrupt officials at all levels help ensure the success of this trade.[3]

From Sarawak to the FBI's Offices in Seattle: Raider of Natural Resources

A Southeast Asian kleptocrat demolished most of one of the world's last major rainforests with financing from some of the world's top financial institutions. These parties maintained their activities even after learning of the ecological damage they were causing. The proceeds of this man's massive personal corruption are dispersed globally, often laundered into real estate in the developed world. The cut trees were purchased by legitimate manufacturers, and the processed woods were bought by consumers on many continents.

Abdul Taib Mahmud, known as the king of the Asian timber mafia, and his family amassed a $15 billion fortune by destroying almost 80 percent of the rainforests of Sarawak in Malaysia, possibly the richest ecosystem in the world. This destruction occurred while he served as chief minister for thirty-three years, starting in 1981.[4] A chilling documentary on this crime, simply entitled *The Borneo Case*, contrasts Taib's opulent lifestyle with the poverty of the inhabitants of the region he decimated.[5] Not only did his crime destroy a paradise, but he intimidated the protesting residents of his territory, a behavior associated with a crime boss more than with the well-educated high-ranking official he was.

Taib did not come from a powerful family, but in fact from one of limited means. As a twenty-seven-year-old, he entered government following graduation from law school at the University of Adelaide in Australia. His entry into the state bureaucracy, just two months before the founding of the Malaysian state in 1963, was aided by an uncle.[6] By 1970, his family had established a dynasty in Sarawak that lasts to this day. As the author of *Money Logging* explains, for the Taib family, logging provided them with the money not only to support their extravagant lifestyle but also to wield power and influence within Malaysia.[7]

The perpetrator of the "biggest environmental crime of our time," according to a former British prime minister, was financed by many of the leading financial institutions in the world.[8] Deutsche Bank loaned $600 million to Taib's government in 2005.[9] At the same time, Deutsche Bank closed the small account of the Bruno Manser Fund without explanation. The Fund was investigating the corruption and illegal logging of the Taib regime. Financiers provided even more support for the Taib government; Goldman Sachs provided a loan of $800 million in 2011.[10] Then major banks profited as the approximately $50 billion in profits from the sale of Borneo's precious trees, shared with Taib's political cronies, was transferred to financial institutions in Zurich, London, Sydney, San Francisco, and Ottawa. Money in UBS accounts went around the world, allowing Taib to segment his money laundering over many jurisdictions.[11]

Money was also transferred into US real estate. Ironically, one of the purchased properties was the Abraham Lincoln building in downtown Seattle, where the FBI northwest regional headquarters moved in 1998. Despite protests that have been held outside the headquarters by environmentalists protesting the rental fees paid to a kleptocrat by the US agency responsible for fighting corruption, the FBI is still occupying these facilities owned by the Taib family.[12] Only in 2017 did a Government Accountability Office (GAO) investigation of governmental rental of office space owned by foreigners point out the owner behind the Seattle property.[13]

Taib is one individual who has done massive damage to the environment, but his counterparts can be found in the Amazon in Brazil, in the rainforests of Indonesia, and in many other locales.[14] Yet he alone is not responsible. He can carry out his activities only with the complicity of many others in the legitimate economy.

Air

The Paris Climate Agreement's goal is to strengthen the global response to the threat of climate change by having the global community pledge to keep the global temperature rise this century well below two degrees Celsius above preindustrial levels. Additionally, the agreement aims to strengthen the ability of countries to deal with the impacts of climate change. Concrete measures are under way to reach these targets, including the development of renewable energy and the establishment of carbon markets, mileage targets, and emission standards for vehicles.[15]

However, the remedies accompanying the Paris Agreement are not "crime-proofed."[16] Policymakers neither planned for nor even anticipated the cunning and innovation of the criminal actors who would target the planet's survival efforts.

Illicit actors, as discussed in chapter 3, have only recently shifted to significant trade in fossil fuel products. ISIS was a wake-up call, but other illicit actors—criminals and terrorists—trade in oil and gas in Latin America, Africa, and the Middle East. Nonstate actor involvement in established energy markets was surprising, but even more unanticipated was the entry of organized criminals and illicit nonstate actors into the new clean economy. Also, no one expected major legitimate companies, like Volkswagen, to engage in criminal collusion at the very top corporate levels to evade governmental emissions regulations.

Billions had been invested in renewables even before the adoption of the agreement.[17] Both licit and illicit actors targeted these new opportunities. Some corporate officials, corrupt bankers, and other malicious facilitators abused the new financial opportunities resulting from the creation of the European carbon market, subsidies for clean energy, and emission controls for vehicles. Other high-level traders found clever ways to trade illegally in ozone-depleting substances (ODSs), which are controlled by the Montreal Protocol.

OZONE TRADERS

Organized criminals have been active participants in the illegal trade of chlorofluorocarbons (CFCs), which complements their existing criminal activity in garbage and harmful waste disposal.[18] Efforts to counter the trade in ozone-depleting substances are one of the few environmental crime success stories, yet they have received little public attention. The phaseout of the production of CFCs, combined with intense regulation and global enforcement, has reduced trade in this environmentally dangerous substance, although the trade apparently still persists in China.

Operation Sky Hole Patching, a campaign to counter the trafficking of ODSs, was started by the Regional Intelligence Liaison Office of the World Customs Organization (WCO) for Asia and the Pacific, which joined with the Asia-Pacific branch of the United Nations Environmental Program (UNEP).[19] This operation yielded positive results. Between 2006 and 2010, participants in this joint environmental-customs operation had made fifty-one seizures of illegal ODS totaling "approximately 730 tons—an average of 183 tons seized per year."[20] The decline in criminal activity has stemmed growth and allowed the healing of the ozone layer.[21] Yet the success of Operation Sky Hole Patching is not total for the planet. Unfortunately, a significant illicit trade persists in hydrofluorocarbons (HFCs).

International efforts to control the HFC trade were adopted because of the refrigerants' potential to cause grave environmental harm.[22] HFC trade is a criminal activity associated with corporate insiders more than crime groups. Therefore, it is more analogous to some illicit cigarette traders who smuggle produce out of the plants where they are employed. Skills, access, and international connections facilitate the growth of the illicit HFC trade.

HFCs are diverted from established factories in Zhejiang, China, that specialize in refrigerants. The illicit traders "even hav[e] facilities to decant ODS from bulk containers into smaller cylinders."[23] The illicit trade includes diverters as well as middlemen, whose trading and brokering of these commodities illegally threatens the success of the Montreal Protocol.[24] False labeling, misdeclaration of commodities, falsified documents, "concealment, fake recycled materials, and transshipment fraud; all have all been identified as methods for smuggling HFCs." A foiled smuggling operation of 39 million tons of "recycled" CFCs from China to Russia revealed the longevity of this activity: these participants had been trading in illegal ODS since the mid-1990s.[25]

ORGANIZED CRIME HIJACKING CLEAN ENERGY

The European Union's efforts to switch to renewable energy provided incentives and funding to build wind and solar facilities, and then the EU guaranteed high rates for the electricity produced. Facility construction favored areas with good winds and open space. But the EU's energy specialists did not crime-proof their program. They failed to consider that the open spaces of Sicily, with excellent wind flows, were lands controlled by the Mafia. Mafia dominance is based on territorial control and corruption of local officials. Therefore, clever mafiosi capitalized on their land, finding in renewable energy a better yield than that from agriculture.

Italian researchers who mapped the location of wind power generators and the boundaries of Mafia territory discovered a strong correlation—wind power development was largely confined to Mafia-controlled land.[26] Therefore, Mafia monopolies, often achieved and maintained through force, also prevail in the new energy economy, eliminating legitimate competitors in this sector from outside the region.

To understand how the EU bureaucrats failed to understand the cunning and forward thinking of La Cosa Nostra, listen to the words of a leading mafioso caught on a wiretap by the Italian government. Like others around the globe, he saw the future advantages of the clean economy:

> "Uncle Vincenzo," implored the businessman, Angelo Salvatore, using a term of affection for the alleged head of Sicily's Gimbellina crime family, 79-year-old Vincenzo Funari, . . . "For the love of our sons, renewable energy is important. . . . It's a business we can live on."[27]

But, as with so many Mafia investments, their concern is not efficient operations or sustainability. Initially, the Mafia did not even care whether the windmills they built were connected to the power grid. Some windmills were constructed so shoddily that they did not work, but they still received EU subsidies.[28] Shifting to this new sector allowed the criminals a means to invest or launder ill-gotten gains. A great deal for them, but bad news for the planet.

To understand the dimensions of the money laundering, meet the individual nicknamed "Lord of the Wind." He is not some mystical sprite out of Shakespeare's *Tempest* but a Sicilian named Vito Nicastri. A former electrician, he had 1.3 billion euros of his assets confiscated after a lengthy legal process that concluded with his conviction in the summer of 2016. How did an electrician-cum-businessman acquire so much in assets? He laundered money for a Mafia boss in Sicily, as well as other organized crime groups. In the Italian government's largest asset confiscation effort, "more than 100 properties, 43 companies operating mainly in the wind-power industry, luxury cars, a 46-foot catamaran, bank accounts and securities" were seized.[29]

ILLICIT CARBON TRADE

Market-based solutions to address climate have been the vehicle of choice for most policymakers seeking to limit the release of carbon dioxide (CO_2) and other green-house gases (GHG) into the air. In carbon trading, sometimes called *emissions trading*, participants trade in "emissions under cap-and-trade schemes, or with credits that pay for or offset GHG reductions."[30] Companies are given permits to release a certain amount of CO_2 into the air. If the company operates within its allowance, it can sell credits, and if it exceeds the allowance, it has to purchase additional permits to cover the excess.[31] This is done by purchasing "units," each of which is equivalent to one ton of CO_2.[32] The governing body for the carbon market distributes or auctions off emissions allowances.

The EU Emissions Trading Scheme was launched in 2005 with optimism—and no anticipation that its weakly regulated system would provide a great opportunity for criminal activity.[33] This naïveté cost the European Union over 5 billion euros (approximately $6.5 billion) and would enrich criminals, terrorists, cyberhackers, and corrupt bankers and traders. The largest European losses were in France, where they totaled approximately 1.6 billion euros.[34]

As one commentator has aptly noted, "Trying to save the world and trying to make money, in other words, are two distinct things. It was fraudsters who saw this sooner than anyone."[35] The diverse participants in this massive fraud hacked into computer registries of carbon credits, filed for illegitimate VAT payments, and made payments to shell companies.[36] The vulnerability of carbon markets is not confined to the crimes described in this section. Interpol believes that the $176 billion carbon market is vulnerable to other forms of criminal penetration, such as securities fraud, transfer mispricing, and the sale of nonexistent carbon credits.[37]

In the spring of 2016, German investigators prepared and distributed a poster stating that between August 2009 and April 2010, Mobeen Iqbal, a Pakistani, caused 136 million euros in losses to the German state by committing value-added tax (VAT) fraud.[38] His companies traded carbon credits free of VAT from one EU member state to another, then resold them with VAT included in the price. Next, the fraudsters sought governmental refunds for the VAT they never paid. They pocketed the VAT and disappeared.[39] "It works astonishingly well," one fraud expert explains, "and can be hard to distinguish from legitimate claims for a refund."[40]

The wanted poster highlighted trade conducted through employees of Deutsche Bank, a bank that once again shows up in shady dealings. Seven bank managers were charged. At sentencing, the judge stated that they had engaged in a "criminal business model." For five years, the bankers processed trades from sham companies by either turning a "blind eye to the 'clear indications' that the transactions were set up to defraud tax authorities or failed to do enough to stop them." Due diligence was not hard to perform. The address of one of the sham companies was a mere five-minute walk from the headquarters of Deutsche Bank's main office in Frankfurt. The bank's penalty was 220 million euros, paid to the German government for the illicit tax refunds. Only one offender was sentenced to prison, a fifty-five-year-old bank manager identified by the investigators as "the boss of some of the younger men in the scam."[41]

A British-Italian case of carbon credit fraud apparently helped fund terrorism. The Italian government accused Yakub Ahmed of Preston,

UK, who was of Pakistani origin, of defrauding the Italian state out of 1.15 billion euros (approximately $1.5 billion in 2010) in VAT, which he allegedly laundered through slush funds and investments in Dubai. The relevance of the Pakistan link became apparent in 2010 when Ahmed's name and company were found in papers picked up by UK and US military personnel when they raided a Taliban base in the mountains between Afghanistan and Pakistan. The prosecutors in Milan believe that the funds were reinvested in the Middle East to disguise the financing of Islamist terrorist organizations.[42]

In France, another carbon credit fraud was perpetrated by a network of international organized criminals with personalities as colorful as those in a Hollywood film.[43] They lived high, indulging in expensive cars, travel, and entertainment. One of the ringleaders had a background in tax fraud, an essential element in this massive crime.[44] The collaborators commuted back and forth to Israel and allegedly made payments to and hosted Prime Minister Benjamin Netanyahu of Israel. After many years of investigation, the French prosecuted the lead perpetrator, Arnaud Mimran, in the summer of 2016, as well as the major money launderer, Mardoché Mouly, who had evaded detention. The third co-conspirator, Samy Souied, was assassinated in a gangland shooting in Paris in 2010. Mardoché Mouly was sentenced in absentia in the summer of 2016 but was extradited from Switzerland at year's end, after being on the run for months.[45] Little of the billion-plus loss from this fraud has been recovered by the French government.

Other participants in the carbon credit fraud included fraudsters and hackers who stole the carbon credits from registries that were maintained on the internet.[46] The British hackers included a high school dropout, thirty-two-year-old Matthew Beddoes, who previously dealt in stolen credit cards, and thirty-eight-year-old Jasdeep Singh Randhawa, a former cigarette smuggler from Leicestershire. Caught when their encrypted entry into UNCOM (the UN Clean Development Mechanism Registry in Bonn, Germany) failed, they both were sentenced by British courts.[47]

A Polish facilitator, Jaroslaw Klapucki, had a brokerage house trading in carbon emissions. He was convicted by the French courts of helping six shell companies sell more than 117 million emission allowances without checking that the companies' tax affairs were in order.[48]

Small-scale Ponzi schemes, sold through the web, tricked investors into buying fictitious carbon credits. Profits from this crime were traced to such favorite locales of criminal proceeds as Latvia, Cyprus, Dubai, and Hong Kong.[49]

The extent and variety of criminality associated with the European carbon market suggest that mitigation strategies to address climate change can work only if they are "crime-proofed." Otherwise, this crucial effort to save the world will continue to be hijacked by corrupt and pernicious nonstate actors, who are always looking for new economic opportunities.

Sea

The sea has been a conduit for illicit trade for millennia. Pirates moved their hijacked cargoes across the seas, and vessels were, and remain, a form of transport of choice for smugglers. But life in the sea is also a victim of illicit trade. The seas are being poisoned by as diverse a range of perpetrators as those destroying the air.

Organized crime, primarily Italian groups, has taken the lead in dumping toxic materials in the Mediterranean Sea and off the coast of Africa. The situation in the sea around Italy is so severe that the activists who follow the ecological crimes of Italian organized crime groups have called its analysis of their activity *Mare Monstrum* (the Sea Monster). There are presently two and a half recorded crimes annually for each kilometer of the Italian coast— dumping pollutants in the sea, illegal fishing, and illegal drainage from often-illicit construction are the prime culprits.[50] Mafia turncoats have confessed to the dumping of radioactive and harmful medical waste in the Mediterranean.[51] The dumpers have also ventured farther from home: the tsunami off the coast of Somalia in 2004 disclosed hazardous radioactive materials that had been disposed of along its coasts.[52] As I have written elsewhere, dumping in turn led to the rise of the Somali pirates because, with the fish disappearing from the sea, fishermen turned to crime as their income from fishing disappeared as well.[53]

Elsewhere in Africa, there is a more direct relationship between terrorism and fishing. Boko Haram has infiltrated the lucrative fishing sector in northeast Nigeria, depriving fishermen of their livelihood and providing themselves with an important revenue stream.[54]

Drug traffickers in the Americas have for many years disguised themselves as tuna fishers, doing significant harm to both tuna and dolphin stocks as they seek to cover their illicit drug smuggling.[55] Now crime groups operating in South America try to compel artisanal fishermen in coastal Ecuador to transport cocaine.[56]

In South Africa, transnational crime networks also contribute to the devastation of sea life. The alliance of Cape Town–based drug gangs and Chinese organized crime groups has contributed to the disastrous overfishing of abalone in South Africa to satisfy the gourmet taste of Chinese consumers.[57]

Yet corporate actors are probably more destructive of fish and their environment than the organized criminal groups. With increased global competition and reduced fish stocks, professional fishermen and fleets face smaller profits and reduced yields.[58] Corporate fishing and state-owned fishing vessels exceed established quotas in many regions of the world to enhance short-term profits.[59] The consequences for global fish stocks have been devastating. Already in 2011, 29 percent of global fish stocks were overfished or extinct, and much more than half of global fish stocks are now fully exploited. On average, 18 percent of the global catch—or as much as 11 million to 26 million tons of fish—are caught illegally each year.[60] West Africa is the region of the globe where illegal fishing is estimated to be highest, at 37 percent. Marine fisheries experts estimate the losses at $2.3 billion annually, an enormous sum for a poor region.[61] In the United States, illegally caught fish are calculated at the high end, ranging between one-fifth and one-third of all imported wild seafood.[62]

Approximately 10 to 12 percent of the global population, most residing in the developing world, is dependent on fishing and fish farming to support their families. Fish and fish products represent

20 percent of the animal protein for three billion people around the world.[63] Stated more dramatically, almost 40 percent of the world's population depends on fish stocks to stay healthy.

The eagerness of the rising middle class in China to consume fish is a driving force for state-owned fishing boats to overfish off the coast of West Africa. Chinese fishermen are also increasingly engaged in illegal fishing in Korea's Western Sea, the East China and South China Seas, the Indian Ocean, and even off the South American coast.[64] Overfishing has prompted violent retaliations against the Chinese boats and their crews. The Indonesian navy has fired on Chinese fishing boats.[65] "South Africa detained three Chinese vessels and arrested nearly 100 crewmen on board for illegally entering the South African Exclusive Economic Zone. In the case of Argentina, its coast guard shot holes in a Chinese vessel that was illegally fishing off its coast."[66]

As we have seen before, one type of illegality facilitates others, setting off a domino effect. When large-scale fishing vessels overfish the coast of West Africa, small-scale local fishermen can no longer make a living. Therefore, they take off on their fishing boats to the Canary Islands and become illegal migrants.[67] The destruction of fish stocks disrupts human livelihoods and results in another form of illicit activity.

Corporate fishing boats pillaging the sea often use trafficked laborers, who are abandoned by the sea captain at the first sign of trouble. A South African case in which seven vessels were brought into the Cape Town harbor for illegal fishing illustrates the problem. The owners of the vessels remain unidentified, but indicators point to a Taiwanese venture capital syndicate that cared nothing about the seventy-five Indonesian workers left on board without money, food, electricity, or clean water. Fortunately, the abandoned workers, in the absence of supplies from their employers, were supported by the local South African community, who used their own limited funds to help the desperate fishermen. The sailors' employer did nothing to support them.[68]

Companies engaging in illegal fishing recruit and retain crews through deception and coercion, subjecting workers to exploitation.

The problem is not confined to Taiwan. Corporate entities in many countries in Asia, including Thailand, South Korea, Singapore, Malaysia, and Russia, mistreat the fishermen they hire.[69] In Thailand, "despite the fact that the fishing industry . . . is an increasingly sophisticated and multi-billion dollar industry, the working conditions for many fishermen continue to be extremely grueling and even life threatening."[70]

How do people at sea become victims of such exploitation? Who facilitates recruitment into such abysmal conditions?[71] Those most immediately responsible are intermediary brokers, recruitment agencies, senior crew, and fishing operators. Myanmar's Rohingya refugees are forced from settlement camps onto Thai fishing industry vessels, where they are abused.[72] Some have been thrown into the sea before or after death.[73] Brokers in Thailand also contract with legitimate fishing companies to deliver a needed number of workers. A good way to obtain potential fishermen is to pay off the debts that they have incurred at karaoke clubs in southern Thailand. Young girls of thirteen to fifteen are trafficked from Myanmar and other neighboring countries, forced to work in bars encouraging customers to buy drinks at inflated prices and selling sexual services at high prices. The recruiters for these vessels pay the debts and acquire the manpower for the fishing expeditions.[74]

Land

The land on which we live and its flora and fauna are being destroyed by man as a result of greed, the desire for conspicuous consumption, and, for some of the lowest-level poachers, the need to eat on a daily basis. Massive construction in India, for instance, has created "sand mafias" that illegally mine large quantities of sand, thereby destroying the waterways necessary for existence.[75]

E. O. Wilson in his book *Half-Earth* suggests that half the planet must be set aside if humans and all other life forms are to survive.[76] But those who assault the planet often prey on the very refuges set aside to preserve ecosystems and diverse species. Some poor Africans living on the land adjoining preserves believe that they have been blessed because of their easy access to the animals in these "protected" locales, which they hunt, consume, and sell.[77] But these poachers of animals, including endangered ones, are just the lowest level of the "destroyers of the planet." Finding viable livelihoods for these individuals who have been deprived of their traditional hunting grounds is just a piece of the puzzle. Much more attention needs to be paid to the perpetrators who decimate vast forests and destroy much land through the dumping of toxic materials and the production of illicit pesticides. As the discussion in the section on the sea revealed, the destroyers include corrupt officials, corporate executives, and crime groups, as well as facilitators who help move and market the earth-destroying commodities and launder the proceeds.

TIMBER

More than thirty offenses related to illegal logging have been identified, including logging in protected areas, logging without permits, logging in excess of what is permitted, logging in excess of quotas, and illegal logging in conflict zones.[78] The crime may be organized and sustained, but its central perpetrators are rarely organized criminals. In some cases, the intermediaries are organized crime, as seen in Siberia and the Far East, but it is corrupt officials colluding with corporate interests who are key to the destruction of the world's last great forests.[79] The proliferation of the illicit timber trade is often a consequence of the fox guarding the henhouse—those charged with protecting the forests are the largest beneficiaries of their sale.

This massive business is operating in many of the world's most precious rainforests, such as Sarawak and Indonesia. Eighty percent of the lumber from the Asia-Pacific region is thought to be illicitly sourced.[80] In Africa, trees in the Democratic Republic of the Congo are a prime target. In the Western Hemisphere, such as Brazil and Peru, rainforests have been extensively hit.[81] Rapid growth has been identified in the Amazon region, after a respite. Cutting increased by up to 103 percent in 2012–2013. These habitats are home to many species of birds, plants, and animals that cannot survive outside of them. Therefore, the damage to ecosystems is permanent.

Serious deforestation is also under way in the vast Russian forests of Siberia and Karelia, and trees from the last remaining large forest in Europe are logged illegally from regions of the embattled Ukraine.[82]

GREED-MOTIVATED DEFORESTATION

The destroyers of Indonesia's timber resources are very similar to the culprits under Taib in Malaysia—responsibility lies with high-level officials. Yet in Indonesia the investigations have been conducted domestically, whereas the Malaysian forest abuse was exposed only by outsiders. In Indonesia, timber crimes have been investigated by the most trusted public institution, the Corruption Eradication Commission (Komisi Pemberantasan Korupsi, KPK). Operating for fourteen years, the KPK has "made a reputation for itself globally for thoroughly investigating, researching, and trying high-level targets," and it has had a high conviction rate.[83] The KPK has prioritized its investigation of the destroyers of Indonesia's forests. In the early 2000s, a parliament member was sentenced to eight years' imprisonment for accepting bribes to allow the conversion of protected forest zones into land where trees could be cut. Subsequently, in 2007, two government officials and their collaborator, the executive of a logging company, were sentenced for illegal logging. The following year, an eleven-year sentence was handed down to a government regent for his role in illegal logging.[84] By 2014, one-third of Indonesia's regents were under investigation for corruption, primarily for the issuance of logging permits in violation of regulations, thereby allowing the expansion of palm oil plantations.[85]

The investigations of the Indonesian anti-corruption agency suggest that companies' underreporting of timber production may have cost Indonesia as much as $9 billion in revenues from 2003 to 2014. Fees and royalties were collected only on approximately 19 to 23 percent of total timber production during these years. Revenue losses of this magnitude could occur only with high-level corruption.[86]

Indonesian police arrested corporate executives for their role in recent devastating and costly fires: they had burned the rainforests they chopped down.[87] The collateral damage was high—half a million respiratory infections were reported in Indonesia after the fires began.[88]

The perpetrators of this environmental crime operate not only at the source but also in transit. Before the crackdown by the KPK, fifteen cargo vessels a month filled with illegally cut timber were moved through the free-trade zones of Singapore, Hong Kong, and Malaysia before being transported to China and other Asian countries. One investigation revealed the involvement of an Indonesian general and brokers in Singapore and Malaysia who produced fake documents to mask the illegal commerce. Traders, shipping agents, and banks were also directly involved in disguising the origin and nature of other timber shipments.[89] The Indonesian Anti-corruption Commission referred to this as organized crime.[90] Certainly, it was highly organized, but it was composed of well-placed individuals of a type not generally associated with a criminal organization.

A similar cast of characters contributed to the illegal deforestation of Papua New Guinea. In 2004, the expulsion of a New Zealand logging company from the Timber Importers Association was "due to its complicity in illegal logging and unsustainable forest management. In 2006, the Government commissioned a review of the logging industry and it concluded that none of the operations evaluated complied with national laws or regulations."[91]

CONFLICT REGIONS AND DEFORESTATION

Regions in conflict cannot protect their natural resources. Today in Africa, Europe, and elsewhere, massive deforestation is accompanying insurgencies and regional conflicts.

Forests in conflict regions in Africa are abused for another purpose—to produce charcoal, which depends on the trees of naturally protected areas. The result is large-scale deforestation, desertification, and famine.[92] Indigent Somalis participate in this trade, which enriches officials and dealers and also benefits dangerous nonstate actors such as militias from the DRC and terrorist groups.[93] The most noted of these is Al-Shabaab, which is estimated to earn between $38 million and $68 million a year from charcoal sales and taxation of charcoal in transit—or 40 percent of its revenues.[94] The transporters move the charcoal across Africa and to the Arabian Peninsula.[95]

Moving to another region of the world, we find similar destroyers of the planet in conflict-ridden Ukraine. Only stumps remain for what was the last virgin forest in Europe, which extended from northern Romania to western Ukraine.[96] The destruction has been under way for the last two decades but has become particularly pronounced since 2005, when large timber factories became operational.[97]

The conflict in Ukraine has facilitated illegal logging. The major Austrian timber firm Holzindustrie Schweighofer benefits from this illegal cutting in Ukraine, because the wood is transferred to its processing facility in Romania. Criminal groups work with corrupt politicians. "They use poor people as fronts for their companies and will run a bulldozer over anyone or anything standing in their way. In the meantime, law enforcement sits on the sidelines as the violence unfolds," report OCCRP's Romana Puiulet and Anna Babinets.[98] As in Sarawak, citizens have mobilized, but with no success.

> The network is opposed in Ukraine by paramilitaries who fight against Russia's expansion. The so-called Cossack Battalion blocks logging trucks on the roads, halts trains loaded with illegal wood and sets up ambushes in the forest.
>
> But it hasn't been enough. The logging cartel is strong and supported by corrupt officials in Kyiv.[99]

In Europe, it is officials, once again, who exploit the natural forests that they are expected to preserve. Instead, they personally profit, depriving the state of massive revenues and the world of the trees needed to sustain global ecosystems. Conflict enhances the opportunities for this corrupt behavior.

BUYERS

Many of us are buyers of illicitly obtained wood, as it goes into the widely available products of IKEA, the third-largest user of timber in the world.[100] Other commercial firms sell products made from illicitly obtained logs as well. A recent prosecution of Lumber Liquidators in the United States revealed that this seller of flooring bought lumber from a Chinese source, despite knowing of its illegal origin.[101] Many buyers of plywood are purchasing illicitly cut timber that has been laundered into a popular consumer item.[102]

Destroyers of Wildlife

The world is now facing a "tsunami of extinction," a consequence of change brought about by human behavior. The chytrid fungus dispersed globally through migration is now demolishing the world's population of frogs, particularly in the tropics of the New World.[103] The warming of the oceans is killing coral.[104] In fact, research has suggested that man has caused 322 extinctions of terrestrial vertebrate species in the last 500 years.[105] "Mammals, birds, and amphibians are currently becoming extinct at rates comparable to the five mass extinctions of the last 500 million years, when "cataclysmic forces"— such as massive meteorite strikes and supervolcano explosions— wiped out vast swaths of life, including the dinosaurs.

The role played by humans in most prior extinctions of species has not been deliberate: instead, the demise of some species has been an inadvertent result of human actions such as habitat destruction, urbanization, agricultural monoculture, or the spread of invasive species. Today, however, humans are playing a greater role in extinctions through both inadvertent and deliberate actions. Tens of thousands of species—including 25 percent of all mammals and 13 percent of birds—are now threatened with extinction because of overhunting, poaching, pollution, loss of habitat, the arrival of invasive species, and other human-caused problems. At this "tipping point" where human population has risen 130 percent in fifty years and is expected to grow by another one-third by 2060, species diversity is threatened unless human patterns of behavior are dramatically changed. Illicit actors, through their agility, speed, and flexibility in both slaughtering and capturing many forms of wildlife, are threatening the very sustainability of many species. Many suggest that we are in an anthropocene epoch—a time when human activities directly impact the earth's geology and ecosystems.[106]

Many diverse individuals contribute to the demise of species. Poor Africans who poach animals, including endangered ones, are just the lowest level of the "destroyers of the planet." Illicit networks of criminals, insurgents, and even terrorists often cooperate with high-level officials to make the global trade work. They hire killers and then move the animal parts thousands of miles to lucrative markets. For example, elephant tusks have been used to buy weapons for Joseph Kony's Lord's Resistance Army (LRA), based in Sudan. His fighters have been poaching in the DRC's Garamba National Park, leading to the death of many of the remaining 20,000 elephants in the park as well as the deaths of numerous park rangers who have sought to protect the animals.[107]

The consequences are severe. The World WISE database, which contains CITES data, reports that over 7,000 species have been traded illegally. Of total seizures, no species represents over 7 percent of the total, reflecting the diverse and perverse impact of the illicit trade.[108] The data collected under the CITES convention between 1999 and 2015 showed that there have been 164,000 seizures from 120 countries on all continents. Mammals and reptiles represent almost 60 percent of the species confiscated. The problem is even greater, however, than these numbers suggest: these data reflect only the transnational trade and not domestic trade, which is outside of CITES jurisdiction.

The desire for animals as a show of wealth and power has contributed to this growth. Traders can make significant profits out of the animal parts they sell.[109] Asia provides a demand not only for ivory and rhino horn but also for Tibetan antelopes, bears and bear bile, pangolins, tigers, reptiles, abalone, marine turtles, sharks, seahorses, coral, and aquarium fish.[110] Pangolin trade is even larger in scale than that of tigers and rhinos, the illegal trade exceeding the legal trade seventy times over.[111] Bear bile is even secured out of American national parks.[112] Gorillas, orangutans, and other apes are heavily traded out of Africa. Much of the trade is going to zoos and private owners in Asia.[113]

Online sales have increased the accessibility not only of ivory but also of many protected animals, plants, and birds.[114] Initial research on online trade conducted by the International Fund for Animal Welfare (IFAW), published in 2008 as *Killing with Keystrokes*, revealed that even a year after eBay outlawed the sale of cross-border ivory trade, 83 percent of ivory identified by investigators was tied to that online source.[115] Subsequent research several years later in Europe indicated that a mere 2 percent of online wildlife offerings in Europe might be compliant with the law. Sales are still occurring on websites such as eBay, although eBay's predominance has declined and shifted to many locally based sites in Europe. Anonymized sellers helped foster the trade. This analysis once again reveals the facilitating role of the new technologies in the growth of illicit trade.[116]

A decade ago, a prize-winning Austrian documentary referred to the contemporary situation in Tanzania as "Darwin's Nightmare," as so many long-lasting species are being rapidly exterminated. In chapter 4 on the rhino horn trade, I advanced the concept of "dysfunctional selection." Contemporary illicit trade in wildlife suggests that the concept is applicable to many more animals than just the rhinoceros.

Destroyers of the Soil

The land is being destroyed by more than just illegal timber harvesting. Producers of illegal pesticides and counterfeit seeds and those who illegally dispose of garbage and toxic and hazardous waste are causing long-term destruction to the land and to human life. The deleterious products are produced on an industrial scale that compounds the harm.

COUNTERFEIT PESTICIDES AND SEEDS

Legal pesticides are expensive to develop.[117] Therefore, there are incentives to produce substitutes more cheaply. Imitation pesticides and counterfeit seeds have become available on a significant scale in the last decade, but an absence of awareness threatens the sustainability of the planet because these products can be very destructive to the soil and to those who apply these products.[118] Inferior counterfeit pesticides are sold. Of even greater concern are harmful compounds that contain banned chemicals and/or mixtures highly toxic to humans, insects, and plant life, which are sold to gullible customers as pesticides.

Quite often counterfeit pesticide products arrive in farmer- or consumer-ready packaging that even the legitimate manufacturer has a difficult time distinguishing from their own labels and packaging. The counterfeit agricultural products are illegally sold in markets, on the street, in neighborhood stores, and over the internet.[119] Once again, online availability enables the dissemination of this illicit and often dangerous commodity.

India is now the fourth-largest producer and sixth-greatest exporter of pesticides in the world, but its counterfeit market is far outpacing its legitimate market in growth. India's fake pesticide industry is expanding at 20 percent per year, while the overall growth rate for sales of legitimate pesticides is only 12 percent. The counterfeit products are made clandestinely and marketed with names that closely resemble the names of legitimate products. That they now account for up to 25 to 30 percent of the $4 billion Indian pesticide market is of significant concern to many sectors of the government, because these pesticides damage soil fertility, harm water supplies, and kill insects that are needed to maintain healthy agriculture.[120]

When I attended a promotional event for Sri Lankan tea in Washington, DC, the tea sellers showed pictures of healthy plantations and pointed out that their teas were grown without harmful pesticides. But the implications of this selling point were lost on most of the audience, who were unaware that the problem of harmful pesticides even exists.

The problem of trade and export of counterfeit pesticides is not confined to India. In China, there are very significant problems of contamination of soil through pollution and dangerous pesticides. The cost to remedy this harm exceeds the world's financial resources.[121] Most of the approximately twenty pesticides that China produces in large amounts are highly toxic and are restricted or banned by the UN's Food and Agriculture Organization (FAO).[122] Despite governmental bans, these highly toxic pesticides continue to be widely used in agriculture, violating safety standards.[123] In 2013, the China Ministry of Public Security reported the seizure of over 3,100 tons of counterfeit pesticides, fertilizers, and agricultural seeds.[124]

Dangerous pesticides from China have been exported to Siberia, not far from production areas on the Mongolian border.[125] Yet Russia also produces its own illegal pesticides. In June 2008, a Russian facility in Kursk was discovered that produced 100 tons of illegal and counterfeit pesticides.[126] The large-scale production reflects the involvement of businessmen and the export of the illegal pesticides suggests that corrupt border personnel may have been facilitating transport.

Dangerous pesticides have been exported to Europe and account for approximately 10 percent of the European market, but in locales in northeastern Europe targeted by criminal networks over 25 percent of the pesticides in circulation are counterfeit.[127] Europol conducted a major operation called Silver Axe in 2016, during which 350 containers were inspected. During this operation, law enforcement agencies from Belgium, France, Germany, Italy, Slovenia, Spain, and the Netherlands discovered 190 tons of illegal or counterfeit pesticides.[128] According to the European Union Intellectual Property Office, these sales are costing the EU about $1.4 billion annually. This loss represents reduced income to legitimate European producers of pesticides and the loss of approximately 2,600 jobs associated with legitimate production.[129]

Counterfeit pesticides are less of a problem in the United States than in Europe, since control over supply chains appears to be more effective. Nonetheless, counterfeit pesticides are now entering the American market, threatening both consumers' lives and farmers' livelihoods. With prices 10 to 20 percent less than authentic products, farmers who have bought these counterfeits have seen significant crop damage because of the unregulated chemicals they contain.[130]

Counterfeit seeds are less of a problem than pesticides, but they are a growing and significant concern as well. In 2011, "30 percent of the estimated 8,700 seed companies operating in China, or 2,610 companies, are believed to be involved in producing and selling counterfeit seeds to farmers."[131]

In Africa, significant penetration of farmers' markets with both counterfeit pesticides and seeds has become a problem. Farmers acquire these fakes at informal markets because they are priced at 20 percent below market rates. Farmers' efforts to save money may sense. But many trade short-term savings for destruction of their entire crop, which leaves the family destitute.

According to a report for the Bill and Melinda Gates Foundation, Ugandan manufacturers lose between $10.7 billion and $22.4 million annually because of counterfeit maize, herbicide, and inorganic fertilizer sales. When considering that the average per capita income of a Ugandan farmer was just $506 in 2012, these losses are staggering for poor farmers, and they undermine the sustainability of rural life, having ripple effects across the country.[132] Yet the African sellers of counterfeit agricultural products, although key to their distribution, may not be aware of the consequences of their action.

Aware of the devastating losses from seeds and pesticides sold at markets, farmers use seeds saved from the previous seasons to sow the following year. This practice results, however, in 90 percent lower crop yields than those obtained from legitimate first-generation hybrid seeds.[133] Therefore, their livelihoods are also jeopardized through their caution.

DISPOSERS OF HAZARDOUS WASTE

Fifteen years ago, the dangerous disposal of waste by the Camorra in their home region near Naples resulted in dramatically increased incidences of cancer.[134] Organized crime figures played an important role in this outcome. The criminal turncoat Carmine Schiavone, one of the leaders of the notorious Casalesi clan in Naples, told a closed parliamentary hearing in 1997 of this dangerous dumping. But organized crime has many accomplices. "In front of the committee he described dumping operations taking place in the dead of night, guarded by men in military uniforms and with the connivance of senior police officers, politicians and businesspeople that burned tons of hazardous waste."[135] In one year, 6,300 fires were set in the region, which was subsequently named the *Terra dei Fuoci* (Land of Fires).[136] But the fires did not disappear after the revelations of the harm. In 2014, firefighters put out 2,400 blazes, and the European Court of Justice fined Italy 20 million euros for its failure to eliminate the dangerous disposal of hazardous waste.[137]

In the southern regions of Camorra domination, Campania and Caserta, there are subregions where illegal waste disposal has made the soil so toxic that spontaneous abortions and appreciably higher rates of child tumors (detected even in infants by age one) are serious problems.[138] This is not just a localized problem. Italian criminal investigations revealed that the Camorra also exports toxic waste. Somalia, a former colony of Italy, was a key foreign victim—once again illustrating that history shapes the present.[139]

Other countries also dispose of hazardous waste in inappropriate ways. President Vladimir Putin, rarely a bearer of bad news, has said that in Russia 30 billion tons of waste is stored at unauthorized dump sites, a situation that could only arise in the presence of high-level corruption. "People are dumping waste where they see fit and how they see fit, and such [unauthorized] dump sites occupy 48 thousand hectares" of land across the country, he said, representing a loss of 6 percent of Russia's GDP.[140]

E-WASTE

The burgeoning use of technology that is rapidly outdated has created another dangerous problem: the disposal of different forms of e-waste (discarded electric and electronic equipment, from computers to small appliances) poses a serious threat to public health, because lead can leach into the soil from batteries and other components and harmful toxins can be released into the environment when plastic is burned.[141]

The developed countries are disproportionately responsible for the 42 million tons of e-waste generated each year, of which only 10 to 40 percent is disposed of properly. E-waste is often diverted to the black market and shipped to China, Indonesia, Thailand, and

Vietnam, countries where there is less regulation, thereby avoiding the costs associated with legitimate recycling.[142] Much of Africa's e-waste is disposed of in Agbogbloshie, Ghana, an Accra suburb inhabited by the city's poorest residents, who "have spent years dismantling, recovering, weighing and reselling parts and metals extracted from the scrapped devices and from the heaps of electronic waste."[143]

The harm is palpable for those who receive the waste. Scientific research in China reveals that children living near e-waste disposal sites are suffering three times the recommended level of lead in the blood. Ghanaian youth who earn money through the recovery of valuable metals from electronic components, mostly by environmentally unsound means, suffer from dangerous quantities of lead in their blood and urine.[144]

Traffickers in Nuclear Materials

Trafficking in nuclear materials can cause great harm to land and to life. It is an activity conducted by many who might be called white-collar criminals—bankers, transport workers, and logistics experts. The bankers employed at BCCI, Banco Nazionale de Lavoro, and HSBC facilitated the financing of nuclear proliferation programs.[145] Iraq under Saddam Hussein "established a special relationship with the Atlanta Branch of the Banca Nazionale de Lavoro," a global Italian government bank that processed billions in Iraqi funds, some of which were used for illicit purchases.[146] The infamous Bank of Credit and Commerce International, the subject of a detailed Senate investigation, was used to transfer funds to support the A. Q. Khan network.[147] Similar patterns were seen more recently in the behavior of ING, Barclays, ABN Amro, Credit Suisse, and HSBC.[148] HSBC, a major British-based bank and facilitator of Iran's nuclear program, was shown to be not only ignoring the illicit activity of its clients but willfully disregarding its own compliance obligations, knowingly facilitating clients' evasion of laws in their home countries, and in several instances actively participating in its clients' criminal activities.[149]

Conclusion

The world's criminals are numerous, flexible, and dispersed. Recent European analyses suggest that they have grown significantly in number. Five thousand organized crime groups are now under investigation in Europe, an increase from 3,400 in 2013.[150] But despite this growth, these groups are not sufficient in number to have caused the extent of damage to the planet's air, sea, land, and inhabitants described in this chapter. Organized crime has always needed officials to survive, and the presence of corrupt officials at many levels of state bureaucracy helps explain the rapid growth of illicit trade.

Some suggest that we are in the midst of a "corruption epidemic," an insight supported by the large numbers of high-level officials represented in the offshore accounts of the "Panama Papers." But even organized criminals and their partners in crime—corrupt officials—working together are still insufficient to explain the rise and diffusion of illicit trade in both the real and virtual worlds. Rather, it takes many more elements of society for illicit trade to flourish—diverse types of businesses, professionals in banking, international commerce, cyber, and law, and consumers who provide a ready market for many of the products traded illicitly. Facilitators from government are key, whether they are military personnel, border guards, or customs officials. But facilitators in the private sector are diverse. They range from the bankers at Deutsche Bank who were part of the conspiracy to sell carbon credits to the recruitment agents who find workers for boats engaging in illegal fishing.

Terrorists and insurgents help destroy the planet as they kill elephants for profit in Africa, deforest Afghanistan and Pakistan, and loot the earth for antiquities that they will traffic.[151] Yet more than nonstate actors benefit from illicit trade. Corporations from many sectors are key facilitators and perpetrators of illicit environmental commerce. Volkswagen, as previously mentioned, harmed the planet and deceived over 11 million purchasers. Mortality rates in Europe will most likely increase where sales were largest.[152] Large corporate fishing companies have boats capable of staying at sea for a long time, compounding the harm they do to fish populations.

Corporations can also be both willing and unwilling facilitators as they transport illicit goods such as counterfeits, natural resources, and harmful pesticides.

The online world, with its focus on increased volume rather than the integrity of its sellers, has been a major driver of illicit commerce harmful to the planet. Dangerous pesticides are bought over the internet, as are furniture and lumber obtained from illegally logged trees. The absence of adequate internet security facilitated the hacking into the carbon registry and the theft of carbon credits.

Political leaders and financial institutions have long escaped scrutiny. Yet in providing loans for development, they are behind the pillaging of the earth's forests. These loans sometimes go toward the construction of roads that facilitate massive deforestation. Furthermore, as intensive investigations resulting in the imposition of multibillion-dollar fines have revealed, international banks launder the money of drug traffickers and facilitate the financial transfers needed to purchase nuclear materials.

Consumers help destroy the planet as they purchase goods without concern for their origins. The poor and often illiterate farmers in Africa and India who purchase inferior pesticides that are harmful to the earth and to themselves are often deceived and not conscious of the consequences of their purchases. The rising middle class in the world is fostering a demand for fish and furniture that cannot be sustained by existing supplies of either fish or lumber.

The growth in illicit trade that harms air, sea, land, and water on a massive scale is not just a violation of global norms. The diverse participants in this trade are also violating our contract with the planet. If this illicit trade continues on such a large scale, human beings as sellers and consumers of the earth's bounty will make life unsustainable for the planet's future billions of inhabitants. In the concluding chapter, I examine what is being done in many sectors to counter those who profit from the destruction of the planet.

8

Summing Up

Many think that greed lies at the heart of illicit trade, believing that human avarice largely explains the search for unauthorized profits. Others blame growth on the rise of regulation. But this book suggests a much more complex picture. Multiple forces have contributed to the rise and abrupt transformation of illicit trade, which is a consequence of many of the most serious and intractable problems in the world. Technology is a driver rather than the cause of the growth of illicit trade. Many states have and continue to gain political advantage through the presence of illicit trade.[1]

Illicit trade not only persists but is escalating in the modern era of increasing global populations, diminishing natural resources, and the phenomenal growth of new technology. The end of the Cold War and the declining role of superpowers and states have enhanced the power of nonstate actors (criminals, terrorists, insurgents), many of whom support themselves through diverse and often converging forms of illegal trade. They have disproportionately benefited from the connectivity afforded by the internet and social media and the anonymity provided by the Dark Web. These new technologies are a boon to those participating in illegal commerce.[2] When misused, they also provide an asymmetric advantage to countries and to non-state actors linked to states.

Addressing the complex sources of illicit trade requires better public policy, based on better understanding of the limits to growth, the impact of climate change, and the consequences of increasing economic disparity within and among countries.[3] States alone are not effective in controlling serious illicit trade that crosses multiple borders and operates in the borderless world of cyberspace.[4]

Why Does Illicit Trade Endure?

In surveying illicit trade over the last four thousand years, the book has shown that there is great consistency over time—at no point in history has illicit commerce ceased to be a problem. Moreover, the problems did not emerge solely in a particular region and subsequently expand to others as a result of contacts with other civilizations. Rather, illicit trade emerged independently in Mesopotamia and was observed among the Aztecs before the Spanish conquest. The universality of this problem suggests that it derives from human nature. But the common features of this trade—the presence of counterfeiting, stolen property, and piracy in so many regions of the world and over so many centuries—suggests that market and trade conditions, as well as state policies, have helped trigger these specific illicit responses. Moreover, illicit trade and smuggling have often contributed to both state-making, as Charles Tilly has written, and to state "unmaking," as many of this book's examples illustrate.[5]

SURVIVAL

Since the dawn of history, human survival has often been difficult. During droughts and wars, whole communities struggle to endure. Illicit trade becomes a tool of survival as people smuggle food, shelter their crops from government officials who seek to requisition them, and subsequently consume and sell what they have hidden. The historic fences, whom we met in chapter 1, often served professional criminals who lived on the fringes of society and lacked access to legitimate professions in the highly stratified societies of the premodern world.

Illicit trade was not always associated with the professional criminal world. Individuals poached animals on royal estates, at times for survival, even though the punishments for this activity were always severe across Eurasia and Europe.[6] Animals were poached when European powers set up colonial rule in Africa and Asia and took over the traditional lands of occupied peoples, denying them access to territory they had long depended on for their livelihoods and sustenance.[7]

Today survival is threatened by some of the same challenges that drove earlier human beings to illicit commerce—extreme weather conditions, conflict, and lack of access to employment. But added to the challenges of contemporary survival are the rapid growth of the world population to 7.4 billion, the decline of the earth's resources, including the fish in the sea, arable land, and forests, and increasing numbers of displaced people.

An estimated 68.5 million people are now displaced as a result of conflicts, natural disasters, or desertification and flooding that have made their traditional homes and homelands uninhabitable. The number of refugees and displaced persons now represents almost 1 percent of the world's population, the highest level since records have been collected.[8] Unfortunately, people are displaced to regions where there is little chance for them to find legal employment or be absorbed into the societies where they have moved. Inadequate aid for the 1 percent of the world's displaced population, who are living at the edge of survival, ensures that some will do anything they need to do to live.

Unfortunately, illicit trade is associated not only with the displaced but also with the disadvantaged. In October 2017, there were major protests in Morocco following the tragic death of a Berber fish vendor in the northern city of Hoceima. The fisherman's unauthorized swordfish catch was confiscated and thrown into a garbage truck because it was caught during a prohibited season. The vendor jumped into the truck to retrieve his fish and died when he was crushed by the compactor.[9]

Unlike the Arab Spring uprisings of 2011, there are no apparent indications of corruption involving the seized fish yet. Nevertheless, the fisherman's death sparked protests across rural Morocco that have been intense and sustained in what had been the most stable of North African countries. Many protest the corruption that makes the poor, like the fisherman, dependent on prohibited goods for their livelihood because the state provides no opportunities for people to make a living legitimately.[10] The tragic death of a poor man caught between his need to live and the state's desire to sustain resources reflects many of the challenges of contemporary illicit trade.

The fisherman's situation is all too common in the contemporary world. There is inadequate legitimate work, particularly for youthful populations. In the absence of viable economic alternatives, and with pervasive corruption, people join the parallel market economy, selling smuggled cigarettes, counterfeits, and other contraband goods. Many participants in gray markets buy and sell these products, as they are not as harshly sanctioned as drugs and arms and are not perceived to be as harmful.[11]

Desperation drives people to do things they would not normally consider, even things that run counter to their morality. They will directly trade prohibited goods or facilitate forbidden trade, serve as drug couriers or cash mules, and place themselves in risky situations. Some do so even with the knowledge that they may be forced to face the consequences of their illegal actions, bringing even more devastation to their already difficult lives. When confronted with medical emergencies, some poor families in India and elsewhere sell their children for a fixed number of years to obtain funds for medical care that will ensure the survival of other family members.[12] This trade in human beings is illegal, but in the absence of alternatives, the altruism of family members is given primacy over law. Altruism is also at work when some refugees from Syria sell a kidney to pay for the smuggling of family members to Europe, where they hope they will have the chance of a better life.

It is not just poverty and extreme conditions that can make people desperate. Individuals who have become drug addicts and do not have access to medical treatment, or who have dropped out of care programs, often engage in illicit trade to secure the drugs on which they have become dependent. Women may sell themselves, and addicts of both sexes may trade drugs to others, to secure funds to support their habits. The exponential growth of drug deaths in the United States in the last thirty-five years—reaching 64,000 in 2016—is in part a result of greater consumption of more potent drugs, especially opioids.[13]

POWER, MONEY, AND ILLICIT TRADE

Illicit trade endures because states, companies, and powerful individuals profit from it. Illicit commerce has helped build, as well as destroy, states. Trading in the illicit economy provides financial advantage in an ever more competitive and globalized world. The profit from this trade can be more than financial. States obtain political advantage as a result of illicit commerce, a phenomenon as old as the raids on the caravans of the Silk Road, the pirate ships of antiquity, and the theft of valuable dyes needed to make expensive trade cloth.

States, now as before, are key actors in illicit trade. In the past, they organized attacks on caravans, sanctioned piracy, and even employed privateers to seize the cargo of ships of rival states at times of conflict. Consequently, when states are complicit, the political will needed for an effective response is absent.

Analysis of the past two centuries reveals that illicit trade, in both reflecting state policies and helping to implement them, has important political consequences. For example, Great Britain, at the height of its global power, used drug smuggling into China to undermine the power structures of another country—a commercial assault that was subsequently followed by a military one. In the Second Opium War in the mid-nineteenth century, American and French forces joined the British, scarring the Chinese political and social consciousness long afterwards. May we be observing the revenge of the opium wars in the massive exportation from China of illegally produced fentanyl to the United States, with addictive and deadly consequences for American consumers?

The problem endures—states use illicit trade to maintain their economies, to acquire advanced technologies they did not develop, and to acquire political advantage. This is particularly true of countries under sanctions. The most notorious current example might be North Korea, possibly the one country in the world most dependent on illicit commerce. It has used this trade to generate revenues in the absence of a functioning legitimate economy. Funds generated through trade in drugs, wildlife parts, and cigarettes and the distribution of counterfeit currency, to name just a few of its illegal products, have allowed North Korea to acquire the apparatus and know-how to build a nuclear weapon, thus gaining the wherewithal to intimidate more powerful and economically advanced countries.[14] A key concern is that North Korea may increase its role in the trade in harmful synthetic drugs, especially to the United States, to engage in "dual-use crime" that provides both financial profits and political advantage.

Other states subject to sanctions routinely engage in illicit commerce and use subterfuge to move money. Iran, while under sanctions, has smuggled oil and was determined by an American court to have moved oil sale proceeds through a Turkish state bank.[15] The Crimean economy, after the Russian invasion, has become a hub of illicit trade, and Sudan survived under sanctions through gold smuggling.[16] States imposing sanctions rarely consider that they must enhance efforts to counter the illicit trade that inevitably grows after sanctions are put in place.

The presence of national governments and state-owned companies in the illicit trade of the cyberworld (discussed later in the chapter) is in dramatic ascendency, yet the problem still remains in the real world.[17] In China, which is the factory to the world, there has been massive growth in the production of counterfeits and their exportation, as indicated by World Trade Organization (WTO) seizure data. These counterfeits, as discussed, include food, baby formula, beverages, pesticides, medicines, purses, clothing, and electronics, just to name a few of the most pervasive categories.[18] These counterfeits not only violate intellectual property rights but have killed many people—as highly potent opioids are consumed, faulty car parts kill numerous drivers in the Middle East, and damaging pesticides permanently harm soils around the world. Elements of the counterfeit trade are harmful to both human life and planetary well-being.

The leaders of many states, and their families, are prime beneficiaries of illicit commerce, often avoiding sanctions by cloaking themselves in the power of the state. We identified this problem with the former president and prime minister of Montenegro, who used his state positions to resist Italian investigators in their attempts to curtail his large-scale cigarette smuggling. At other times, often for reasons of political expediency, governments ignore the illicit trade of national leaders in the name of "national security." This was certainly the case when the United States and its allies tolerated the drug trade of the Karzai family, in the name of larger political objectives. The consequence of this willful blindness was to see the hard-won efforts to oust the Taliban eroded by accommodation to the criminality and corruption of the Afghan leadership. The Afghan heroin business doubled in 2016, according to the UNODC, from its level the previous year and now represents $3 billion annually, or about 16 percent of the country's gross domestic product.[19] The consequences of this trade are felt globally.

One need not go to the heads of states to meet the powerful facilitators of illicit activity. Illicit trade could not be carried out without both high-level and lower-level forms of corruption. Transnational corruption has facilitated its global growth.

Corruption-facilitated illicit trade undermines governance, the economy, health, the social order, and sustainability in all regions of the globe. Illicit actors intentionally penetrate the state, often entering legislative bodies to shape laws in their favor. They join the security apparatus, ministries of justice, judiciaries, law enforcement—particularly customs and border patrol—to ensure the absence of effective law enforcement. Legal provisions preventing the prosecution of legislators and state officials serve as an added incentive to "engage in government service." Some have described this as state capture. Once, kings could be ransomed after they were taken by their enemies. But with contemporary state capture, there is little chance of release. Few countries have

managed to oust the illicit networks once they have become en-
tangled in governmental structures.[20]

Like corruption, fear is a great motivator of human conduct. Illicit trade has often been accompanied by violence, whether it was
terrifying pirates, the cutthroat fences of Elizabethan and Dicken-
sian England, or, more recently, brutally vengeful drug traffickers.
The wealth and power of the networks behind illegal commerce enables them to reach high officials. Threats by criminal traders against
government ministers, civil servants, and their families often result
in co-optation, death, or exile. The many who choose the first rather
than the last two are complicit in not just the hollowing out of the
state but its capitulation.

STATE POLICY AND ILLICIT TRADE

Tax evasion has always been an important incentive for many
traders who sell highly taxed commodities sought by consumers.
This is well documented by the emerging field of historical analysis
of contraband and smuggling. In the past, as well as now, regulations on trade perceived as unfair or unacceptable to citizens became major drivers of smuggling and illicit commerce. Today there
are ever-greater bureaucratic obstacles to trade, as the number
of countries in the world has increased and each sovereign state
has its own tax rates and policies. Regulatory policy combined
with a concomitant rise in the number of borders creates greater
incentives to smuggle. Therefore, evading taxes remains an ongoing driver of illicit trade, particularly for products such as alcohol,
cigarettes, and luxury commodities, which have consistently been
taxed at high rates.

TRUST AND MARKETPLACES

Trust was key in the markets of the past, where individuals traded
tangible goods. Historically, in environments with little trust, mechanisms developed to ensure the quality of the products sold. A widely
recognized analysis of the rise of the Mafia in Sicily explains that

this criminal organization grew through its provision of services—its certification of horses and other valuable commodities sold in the markets of Sicily that were characterized by little trust.[21] Now we have rating systems for products sold online, both the web and the Dark Web, but no one to certify the authenticity or the objectivity of the ratings, or the risks posed by the products.[22] The regulations that apply to the sale of products in real markets and cyberspace do not apply in the virtual world. *Caveat emptor* (buyer beware) applies, but most citizens are not aware that what is sold in online platforms is not subject to oversight. Citizen knowledge of risks must be expanded as online marketplaces continue to grow, offering many more products that could place buyers at risk.[23]

NON-STATE ACTORS AND ILLICIT TRADE

Illicit trade plays a significant role in the power and economic equations not only of states but also of nonstate actors. Rebels, revolutionaries, insurgents, terrorists, and criminals understand the utility of illicit trade not just as an income source but also as a means of obtaining leverage over society. In some cases, engaging in smuggling is a sign of patriotism, an assertion of national interests over those of a foreign power. When this is the case, there is a pride in smuggling. In other situations, smuggling is merely a means to an end.

CONFLICTS AND ILLICIT TRADE

Revolutionaries fighting against autocratic rulers and colonial powers have relied on illicit trade for financing and arms. This was true in the Mexican and American Revolutions in North America and in the later colonial struggles in Africa and Asia. Since the end of the Cold War, and again after the Arab Spring of 2011, we have had an ever-expanding number of conflicts, and the lives of ever more people have been uprooted by these conflicts. The contributions to illicit trade of the Balkan Wars, the insurgencies in the DRC, and the ongoing conflicts in Syria and Iraq should not be underestimated. Each of these conflicts has resulted in instability and destruction, but in different ways.[24] A legacy of illicit commerce in the Balkans during the conflict there was the emergence of long-standing criminal networks in Europe. These now play a key role in contemporary drug, arms, and human trafficking, as well as in human smuggling within and into Europe.

The conflict in the DRC has resulted in massive poaching of elephants, giraffes, and other wildlife for sale outside of Africa.[25] A massive arms trade within the country and the region has facilitated the slaughter of animals as well as the murder of the rangers who seek to protect the wildlife. The mining of the conflict mineral coltan, an essential element of cell phones and other electronics, by workers and children, in slavelike conditions, in the DRC clearly illustrates the link between conflict, illicit trade, and global human consumption of illicitly sourced products.

The massive illicit revenues from oil sales by ISIS, other terrorist groups, and officials of the Assad government have contributed to the prolongation of the Syrian conflict. Of the once-total population of 22 million in Syria, six in ten had been displaced from their homes by 2016, the highest percentage ever recorded for a single country.[26] Most of these people have nothing to return to because of the massive infrastructure destruction. In the absence of a viable and legitimate economy, the entrenched illicit networks perpetuate violence and destruction. As has been identified in earlier studies of conflict, greed rather than grievance is central to the duration of the Syrian conflict.[27]

TERRORISM AND ILLICIT TRADE

Terrorists, once largely supported by states, moved heavily into the drug trade as a revenue source after the superpower conflict ended in 1991. More recently, terrorists have diversified their trade commodities, as epitomized by the oil trading of ISIS. The United Nations Security Council, in late 2014 and early 2015, recognized this transition in resolutions 2195 and 2199, which articulate the links between transnational crime, illicit trade in diverse commodities, and the funding of terrorism.[28] The rare consensus within the leadership body of the United Nations reflects the universality of the problem across the globe.

Illicit commerce funds not only terrorism at the center of conflicts such as in Iraq, Syria, Afghanistan, Libya, and West Africa, but also smaller-scale terrorist attacks in developed countries, such as have been seen in France, Belgium, and Spain. Small-scale illicit trade in drugs, counterfeits, cigarettes, and other commodities has helped finance many of the terrorists and their attacks in recent years in Continental Europe. Moreover, a hybrid criminal-terrorist is increasingly observed: a preponderance of today's European terrorists have criminal pasts, often in small-scale illicit commerce.[29] The pattern has apparently been observed elsewhere but is not as well documented as in Europe, where perpetrators' pasts and networks are examined intensively.

RESPECT FOR THE LAW AND ILLICIT TRADE

Terrorism is a violent and overt form of resistance to state authority, but illicit trade not tied to such visible acts of resistance as terrorism may also have less apparent political dimensions. Returning to the rhino case study, detailed interviews of individuals involved in the trade in South Africa revealed that traders, both black Africans who lived near the parks and white farmers who bred rhinoceroses, did not acknowledge the validity of the law.[30] For the black South Africans, the parks were created through colonial expropriation of their native lands, and for white farmers, the criminalization of the trade deprived them of a revenue source without compensation.

The rhino horn example clearly illustrates a more universal problem. Individuals participate in illicit trade because they do not recognize the validity either of state laws or of transnational legal codes. The discussion of Dread Pirate Roberts revealed that the mastermind of the online marketplace Silk Road in the Dark Web was a libertarian who did not acknowledge the validity of drug prohibition laws.[31] In other contexts, individuals do not recognize state monopolies, whether of the type given to kings, as we saw in pre-revolutionary France, or the type assumed by dictators today. Therefore, smuggling is sometimes a form of nonviolent individual resistance.

OPPORTUNISM AND ENTREPRENEURSHIP

Much of illicit trade, like its legitimate counterpart, is motivated by profit rather than politics. The profits for those at the top of the illicit pyramid are enormous. Illicit entrepreneurs can make large profits as they traffic in, or produce, illicit and/or deliberately harmful products, such as old and new forms of narcotic and addictive drugs, illicit pesticides, or products that ransom or enslave computers. Some major drug traffickers—not just in cocaine but also in painkillers—have become billionaires.[32] But there are many more diverse beneficiaries.

Unfortunately, human entrepreneurship has often been channeled into copying the successful commodities of competitors rather than in developing unique new products to trade in markets, leading to the massive rise of counterfeiting that the global community faces these days. Counterfeiting is more than trademark violations; it sometimes includes the production of illicit goods with great potential harm to purchasers. In late 2016, one million counterfeit copies of the potentially deadly painkiller Xanax were confiscated in the Bronx after being purchased over the Dark Web.[33] Illicit trade is also going on in intellectual property and the products of the future.

Corporations ensure their competitiveness in an increasingly global marketplace by participating in illicit commerce. Volkswagen sold 11 million cars worldwide equipped with software that turned off the emissions controls when the car was being driven. Without this software, these cars did not meet emission standards and could not be sold. After being investigated in both the United States and the European Union, Volkswagen paid a $2.8 billion fine at the time of its conviction.[34] Purdue Pharma, the privately held company selling oxycontin, a key drug abused in the opioid epidemic, generated $1 billion to $3 billion annually for the Sackler family and the company; its top executives were successfully prosecuted for misrepresenting the impact of this opioid.[35] The owners of Backpage

generated annual bonuses for themselves of $10 million by conniv-
ing with a Philippine online outsourcing company, Avion, to mask
that they were marketing juveniles for sexual exploitation on their
website in the United States, the United Kingdom, and Australia, in
violation of American human trafficking laws.[36] These are just some
of the corporations investigated or sanctioned for their role in illicit
commerce.

Civil cases against major banks for laundering the proceeds of the
drug trade and against United Parcel Service for illegally shipping
cigarettes reflect the range of businesses that facilitate illicit trade.
These cases transpired in the United States and western Europe despite the existence of well-developed and -funded investigative apparatuses and legal systems. In other parts of the world, corporations
and Chinese state-owned fishing vessels engage in illegal fishing and
companies transport harmful pesticides, but countries may only be
able to seize the ship or impound the cargo. They lack any capacity
to hold the company to account. Therefore, they fail to realize one
of the fundamental principles of deterrence, articulated by Cesare
Beccaria a few centuries ago: the certainty of punishment is more
important than its severity.[37] In not adhering to this principle, these
countries ensure the perpetuation of these harmful practices.

High-level officials can often benefit greatly from their involvement in illicit trade. Chapter 7, "Destroyers of the Planet," revealed
the vast profits made by Southeast Asian officials involved in the
illicit timber trade. Narcotics trafficking has brought large sums to
corrupt heads of state and their families in Latin America, Africa,
and Asia. High-level corrupt officials protecting illicit commerce can
receive tens of millions of dollars in bribes and protection money.
They also trade in influence, an increasingly prevalent form of corruption that does not involve the transfer of tangible goods or money
but does provide for the acquisition of power and often subsequent
financial advantage and wealth in some form.

Individuals and corporations persist in this activity because they
rarely suffer reputational damage. Quite the reverse. As our historical
analysis shows, leading American figures and their families engaged
in smuggling for profit in the past without suffering opprobrium.

The same is true elsewhere. The famous Italian novel *The Leopard* realistically depicts Sicilian society in the mid-nineteenth century in recounting the story of the marriage of a mafioso's daughter into the Sicilian nobility.[38] Similar marriages have occurred more recently in Colombia and Mexico. The offspring of these blended families of the leaders of the criminal economy now dominate the tops of these stratified societies.

Today the reputations of those who have earned their money from illicit trade or its facilitation can be varnished through philanthropy. Many of the major foundations in the United States were started by so-called robber barons. Presently, many museums in major cities have wings or buildings named after individuals who earned their money in dark commerce.[39] Dubious corporate sponsors support individual exhibitions; many sponsors have previously been sanctioned for their participation in illicit trade and accompanying malfeasance. Universities are often more careful in conducting due diligence on the source of donors' funds, but not all the time. For instance, Dmitry Firtash contributed $6 million to Cambridge University, starting in 2010, to develop Ukrainian studies. Long a shady figure, his high-level protection in Ukraine vanished after a change in government. After he had fallen out of favor, he was arrested in Austria in 2017 as a result of many investigations in the United States and Spain for his involvement in international organized crime.[40]

CULTURE

Another reason illicit trade persists is that its perpetrators are often glorified in popular culture. In pre-revolutionary France (discussed in chapter 1), the smuggler Louis Mandrin was glorified in many songs of the era.[41] More recently, the *narcocorrido* emerged, a Spanish-language song extolling drug traffickers in Latin America. Recently in Russia, the tradition of the *chanson*—Russian-language songs emanating from the prison camp culture of the Stalin period—is perpetuated in songs extolling the criminal activity of high-level criminals.[42] In the United States, the glorification of the pimp culture, in song and film, has become so pervasive that you can go to the internet and find the top twenty songs extolling human traffickers, with titles such as "P.I.M.P." and "Bad Girls."[43] Just Google "pimps in films" and many sites appear, offering the viewer films that celebrate the pimp dating back almost five decades.[44] The glorification of the criminal world and its role in smuggling, the drug trade, and human trafficking, in the Russian, Latin American, and historic French context, indicates that popular culture helps perpetuate tolerance for this activity. In contrast, the American glorification of the criminal world is not sui generis but generated by the powerful and well-financed film and music industries.

What Comes Next?

The problems are already severe, but we can anticipate further serious challenges in the coming years that may exacerbate already serious problems for the earth's inhabitants. No category of crime has shown marked decline, apart from the illicit trade in CFCs. The illicit trade in species is expanding in numbers, as markets for endangered and protected species become even more geographically dispersed, and criminal trade of the vital resources of the planet is also escalating.

Antiquities smuggling has expanded dramatically, not only of objects from the famed sources of Western civilization in what was once Mesopotamia, now known as Syria and Iraq, but also of the objects of pre-Colombian civilizations of the New World. Human beings are moving, in response to violence, civil conflict, climate change, and an absence of employment. Mass displacement is at an all-time high, accompanied by its illicit elements, human smuggling and trafficking, and the forces driving illegal migration are not dissipating but intensifying. As individuals increasingly contract with smugglers to move them across borders, the territorial integrity of states remains challenged.

The new technology and its ability to rapidly expand illicit trade, particularly through online markets and the Dark Web, will continue to challenge the state in important ways. The private sector's ownership of social media and online platforms provides new challenges to their regulation. These new businesses that enhance connectivity are more interested in producing a profit than in spending money to ensure the security of their users or to filter out malicious traders and abusers. Attention has recently been paid to the propagation of false news and terrorist recruitment through these media, but insufficient attention has been brought to their role in expanding pernicious illicit commerce in the virtual world and through social media. Cryptocurrencies, some devised specifically to evade state regulation and facilitate illicit trade, will be increasingly used by illicit nonstate actors for illegal commerce. These readily accessed currencies can facilitate global financial movements by individuals who cannot use traditional banking easily or affordably, but the unregulated expansion of these currencies provides many opportunities for even more abuse in the future.

As the "Internet of Things" becomes pervasive in future decades and individuals become increasingly connected, societies will be all the more vulnerable to the illicit traders who traffic in commodities, based on algorithms that hijack passwords, propagate malware, and steal identities. These new readily traded tools of cybercriminals have already caused billions in damage to individuals, institutions, and companies. Intellectual property theft will expand as cybercriminals and state-sponsored criminals break into computers to steal and trade future inventions and products. This criminal activity will have a major impact on global economic competition.

The Weberian concept that the state should have a monopoly on violence is defied by the expanding illicit trade in arms, a problem worsening with the advent of 3-D printing, which may facilitate access and trade in weapons outside of any controls. North Korea's nuclear program, which challenges global security, has been financed in part by illicit commerce. It may be a harbinger of the means by which rogue states survive in the international order.

Narcotics traffickers are finding new customers as they produce an ever-larger array of new products to sell. Many of these new drugs are synthetics, rather than drugs derived from agricultural production, and are created through the innovation of highly skilled individuals in the most profitable sectors of illicit trade. This shift deprives farmers of revenue and reduces the complexity of supply chains, allowing manufacture closer to customers. In the future, there may be greater abuse of medical products, custommade drugs, and drugs like fentanyl. The violence, corruption, and health risks associated with these drugs are not likely to subside in the future, despite the movement of trade into the cyberworld. The many underemployed and dissatisfied youths provide a willing market for these products. With the increasing mechanization of daily life, such as self-driving vehicles, there may be many economically displaced individuals, especially in the developed world, who begin consuming drugs. The focus of drug policies on enforcement rather than prevention, treatment, and economic development suggests no abatement in widespread drug abuse internationally.

The exacerbating impacts of climate change, seen particularly in sub-Saharan Africa, the Middle East, Pakistan, and the Bay of Bengal, will create conditions that foster emigration. Few countries are willing to take displaced and desperate people. Therefore, residents of these vulnerable regions, searching for locales where there is water to drink, inhabitable land, and stability, will resort even more to smugglers to facilitate their movement. But the areas to which they move, if unprepared for these new settlers, may be destabilized by the mass migrations to come. Human trafficking and smuggling will be defining issues of the twenty-first century.[45]

Illicit trade's impact on the sustainability of the planet will compound the other environmental challenges caused by growing populations, deforestation, and climate change. Unfortunately, illicit traders have already shown their capacity to capitalize on the resource scarcity of our planet by seeking to capitalize on the global community's efforts to mitigate the impact of climate change. Addressing these challenges requires both strategy and large-scale financial resources. Unfortunately, much of the trillions of dollars needed to bring about meaningful change is located in offshore locales, where the holders of these funds evade taxes rather than contribute the resources needed to implement meaningful change at a critical moment for the planet.

This summation looks dire. In the final chapter, I will look at diverse ways of trying to reverse the tragic trajectory of many forms of illicit trade. Can the new technologies dramatically transforming trade be restrained to limit their illicit exponential growth? Can we find the political will and the commitment of the citizens of different societies to address the rapidly accelerating growth of so many forms of illicit trade?

Conclusion

COUNTERING THE CHALLENGES
POSED BY ILLICIT TRADE

Combating the explosive growth of illicit trade requires diverse and sometimes unconventional approaches that transcend previously taken measures. Steps must be taken at the global, national, and even community level.[1] The Paris Agreement on climate change was signed by 195 countries of the planet (although President Trump is now going through a multiyear process to withdraw from it), all of whom agreed to controls limiting carbon emissions, thereby slowing the extent of climate change. Is the global community also ready to work together to address dark commerce and the factors contributing to its growth? Countering illicit trade may not be as dependent on a global agreement as the Paris accord, but it requires serious and concerted action to address the large-scale environmental and natural resource crime that is undermining sustainability and driving the exponential growth in online trade, especially in the Dark Net, and through social media.

Inadequate measures to regulate trade, in both the real and virtual worlds, have resulted in supply chains lacking transparency. This has led to outsourcing to manufacturers that use trafficked labor and allowed platforms in the virtual world to sell items that are harmful, inauthentic, or not authorized for sale. In the absence of regulation, items such as antiquities, counterfeits, fentanyl and other very harmful synthetic drugs, and the body parts of endangered wildlife are readily available for purchase online.

Greater regulation of online platforms and cryptocurrencies that facilitate the exponential growth of illicit commerce in cyberspace is needed. At present, the most economically powerful countries in the G-7 and the G-20 have yet to make these issues a priority. Illicit commerce needs to be a more central concern for these important policy groups.

Two decades ago, Susan Strange noted that markets have outgrown governments; illicit trade and entrepreneurship exemplify this problem.[2] Moreover, states and multinational institutions alone cannot respond to the challenges posed by the illicit economy, because pernicious nonstate actors interact and collaborate with corrupt state officials across diverse jurisdictions. Many sectors of the business community need to respond significantly and consistently to the problems posed by illicit trade, but unfortunately, some serve willingly or inadvertently as facilitators of this deleterious commerce. Civil society, acting through local communities and multinational NGOs, must be a key actor in curbing harmful illegal commerce. Investigative journalists are key in exposing dark commerce, its perpetrators, and its routes.

No Grand Strategy

No grand strategy is capable of arresting illicit trade, nor is there any single means to slow its present rapid evolution. Illicit trade encompasses many more activities than just arms, drugs, and human trafficking, and our failure to recognize this problem contributes to our poor and ineffective responses. We need to stop stovepiping our reactions: it is only the responders, not the perpetrators, who categorize illicit trade. Unless the international community addresses the full range of illegal commerce, the perpetrators and facilitators of illicit trade, after evaluating the risks and rewards of entering new illicit markets, will merely shift to different commodities.

Illicit trade cannot be addressed by the overarching strategies used in the past by military leaders and heads of state to counter the threats faced by their societies. The conventional approach is to harness the coercive security apparatus of states and multinational organizations—to use military or law enforcement to combat problems. Investigating and punishing the perpetrators is not sufficient. Mitigating the harm to the environment and to human security caused by illicit trade requires prevention, resilient communities, and strategies to stem the supply and distribution of illegally traded products. It also requires giving individuals incentives to stay in their countries of origin. For example, a modern-day Marshall Plan may be needed to ensure that everyone has legitimate employment opportunities in their home country. Punishing the perpetrators of illicit trade may deter others, but it does not reverse the permanent harm that has already been done to individuals who must flee their homes, nor does it address the damage to life on earth through forms of illicit trade.

The Trans-Pacific Partnership (TPP), adopted in 2016 after eleven years of negotiations, tries to increase transparency, ensure the integrity of supply chains, and reduce corruption among the dozen signatory countries, which have close to 800 million in population. One of President Trump's first acts was to withdraw from this partnership, illustrating the difficulty of relying on collaborative action by governments in the contemporary period.[3] In recent decades, the slow pace of adoption and controversial nature of trade agreements and regulations have allowed illicit trade to expand.[4]

To develop strategies to counter the challenges of illicit commerce, we must not only address the present problems but also anticipate future negative developments, however challenging that may be in an era of rapid transformation in illegal commerce, both in cyberspace and in the commodities of illicit traders. The key to meeting this challenge is developing the political will to ensure that needed strategies will be adopted and implemented. Changing economic incentives and disincentives to encourage behavior in the desired direction to nudge people is also essential.[5]

Certain realities that limit our ability to take these actions are unlikely to change in the coming decades: increasing global population; state-based legal systems and governance focused on national rather than transnational laws; the increasing impact and disruption of life by new technologies; corruption at all levels of society; enduring income inequalities within and among countries; gender inequality; the endurance of regional conflicts; the continued importance of nonstate actors, including multinational corporations; greater resource scarcity; and the increasing impact of climate change[6]

Countering illicit trade requires the input of crime specialists, but it also requires action and involvement from a much broader community.[7] It necessitates more than controlling the size of the world's population and the demands that the planet's inhabitants make on its resources. Stemming the growth of illicit trade demands a rethink of the financial system to provide more transparency, strong anticorruption measures, and the targeting of the diverse facilitators that perpetuate illicit commerce. Furthermore, it requires a corporate culture, especially in the rapidly evolving tech world, more committed to curbing trade in outlawed commodities and ensuring the transparency of supply chains.

We need to focus more on human security and resilient communities to ensure that women, children, and the displaced, now disproportionately victims of illicit trade, do not suffer in such large numbers in the future. Corruption is key to the perpetration of illicit trade, and its control needs to be at the core of all strategies to combat this commerce. The women active in anti-corruption movements globally therefore have a key role to play in combating dark commerce.

Policymakers who seek to address these broader challenges must understand and incorporate the phenomenon of illicit trade into their analyses. Where do we start to preserve the planet and the lives of the species inhabiting it? What has worked in the past? What might have lessons for the future? Can a more business- or community-oriented approach, rather than a state-based methodology, help address illicit trade?

Legal and Regulatory Policy

Since the introduction of the UN Convention against Transnational Organized Crime and its related protocols in late 2000, the lead approach to the most severe forms of illicit trade has been enhanced use of the criminal law and process. In this environment, the benchmark of success is the number of perpetrators arrested, charged, and sentenced. Yet this may not be the most appropriate measure of success. Prosecutions are limited and have rarely proven an effective deterrent.

In the nearly two decades since the adoption of the Convention, human trafficking, for example, has evolved from an issue of human rights to a criminal act sanctioned by almost all countries in the world. The failure to harmonize laws has helped perpetuate this activity, and many traffickers bifurcate their activities among different jurisdictions, knowing that the absence of consistent laws makes prosecution of their activity difficult.

Illustrative of the extreme disparity of legal response to human trafficking are the responses of two high-income countries of the European Union. Sweden has criminalized the purchase of sexual services, whereas the Netherlands has legalized the maintenance of brothels, provided that their employees have work permits.[8] Neither policy has ended human trafficking. Moreover, the recent arrival in Sweden of smuggled migrants has undermined enforcement efforts, as these vulnerable people are subject to diverse forms of human exploitation.[9]

Relying primarily on a coercive response to illicit trade has other limitations. The criminal networks and supply chains for illicit products are global, whereas no international police force presently exists. Enforcement relies on a state-based system, whereas the criminals function multinationally. Nowhere is this more evident than in the cyberworld. In this anonymized world, the locale of the perpetrators is not known and sometimes is unknowable.

Many legal responses to illicit traders are based on outdated conceptions, such as going after perpetrators as if they headed hierarchical criminal organizations. More often, however, as criminal organizations have evolved, we are looking at network structures rather than top-down organizations. Criminal networks today more closely resemble the new distributed corporate structures of the technology world than the older hierarchical structures of a Ford or a Xerox. Thus, the naming of kingpins through the Foreign Narcotics Kingpin Designation Act, in place since 1999 in the United States, focuses on removing the heads of traditional criminal organizations, but implementation of the act in Latin America has failed because taking out "kingpins" merely provides a key promotion opportunity for underlings.[10] Moreover, this enforcement approach sometimes leads to the proliferation of harmful organizations rather than the elimination of consolidated ones. Legal responses to illicit trade must reflect an understanding of the nature of the problem that often can only be achieved through research. Current research helps us understand the need to focus on illicit and facilitating networks as a means to combating illicit trade.[11]

State and multinational institutions often cannot effectively combat the illicit economy because malicious nonstate actors interact and collaborate with corrupt officials. Indeed, smuggling research reveals the centrality of state authorities to this trade.[12] In many countries, institutions are undermined from both within and without. Corruption in law enforcement, the judiciary, border patrols, custom services, and the military undermines the possibility of an effective response to illicit commerce. Therefore, an international criminal court that focuses on anti-corruption may help address dark commerce where there are no internal actors or institutions capable of checking state corruption.[13]

Military missions and peacekeepers authorized to enter conflict regions often lack the training or the capacity to combat illicit trade, and in the worst cases they are complicit in its commission. Participants in peacekeeping efforts in the Balkans, for instance, trafficked women.[14] Officers, operating under orders, may purchase smuggled oil to complete combat missions. The impunity of corrupt officials and peacekeepers must not be tolerated. Anti-corruption strategies must be at the core of combating illicit trade, in both law enforcement and the military.

Criminal law has been put to extensive use against diverse forms of illicit trade only recently. In the past, administrative law and regulations were the prime mechanisms used to counter illicit trade. Some analysts believe that prohibition regimes and high tax rates have been conducive to the growth of illicit trade; they argue that increased regulation has created illegal commerce because individuals and groups are seen as seeking to force their morality on others.[15] To these critics, illicit trade is simply a response to governmental regulation.[16] This book offers a contrary view—that some regulation, particularly in the environmental area seeking to protect natural resources, stems not from morality but from scientific analyses of the measures needed to sustain life on the planet.

Far too little attention has been paid by states to optimizing tax rates. Cigarettes are one of the most commonly bought illicit commodities, but there has been limited analysis by state bodies or independent researchers to determine the tax rates that drive citizens to purchase items outside of regulated markets. The disparities in tax rates in different US states or different countries in Europe are conducive to cigarette smuggling. For example, cigarettes are smuggled from North Carolina, where they are lightly taxed, to Michigan, where they are highly taxed, providing a funding mechanism for both criminals and terrorists.[17] France is a center of smuggled cigarettes in Europe in part because of its high tax rates relative to neighboring states.

Research and analysis can go a long way in helping us develop rational policies. But analyses of corruption and illicit markets were almost absent from the economics literature twenty-five years ago, and the situation has not improved dramatically since.[18]

The regulations protecting the pharmaceutical industry in the United States combine with widespread lack of insurance to compel some citizens to turn to illicit markets to obtain needed prescription drugs, as is the case in the developing world. The answer to this growth in illicit trade in medicines is not just better regulatory policies, or crackdowns on the illicit online pharmacies that sell these drugs, but improving access to health care and making medicine more affordable. As this discussion on responses will repeatedly show, effective answers to illicit trade require not just reactions to specific actions but often strategies that approach the problem with a completely different toolbox.

Awareness and Education

The full consequences of the growth and dramatic transformation of illicit commerce in the past thirty years are poorly understood, as few understand the significance of the shift to online and social media platforms and the targeting of the earth's resources. Citizens must demand greater consumer protections and greater vigilance over online platforms to ensure that they take responsibility for what they sell. Public-private partnerships are key to obtaining this result.

The opioid epidemic is growing exponentially in the United States because too few young people understand the threat to their lives posed by the drugs they consume. Education and information campaigns have not been sufficient to counter this dangerous and profitable form of illicit trade run by transnational criminals. The United States is not the only locale that has failed to effectively inform its citizens about the dangers of opioids, but its failure stands out because of the unique level of fatalities from illegal drug consumption in this country.

The billions of people now participating in, and victimized by, illicit trade must be educated about and made aware of the prevalence and costs of illicit trade—not just narcotics and prescription opioids but also unregulated pharmaceutical drugs. Social and online media can, and should, play a key role. If false news can reach hundreds of millions of readers, we can also design information alerts on the threats of illicit trade. Public service announcements by celebrities to try to prevent the consumption of rhino horn have been just the first step in outreach on that issue, but they seem to have had some success in raising awareness in Asia of the costs of this trade and in introducing shame, which is key to controlling illicit commerce in that cultural context.[19]

Multilateral organizations, such as the International Labour Organization (ILO), the International Organization for Migration

(IOM), the Organization for Economic Cooperation and Development (OECD), the Organization for Security and Cooperation in Europe (OSCE), and the United Nations Office on Drugs and Crime (UNODC), also use press conferences, online and social media, and meetings to raise awareness of the personal, social, and economic costs of illicit trade. Some of these organizations specialize: the IOM tackles human smuggling, and ILO focuses on labor issues. Others, such as OECD, have taken a more holistic approach, setting up a significant working group on illicit trade whose participants come from government, civil society, academia, business, and multilateral organizations.[20] Unfortunately, other multinational organizations, such as the World Trade Organization, have focused on trade liberalization and pay insufficient attention to illicit commerce.[21]

Popular culture needs not only to question its glorification of the illicit but also to raise awareness about its harms. Hollywood in the 1930s, through its gangster movies, exposed the pernicious impact of organized crime on community violence and municipal corruption. Today diverse forms of entertainment media must rise to the challenge and contribute to the solution, not just the problem.

Fortunately, some recent movies on human trafficking have raised awareness of the pervasiveness of the problem and the harm it causes. These films, produced in many regions of the world and shown to local and international audiences, reveal the brutality of human trafficking and acute labor exploitation in many regions.[22] These films often show that those suffering are not just the victims but also their families and even their entire community. Broader exposure to these films, as well as television shows such as *Ozark* and *Breaking Bad*, which address the drug trade and the violence related to it, also helps to raise awareness.

Religious institutions in many regions of the world help communicate the harms caused by illicit trade in drugs, people, and other commodities. The heads of many communities of faith have addressed the illicit commerce harming the larger community, and some have mobilized members of their congregations to work against this destructive phenomenon. Two decades ago, religious leaders in Sicily and Colombia collaborated on programs to keep community members out of the drug trade and safe from addiction in environments in which drug trafficking was pervasive.[23] Religious leaders have even been threatened for opposing the drug trade. More than twenty priests in Sicily acknowledged that they were intimidated, and the archbishop of Guadalajara, Mexico, was killed in a drug-related shooting in 1995.[24]

Diverse civil society groups play a key role in preventing and even combating illicit trade in its different forms. Kailash Satyarthi, who won the Nobel Peace Prize in 2014 for freeing Indian children from slavery-like conditions, mobilized massive marches to counter this form of trafficking, at great risk not only to himself but to members of his family.[25]

Some groups, such as TRAFFIC of the World Wildlife Fund and numerous other anti-trafficking groups, are dedicated exclusively to combating a single form of illicit trade. By contrast, the actions of many other groups against illicit trade are part of a larger mission. This is characteristic of larger conservation organizations, groups seeking to address victims of conflict, and humanitarian organizations seeking to aid refugees and migrants. Specialized groups focus on the issue of supply chains and human consumption, campaigning against the sale of goods produced by trafficked laborers, the sale of unsustainable and threatened fish, or the exploitation of children used to produce the cocoa that goes into chocolate.[26] Many NGOs have effective dissemination strategies that drive home the size and severity of human smuggling, arms trade, and poaching—to name a few of their key messaging topics. Campaigns launched by citizen groups to buy sustainable products and purchase fair-trade items not only raise consumer consciousness but also ensure that corporations are more diligent about their supply chains.

Powerful actions against illicit trade operate less visibly at the community level, but are key to developing resilient communities and ensuring the sustainability of life. For example, local organizations such as farmers' cooperatives educate their members on the specific harms of illicitly traded products, such as counterfeit pesticides. In India, some empowered community groups establish buying programs for their members to ensure the purchase and delivery of quality products.[27] Cumulatively, these local organizations reach tens of millions of farmers. Similar community efforts, as will be discussed, are being initiated to preserve fish in the sea as well as the quality of the soil. Significant innovations are also being implemented in Africa—for example, using cell phones to alert potential victims to the threat of counterfeit medications, which is a significant problem in countries where substandard medicines are rampant.[28]

Outreach in developed countries can be conducted through exhibitions, which can be an effective messaging strategy: surveys reveal that museums are among the most trusted of institutions. For example, the highly visited Victoria and Albert Museum (V&A) in London has a permanent exhibition that includes description and illustration of the historical smuggling of expensive textiles. A recent exhibition on plywood at the V&A had a whole section on supply chains for illegally logged timber, showing how timber from protected tree species is turned into plywood that is used by unaware consumers, as those felling the trees deliberately disguise the illicit origin of the timber.[29]

Modern art museums that focus on contemporary themes are replete with examples of the centrality of illicit trade to contemporary life. In Paris, a recent exhibition of African art at the Louis Vuitton Foundation had a whole room of decorated plastic containers previously used to smuggle oil.[30]

Investigative journalists are on the front line in combating illicit trade, often at great risk to their lives. Maltese journalist Daphne Caruana Galizia, a member of the Panama Papers team and part of an oil smuggling investigation team, was blown up in her car by a bomb in mid-October 2017.[31] Her murder was unusual, as she was working in a member state of the EU. The Committee to Protect Journalists reports that, regrettably, 46 journalists died in 2017, many residing in the developing world, where corrupt officials and organized crime can strike out with impunity at the journalists who expose their activities.[32] This problem is not recent. Between 2006 and 2016, 930 journalists were killed worldwide—or approximately one every four days.[33]

Despite the enormous risks to their lives, journalists are increasingly banding together to share information and train their colleagues on how to better investigate crime and illicit trade in groups such as the International Consortium of Investigative Journalists (ICIJ), the Global Investigative Journalism Network (GJIN), and the Organized Crime and Corruption Reporting Project (OCCRP).[34] None of these groups existed in its present form more than fifteen years ago, but their increasing membership and global reach reveal their vitality and the appreciation of the need for effective journalism to root out corruption, crime, and illicit commerce.

Illicit trade has negatively affected many businesses, especially through the smuggling and counterfeiting of their goods. Most large companies choose to address this problem exclusively in reference to their own organization's needs. They create significant units staffed to combat illicit trade in the commodity they produce. But few have made the larger problem of illicit trade a corporate priority. An exception is Philip Morris International (PMI), which has focused on illicit trade through conferences, research support, and the establishment of a $100 million fund to combat illicit trade and related crimes.[35] Less visible have been the lead actors in the pharmaceutical industry, although the decades-old Pharmaceutical Security Institute tries to increase knowledge about the prevalence and costs of counterfeit medicines.[36] Both the International Chamber of Commerce and the US Chamber of Commerce have raised the visibility of the counterfeiting problem, but this has not been a priority of these business bodies. Businesses are cooperating with governments and NGOs through the OECD Task Force on Countering Illicit Trade.[37] More corporations with products traded in both the real and virtual worlds must become active in working against illicit trade, not just for their personal corporate interests but also as part of a broader strategy of corporate social responsibility.

Changing the Environment and the Mentality Facilitating Illicit Trade

Communities can and should create environments less conducive to harmful commerce. Bristol, a southern port city in England, provides an excellent example. Bristol was a major slave-trading center before this commerce became illegal. Many rural women from southwest England were shipped to Ireland to be slaves before the Norman Conquest in AD 1066. After the conquest, this conduct was prohibited by church leadership and the Crown, but the trade continued, through subterfuge, for a significant period. Bristol's tradition as a hub for slave trading continued, and leaders of the city subsequently played a key role in the African slave trade.[38] In fact, the cathedral now contains a sign indicating, with regret, that one of its largest donors made his fortune trading slaves. Memorials, wall murals, and signs throughout the city recall this dark element of the city's commerce. Along with the slave trade, other illegal forms of activity thrived; the famous pirate novel of Robert Louis Stevenson, *Treasure Island*, is set along the docks of the city. But Bristol has been transformed, and now it is a bustling city based on the legitimate economy. Not only does it repent for its long history of slave trade and piracy, but a Michelin-starred restaurant now serves customers close to the setting of Stevenson's famous novel.

Environmental transformation is not confined to the developed world. Singapore was once a prominent center of illicit trade in Southeast Asia. The Malaccan Straits, which divide Singapore and Malaysia from Indonesia, were the locus of significant smuggling of goods and people, an activity that colonial authorities attempted to curb.[39] Smuggling proliferated as a form of resistance to colonial rule and the imposition of borders by foreign rulers.[40] But now Singapore is distinguished for its low levels of corruption and the integrity of its trade. Only the free-trade zone of Singapore still recalls the smuggling past of this now economically powerful island of integrity, in a region whose neighboring states score poorly on the Transparency International's Corruption Perception Index. Yet free-trade zones remain a problem for the trans-shipment not only of counterfeit consumer items but of strategic items necessary for WMD proliferation, such as is seen with North Korea.[41]

The transformation of Bristol and Singapore from centers of illicit trade to cities whose affluence is based on a legitimate economy came about not just because of changes in government and economics. It required a change in the mentality of the citizens.

Naming and shaming can play a significant role in changing behavior. The *Trafficking in Persons Report* issued annually by the US State Department has achieved some success by placing governments on the trafficking watch list or reducing their ranking for poor performance. Colombians who found themselves unable to travel or who were confronted with embarrassing situations at border control while traveling overseas eventually pressured their government to do more against drug trafficking. The reputation of Hobby Lobby, a company that has bought antiquities for its new Bible Museum, was damaged following the imposition of sanctions for its illicit trade in antiquities. References to this case accompanied the opening of the museum in Washington.[42]

Behavioral change is possible, as suggested by the research of Richard Thaler, the 2017 Nobel Prize–winning economist. Thaler, known for his "nudge" theory, believes that people can be prompted to change their behavior. If people have been encouraged to pay their taxes, donate organs, and be more conscious of their health, they can also be nudged to help solve some of the world's problems.[43] Nudge theory has not yet been broadly applied to countering illicit trade. Can people be nudged not to buy rhino horn or ivory tusks? Examining ways to nudge consumers, producers, and facilitators of illicit trade toward behavior that might be more salutary, for both people and the planet, is certainly a worthwhile objective.

States and Illicit Trade

Nudging will not work when states and their leaders engage in illicit trade, whether for the good of the state or their personal benefit. When illicit trade serves the purposes of war or can be weaponized as a tool of war, moving human behavior to a more desired outcome is not likely. Diplomacy is key to the behavioral transformation of states; many hours of bilateral and multilateral negotiations have been spent trying to force states to curb drug production, the manufacture of counterfeits, or the smuggling that supports unauthorized nuclear programs, such as those in Iran, Pakistan, and North Korea.

Diverse tools often associated with wars rather than commerce have been used to counter harmful forms of illicit trade, including military actions, sanctions, trade blockades, and embargos. State power and policy have been adapted to the cyber age, contributing to the rise of cyber-conflict, or cyberwar. The present-day analogue of the privateers of the past and the opium wars of the mid-nineteenth century may be cyberwar, where illicit trade is used as a weapon. Recognizing that this problem has historical precedents may be useful in developing effective counterstrategies.

Specific Strategies

Conducting research and analysis, limiting corruption, initiating rational legal and economic policies, promoting behavioral change for individuals, communities, and corporations, developing resilient communities—all may reduce illicit trade. Yet more specific recommendations to address illicit trade might have significant success in reversing its present trajectory. The following suggestions focus particularly on two areas where change is most needed—environmental and cyber-related illicit trade.

COMBATING ENVIRONMENTAL CRIME

The effort to combat environmental crime does not have many success stories. One of the most noted is the termination of illicit trade in chlorofluorocarbons. Enforcement of the Montreal Protocol—its ban on the production of CFCs as well as its trade provisions—has allowed the ozone layer to mend.[44] Scientists, policymakers, and law enforcers had to work together for a few decades to achieve tangible results, but the success of this effort shows that it can be done.

There are other examples from the timber, wildlife, and fishing sectors. None have yielded remarkable reversals, as with CFCs, but they have had considerable impact on reducing illicit trade and have contributed to sustainability.

Brazil, starting in 2005, was able to dramatically reverse the deforestation of its rainforest by taking several key measures. The plan required greater intragovernmental cooperation but also provided incentives for sustainable economic activities. Enforcement of laws, interventions in soy and beef supply chains, restrictions on access to credit, and expansion of protected areas appear to have contributed to a 70 percent decline in deforestation.[45] Under these plans implemented by the Brazilian government, it ceased to be in the farmers' financial interests to grow soy and raise cattle. An understanding of supply chains and market mechanisms resulted in dramatic declines in illegal timber harvesting, at least in the short term.

A different approach was tried in Indonesia. The country's empowered anti-corruption agency, the Corruption Eradication Commission, one of the most effective of its kind in the world, targeted the facilitators of the massive deforestation who caused billions in losses of revenues to the Indonesian government between 2003 and 2014.[46] Indonesia's approach illustrates the principle that attacking related problems can successfully diminish illicit trade.

African Parks has had positive results in protecting wildlife. This organization builds a constituency for the preservation of wildlife by providing services for the communities around the ten parks it manages in eight African countries. Seeking to change the economic incentives of those living near the parks, African Parks makes the benefits realized by sustaining the parks greater than those from poaching the animals. Medical care and education are provided to those living near the parks, and visits to the parks are provided at no cost to their children. Over 4,500 people living in proximity to the parks are directly employed in them. But the number benefiting from the parks is far greater, as African Parks "estimate[s] that as many as 2.1 million people who live around the parks and in the region, benefit from the parks' existence and their effective management."[47]

African Parks's advocacy for a conservation-led economy has had considerable success in curbing poaching, except in the highly violent DRC. The foundation has a very different perspective from South Africa, which has done little to enhance sustainability in local communities around parks.

Tourism presently represents about 7 percent of GDP in Africa. If this revenue flowed not just to tour companies and upscale hotels but to communities, it could change the incentive structures for wildlife preservation.[48] Members of local communities would realize that they had more to gain from preserving animals than from poaching.

The Nobel Prize–winning economist Elinor Ostrom's research revealed that local communities in Africa, Asia, Europe, and the United States would not destroy their commonly held resources if they shared and were committed to a management system. Visiting the rich sea off the Maine coasts, where fishermen have ample supplies of lobsters to collect, I recalled Ostrom's insights into how local regulation can ensure more supply for all. Lobstermen have developed rules on the size of the lobsters that can be caught—younger ones must be returned to the sea to grow and propagate—and insights from Ostrom explain why this system works:

> Maine lobster fishermen use this system when another man sets his traps on their patch. It's a warning to the poacher that he's been found out. If he persists, he receives a visit at home. If that doesn't convince him to mend his ways, he can expect a whole range of other sanctions, up to the destruction of his boat.[49]

In this case, sanctions are not left to the state, and local community controls help ensure the preservation of valuable community resources. This is possible when the violators are members of the community who cannot escape the enforcement of local norms.

Where community controls are insufficient because foreigners are harming fish stocks, other strategies are needed. One of the most overfished regions of the world is the west coast of Africa, where large fishing trawlers, often owned by Chinese state-owned companies, deplete the sea of the fish needed by the local community for consumption and income. Both human and security challenges have ensued.[50] One response has come from the Natural Resources

Defense Council, a major American NGO. The NRDC has a China program that seeks to improve the availability of Chinese fish stocks. If the Chinese can enhance their domestic supplies, they will be less likely to go after fish in other regions of the world.[51]

In 2009, after years of delay and negotiation, the United Nations took action to address rogue fishing by adopting a new act—the Agreement on Port State Measures (PSMA) to Prevent, Deter, and Eliminate Illegal, Unreported, and Unregulated (IUU) Fishing.[52] Working to counter the $23 billion generated annually from illicit fishing, this treaty "restricts port access to fishing vessels that fail to comply with a set of rules, including proof that they have proper operating licenses and transparent disclosure of the species and quantity of fish caught."[53] It adds greater scrutiny to industrial fishing trawlers that deplete the sea, possibly bringing shame to Asian countries, the key perpetrators of this activity. Shaming, as previously mentioned, has proved helpful in slowing illicit trade in environmental products.

In addition to UN action, the European Union has recently enacted new legislation to focus on sustainable fishing.[54] To ensure the sustainability of marine resources, European policymakers are implementing fisheries management systems for both European boats and foreign boats operating in European waters.[55]

The Fisheries Transparency Initiative, a new public-private partnership, was launched in 2015 to work with states, fishing companies, civil society, workers, and consumers to ensure the sustainability of fish stocks. Oversight of fishery practices by this NGO would enhance governmental capacity in countries with limited capabilities to protect fish stocks off their coasts. Building on models from the extractive industries sector, the Initiative has had a strong initial focus on West Africa, where the problems are particularly acute.[56]

In the United States, the influential NRDC focuses on the development of law and enforcement mechanisms through fishing councils, courts, and Congress to set fishing limits on certain fish, "rebuild depleted fish stocks and strengthen safeguards against destructive fishing practices."[57] Its efforts have been complemented by those of many other NGOs, such as Oceana, Greenpeace, and the Monterey

Bay Seafood Watch, which guides consumers in purchasing sustainable fish.[58] The technology being used to counter the fish threat will be discussed later in the chapter.

CONTROLLING TECHNOLOGY AND HARNESSING IT FOR GOOD

The new technology of the web, the Dark Web, and social media have been major enablers of both licit and illicit trade. The internet, as previously mentioned, was first developed by the military but is now dominated by major companies such as Google, Amazon, and Facebook. New social media, such as Twitter, Snapchat, and Reddit, are also owned and maintained by the private sector. Yet these new forms of technology sell illicit products, provide ways to facilitate their movement, and help launder the proceeds of their sale. They are enablers of good, by promoting connectivity, but also accelerators of deleterious forms of illicit trade.

With private ownership of online marketplaces, internet service providers (ISPs), and social media companies, cyberspace cannot be regulated exclusively by government but requires the cooperation of the private sector, which is inherently more interested in profit than in good governance. Thus, reducing illicit trade will be difficult to achieve unless fruitful public-private partnerships are formed, and measures are adopted, to protect citizens and human security and not just the financial interests of the major owners and providers of the new media. This challenge falls particularly on the United States, where the owners of the major commercial platforms and the social media are based and Alibaba, the major online seller in China, is listed on the New York Stock Exchange. Alibaba does retain former Chinese law enforcement officers to vet its sellers and sales, but it needs to do more, as it faces pressure for selling many counterfeit items on the internet.[59]

A seemingly obscure legal provision, section 230 of the 1996 Communications Decency Act, curbs governmental interference in interactive media. By excluding online platforms from responsibility for the information they provide or the products they sell, harmful state and nonstate actors have an asymmetric advantage in the media increasingly central to citizen purchases and news. It is this provision that has facilitated the dissemination of false news. What is particularly relevant to this book is that it has allowed technology-facilitated human trafficking to flourish and malicious products such as harmful pharmaceuticals to be sold through the internet.[60] In the face of threats to both democracy and human life, there may be greater pressure in coming years, from civil society or government, for regulation of tech giants such as exist now in utilities and newspapers.[61]

Controls on tech companies, including the owners of web platforms and social media, have originated more from authoritarian states than in response to human security. For example, controls in China suppress human rights and free expression more often than they limit illicit sales.

In the coming years, greater attention to the web, social media, and digital currencies or cryptocurrencies will be needed as these are increasingly used to make illegal purchases in cyberspace. Existing currencies that provide more anonymity, such as Monero, Dash, and Zcash, as well as China's AliPay, Russia's WebMoney, and Kenya's M-Pesa, are subject to greater misuse than Bitcoin.[62] Public-private partnerships are key to effectively regulating these currencies and curbing the abuse of online platforms. Corporate hosts need to be more active in controlling their own content.

Technology accelerates connectivity as well as access to markets, goods, and victims, but it can also be a force that helps counter illicit trade. As President Obama said at the 2012 Clinton Global Initiative, "We're turning the tables on the traffickers. Just as they are now using technology and the Internet to exploit their victims, we're going to harness technology to stop them . . . to develop tools that our young people can use to stay safe online and on their smart phones."[63]

Tools to combat illicit trade cannot be built in isolation. They must be developed in conjunction with people who understand the dynamics of illicit trade, transnational crime, and money laundering. By combining substantive knowledge with technical capacity, progress can be made in combating illicit trade.

Computer specialists are equipping themselves with new instruments, such as the previously mentioned Memex data maps used by DARPA, to combat the key participants in illicit trade in cyberspace. Conducting large-scale network analysis allows investigators to evaluate the centrality of participants in networks, permitting a focus on key personnel rather than less important participants.

Apps provide anonymity to human smugglers as they guide clients. "They amount to a digital infrastructure comparable to roads and trains in refugees' journeys."[64] Instead of being vulnerable to theft in transit by predatory criminals, refugees can use apps to transfer funds more safely.

Apps readily available on cell phones are also used to disclose human trafficking.[65] TraffickCam, an app developed in 2015 by a private meeting management company, allows individuals to upload hotel room photos in the hope of being matched with advertisements for sexual services.[66] The LaborVoices app permits real-time crowdsourcing of factory sites to report incidents of illegal migrant and child labor exploitation. It provides monitoring in a less visual way than on-the-ground observers, who often can be diverted from full oversight of labor conditions.[67] Companies importing products from developing countries can more easily detect abusive practices of suppliers.

Another example of the ways in which some corporations are using technology to help counter serious illicit trade is the technology being used to address the problem of abusive fishing practices. In late 2016, Oceana, Google, and SkyTruth launched Global Fishing Watch, a big data technology platform that leverages satellite data to create the first global view of commercial fishing. Sixty thousand commercial vessels equipped with automatic identification system (AIS) technology have been tracked.[68] Global Fishing Watch maps allow users to "visualize the hot spots around the world and see where illegal fishing or overfishing is taking place. It shows a vessel's name, type and country of origin, and also tracks its movements."[69]

Technology is also being used to track the transparency of supply chains for timber. Some companies provide tools, on a commercial basis, that enable the monitoring of wood from the source of timber to the point of export. This helps ensure that the timber was logged legally and the wood is sustainable.[70]

PUBLIC-PRIVATE PARTNERSHIPS

The partnerships between the business world, government enforcers, and civil society are key to addressing illicit trade—an especially acute problem with the rise of cyber-facilitated crime. Much crime is now committed through privately owned channels. Therefore, the state-based system—the basis of security since the 1648 Treaty of Westphalia ending the Thirty Years' War—is no longer as relevant. Efforts are being made to expand borders to include not just the physical perimeters of each country but the locale from which goods are shipped.[71]

Today, with global supply chains and vast movements of people, states and multinational organizations must find new ways to cooperate and even collaborate with the private sector. Too little information-sharing occurs between the public and private sectors, although communications, commerce, and money increasingly flow through private channels, many of which are not visible or accessible to law enforcement. Policing and military activities are often based only on the actions observed by law enforcement and the borders controlled by governments, whereas the illicit trade today and its accompanying illegal financial flows are difficult to discern or even unknowable without the cooperation of the private sector.

Response to the abuse of new technology has been fragmented and slow and has not kept pace with the hijacking by pernicious actors of innovative developments. New strategies for public-private partnership have been developed in the past two decades to address these new challenges. For example, one of the first illicit activities to grow with the introduction of the internet was the distribution of child pornography. Since 2006, the US Financial Coalition Against Child Pornography (FCACP) has brought together financial institutions in the United States to halt the purchase of this forbidden item. "The US FCACP's membership includes the country's leading banks, credit card companies, electronic payment networks, third-party-payments companies, and Internet services companies, making up 90% of the US payments industry."[72] Ever alert to recent developments, this organization combats the use of digital currencies for the purchase of child pornography. This approach has expanded to the Asia-Pacific region and Europe.[73] The European Financial Coalition (EFC) brings together the major credit card companies, Google, Microsoft, and Europol to fight online commercial exploitation of children.[74]

Thorn, a tech NGO, is combining the efforts of more than twenty international NGOs, more than forty tech partners, and five thousand law enforcement officers in all fifty US states and more than eighteen countries. Engaged in a deterrence program in the United States and abroad, Thorn participants communicate directly with people searching for child sexual material by disrupting their sense of anonymity and encouraging them to seek help. Through this effort, they "aim to change behavior and increase accountability."[75] This effort seeks to counter the anonymity of cyberspace that facilitates such abuse, but similar efforts may not be permissible in many other countries because of privacy laws.

Coalitions of financial institutions, first in New York and more recently in other regions of the United States, data-mine credit card and other financial data based on the footprints of human trafficking, such as charges to nail salons in the middle of the night, hours when these businesses are closed.[76] More recently, this approach was used with success to find human traffickers during Super Bowl weekend in 2018; in the days around the game, ads for sexual services increase by a factor of five to ten.[77]

Tech companies have funded research and supplied software, expertise, and assistance in conducting network analysis to fight human trafficking.[78] Algorithmic mining of big data, first used to fight human trafficking, has been also used to combat illicit wildlife trade.

The California Transparency in Supply Chain Act, which came into force in 2012, helps prevent the sale of goods manufactured by trafficked laborers. It requires all businesses with over $100 million in annual revenues globally "to disclose information regarding their efforts to eradicate human trafficking and slavery within their supply chains on their website, or, if a company does not have a website, through written disclosures."[79] Although enacted only by a single state, the almost 40 million residents of California provide a market that cannot be ignored by most significant businesses. Therefore, the passage of this law in one state impacts the rest of the country and even other countries. It allows purchasers to be more responsible and forces companies to understand their supply chains better. Unfortunately, an absence of enforcement makes this mandate less effective than it could be.

Public-private partnerships that disrupt global cybercrime were seen already in 2005, when Microsoft disclosed that Morocco and Turkish-based individuals were responsible for the release of the computer worm Zotob, which disrupted over one hundred American companies. Collaboration among Microsoft, the FBI, and Turkish and Moroccan law enforcement authorities facilitated the arrest and subsequent sentencing of the perpetrators, which would not have been possible without cooperation from the corporate world.[80]

The takedown of Avalanche, the criminal network that facilitated the spread of diverse forms of malware (discussed in chapter 5), occurred with the support of Symantec Corporation and other private security and IT companies. Symantec's research on ransomware enabled it to reverse-engineer the malware and permitted investigators to understand relationships among the disseminators of this harmful product, thereby facilitating the identification and arrest of the criminals running key nodes in the network.[81]

Many tech innovators are developing apps and other tools to increase monitoring of illicit activities and alert companies to problems in their supply chains. Blockchain technology—also known as *distributed ledger technology*, the technology underlying all cryptocurrencies, including Bitcoin)—can be used to validate all critical steps in a product's entire supply chain, from manufacturer to consumers; this technology is especially helpful in the pharmaceutical arena.[82] Using blockchain technology, it is possible to "build tamper-proof, decentralized records of flow of commodities and materials across a supply chain by using trusted stakeholders to validate flows and movements."[83]

Many others are exploring the construction of supply chain management systems that use blockchain to create tamper-proof supply chain records of the ownership and provenance of traded goods. Such a system depersonalizes the trust that has been at the heart of licit trade for millennia. Everledger, a London-based company, is working on creating such a system for the diamond industry, and other companies are looking at systems for artworks, pharmaceuticals, and other frequently traded goods.[84] The potential for blockchain to secure supply chains and financial transactions has engaged investors, the World Bank, and the tech community.[85]

Larger tech companies are also addressing tech-facilitated crime, particularly crime related to human exploitation. Unfortunately, online platforms and social media, such as Facebook and Twitter, still remain major enablers, and they have proved unwilling or unable to invest in efforts to control the abuse they facilitate. Citizen pressure on government for greater regulation, shareholder activism—such as has been directed at Apple to encourage it not to produce its products in factories that exploit laborers—and media exposure of abuses and solutions are all needed to make the new online platforms not just facilitators of illicit trade but more active participants in its prevention and disruption.

CURBING CORRUPTION AND CRIME AND FOLLOWING THE MONEY

The United Nations and its member states have prioritized law enforcement and coercive methods over other strategies against illicit trade. Greater coercion and authoritarian controls are often the measure of choice, as epitomized by President Rodrigo Duterte of the Philippines, under whose rule many have been killed in his war on drugs. But, as was seen in pre-revolutionary France and in the Soviet period, harsh penalties against illegal traders do not eliminate the problem, especially when illicit trade is systemic and high-level facilitators remain untouched.

State-based legal systems are not equipped to tackle an increasingly globalized illicit trade that operates across multiple borders in both the real and virtual worlds. Therefore, international collaboration is key, as seen in the takedown of Avalanche and other cross-border cybercrimes. Differences in legal codes have been overcome as law enforcement of many different countries have learned to collaborate. Transnational legal mechanisms have evolved to address illicit wildlife trade globally—such as CITES, which operates under the UN. But CITES was not created explicitly to address crime, and it calls upon law enforcement to respond to "illicit" rather than "illegal" trade, which is not a priority in many countries.[86]

Despite the increased collaboration, pervasive corruption and income inequality ensure that there is no certainty of punishment for the perpetrators of illicit trade. Severe punishment is reserved for those without power, whereas the sanctioning of top corporate or government officials or wealthy individuals is rare. Mexico has incarcerated some of its top drug traffickers, and the International Criminal Court (ICC) has sanctioned governmental leaders who are also responsible for illicit trade, but these examples are few and far between.

The criminal process must be used to address illicit trade—to disrupt its routes, its key facilitators, and the major networks behind its activities. Newly developed analytical tools can help locate and target the key nodes. But of equal, and possibly greater, effect would be to target the corruption that facilitates illegal commerce and the corrupters who make this trade run. To accomplish this objective, it is necessary to curtail offshore havens and money laundering into real estate, where key figures of illicit trade park their money with impunity.

Large sums exit the developing world annually, enabled by the use of anonymous and shell companies that mask the owners' identities. Many countries do not require that companies be registered with their beneficial owners, making it impossible to know who actually owns the account. Global Financial Integrity estimates that, between 2005 and 2014, illicit financial flows (IFFs) in and out of developing countries were "worth at least 14.1 to 24.0 percent of developing country trade, on average, per year."[87]

The importance of offshore centers to illegal commerce until recently could only be hypothesized. Recent massive document leaks have revealed that these locales not only help the super-rich evade billions in taxes but also serve as repositories of ill-gotten gains from corruption and participation in illicit trade.[88] The Panama Papers and the Paradise Papers exposing offshore accounts in the Bahamas identified the specific beneficiaries of illicit trade—transnational criminals, terrorists, and past and present high-level officials.[89] In fact, Europol linked almost 3,500 suspected criminals, smugglers, and terrorists in its database to names in these files. Analyses by Colombians and others have revealed that trade-based money laundering has been key to the movement of money to these locales.[90] Therefore, illegal commerce plays a dual role in these havens. It is both the source of the money and the means used to transfer ill-gotten gains.

Clearly, a key strategy to control illicit trade and corruption is to end offshore havens, which are now depositories for a significant amount of the world's wealth, which is not being put to productive use, often depriving the poorest countries of the world of resources needed to create sustainable communities.

Facilitators in law, finance, and transport also profit, as money made through illicit trade does not stay exclusively in the criminal economy: billions are laundered through well-established banks and into high-end real estate in many major financial centers of the world—London, New York, Miami, and Dubai.[91] The enormous amount of money invested in these sectors is a clue that we must prioritize illicit financial flows and enhance financial enforcement. Following the money needs to be a key adage in combating illicit trade and its proceeds. Sustainable development cannot occur in the world when such significant resources are looted.

Concluding Thoughts

The diverse and creative responses to growing illicit trade highlighted in this chapter show the human ingenuity that could be brought to bear in countering what the National Book Award speech of Annie Proulx characterized as "the accelerating destruction of the natural world and the dreadful belief that only the human species has the . . . permission to take anything it wants from nature, whether mountaintops, wetlands or oil."[92]

Strategies to counter illicit trade must educate the world's population and draw on the insights of human psychology, economics, and application of legal norms. Exceptional individuals risk their lives for this objective, such as the activists and investigative journalists who counter and document human trafficking, the drug trade, illegal timber harvesting, and illicit financial flows. Each year many honest law enforcement and park rangers who work on the front lines against illicit trade die in the line of duty trying to save human lives and protected species. New technology and data analytics tools are being developed by government and the private sector to counter the growth of illicit trade, particularly in the cyberworld. Many individuals are involved at the local level in their communities to prevent harm to all forms of life. But why is there no collective or coordinated response? Is it time to alter how we view this subject and to cast aside the term "illicit"? Do its negative implications and connotations lead to misunderstandings? Do we need a new paradigm to address a problem that threatens our futures?

The challenges are great and the windows of opportunity to reverse the planet's present tragic course are limited. Let us hope that the mundane but important acts of ordinary citizens, combined with the extraordinary acts of the few, help reverse the current growth trajectory of dark commerce. We do not want a future where there is no trade of any form, nor "jobs on a dead planet."[93]

NOTES

Acknowledgments

1. E. O. Wilson, *Half-Earth: Our Planet's Fight for Life* (New York: W. W. Norton & Co., 2016).

2. Peggy E. Chaudhry, ed. *Handbook of Research on Counterfeiting and Illicit Trade* (Cheltenham, UK: Edward Elgar, 2017).

3. H. Richard Friman and Peter Andreas, *The Illicit Global Economy and State Power* (Lanham, MD: Rowman & Littlefield, 1999); R. T. Naylor, *Bankers, Bagmen, and Bandits: Business and Politics in the Age of Greed* (Montreal: Black Rose Books, 1990); R. T. Naylor, *Wages of Crime: Black Markets, Illegal Finance, and the Underworld Economy* (Ithaca, NY: Cornell University Press, 2002); Fernand Braudel, *Civilization and Capitalism, 15th–18th Century*, 3 vols. (New York: Harper & Row, 1982–1984); K. N. Chaudhuri, *Trade and Civilisation in the Indian Ocean: An Economic History from the Rise of Islam to 1750* (Cambridge: Cambridge University Press, 1985); Manuel Castells, *The Internet Galaxy: Reflections on the Internet, Business, and Society* (Oxford: Oxford University Press, 2001).

4. Moisés Naím, *Illicit: How Smugglers, Traffickers, and Copycats Are Hijacking the Global Economy* (New York: Doubleday, 2005); Raymond Fisher and Edward Miguel, *Economic Gangsters: Corruption, Violence, and the Poverty of Nations* (Princeton, NJ: Princeton University Press, 2008).

5. Peter Grabosky, *Cybercrime* (Oxford: Oxford University Press, 2015); David S. Wall, *Cybercrime: The Transformation of Crime in the Information Age* (Cambridge: Polity Press, 2007); Misha Glenny, *DarkMarket: Cyberthieves, Cybercops, and You* (New York: Alfred A. Knopf, 2011); Brian Krebs, *Spam Nation: The Inside Story of Organized Cybercrime—from Global Epidemic to Your Front Door* (Naperville, IL: Sourcebooks, 2014); Marc Goodman, *Future Crimes: Everything Is Connected, Everyone Is Vulnerable, and What We Can Do About It* (New York: Doubleday, 2015); Xavier Raufer, *Cyber-criminologie* (Paris: CNRS [Centre National de la Recherche Scientifique] Éditions, 2015).

6. A small selection includes Alexis Aronowitz, *Human Trafficking, Human Misery: The Global Trade in Human Beings* (Westport, CT: Praeger, 2009); Ko-Lin Chin, *The Golden Triangle: Inside Southeast Asia's Drug Trade* (Ithaca, NY: Cornell University Press, 2009); Cláudia Costa Storti and Paul de Grauwe, eds., *Illicit Trade and the Global Economy* (Cambridge, MA: MIT Press, 2012); Vanda Felbab-Brown, *Shooting Up: Counterinsurgency and the War on Drugs* (Washington, DC:

Brookings Institution, 2009); Rensselaer W. Lee II, *The White Labyrinth: Cocaine and Political Power* (New Brunswick, NJ: Transaction Publishers, 1990); John M. Sellar, *The UN's Lone Ranger: Combating International Wildlife Crime* (Dunbeath, UK: Whittles Publishing, 2014); Michael J. Lynch et al., *Green Criminology: Crime, Justice, and the Environment* (Berkeley: University of California Press, 2017); Vanda Felbab-Brown, *The Extinction Market: Wildlife Trafficking and How to Counter It* (Washington, DC: Brookings Institution, 2017).

7. Carlo Morselli, *Crime and Networks* (New York: Routledge, 2014); Manuel Castells, ed., *The Network Society: A Cross-Cultural Perspective* (Cheltenham, UK: Edward Elgar, 2004); Manuel Castells, *The Rise of a Network Society* (Cambridge, MA: Blackwell Publishers, 1996).

8. Ko-lin Chin, *Going Down to the Sea: Chinese Sex Workers Abroad* (Chiang Mai, Thailand: Silkworm Books, 2014); Ko-lin Chin and James O. Finckenauer, *Selling Sex Overseas: Chinese Women and the Realities of Prostitution and Global Sex Trafficking* (New York: New York University Press, 2012); Stephen Ellis, *This Present Darkness: A History of Nigerian Organised Crime* (Oxford: Oxford University Press, 2016).

9. Amar Farooqui, *Smuggling as Subversion: Colonialism, Indian Merchants, and the Politics of Opium, 1790–1843* (Lanham, MD: Lexington Books, 2005); Peter Ward Fay, *The Opium War, 1840–1842: Barbarians in the Celestial Empire in the Early Part of the Nineteenth Century and the War by Which They Forced Her Gates Ajar* (Chapel Hill: University of North Carolina Press, 1997); J. Y. Wong, *Deadly Dreams: Opium, Imperialism, and the Arrow War (1856–1860) in China* (Cambridge: Cambridge University Press, 1998); Michael Kwass, *Contraband: Louis Mandrin and the Making of a Global Underground* (Cambridge, MA: Harvard University Press, 2014): George T. Díaz, *Border Contraband: A History of Smuggling across the Rio Grande* (Austin : University of Texas Press, 2015).

Introduction: The Fundamental Transformation of Illicit Trade

1. Viviana Zelizer, *The Social Meaning of Money: Pin Money, Paychecks, Poor Relief, and Other Currencies* (Princeton, NJ: Princeton University Press, 2017).

2. Edoardo Grendi, "Counterfeit Coins and Monetary Exchange Structures in the Republic of Genoa during the Sixteenth and Seventeenth Centuries," in *History from Crime*, ed. Edward Muir and Guido Ruggiefro (Baltimore: Johns Hopkins University Press, 1994), 170–205; "Illicit Financial Flows," Global Financial Integrity, http://www.gfintegrity.org/issue/illicit-financial-flows/, accessed September 22, 2018.

3. "Number of Monthly Active WhatsApp Users Worldwide from April 2013 to December 2017," Statistics Portal, https://www.statista.com/statistics/260819/number-of-monthly-active-whatsapp-users/, accessed February 3, 2017.

4. Larry Greenemeier, "Human Traffickers Caught on Hidden Internet," *Scientific American*, February 8, 2015, https://www.scientificamerican.com/article/human-traffickers-caught-on-hidden-internet/; see also the accompanying

visualization of the international links, "*Scientific American* Exclusive: DARPA Memex Data Map," https://www.scientificamerican.com/slideshow/scientific-american-exclusive-darpa-memex-data-maps/, accessed July 13, 2017; Channing May, *Transnational Crime and the Developing World* (Washington, DC: Global Financial Integrity, 2017), xi.

5. Ransomware is extensively used in India; see "Net Losses Estimating the Global Cost of Cybercrime: Economic Impact of Cybercrime II," Center for Strategic and International Studies (CSIS), June 2014, 15, https://www.sbs.ox.ac.uk/cybersecurity-capacity/system/files/McAfee%20and%20CSIS%20-%20Econ%20Cybercrime.pdf. A major analyst of the Dark Web suggests that 10 percent of its content consists of this stolen material.

6. See CSIS, "Net Losses," 15.

7. Anthony Cuthbertson, "Ransomware Attacks Rise 250 Percent in 2017, Hitting US Hardest," *Newsweek*, May 23, 2017, http://www.newsweek.com/ransomware-attacks-rise-250-2017-us-wannacry-614034; Jessica Davis, "Ransomware: See the 14 Hospitals Attacked So Far in 2016," *Healthcare IT News*, October 5, 2016, http://www.healthcareitnews.com/slideshow/ransomware-see-hospitals-hit-2016, accessed November 11, 2016; April Glaser, "US Hospitals Have Been Hit by the Global Ransomware Attack," *recode*, June 27, 2017, https://www.recode.net/2017/6/27/15881666/global-eu-cyber-attack-us-hackers-nsa-hospitals, accessed November 11, 2017; Al Baker, "A Rush to Attack Digital Villainy," *New York Times*, February 6, 2016.

8. Joe Mandak, "Prosecutor's Office Paid Bitcoin Ransom in Cyberattack," PhysOrg, December 5, 2016, https://phys.org/news/2016-12-prosecutor-office-paid-bitcoin-ransom.html, accessed July 15, 2017; United States of America vs. flux and flux 2, complaint filed November 28, 2016, in US District Court, Western District of Pennsylvania, https://www.justice.gov/opa/page/file/915216/download, accessed July 15, 2017; "'Avalanche' Network Disrupted in International Cyber Operation," Europol, December 1, 2016, https://www.europol.europa.eu/newsroom/news/%E2%80%98avalanche%E2%80%99-network-dismantled-in-international-cyber-operation, accessed February 1, 2017. This is the Avalanche case discussed in chapter 5.

9. UNODC, "United Nations Convention against Transnational Organized Crime and the Protocols Thereto," 2004, https://www.unodc.org/documents/treaties/UNTOC/Publications/TOC%20Convention/TOCebook-e.pdf. Adopted as General Assembly Resolution 55/25 on November 15, 2000, the UN Convention against Transnational Organized Crime is the main international instrument in the fight against transnational organized crime. It was opened for signature by member states at a high-level political conference convened in Palermo, Italy, in December 2000; see also Asif Efrat, *Governing Guns, Preventing Plunder: International Cooperation against Illicit Trade* (Oxford: Oxford University Press, 2012).

10. Susan Strange, *Retreat of the State: Diffusion of Power in the World Economy* (New York: Cambridge University Press, 1996).

11. David Chaikin and Jason C. Sharman, *Corruption and Money Laundering: A Symbiotic Relationship* (New York: Palgrave Macmillan, 2009).

12. Ziming Zhao, Mukund Sankaran, Gail-Joon Ahn, Thomas J. Holt, Yiming Jing, and Hongxin Hu, "Mules, Seals, and Attacking Tools: Analyzing 12 Online Marketplaces," *IEEE Security and Privacy* 14, no. 3 (2016): 32–43, http://doi .ieeecomputersociety.org/10.1109/MSP.2016.46.

13. "Avalanche Network Dismantled in International Cyber Operation," US Department of Justice, Office of Public Affairs, December 5, 2016, https:// www.justice.gov/opa/pr/avalanche-network-dismantled-international-cyber -operation, accessed November 11, 2017.

14. In October 2017, I discussed this case with members of Ukraine's anti-corruption agency who were not even aware of this case.

15. Steve Kovach, "FBI Says Illegal Drugs Marketplace Silk Road Generated $1.2 Billion in Sales Revenue," *Business Insider*, October 2, 2013, http://www .businessinsider.com/silk-road-revenue-2013-10, accessed August 22, 2017.

16. Christian Nellemann et al., eds., *The Rise of Environmental Crime—A Growing Threat to Natural Resources, Peace, Development, and Security: A UNEP/ INTERPOL Rapid Response Assessment*, United Nations Environment Program (UNEP), 2016, https://wedocs.unep.org/bitstream/handle/20.500.11822/7662 /-The_rise_of_environmental_crime_A_growing_threat_to_natural_resources _peace%2c_development_and_security-2016environmental_crimes.pdf.pdf ?sequence=3&isAllowed=y.

17. Kathleen Garrigan, "Going Tuskless," African Wildlife Foundation, February 4, 2015, http://www.awf.org/blog/going-tuskless, accessed August 10, 2017; Amy Yee, "Poaching Leaving Elephant Daughters in Charge," *New York Times*, July 4, 2016, https://www.nytimes.com/2016/07/05/science/female-elephants -follow-in-their-mothers-footsteps.html, accessed August 10, 2017.

18. David E. Kaplan and Alec Dubro, *Yakuza Japan's Criminal Underworld* (Berkeley: University of California Press, 1987); James B. Jacobs et al., *Gotham Unbound: How New York City Was Liberated from the Grip of Organized Crime* (New York: New York University Press, 1999).

19. Max Roser and Esteban Ortiz-Ospina, "World Population Growth," Our World in Data, 2013, updated April 2017, https://ourworldindata.org/world -population-growth/, accessed June 11, 2017. The Global Footprint Network shows that we need about one and a half worlds to provide the resources we use annually and absorb the waste generated by the world's population; see *Living Planet Report 2014: Species and Spaces, People and Places*, WWF International, 9, https://www.wwf.or.jp/activities/data/WWF_LPR_2014.pdf, accessed June 16, 2017.

20. Nellemann et al., *The Rise of Environmental Crime*, 7.

21. "Entrepreneurship" is defined as the capacity and willingness to de-velop, organize, and manage a business venture along with any of its risks in order to make a profit; "Entrepreneurship," BusinessDictionary, http://www .businessdictionary.com/definition/entrepreneurship.html, accessed August 22,

2017. Illicit entrepreneurs do the same to make a profit, yet the key difference is that they engage in illicit activity.

22. Francisco Calderoni, "The Analysis and Containment of Organized Crime and Transnational Organized Crime: An Interview with Ernesto U. Savona," *Trends in Organized Crime* 18, nos. 1–2 (June 2015): 128–142.

23. UNESCO established the Convention on the Means of Prohibiting and Preventing the Illicit Import, Export, and Transfer of Ownership of Cultural Property in 1970; "Illicit Trafficking of Cultural Property," UNESCO, http://www .unesco.org/new/en/culture/themes/illicit-trafficking-of-cultural-property /1970-convention/, accessed February 3, 2017.

24. *Illicit Trade Report 2013*, World Customs Organization, www.wcoomd .org/~/media/wco/public/global/pdf/topics/enforcement-and-compliance /activities-and-programmes/illicit-trade-report/illicit-2013-_-en_lr2.pdf?la=en, accessed February 3, 2017.

25. Asif Efrat, *Governing Guns, Preventing Plunder: International Coopera-tion against Illicit Trade* (Oxford: Oxford University Press, 2012), 5; H. Richard Friman and Peter Andreas, "Introduction: International Relations and the Illicit Global Economy," in *The Illicit Global Economy and State Power*, ed. H. Richard Friman and Peter Andreas (Lanham, MD: Rowman and Littlefield, 1999), 5–6.

26. "Countering Illicit Trade," EU-OECD High Level Seminar on Countering Illicit Trade, March 9, 2018, http://www.oecd.org/gov/risk/illicit-trade.htm, ac-cessed August 22, 2017.

27. Phil Williams, "Crime, Illicit Markets, and Money Laundering," in *Chal-lenges in International Governance*, ed. P. Simmons and C. Ouderen (Washington, DC: Carnegie Endowment, 2001), 107.

28. Jack Radisch, "Illicit Trade: Convergence of Criminal Networks," in OECD, *Illicit Trade: Converging Criminal Networks*, OECD Reviews of Risk Man-agement Policies (Paris: OECD Publishing, 2016), 19–21.

29. Williams, "Crime, Illicit Markets, and Money Laundering."

30. "New UNODC Campaign Highlights Transnational Organized Crime as a US$870 Billion a Year Business," UNODC, July 16, 2012, https://www.unodc.org /unodc/en/frontpage/2012/July/new-unodc-campaign-highlights-transnational -organized-crime-as-an-us-870-billion-a-year-business.html, accessed August 22, 2017.

31. Williams, "Crime, Illicit Markets, and Money Laundering."

32. Michael Mikluacic and Jacqueline Brewer, eds., *Convergence: Illicit Net-works and National Security in the Age of Globalization* (Washington, D.C.: Na-tional Defense University Press, 2013).

33. Mikluacic and Brewer, *Convergence*.

34. Tom Behan, *The Camorra* (London: Routledge, 2016); Roberto Saviano, *Gomorrah: A Personal Journey into the Violent International Empire of Naples' Or-ganized Crime System* (New York: Farrar, Straus and Giroux, 2006).

35. "Lumber Liquidators Inc. Sentenced for Illegal Importation of Hardwood and Related Environmental Crimes," US Department of Justice, Office of Public

Affairs, February 1, 2016, https://www.justice.gov/opa/pr/lumber-liquidators-inc-sentenced-illegal-importation-hardwood-and-related-environmental, accessed June 28, 2016; Ian Urbina, "Nestlé Reports on Abuses in Thailand's Seafood Industry," *New York Times*, November 23, 2015, http://www.nytimes.com/2015/11/24/business/nestle-reports-on-abuses-in-thailands-seafood-industry.html, accessed January 24, 2017; Ida Karlsson, "IKEA under Fire for Ancient Tree Logging," *Guardian*, May 29, 2012, https://www.theguardian.com/environment/2012/may/29/ikea-ancient-tree-logging, accessed May 14, 2018.

36. "Shadow Economy," BusinessDictionary, http://www.businessdictionary.com/definition/shadow-economy.html, accessed August 18, 2017.

37. Guilbert Gates, Jack Ewing, Karl Russell, and Derek Watkins, "How Volkswagen's 'Defeat Devices' Worked," *New York Times*, March 16, 2017, https://www.nytimes.com/interactive/2015/business/international/vw-diesel-emissions-scandal-explained.html?mcubz=1, accessed August 22, 2017.

38. Sarah Bracking, *The Financialisation of Power: How Financiers Rule Africa* (London: Routledge, 2016), 111–113; John A. Cassara, *Trade-Based Money Laundering: The Next Frontier in International Money Laundering Enforcement* (New York: John Wiley & Sons, 2016), 13–31, 111–124.

39. Jean-François Gayraud, *Le Nouveau capitalisme criminel* (Paris: Odile Jacob, 2014).

40. Bonnie Christian, "Stephen Hawking Believes We Have 100 Years Left on Earth—and He's Not the Only One," *Wired*, May 19, 2017, http://www.wired.co.uk/article/stephen-hawking-100-years-on-earth-prediction-starmus-festival, accessed August 22, 2017.

Chapter 1. Illicit Trade: Past as Prologue

1. Ira Spar, ed., *Cuneiform Texts in the Metropolitan Museum of Art*, vol. 1, *Tablets, Cones, and Bricks of the Third and Second Millennia BC* (New York: Metropolitan Museum of Art, 1988). I was trained by Ira Spar on these documents for a class I taught on Western Legal Tradition.

2. Ibid.

3. Joshua J. Mark, "The Sea Peoples," Ancient History Encyclopedia, September 2, 2009, http://www.ancient.eu/Sea_Peoples/, accessed August 12, 2017; Jenni Irving, "Pirates in the Ancient Mediterranean," Ancient History Encyclopedia, August 23, 2102, http://www.ancient.eu/Piracy/, accessed August 12, 2017.

4. *Le Code de Hammurabi et les trésors du Louvre, Dossier d'Archeologie* 299 (November 2003).

5. Provision 7 of Hammurabi's Code of Laws, excerpted from the original electronic text at K. C. Hanson's *Collection of Mesopotamian Documents*, http://history.hanover.edu/courses/excerpts/165hammurabi.html, accessed June 10, 2017.

6. Ira Spar, "Daily Life in Ancient Mesopotamia," *Calliope* 11, no. 3 (2000): 18; Iraq's Ancient Past, "The Royal Cemetery," University of Pennsylvania Museum

of Archaeology and Anthropology, http://www.penn.museum/sites/iraq/?page _id=26, accessed June 10, 2017.

7. For example, see a performance on September 20, 1968, by The Doors at https://www.youtube.com/watch?v=afmE_4L17t8, accessed June 10, 2017.

8. J. M. Beattie, *Crime and the Courts in England 1660–1800* (Oxford: Clarendon, 1986), 55–59; Gerald Howson, *Thief-Taker General: The Rise and Fall of Jonathan Wild* (New York: St. Martin's Press, 1970).

9. Carl B. Klockars, *The Professional Fence* (New York: Free Press, 1974). Another major work on fences is Darrell J. Steffensmeier, *The Fence in the Shadow of Two Worlds* (Totowa, NJ: Rowman & Littlefield, 1986).

10. Laura Spandanuta, "Retailers Fight E-fencing," *Security Management*, February 1, 2008, https://sm.asisonline.org/Pages/Retailers-Fight-EFencing.aspx, accessed June 10, 2017; see also Kristin M. Finklea, "Organized Retail Crime," Congressional Research Center, December 11, 2012, https://fas.org/sgp/crs/misc /R41118.pdf, accessed June 10, 2017.

11. Ana Serafin Smith, "Retailers See Increase in Organized Retail Crime," National Retail Federation, October 18, 2016, https://nrf.com/media/press-releases /retailers-see-increase-organized-retail-crime, accessed January 5, 2018.

12. I reviewed these websites on August 6, 2016.

13. Maxine Bernstein, "Vancouver Couple Headed to Court, Accused of Using eBay to Market Shoplifted Goods," *Oregonian*, July 15, 2012, http://www .oregonlive.com/clark-county/index.ssf/2012/07/vancouver_couple_headed_to _cou.html, accessed June 10, 2017.

14. Ronald S. Stroud, "An Athenian Law on Silver Coinage," *Hesperia: The Journal of the American School of Classical Studies at Athens* 43, no. 2 (April–June 1974): 171.

15. Spar, *Cuneiform Texts in the Metropolitan Museum of Art*; Jürgen Renn, "The Globalization of Knowledge in the Ancient Near East," in *Melammu: The Ancient World in an Era of Globalization*, ed. Markham J. Geller, Max Planck Research Library for the History and Development of Knowledge, Proceedings of the Sixth Symposium of the Melammu Project, Sophia, Bulgaria, September 1–3, 2008, Edition Open Access, 2014, 1–3, http://edition-open-access.de /media/proceedings/7/Proceedings7.pdf, accessed August 7, 2017; Maria Grazia Masetti-Rouault, "Globalization and Imperialism: Political and Ideological Reactions to the Assyrian Presence in Syria (IXth–VIIIth Century BCE)," in Geller, *Melammu*, 65.

16. Mohammed Maraqten, "Dangerous Trade Routes: On the Plundering of Caravans in the Pre-Islamic Near East," *ARAM* 8 (1996): 221.

17. Andrea Carli, "Counterfeiting an Ancient Problem, 2,000 Years Ago the First Brand Said 'Made in Rome,'" *Il Sole 24 Ore*, May 21, 2016, http://www .italy24.ilsole24ore.com/art/arts-and-leisure/2016-05-12/made-rome-174207 .php?uuid=ADFM6bG, accessed June 10, 2017.

18. "Pliny the Elder," BrainyQuote, http://www.brainyquote.com/quotes /quotes/p/plinytheel104974.html, accessed June 10, 2017.

19. Steven E. Sidebotham, *Roman Economic Policy in the Erythra Thalassa: 30 BC–AD 217* (Leiden: Brill Academic Publishers, 1986), 21.

20. Peggy E. Chaudry and Alan Zimmerman, *Protecting Your Intellectual Property Rights: Understanding the Role of Management, Governments, Consumers, and Pirates* (New York: Springer, 2013), 8.

21. Stroud, "An Athenian Law on Silver Coinage," 171.

22. Stroud, "An Athenian Law on Silver Coinage," 171.

23. Stroud, "An Athenian Law on Silver Coinage," 178.

24. Stroud, "An Athenian Law on Silver Coinage," 177.

25. Stroud, "An Athenian Law on Silver Coinage," 175.

26. Zhen Zin, *Study on Ancient Chinese Counterfeit Money* (Zhejiang: Zhejiang University Press, 2008). As Zhen points out, as does Stroud, ancient governments also often produced their own fake currency to advance their economic interests.

27. David Biello, "Fact or Fiction? Archimedes Coined the Term 'Eureka!' in the Bath," *Scientific American*, December 8, 2006, http://www.scientificamerican.com/article/fact-or-fiction-archimede/, accessed June 10, 2017.

28. "Archimedes' Principle," Encyclopedia Britannica, https://www.britannica.com/science/Archimedes-principle, accessed June 10, 2017.

29. Philip de Souza, "Greek Piracy," in *The Greek World*, ed. Anton Powell (London: Routledge, 1995), 180.

30. De Souza, "Greek Piracy," 181.

31. Nicolas D. Smith, "Aristotle's Theory of Natural Slavery," *Phoenix* 37, no. 2 (Summer 1983): 109–122.

32. Philip de Souza, *Piracy in the Graeco-Roman World* (Cambridge: Cambridge University Press, 1999), 63.

33. De Souza, "Greek Piracy," 187–189.

34. Maraqten, "Dangerous Trade Routes," 213–236; for maps of these trade routes that also were used in the Islamic period as pilgrimage routes, see Ali Ibrahim Al-Ghabban et al., *Roads of Arabia: Archaeology and History of the Kingdom of Saudi Arabia* (Washington, DC: Freer/Sackler, 2012), 424, 478.

35. Maraqten, "Dangerous Trade Routes," 233.

36. Maraqten, "Dangerous Trade Routes," 233.

37. Maraqten, "Dangerous Trade Routes," 218–219.

38. Peter Hopkirk, *Foreign Devils on the Silk Road: The Search for the Lost Cities and Treasures of Chinese Central Asia* (Amherst: University of Massachusetts Press, 1980), 19.

39. Maraqten, "Dangerous Trade Routes," 213–236; de Souza, "Greek Piracy," 179–198.

40. Maraqten, "Dangerous Trade Routes," 223.

41. De Souza, "Greek Piracy," 179–198.

42. Martin N. Murphy, *Small Boats, Weak States, Dirty Money: Piracy and Maritime Terrorism in the Modern World* (New York: Columbia University Press, 2010), 10–11.

43. Charles Tilly, "War Making and State Making as Organized Crime," in *Bringing the State Back*, ed. Peter Evans, Dietrich Rueschemeyer, and Theda Skocpol (Cambridge: Cambridge University Press, 1985), 173.

44. Luigi Mendola, "Historic Families: Grimaldi," Best of Sicily, 2011, http://www.bestofsicily.com/mag/art386.htm, accessed June 10, 2017.

45. Michael P. Scharf and Michael A. Newton, eds., *Prosecuting Maritime Piracy: Domestic Solutions to International Crimes* (Cambridge: Cambridge University Press, 2015),124–125; Thomas W. Gallant, "Brigandage, Piracy, Capitalism," in *States and Illegal Practices*, ed. Josiah McC. Heyman (Oxford: Berg, 1999), 25–61.

46. Jennifer L. Schenker, "The Infoanarchist," *Time*, July 17, 2000, http://content.time.com/time/world/article/0,8599,2056230,00.html, accessed June 10, 2017.

47. Sam Jones, "Licensed to Hack: The Rise of the Cyber Privateer," March 16, 2017, *Financial Times*, https://www.ft.com/content/21be48ec-0a48-11e7-97d1-5e720a26771b; Brian Whitenton, "The Difference between Pirates, Privateers, and Buccaneers, Part 1," Mariners' Museum and Park, March 20, 2012, http://www.marinersmuseum.org/blog/2012/09/the-difference-between-pirates-privateers-and-buccaneers-pt-1/, accessed September 23, 2017; Janice E. Thomson, *Mercenaries, Pirates, and Sovereigns: State-Building and Extraterritorial Violence in Early Modern Europe* (Princeton, NJ: Princeton University Press, 1994), 21.

48. Ben Johnson, "Sir Francis Drake," Historic UK, http://www.historic-uk.com/HistoryUK/HistoryofEngland/Sir-Francis-Drake/, accessed June 10, 2017. For Drake's role in piracy connected to the cochineal and textile industries, see Amy Butler Greenfield, *A Perfect Red: Empire, Espionage, and the Quest for the Color of Desire* (New York: HarperCollins, 2005), 113.

49. Ellen Nakashima, "Justice Department Charges Russian Spies and Criminal Hackers in Yahoo Intrusion," *Washington Post*, March 15, 2017.

50. "Money: Fakes and Forgeries," British Museum, http://www.britishmuseum.org/explore/themes/money/fakes_and_forgeries.aspx, accessed June 10, 2017.

51. Thomas Y. Allsen, *The Royal Hunt in Eurasian History* (Philadelphia: University of Pennsylvania Press, 2006).

52. Allsen, *The Royal Hunt in Eurasian History*.

53. David Ross, "Robin Hood," Britain Express, http://www.britainexpress.com/Myths/robin-hood.htm, accessed June 10, 2017.

54. Fernand Braudel, *Civilization and Capitalism, 15th–18th Century*, vol. 2, *The Wheels of Commerce*, trans. Siân Reynolds (New York: Harper & Row, 1979).

55. Suraiya Faroqhi, "Ottoman Cotton Textiles, 1500s to 1800: The Story of a Success That Did Not Last," paper presented at GEHN conference, University of Padua, November 17–19, 2005, http://www.lse.ac.uk/Economic-History/Assets/Documents/Research/GEHN/Padua/PaduaFaroqhiPaper.pdf.

56. K. N. Chaudhuri, *Trade and Civilisation in the Indian Ocean: An Economic History from the Rise of Islam to 1750* (Cambridge: Cambridge University Press, 1985), 9.

57. Michael Kwass, "Smuggling, Rebellion, and the Origins of Global Capitalism," Harvard University Press blog, July 28, 2014, http://harvardpress.typepad.com/hup_publicity/2014/07/smuggling-rebellion-and-the-origins-of-global-capitalism-michael-kwass.html, accessed January 26, 2017.

58. See, for example, James D. Tracy, ed., *The Rise of Merchant Empires: Long-Distance Trade in the Early Modern World, 1350–1750* (Cambridge: Cambridge University Press, 1990); Maria Fusaro, *Political Economies of Empire in the Early Modern Mediterranean: The Decline of Venice and the Rise of England 1450–1700* (Cambridge: Cambridge University Press, 2015); and Braudel, *Civilization and Capitalism: The Wheels of Commerce*.

59. For a discussion of the consumer revolution of the eighteenth century, see Michael Kwass, *Contraband: Louis Mandrin and the Making of a Global Underground* (Cambridge, MA: Harvard University Press, 2014), 2, 20.

60. Kwass, *Contraband*.

61. Braudel, *Civilization and Capitalism: The Wheels of Commerce*, 152.

62. E. Douglas Bebb, *Wesley: A Man with a Concern* (Eugene, OR: Wipf and Stock, 2016), 35–36.

63. Alan L. Karras, *Smuggling: Contraband and Corruption in World History* (Lanham, MD: Rowman and Littlefield, 2010), 21.

64. Sergei Antonov, "Criminal Capitalism in Imperial Russia: Counterfeiters, Merchants, and Gendarmes," address at NYU Jordan Center for the Advanced Study of Russia, February 5, 2016, http://jordanrussiacenter.org/event/sergei-antonov/, accessed June 11, 2017.

65. Antonov, "Criminal Capitalism in Imperial Russia."

66. Caroline Spence, "Smuggling in Early Modern France," master's thesis, University of Warwick, September 2010, 3, https://warwick.ac.uk/fac/arts/history/ecc/emforum/projects/disstheses/dissertations/spence-caroline.pdf.

67. Karras, *Smuggling*; Peter Andreas, *Smuggler Nation: How Illicit Trade Made America* (Oxford: Oxford University Press, 2013).

68. Maria Pia Pedani, "Ottoman Merchants in the Adriatic Trade and Smuggling," *Acta Histriae* 16 (2008): 1–2, 163–164. In *Heroin, Organized Crime, and the Making of Modern Turkey* (Oxford: Oxford University Press, 2014, 2, 42), Ryan Gingeras shows that smuggling was present before 1800 but has accelerated since then.

69. Andreas, *Smuggler Nation*, 45–60.

70. Victor Enthoven, "'That Abominable Nest of Pirates': St. Eustatius and the North Americans, 1680–1780," *Early American Studies* 10, no. 2 (2012): 291–293; Christian J. Koot, "Smuggling in Early America," Oxford Research Encyclopedias, January 2016, DOI:10.1093/acrefore/9780199329175.013.263, accessed June 11, 2017.

71. "Legal Papers of John Adams, Vol. 2," The Adams Papers: Digital Edition, https://www.masshist.org/publications/apde2/view?id=ADMS-05-02-02-0006-0004-0001, accessed June 11, 2017.

72. Koot, "Smuggling in Early America," citing Thomas Hutchinson to Thomas Pownall, January 29, 1769, quoted in Benjamin L. Carp, *Defiance of the*

Patriots: The Boston Tea Party and the Making of America (New Haven, CT: Yale University Press, 2010), 72. See also Carp, *Defiance of the Patriots*, 17, 71–73, 76–77; Jane Merritt, "Tea Trade, Consumption, and the Republican Paradox in Pre-Revolutionary Philadelphia," *Pennsylvania Magazine of History and Biography* 128, no. 2 (April 2004): 128–130.

73. Mark Karlin, "Smuggling and Illicit Trade Have Always Been an Essential Element of the US Economy," *Truthout*, July 31, 2014, http://www.truth-out.org/progressivepicks/item/25273-smuggling-and-illicit-trade-have-always-been-an-essential-component-of-the-us-economy, accessed June 11, 2017.

74. "The Beginnings of Revolutionary Thinking: 7d. Smuggling," U.S. History, http://www.ushistory.org/us/7d.asp, accessed June 11, 2017.

75. Leslie Bethell, *The Cambridge History of Latin America* (Cambridge: Cambridge University Press, 1984), 589–599.

76. Bethell, *The Cambridge History of Latin America*, 458.

77. Robert S. Kent, *Latin America: Regions and Peoples* (New York: Guilford Press, 2006), 324.

78. Dan Bethencourt, "Gold Refiner's Sales Team Tricked Compliance Staff into Approving Illegal Acquisitions," September 14, 2017, ACAMS/MoneyLaundering.com, http://www.moneylaundering.com (copy provided to author); United States of America v. Samer H. Barrage and Renato J. Rodriguez, filed in US District Court for the Southern District of Florida, March 21, 2017.

79. For example, see Eric Tagliacozzo, *Secret Trades, Porous Borders: Smuggling and States along a Southeast Asian Frontier, 1865–1915* (New Haven, CT: Yale University Press, 2005).

80. Kwass, *Contraband*: see also Spence, "Smuggling in Early Modern France."

81. Kwass, *Contraband*, 229.

82. Kwass, *Contraband*, 229.

83. For a discussion of private violence, see Alejandro Colás and Bryan Mabee, eds., *Mercenaries, Pirates, Bandits, and Empires: Private Violence in Historical Context* (London: Hurst & Co., 2010).

84. Kwass, *Contraband*, 229.

85. Denis C. Twitchett and Frederick W. Mote, eds., *The Cambridge History of China*, vol. 8, *The Ming Dynasty 1368–1644, Part 2* (Cambridge: Cambridge University Press, 1998), 341.

86. Philip D. Curtin, *Cross-Cultural Trade in World History* (Cambridge: Cambridge University Press, 1984), 1–6.

87. Frederico Varese, *Mafias on the Move: How Organized Crime Conquers New Territory* (Princeton, NJ: Princeton University Press, 2011); Juan Carlos Garzón, Marianna Olinger, Daniel M. Rico, and Gema Santamaría, *La Diáspora criminal: La Difusion transnacional del crimen organizado y cómo contener su expansion* (Washington, DC: Woodrow Wilson Center Latin American Program, 2013).

88. Jackson Miller, Varun Vira, and Mary Utermohlen, "Species of Crime: Typologies and Risk Metrics for Wildlife Trafficking," C4ADS, May 2015, http://static1.squarespace.com/static/566ef8b4d8af107232d5358a/t

/56af8242cf80a1474b572b85/1454342724100/Species+of+Crime.pdf, accessed June 11, 2017.

89. Malia Politzer and Emilie Kassie, "21st Century Gold Rush: How the Refugee Crisis Is Changing the World Economy," *Huffington Post/Highline*, December 21, 2016, http://highline.huffingtonpost.com/articles/en/the-21st-century-gold-rush-refugees/#/niger, accessed June 11, 2017.

90. Curtin, *Cross-Cultural Trade in World History*, 1–6.

91. Tagliacozzo, *Secret Trades, Porous Borders*.

92. Koot, "Smuggling in Early America."

93. Patrick Hunt, "Byzantine Silk: Smuggling and Espionage in the 6th Century CE," Altmarius, July 13, 2012, http://altmarius.ning.com/profiles/blogs/byzantine-silk-smuggling-and-espionage-in-the-6th-century-ce, accessed June 10, 2017; Braudel, *Civilization and Capitalism: The Wheels of Commerce*.

94. Karras, *Smuggling*, 29–30.

95. Greenfield, *A Perfect Red*, 45; In *Turkmen Carpets: A New Perspective* (Basel: Jürg Rageth and Freunde Des Orienteppichs, 2016), Jürg Rageth and his coauthors use carbon dating to establish the presence of cochineal.

96. Greenfield, *A Perfect Red*, 113.

97. Greenfield, *A Perfect Red*, 113–114.

98. "Red Scales in the Sunset: Cochineal," http://www.qbgdocents.org/Other_docs/Cochineal%201.pdf, accessed June 11, 2017; Greenfield, *A Perfect Red*. Cochineal also was exported to the Philippines and China.

99. Fernand Braudel, *Afterthoughts on Material Civilization and Capitalism*, trans. Patricia M. Ranum (Baltimore: Johns Hopkins University Press, 1977), 88.

100. Marco Musumeci, Vittoria Luda di Cortemiglia, and Elena D'Angelo, *Counterfeiting as an Activity Managed by Transnational Organised Crime and the Possible Re-use of Seized Assets for the Promotion of Intellectual Property and Economic Growth*, United Nations Interregional Crime and Justice Research Institute (UNICRI), 2014.

101. Braudel, *Afterthoughts on Material Civilization and Capitalism*; see also Fusaro, *Political Economies of Empire in the Early Modern Mediterranean*, 77–78.

102. Kate Finnigan, "Flower Power! Why Chintz Is Back in Fashion," *Telegraph*, May 7, 2016, https://www.telegraph.co.uk/fashion/style/flower-power-why-chintz-is-back-in-fashion.

103. Kwass, *Contraband*; Spence, "Smuggling in Early Modern France," 3.

104. Woodruff Smith, *Consumption and the Making of Respectability, 1600–1800* (London: Routledge, 2012), 259, n. 88.

105. Kwass, *Contraband*, 10–11; see also Karras, *Smuggling*; Tagliacozzo, *Secret Trade, Porous Borders*; Johan Mathew, *Margins of the Market: Trafficking and Capitalism across the Arabian Sea* (Berkeley: University of California Press, 2016); Robert Crews, "Trafficking in Evil? The Global Arms Trade and the Politics of Disorder," in *Global Muslims in the Age of Steam and Print, 1850–1930*, ed. James Gelvin and Nile Green (Berkeley: University of California Press, 2014), 121–142.

106. Koot, "Smuggling in Early America."

107. Andreas, *Smuggler Nation*, 155.

108. Andreas, *Smuggler Nation*, 154–174.

109. "Uzbekistan: Tier 3," in US Department of State, Office to Monitor and Combat Trafficking in Persons, *Trafficking in Persons Report 2016*, June 2016, https://www.state.gov/j/tip/rls/tiprpt/countries/2016/258890.htm, accessed June 16, 2017.

110. "Children Found Sewing Clothing for Wal-Mart, Hanes, & Other US & European Companies," Harvard University, Labor and Worklife Program, http://www.globallabourrights.org/reports/200610-IGLHR-Child-Labor-Is-Back.pdf; Steven Greenhouse and Michael Barbaro, "An Ugly Side of Free Trade: Sweatshops in Jordan," *New York Times*, May 3, 2006, http://www.nytimes.com/2006/05/03/business/worldbusiness/03clothing.html, accessed June 16, 2017. On Vietnamese in Jordan, see "Vietnamese Workers Abroad: A Rights Watch," Boat People SOS (blog), March 27, 2008, https://vietnameseworkersabroad.wordpress.com/about/, accessed June 16, 2017; see also "List of Goods Produced by Child Labor or Forced Labor," US Department of Labor, September 30, 2016, https://www.dol.gov/ilab/reports/child-labor/list-of-goods/, accessed June 16, 2017.

111. Koot, "Smuggling in Early America," citing Adam Smith, *An Inquiry into the Nature and Causes of the Wealth of Nations* [1776], ed. R. H. Campbell and A. S. Skinner (Indianapolis, IN: Liberty Classics, 1976), 898; Joshua M. Smith, *Borderland Smuggling: Patriots, Loyalists, and Illicit Trade in the Northeast, 1783–1820* (Gainesville: University Press of Florida, 2006).

Chapter 2. The Making of Modern Illicit Trade: From 1800 to the End of the Cold War

1. Karras, *Smuggling*, 73.

2. William Bristow, "Enlightenment," in Stanford Encyclopedia of Philosophy, August 20, 2010 https://plato.stanford.edu/archives/sum2011/entries/enlightenment/, accessed May 31, 2017.

3. Carolyn Nordstrom, *Global Outlaws: Crime, Money, and Power in the Contemporary World* (Berkeley: University of California Press, 2007); Mathew, *Margins of the Market*.

4. Tagliacozzo, *Secret Trades, Porous Borders*; Mathew, *Margins of the Market*; Chaudhuri, *Trade and Civilisation in the Indian Ocean*; Muriel Laurent, *Contrabando en Colombia en el siglo xix: Prácticas y discursos de resistencia y reproducción* (Bogotá: Universidad de los Andes, Facultad de Ciencias Sociales, Departamento de Historia, CESO, Ediciones Uniandes, 2008), https://appsciso.uniandes.edu.co/sip/data/pdf/Contrabando_en_Colombia_siglo_XIX.pdf, accessed June 12, 2017.

5. James H. Mills and Patricia Barton, "Introduction," in *Drugs and Empires: Essays in Modern Imperialism and Drugs*, ed. James H. Mills and Patricia Barton (Houndsmills, UK: Palgrave Macmillan, 2007), 1.

6. Yücel Yeşılgöz and Frank Bovenkerk, "Urban Knights and Rebels in the Ottoman Empire," in *Organised Crime in Europe: Concepts, Patterns, and Control Policies in the European Union and Beyond*, ed. Cyrille Fijnaut and Letizia Paoli (Dordrecht: Springer, 2004), 181–224; Gingeras, *Heroin, Organized Crime, and the Making of Modern Turkey*, 19–52.

7. Gingeras, *Heroin, Organized Crime, and the Making of Modern Turkey*; Peter Tinti and Tuesday Reitano, *Migrant, Refugee, Smuggler, Saviour* (London: Hurst, 2016).

8. Lindita Arapi, "The Balkan Route to Western Europe for Yugoslavia Guns," DW, December 5, 2015, http://www.dw.com/en/the-balkan-route-to-western -europe-for-yugoslavia-guns/a-18896280, accessed June 12, 2017.

9. "Top 10 Plundered Artifacts," *Time*, http://content.time.com/time/specials /packages/completelist/0,29569,1883142,00.html, accessed June 12, 2017.

10. Efrat, *Governing Guns, Preventing Plunder*, 115–136. Because many countries did not pass laws in accordance with the UNESCO Convention for thirty years, an active trade in antiquities continued.

11. Rachel Shabi, "Looted in Syria—and Sold in London: The British Antiques Shops Dealing in Artefacts Smuggled by Isis," *Guardian*, July 3, 2015, https:// www.theguardian.com/world/2015/jul/03/antiquities-looted-by-isis-end-up-in -london-shops, accessed June 12, 2017; "Committee Reports: H. Rept. 114-380: Prevent Trafficking in Cultural Property," 114th Cong., 1st sess., Congress.gov, December 15, 2015, https://www.congress.gov/congressional-report/114th-congress /house-report/380/1, accessed June 12, 2017; Neil Brodie, "Syria and Its Regional Neighbors: A Case of Cultural Property Protection Policy Failure?," *International Journal of Cultural Property* 22, nos. 2–3 (2015): 317–335; Neil Brodie, "The Internet Market in Antiquities," in *Countering Illicit Traffic in Cultural Goods: The Global Challenge of Protecting the World's Heritage*, ed. France Desmarais (Paris: International Council of Museums [ICOM], 2015), 11–20; Nathan Elkins, "The Trade in Fresh Supplies of Ancient Coins: Scale, Organization, and Politics," in *All the King's Horses: Essays on the Impact of Looting and the Illicit Antiquities Trade on Our Knowledge of the Past* (Washington, DC: Society for American Archaeology Press, 2012), 91–107.

12. Rosaleen Duffy, *Nature Crime: How We're Getting Conservation Wrong* (New Haven, CT: Yale University Press, 2010).

13. N. D. Smith, "Aristotle's Theory of Natural Slavery," in *A Companion to Aristotle's Politics*, ed. David Keyt and Fred Miller (Oxford: Oxford University Press, 1991), 142–155; John Locke, "Of Slavery," chap. 4 in *Second Treatise on Government* (New York: Hafner Library of Classics, 1947), 132–133; Jill Frank, "Citizens, Slaves, and Foreigners: Aristotle on Human Nature," *American Political Science Review* 98, no. 1 (2004): 91–104.

14. "The 1807 Act and Its Effects," Abolition Project, http://abolition.e2bn .org/slavery_113.html, accessed June 13, 2017.

15. For the Spanish Crown's involvement in the slave trade, see Andrés Reséndez, *The Other Slavery: The Uncovered Story of Indian Enslavement in America* (Boston: Houghton Mifflin Harcourt, 2016), 44.

16. Hugh Thomas, *The Slave Trade: The Story of the Transatlantic Slave Trade: 1440–1870* (New York: Simon & Schuster, 1997); James A. Rawley, *The Transatlantic Slave Trade: A History* (New York: W. W. Norton & Co., 1981).

17. Joel Quirk, *The Anti-Slavery Project: From the Slave Trade to Human Trafficking* (Philadelphia: University of Pennsylvania Press, 2011), 33.

18. David Brion Davis, *The Problem of Slavery in the Age of Revolution, 1770–1823* (Ithaca, NY: Cornell University Press, 1975), 43–51.

19. Seymour Drescher, *Capitalism and Antislavery: British Mobilization in Comparative Perspective* (New York: Oxford University Press, 1987), 166. Drescher suggests that it was the concept of benevolence combining with the fervor of the evangelicals to form a powerful abolitionist movement that eliminated the slave trade.

20. Drescher, *Capitalism and Antislavery*, 54.

21. Davis, *The Problem of Slavery in the Age of Revolution*, 32.

22. Andreas, *Smuggler Nation*, 130. The National Archives contains numerous trial records and ship records of illicitly transported slaves to the United States; see "The Slave Trade," National Archives, https://www.archives.gov/education /lessons/slave-trade.html, accessed August 17, 2016.

23. Andreas, *Smuggler Nation*, 134.

24. Andreas, *Smuggler Nation*, 133–143.

25. Quirk, *The Anti-Slavery Project*, 60.

26. Quirk, *The Anti-Slavery Project*, 61.

27. "Net ODA," OECD Data, https://data.oecd.org/oda/net-oda.htm, accessed May 29, 2017.

28. "Military Expenditure (% of GDP)," World Bank, http://data.worldbank .org/indicator/MS.MIL.XPND.GD.ZS, accessed June 13, 2017.

29. *The British and Foreign Anti-Slavery Reporter*, vol. 6 (London: Lancelot Wild, 1845), 221.

30. F. George Kay, *The Shameful Trade* (London: Muller, 1967), 129; Leslie Bethell, *The Abolition of the Brazilian Slave: Britain, Brazil, and the Slave Trade Question, 1807–1869* (Cambridge: Cambridge University Press, 1970); "The Abolition of the Slave Trade," Schomburg Center for Research in Black Culture, http://abolition.nypl.org/print/illegal_slave_trade/, accessed May 29, 2017.

31. Deryck Scarr, *Slaving and Slavery in the Indian Ocean* (Houndsmills, UK, and New York: Macmillan Press and St. Martin's Press, 1998).

32. Immanuel Wallerstein, "The Three Stages of African Involvement in the World-Economy," in *The Political Economy of Contemporary Africa*, ed. C. W. Gutkind and Immanuel Wallerstein (Beverly Hills, CA: Sage Publications, 1976), 40.

33. Wallerstein, "The Three Stages of African Involvement in the World-Economy," 40; Thomas, *The Slave Trade*, 564.

34. Mathew, *Margins of the Market*, 53–54, 55.

35. For a picture of this sign, see "Stone Town Slave Market in Zanzibar," SHABL, April 5, 2011, http://stophavingaboringlife.com/stone-town-slave -market-in-zanzibar/, accessed June 13, 2017.

36. Mathew, *Margins of the Market*, 54–55.

37. Kate Parlett, *The Individual in the International Legal System: Continuity and Change in International Law* (Cambridge: Cambridge University Press, 2011), 288.

38. "British-American Diplomacy: Treaty between United States and Great Britain for the Suppression of the Slave Trade; April 7, 1862," Yale Law School, Avalon Project, http://avalon.law.yale.edu/19th_century/br1862.asp, accessed June 13, 2017.

39. Saul David, "Slavery and the 'Scramble for Africa,'" BBC History, February 17, 2011, http://www.bbc.co.uk/history/british/abolition/scramble_for_africa_article_01.shtml, accessed June 13, 2017.

40. Louise Shelley, *Human Trafficking: A Global Perspective* (Cambridge: Cambridge University Press, 2010), 146; Sterling Seagrave, *Lords of the Rim: The Invisible Empire of the Overseas Chinese* (New York: G. P. Putnam's Sons, 1995).

41. R. T. Naylor, *Counterfeit Crime: Criminal Profits, Terror Dollars, and Nonsense* (Montreal: McGill–Queen's University Press, 2014).

42. Amitav Ghosh, *Flood of Fire* (New York: Farrar, Straus and Giroux, 2015), *River of Smoke* (New York: Farrar, Straus and Giroux, 2011), and *Sea of Poppies* (New York: Farrar, Straus and Giroux, 2008), all discuss the Indian-Chinese opium trade. *Flood of Fire* focuses on China at the time of the First Opium War.

43. "*Sea of Poppies*," Amitav Ghosh, http://www.amitavghosh.com/seapoppies.html, accessed June 13, 2017.

44. Kate Boehme, "Smuggling India: Deconstructing Western India's Illicit Export Trade, 1818–1870," *Journal of the Royal Asiatic Society*, 2015, https://www.repository.cam.ac.uk/bitstream/handle/1810/246788/Boehme-2015-Journal_of_the_Royal_Asiatic_Society.pdf, accessed June 13, 2017.

45. Amar Farooqui, "Opium and the Trading World of Western India in the Early Nineteenth Century," in *Drugs and Empires: Essays in Modern Imperialism and Drugs*, ed. James H. Mills and Patricia Barton (Houndsmills, UK: Palgrave Macmillan, 2007), 83–100; Amar Farooqui, *Smuggling as Subversion: Colonialism, Indian Merchants, and the Politics of Opium, 1790–1843* (Lanham, MD: Lexington Books, 2005); William O. Walker III, "'A Grave Danger to the Peace of the East': Opium and Imperial Rivalry in China, 1895–1920," in Mills and Barton, *Drugs and Empires*, 185–203; Simon Harvey, *Smuggling: Seven Centuries of Contraband* (London: Reaktion Books, 2016), 151–175.

46. Chaudhuri, *Trade and Civilisation in the Indian Ocean*, 109. India trade records from the sixteenth century already revealed that opium moved along with other high-value items.

47. J. Y. Wong, *Deadly Dreams: Opium, Imperialism, and the Arrow War (1856–1860) in China* (Cambridge: Cambridge University Press, 1998), 369–374.

48. Hsin-pao Chang, *Commissioner Lin and the Opium War* (Cambridge, MA: Harvard University Press, 1964).

49. For the mechanisms of smuggling and Chinese complicity, see Peter Ward Fay, *The Opium War, 1840–1842: Barbarians in the Celestial Empire in the Early Part of the Nineteenth Century and the War by Which They Forced Her Gates Ajar*

NOTES TO CHAPTER 2 **267**

(Chapel Hill: University of North Carolina Press, 1997), 44–46; see also Karl E. Mayer, "The Opium War's Secret History," *New York Times*, June 28, 1997, http://www.nytimes.com/1997/06/28/opinion/the-opium-war-s-secret-history.html, accessed June 13, 2017.

50. Mayer, "The Opium War's Secret History."

51. Frank Dikötter, Lars Laaman, and Xun Zhou, "China, British Imperialism, and the Myth of the 'Opium Plague,'" in Mills and Barton, *Drugs and Empires*, 19–38. See also Frank Dikötter, "'Patient Zero': China and the Myth of the Opium Plague,'" October 24, 2003, http://www.frankdikotter.com/publications/the-myth-of-opium.pdf.

52. Wong, *Deadly Dreams*.

53. Mayer, "The Opium's War Secret History"; Andreas, *Smuggler Nation*, 254.

54. I gleaned this information from a tour of the historic Roosevelt home on Campobello Island on September 21, 2016.

55. In the film *Art Trafficking* (Arte France, 2016), Tania Rakhmanova discusses heads stolen from the Forbidden Palace and found in prominent French collections. I saw this interesting film on an airplane flight in 2017. For information on the film, see "Art Trafficking," an *Al-Jazeera* special series, March 17, 2017, http://www.aljazeera.com/programmes/specialseries/2017/02/art-trafficking-170228090044987.html, accessed May 29, 2017.

56. Efrat, *Governing Guns, Preventing Plunder*, 227–238.

57. "Illicit Drug Markets: Situations and Trends," *World Drug Report 2016*, UNODC, 2016, 26–42, http://www.unodc.org/doc/wdr2016/WDR_2016_Chapter_1.pdf, accessed May 31, 2017.

58. Andreas, *Smuggler Nation*, 98–112.

59. World Intellectual Property Organization (WIPO), "International Treaties and Conventions on Intellectual Property," chap. 5 in *Intellectual Property Handbook*, 2004, 241–242, http://www.wipo.int/export/sites/www/about-ip/en/iprm/pdf/ch5.pdf, accessed June 13, 2017. The first eleven signatories were Belgium, Brazil, El Salvador, France, Guatemala, Italy, the Netherlands, Portugal, Serbia, Spain, and Switzerland. When Great Britain, Tunisia, and Ecuador joined in 1884, all of the signatories were now highly industrialized countries. See also Efrat, *Governing Guns, Preventing Plunder*, 263–266.

60. Efrat, *Governing Guns, Preventing Plunder*, 262.

61. This concern has been expressed by doctoral students in technical fields at George Mason University where I teach, and they have been exempted from the rule that dissertations are to be filed online.

62. "What We Investigate: Intellectual Property Theft/Piracy," Federal Bureau of Investigation (FBI), https://www.fbi.gov/investigate/white-collar-crime/piracy-ip-theft, accessed June 13, 2017.

63. Linton Weeks, "Hats Off to Women Who Saved the Birds," NPR History Dept., July 15, 2015, http://www.npr.org/sections/npr-history-dept/2015/07/15/422860307/hats-off-to-women-who-saved-the-birds, accessed June 13, 2017.

64. Barry Yeoman, "Why the Passenger Pigeon Went Extinct," *Audubon*, May/June 2014, http://www.audubon.org/magazine/may-june-2014/why-passenger-pigeon-went-extinct, accessed June 13, 2017.

65. "The First Venture Capitalists: Fin-Tech," *Economist*, January 2, 2016, http://www.economist.com/news/finance-and-economics/21684805-there-were-tech-startups-there-was-whaling-fin-tech, accessed June 13, 2017.

66. "Key Documents," International Whaling Convention, https://iwc.int/convention, accessed August 7, 2017.

67. Robert Crews, "Trafficking in Evil? The Global Trade and the Politics of Disorder," in *Global Muslims in the Age of Steam and Printing*, ed. James L. Gelvin and Nile Green (Berkeley: University of California Press, 2014), 121.

68. George T. Díaz, *Border Contraband: A History of Smuggling across the Rio Grande* (Austin: University of Texas Press, 2015), 65–88.

69. Díaz, *Border Contraband*, 73.

70. Díaz, *Border Contraband*, 126–137.

71. Crews, "Trafficking in Evil?," 122.

72. Harvey, *Smuggling*, 222–227.

73. Michael T. Klare, *Resource Wars: The New Landscape of Global Conflict* (New York: Henry Holt and Co./Metropolitan Books, 2001).

74. Avi Brisman, Nigel Smith, and Rob White, "Toward a Criminology of Environment-Conflict Relationships," in *Environmental Crime and Social Conflict: Contemporary and Emerging Issues*, ed. Avi Brisman, Nigel Smith, and Rob White (Burlington, VT: Ashgate Publishing Co., 2015), 18–19; Aaron Fichtelberg, "Resource Wars, Environmental Crime, and the Laws of War: Updating War Crimes in a Resource Scarce World," in Brisman, Smith, and White, *Environmental Crime and Social Conflict*, 177–195.

75. The 1921 convention was called the International Convention for the Suppression of the Traffic in Women and Children, and the 1933 convention was titled International Convention for the Suppressions of the Traffic in Women of Full Age. These followed from the adoption in 1910 of the International Convention for the Suppressions of the White Slave Traffic.

76. The Single Convention on Narcotic Drugs was adopted by the UN in 1961 and amended in 1972; "Legal Framework for Drug Trafficking," UNODC, https://www.unodc.org/unodc/en/drug-trafficking/legal-framework.html, accessed May 24, 2017.

77. John M. Sellar, *The UN's Lone Ranger: Combating International Wildlife Crime* (Dunbeath, UK: Whittles Publishing, 2014), 7–11. The Montreal Protocol on Substances That Deplete the Ozone Layer (a protocol to the Vienna Convention for the Protection of the Ozone Layer) is an international treaty designed to protect the ozone layer by phasing out the production of numerous substances that are responsible for ozone depletion. It was agreed to on August 26, 1987, and entered into force on August 26, 1989; see "The Montreal Protocol on Substances That Deplete the Ozone Layer," UNEP, Ozone Secretariat, http://ozone.unep.org/en/treaties-and-decisions/montreal-protocol

-substances-deplete-ozone-layer, accessed June 13, 2017; Jennifer Clapper, "Illicit Trade in Hazardous Wastes and CFCs: International Responses to Environmental 'Bads,'" in Friman and Andreas, *Illicit Global Economy and State Power*, 91–123. For a list of treaties related to WMDs, see "Treaties and Regimes," Nuclear Threat Initiative (NTI), http://www.nti.org/learn/treaties-and-regimes /treaties/, accessed June 13, 2017.

78. The Basel Convention on the Control of Transboundary Movements of Hazardous Wastes and Their Disposal was adopted on March 22, 1989; "Text of the Convention," UNEP, Basel Convention, http://www.basel.int /TheConvention/Overview/TextoftheConvention/tabid/1275/Default.aspx, accessed June 13, 2017; K. R. Stebbins, "Garbage Imperialism: Health Implications of Dumping Hazardous Wastes in Third World Countries," *Medical Anthropology* 15, no. 1 (1992): 81–102; C. A. Anyinam, "Transboundary Movements of Hazardous Wastes: The Case of Toxic Waste Dumping in Africa," *International Journal of Health Services* 21, no. 4 (1991): 759–777; Donald J. Rebovich, *Dangerous Ground: The World of Hazardous Waste Crime* (New Brunswick, NJ: Transaction Publishers, 1992); Andrew Szasz, "Corporations, Organized Crime, and the Disposal of Hazardous Waste: An Examination of the Making of a Criminogenic Regulatory Structure," *Criminology* 24, no. 1 (1986): 1–27.

79. Rebecca Onion, "Nifty Methods for Smuggling Contraband, from a Manual for World War II–Era British Spies," *Slate/The Vault*, December 5, 2014, http:// www.slate.com/blogs/the_vault/2014/12/05/history_of_spycraft_manual_for _british_spies_during_wwii.html, accessed June 13, 2017.

80. Carol Vogel, "Lauder Pays $135 Million, a Record, for a Klimt Portrait," *New York Times*, June 19, 2006, http://www.nytimes.com/2006/06/19/arts /design/19klim.html, accessed June 13, 2017.

81. Matt Vasilogambros, "The Still-Missing Nazi Gold Train," *Atlantic*, August 24, 2016, http://www.theatlantic.com/news/archive/2016/08/poland-nazi -gold-train/497231/, accessed June 13, 2017.

82. Suryatapa Bhattacharya, "Highlighting the Heroes of India's Freedom Fight," *National*, August 17, 2013, http://www.thenational.ae/news/world/south -asia/highlighting-the-heroes-of-indias-freedom-fight, accessed June 13, 2017; "Hindu Conspiracy Cases: Activities of the Indian Independence Movement in the US, 1908–1933," Gale, https://www.gale.com/c/the-hindu-conspiracy-cases -activities-of-the-indian-independence-movement-in-the-us-1908-1933.

83. See also Julian Rademeyer, *Killing for Profit: Exposing the Illegal Rhino Horn Trade* (New York: Random House, 2012), 45–62; Bram Buscher and Maano Ramutsindela, "Green Violence: Rhino Poaching and the War to Save Southern Africa's Peace Parks," *African Affairs* 115, no. 458 (2016): 5; Annette Hübschle, "A Status Symbol to Die For," in "The Black Market as a Gray Zone," *Culture and Society: Illegal Markets*, Max Planck Institute for the Study of Societies, January 15, 2015, 73–75, https://www.mpg.de/9093473/W005_culture_society _070-077.pdf, accessed June 14, 2017; Annette Michaela Hübschle, "A Game of Horns: Transnational Flows of Rhino Horn," International Max Planck Research

School, 2016, http://pubman.mpdl.mpg.de/pubman/item/escidoc:2218357:5 /component/escidoc:2261029/2016_IMPRSDis, accessed June 14, 2017.

84. "Decolonization of Asia and Africa, 1945–60," US Department of State, Office of the Historian, https://history.state.gov/milestones/1945-1952/asia-and -africa.

85. Eric Hobsbawm, *Primitive Rebels: Studies in Archaic Forms of Social Movement in the 19th and 20th Centuries* (Manchester, UK: Manchester University Press, 1959).

86. Thor Hanson, Thomas M. Brooks, Gustavo A. B. da Fonseca, Michael Hoffmann, John F. Lamoreux, Gary Machlis, Cristina G. Mittermeier, Russell A. Mittermeier, and John D. Pilgrim, "Warfare in Biodiversity Hotspots," *Conservation Biology* 23, no. 3 (2009): 578–587.

87. John E. Thomas Jr., "Narco-Terrorism: Could the Legislative and Prosecutorial Responses Threaten Our Civil Liberties?," *Washington and Lee Law Review* 66 (2009): 1885–1886, http://law2.wlu.edu/deptimages/Law%20Review /66-4ThomasNote.pdf.

88. Shaun Rein, "No, China Will Absolutely Not Collapse," *Forbes*, March 2, 2010, http://www.forbes.com/2010/02/03/china-economy-bubble-leadership -citizenship-rein.html, accessed June 13, 2017; Greg Grossman, "The Second Economy of the USSR," *Problems of Communism* 26 (September/October 1977): 25–40.

89. Grossman, "The Second Economy in the USSR"; Michael Alexeev, "The Russian Underground Economy in Transition," National Council for Soviet and East European Research, November 20, 1995, https://www.ucis.pitt.edu/nceeer /1995-809-04-Alexeev.pdf, accessed June 13, 2017; Konstantin M. Simis, *USSR— the Corrupt Society: The Secret World of Soviet Capitalism* (New York: Simon & Schuster, 1982).

90. Alena V. Ledeneva, *Russia's Economy of Favours: Blat, Networking, and Informal Exchange* (Cambridge: Cambridge University Press, 1998); Caroline Humphrey, *The Unmaking of Soviet Life* (Ithaca, NY: Cornell University Press, 2002).

91. Alena V. Ledeneva, *How Russia Really Works: The Informal Practices That Shape Post-Soviet Politics and Business* (Ithaca, NY: Cornell University Press, 2006).

92. Prema-chandra Athukorala, ed., *The Rise of Asia: Trade and Investment in Global Perspective* (Abingdon, UK: Routledge, 2011); Gideon Rachman, *Easternization: Asia's Rise and America's Decline: From Obama to Trump and Beyond* (New York: Other Press, 2017).

93. Vint Cerf, "A Brief History of the Internet and Related Networks," Internet Society, http://www.internetsociety.org/internet/what-internet/history -internet/brief-history-internet-related-networks, accessed June 13, 2017.

94. "The Invention of the Internet," History, http://www.history.com/topics /inventions/invention-of-the-internet, accessed June 13, 2017.

95. Zeynep Tufekci, "The Looming Digital Meltdown," *New York Times*, January 6, 2018, https://www.nytimes.com/2018/01/06/opinion/looming-digital -meltdown.html, January 8, 2018.

96. "A Brief History of NSF and the Internet," National Science Foundation (NSF), August 13, 2003, https://www.nsf.gov/news/news_summ.jsp?cntn_id= 103050, accessed June 13, 2017.

97. Author's interviews with early participants in the development of the internet. In the mid-1980s, the NSF became involved in the development of the internet, contributing a system to improve communications that today is a backbone of its operations.

98. Sarah Deming, "The Economic Importance of Indian Opium and Trade with China on Britain's Economy, 1843–1890," Whitman College Economics Working Paper 25, Spring 2011, 4, https://www.whitman.edu/economics /Workingpapers/content/WP_25.pdf, accessed June 13, 2017.

99. Braudel, *Afterthoughts on Material Civilization and Capitalism*.

100. Jerrold Seigel, *Modernity and Bourgeois Life: Society, Politics, and Culture in England, France, and Germany since 1750* (Cambridge: Cambridge University Press, 2012).

101. William Beinart, "Empire, Hunting, and Ecological Change in Southern and Central Africa," *Past and Present* 1990, no. 128 (1): 162–186.

Chapter 3. How Did We Get Here?
Drivers of the Post–Cold War Expansion

1. See, for example, Moisés Naím, *Illicit: How Smugglers, Traffickers, and Copycats Are Hijacking the Global Economy* (New York: Doubleday, 2005).

2. Nils Gilman, Jesse Goldhammer, and Steve Weber, *Deviant Globalization: Black Market Economy in the 21st Century* (New York: Continuum, 2011); Alain Bauer and Xavier Raufer, *The Dark Side of Globalization* (Paris: CNRS [Centre National de la Recherche Scientifique] Éditions, 2009).

3. For more on this, see my earlier work, Louise I. Shelley, *Dirty Entanglements: Corruption, Crime, and Terrorism* (Cambridge: Cambridge University Press, 2014), 64–96; see also Chaikin and Sharman, *Corruption and Money Laundering*; Sarah Chayes, *Thieves of State: Why Corruption Threatens Global Security* (New York: W. W. Norton & Co., 2015); Sarah Chayes, "Corruption, Violent Extremism, Kleptocracy, and the Dangers of Failing Governance," Carnegie Endowment for International Peace, June 30, 2016, http://carnegieendowment.org /2016/06/30/corruption-violent-extremism-kleptocracy-and-dangers-of-failing -governance-pub-63982, accessed August 7, 2017; Kelly M. Greenhill, "Kleptocratic Independence: Trafficking, Corruption, and the Marriage of Politics and Illicit Profits," in *Corruption, Global Security, and World Order*, ed. Robert I. Rotberg (Cambridge, MA: World Peace Foundation and American Academy of Arts and Sciences, 2009), 96–124.

4. Vanda Felbab-Brown, *Shooting Up: Counterinsurgency and the War on Drugs* (Washington, DC: Brooking Institution Press, 2009), 13–33.

5. On Iran, see R. T. Naylor, *Patriots and Profiteers: On Economic Warfare, Embargo Busting, and State-Sponsored Crime* (Toronto: McClelland & Stewart,

1999), 227–296. For more recent analyses of sanction-busting, see Sam Dagher, "Smugglers in Iraq Blunt Sanctions against Iran," *New York Times*, July 9, 2010, http://www.nytimes.com/2010/07/09/world/middleeast/09kurds.html, accessed May 31, 2017; Benoît Vitkine, "Smugglers Profit from Ukraine's Dirty War," *Guardian*, November 3, 2015, https://www.theguardian.com/world/2015/nov/03/ukraine-smuggling-blockade-luhansk-separatists, accessed June 15, 2017; Colum Lynch, "Shutting Down Iran's Nuclear Smugglers," *Foreign Policy*, July 1, 2015, http://foreignpolicy.com/2015/07/01/shutting-down-irans-tehran-nuclear-smugglers-security-council-united-nations/; Benjamin Weiser, "US Urges No Bail for Reza Zarrab in Iran Sanctions Case," *New York Times*, May 25, 2016, https://www.nytimes.com/2016/05/26/world/middleeast/us-urges-no-bail-for-reza-zarrab-in-iran-sanctions-case.html, accessed May 31, 2016; Liana Sun Wyler and Dick K. Nanto, "North Korean Crime-for-Profit Activities," Congressional Research Service, August 25, 2008, https://fas.org/sgp/crs/row/RL33885.pdf, accessed June 15, 2017.

6. Juan C. Zarate, *Treasury's War: The Unleashing of a New Era of Financial Warfare* (New York: Public Affairs, 2013), 321–356; Paul Rexton Kan, Bruce E. Bechtol Jr., and Robert M. Collins, "Criminal Sovereignty: Understanding North Korea's Illicit International Activities," US Army War College, Strategic Studies Institute, March 2010, http://www.strategicstudiesinstitute.army.mil/pdffiles/PUB975.pdf, accessed June 15, 2017.

7. "About 475 Thousand Persons Were Killed in 76 Months of the Syrian Revolution and More Than 14 Million Were Wounded and Displaced," Syrian Observatory for Human Rights, July 16, 2017, http://www.syriahr.com/en/?p=70012, accessed August 17, 2017.

8. John Wendle, "The Ominous Story of Syria's Climate Refugees," *Scientific American*, December 17, 2015, http://www.scientificamerican.com/article/ominous-story-of-syria-climate-refugees/, accessed August 15, 2017.

9. Wendle, "The Ominous Story of Syria's Climate Refugees."

10. "Drought in the Fertile Crescent," NASA Earth Observatory, April 30, 2008, https://earthobservatory.nasa.gov/NaturalHazards/view.php?id=20010, accessed August 15, 2017.

11. NASA Earth Observatory, "Drought in the Fertile Crescent"; Colin P. Kelley et al., "Climate Change in the Fertile Crescent and Implications of the Recent Syrian Drought," *Proceedings of the National Academy of Sciences of the United States of America* 112, no. 11 (2015): 3241–3246, http://www.pnas.org/content/112/11/3241.full, accessed March 6, 2016.

12. "World Urbanization Prospects: The 2014 Revision: Highlights," ST/ESA/SER.A/352, United Nations, Department of Economic and Social Affairs, Population Division, 2, http://esa.un.org/unpd/wup/highlights/wup2014-highlights.pdf, accessed August 15, 2017.

13. Kelley et al., "Climate Change in the Fertile Crescent and Implications of the Recent Syrian Drought."

14. Campbell Fraser, "Human Organ Trafficking: Understanding the Changing Role of Social Media and Dark Web Technologies 2010–2015," seminar,

George Mason University, Terrorism, Transnational Crime, and Corruption Center (TraCCC), January 21, 2016, http://traccc.gmu.edu/events/events-2014 -2017/, accessed August 22, 2017; author's conversations with Campbell Fraser.

15. See my previous book, Shelley, *Dirty Entanglements*.

16. Paul J. Smith, *The Terrorism Ahead: Confronting Transnational Violence in the 21st Century* (London: Routledge, 2015), 151–152.

17. Mats Berdal and David M. Malone, eds., *Greed and Grievance: Economic Agendas in Civil Wars* (Boulder, CO: Lynne Rienner Publishers, 2000).

18. Fred Pearce, "Armed Conflict Wipes Out Wildlife in Libya and Syria," *New Scientist* (February 20, 2016): 11.

19. "IS Threat to Syria's Northern Bald Ibis Near Palmyra," *BBC News*, May 25, 2015, http://www.bbc.com/news/world-middle-east-32872350, accessed June 15, 2017.

20. Musumeci, Cortemiglia, and D'Angelo, *Counterfeiting as an Activity Managed by Transnational Organised Crime*, 37.

21. Aryn Baker, "How Climate Change Is Behind the Surge of Migrants to Europe," *Time*, September 7, 2015, http://time.com/4024210/climate-change -migrants/, accessed June 16, 2017; *Livelihood Security: Climate Change, Conflict, and Migration in the Sahel*, UNEP, 2011, postconflict.unep.ch/publications /UNEP_Sahel_EN.pdf, accessed June 16, 2017.

22. Susan F. Martin, *International Migrations: Evolving Trends from the Early Twentieth Century to the Present* (New York: Cambridge University Press, 2014), 214–234; Damian Carrington, "Climate Change Will Stir 'Unimaginable' Refugee Crisis, Says Military," *Guardian*, December 1, 2016, https://www.theguardian .com/environment/2016/dec/01/climate-change-trigger-unimaginable-refugee -crisis-senior-military, accessed June 16, 2017; author's many personal discussions with Major General Munir Muniruzzaman, chairman of the Global Military Advisory Council on Climate Change (http://gmaccc.org/, cited by Carrington). On the rise of the smuggling and trafficking of Bengalis to the United Kingdom and Italy, see Nishtha Chugh, "Bangladeshi Migrants Eke Out a Living in Rome," *Al-Jazeera*, November 6, 2014, http://www.aljazeera.com/indepth/features /2014/11/bangladeshi-migrants-italy-boat-economy-201411611232371682.html, accessed April 14, 2017.

23. "Worldwide Displacement Hits All-Time High as War and Persecution Increase," UNHCR, June 18, 2015, http://www.unhcr.org/558193896.html, accessed June 15, 2017.

24. Adrian Edwards, "Global Forced Displacement Hits Record High," UNHCR, June 20, 2016, http://www.unhcr.org/en-us/news/latest/2016 /6/5763b65a4/global-forced-displacement-hits-record-high.html, accessed June 15, 2017.

25. Nazia Hussain, "Tracing Order in Seeming Chaos: Understanding the Informal and Violent Political Order of Karachi," PhD diss., George Mason University, spring 2016, 127–131; "The Water Mafia Is Sucking India Dry," *Hindustan Times*, May 3, 2016, http://www.hindustantimes.com/editorials/the-water-mafia -is-sucking-india-dry/story-iTe8Frdg3slqxSp4o2MhwM.html, accessed June 15,

2017; AFP, "The 'Water Mafias' That Suck Karachi Dry," *Dawn*, October 4, 2015, https://www.dawn.com/news/1210853, accessed June 15, 2017.

26. Marc Goodman, *Future Crimes: Everything Is Connected, Everyone Is Vulnerable, and What We Can Do About It* (New York: Doubleday, 2015); Misha Glenny, *DarkMarket: Cyberthieves, Cybercops, and You* (New York: Alfred A. Knopf, 2011).

27. Joshua Baron, Angela O'Mahony, David Manheim, and Cynthia Dion-Schwarz, *National Security Implications of Virtual Currency: Examining the Potential for Non-State Actor Deployment*, RAND Corporation, 2015, http://www.rand.org/content/dam/rand/pubs/research_reports/RR1200/RR1231/RAND_RR1231.pdf, accessed June 16, 2017; Analytical Services, Inc. (ANSER), *Risks and Threats of Cryptocurrencies*, RP-14-01.03.03-02, US Department of Homeland Security, Homeland Security Studies and Analysis Institute, December 31, 2014, https://www.anser.org/docs/reports/RP14-01.03.03-02_Cryptocurrencies%20508_31Dec2014.pdf, accessed June 16, 2017.

28. *Trade in Counterfeit and Pirated Goods: Mapping the Economic Impact*, OECD, April 18, 2016, 34, DOI:http://dx.doi.org/10.1787/9789264252653-en.

29. Nick Bilton, *American Kingpin: The Epic Hunt for the Criminal Mastermind behind the Silk Road* (New York: Random House/Portfolio, 2017), 42–43.

30. United Nations, "Addressing Security Council, UN Secretary General Calls for Recommitment to Eradicating Weapons of Mass Destruction 'Once and for All,'" August 25, 2016, https://www.un.org/press/en/2016/sgsm17996.doc.htm; see also the FBI presentation at a French-American law enforcement sharing conference, Washington, DC, April 2015; Goodman, *Future Crimes.*

31. US Department of Justice, "Avalanche Network Dismantled in International Cyber Operation."

32. "AlphaBay, the Largest Online 'Dark Market,' Shut Down," US Department of Justice, Office of Public Affairs, July 20, 2017, https://www.justice.gov/opa/pr/alphabay-largest-online-dark-market-shut-down, accessed February 19, 2018.

33. Geralda Odinot et al., "Cyber-OC in the Netherlands," in *Cyber-OC—Scope and Manifestations in Selected EU Member States*, ed. Gergana Bulanova-Hristova et al. (Magdeburg: BKA, 2016), 42.

34. Bilton, *American Kingpin.*

35. Odinot et al., "Cyber-OC in the Netherlands," 42.

36. Andy Greenberg, "Collected Quotations of the Dread Pirate Roberts, Founder of Underground Drug Site Silk Road and Radical Libertarian," *Forbes*, April 29, 2013, https://www.forbes.com/sites/andygreenberg/2013/04/29/collected-quotations-of-the-dread-pirate-roberts-founder-of-the-drug-site-silk-road-and-radical-libertarian/#2b9525c31b0c, accessed August 22, 2017.

37. "Child Pornography," US Department of Justice, Criminal Division, updated July 25, 2017, https://www.justice.gov/criminal-ceos/child-pornography, accessed August 22, 2017,

38. Bilton, *American Kingpin*, 42–43.

39. Bilton, *American Kingpin*, 45.

40. Bilton, *American Kingpin*, 186.

41. Steve Kovach, "FBI Says Illegal Drugs Marketplace Silk Road Generated $1.2 Billion in Sales Revenue," *Business Insider*, October 2, 2013, http://www.businessinsider.com/silk-road-revenue-2013-10, accessed August 22, 2017.

42. "Ross Ulbricht, A/K/A 'Dread Pirate Roberts,' Sentenced in Manhattan Federal Court to Life in Prison," US Department of Justice, US Attorney's Office, Southern District of New York, May 29, 2015, https://www.justice.gov/usao-sdny/pr/ross-ulbricht-aka-dread-pirate-roberts-sentenced-manhattan-federal-court-life-prison, accessed August 22, 2017.

43. Bilton, *American Kingpin*, 307–309.

44. Bilton, *American Kingpin*, 180–183.

45. Andy Greenberg, "Ross Ulbricht's Lawyers Say They Have Found Another Corrupt Agent on Silk Road Case," *Wired*, November 29, 2016, https://www.wired.com/2016/11/ross-ulbrichts-lawyers-point-another-corrupt-agent-silk-road-case/. I attended a conference on the Dark Net in January 2017 at which a speaker, one of the Baltimore investigators of Silk Road, said that he had observed his colleague going rogue.

46. "Taking Stock of the Online Drug Trade," RAND Corporation, August 5, 2016, https://www.rand.org/randeurope/research/projects/online-drugs-trade-trafficking.html, accessed August 18, 2017.

47. Joseph Cox, "The Secret Life of a Silk Road 2.0 Mastermind," *Vice/Motherboard*, March 10, 2017, https://motherboard.vice.com/en_us/article/3dad83/the-secret-life-of-a-silk-road-20-mastermind, accessed August 16, 2016.

48. "Strategic Insights Series: EUROPOL Executive Director Robert Wainwright: Takedown of Dark Web Market Giants AlphaBay and Hansa," George Washington University, Center for Cyber and Homeland Security, July 2017, https://cchs.gwu.edu/sites/cchs.gwu.edu/files/Europol-Wainwright-QA-July2017.pdf, accessed August 3, 2017.

49. "Victim of Identity Theft, 2014," NCJ 248991, US Department of Justice, Bureau of Justice Statistics, Office of Justice Programs, September 2015, https://www.bjs.gov/content/pub/pdf/vit14_sum.pdf, accessed August 22, 2017. I have been a victim myself of identity theft as a result of a break-in and data breach of my health insurer's records.

50. "Estonian Cybercriminal Sentenced for Infecting 4 Million Computers in 100 Countries with Malware in Multimillion-Dollar Fraud Scheme," US Department of Justice, US Attorney's Office, Southern District of New York, April 26, 2016, https://www.justice.gov/usao-sdny/pr/estonian-cybercriminal-sentenced-infecting-4-million-computers-100-countries-malware, accessed August 19, 2017.

51. Comments by American security specialists at the US-France Cooperative Futures Forum "Anticipating Transnational Threats and Risks," Washington, DC, April 28–29, 2015.

52. Yael Werner and Lars Korsell, "Cyber-OC in Sweden," in Bulanova-Hristova et al., *Cyber-OC—Scope and Manifestations in Selected EU Member States*, 105–106.

53. *2016 Internet Security Threat Report*, Symantec, April 2016, 6, https://www.symantec.com/content/dam/symantec/docs/reports/istr-21-2016-en.pdf, accessed June 16, 2017.

54. For a fuller discussion, see Shelley, *Dirty Entanglements*, 64–65; Lionel Beehner, "The Effects of 'Youth Bulge' on Civil Conflicts," Council on Foreign Relations, April 13, 2007, https://www.cfr.org/backgrounder/effects-youth-bulge-civil-conflicts, accessed August 7, 2017.

55. Thomas Piketty, *The Economics of Inequality*, trans. Arthur Goldhammer (Cambridge, MA: Belknap Press of Harvard University Press, 2015).

56. Deborah Hardoon, "An Economy for the 99 Percent," Oxfam, January 16, 2017, http://policy-practice.oxfam.org.uk/publications/an-economy-for-the-99-its-time-to-build-a-human-economy-that-benefits-everyone-620170, accessed August 8, 2017.

57. Larry Elliott, "World's Eight Richest People Have Same Wealth as Poorest 50%," *Guardian*, January 15, 2017, https://www.theguardian.com/global-development/2017/jan/16/worlds-eight-richest-people-have-same-wealth-as-poorest-50, accessed August 8, 2017.

58. Sebastian Smith, "Brazil Protesters Demand Anti-Corruption Drive 'Go All the Way,'" *Guardian*, March 26, 2017, http://guardian.ng/news/brazil-protesters-demand-anti-corruption-drive-go-all-the-way/; Elizabeth Roberts, "Russia's Anti-Corruption Protests Explained," *CNN*, June 12, 2017, https://www.cnn.com/2017/06/12/europe/russia-protests-qa/index.html; Ed Adamcyzk, "Anti-Corruption Protests Call on South Africa's Zuma to Resign," *UPI*, November 2, 2016, http://www.upi.com/Top_News/World-News/2016/11/02/Anti-corruption-protests-call-on-South-Africas-Jacob-Zuma-to-resign/7441478087436/, accessed June 16, 2017; Kate Bateman and Charles Davidson, "America Must Continue the Fight against Kleptocracy around the Globe," *The Hill*, June 5, 2017, http://thehill.com/blogs/pundits-blog/international/336361-america-must-continue-the-fight-against-kleptocracy-around, accessed June 15, 2017.

59. Homi Kharas, "The Unprecedented Expansion of the Global Middle Class: An Update," Global Economy and Development Working Paper 100, Brookings Institution, February 2017, https://www.brookings.edu/wp-content/uploads/2017/02/global_20170228_global-middle-class.pdf, accessed February 20, 2018.

60. Kris Maher, "Demand for Ginseng Boosts Prices, Tempts Poachers," *Wall Street Journal*, September 17, 2014, https://www.wsj.com/articles/demand-for-ginseng-boosts-prices-tempts-poachers-1410971637, accessed June 15, 2017; author's interview with National Park Service ranger and investigator, September 2016; "Pangolin," WWF, http://www.worldwildlife.org/species/pangolin, accessed June 16, 2017; "White Abalone," NOAA Fisheries, https://www.fisheries.noaa.gov/species/white-abalone, May 14, 2018.

61. Marianna Grigoryan, "Private Zoos Boasting Exotic Animals—The New Status Symbol of Armenia's Elite," *Guardian*, October 30, 2014, https://www.theguardian.com/world/2014/oct/30/armenia-zoo-exotic-animals, accessed June 16, 2017; John Roach, "'Blood Diamonds' and How to Avoid Buying Illicit Gems," *National*

Geographic News, December 8, 2006, http://news.nationalgeographic.com/news /2006/12/061208-blood-diamonds.html, accessed June 16, 2017.

62. Kieran Guilbert, "Number of Women Convicted for Human Trafficking 'Exceptionally High'—UN," *Reuters*, November 24, 2014, http://news.trust .org //item/20141124163933-6vy1j/, accessed August 10, 2017.

63. Guilbert, "Number of Women Convicted for Human Trafficking."

64. Shelley, *Human Trafficking*, 56.

65. The Deep Web—also referred to as the "invisible web" or the "hidden web"—is part of the World Wide Web whose contents are not indexed by standard search engines for any reason. Larry Greenemeier, "Human Traffickers Caught on Hidden Internet," *Scientific American*, February 8, 2015, https://www .scientificamerican.com/article/human-traffickers-caught-on-hidden-internet/. Accompanying Greenemeier's article is a visualization that reveals the international links: "*Scientific American* Exclusive: DARPA Memex Data Maps," https:// www.scientificamerican.com/slideshow/scientific-american-exclusive-darpa -memex-data-maps/, accessed July 13, 2017.

66. Greenemeier, "Human Traffickers Caught on Hidden Internet," 10.

67. "Garment Factory Owner Convicted in Largest Ever Human Trafficking Cased Prosecuted by the Department of Justice," US Department of Justice, February 21, 2003, https://www.justice.gov/archive/opa/pr/2003/February/03_crt _108.htm, accessed June 16, 2017.

68. "Garment Factory Owner Sentenced to 40 Years for Human Trafficking," US Department of Justice, June 23, 2005, https://www.justice.gov/archive/opa /pr/2005/June/05_crt_335.htm, accessed August 8, 2017.

69. Robert Legvold, "Corruption, the Criminalized State, and Post-Soviet Transitions," in Rotberg, *Corruption, Global Security, and World Order*, 194–238; Christoph H. Stefes, *Understanding Post-Soviet Transitions: Corruption, Collusion, and Clientelism* (New York: Palgrave Macmillan, 2006).

70. Graham Allison, *The Ultimate Preventable Catastrophe* (New York: Henry Holt and Co., 2004); Matthew Bunn, *Securing the Bomb 2010: Securing All Nuclear Materials in Four Years*, Harvard University, Harvard Kennedy School, Belfer Center for Science and International Affairs, April 2010, 34. http://www .nti.org/media/pdfs/Securing_The_Bomb_2010.pdf?_=1317159794, accessed June 15, 2017.

71. Louise Shelley and Robert Orttung, "Criminal Acts," *Bulletin of the Atomic Scientist* (September/October 2006): 22–23; Alexander Kupatadze, "Organized Crime and the Trafficking of Radiological Materials," *Nonproliferation Review* 17, no. 2 (July 2010): 219–234; "CNS Global Incidents and Trafficking Database," NTI, March 29, 2017, http://www.nti.org/analysis/reports/cns-global-incidents -and-trafficking-database/, accessed August 7, 2017.

72. Stephen Brain, "The Environmental History of Russia," *Environmental Science*, November 2016, DOI:10.1093/acrefore/9780199389414.013.355.

73. Thomas Firestone, "Criminal Corporate Raiding in Russia," *International Lawyer* 42, no. 4 (Winter 2008): 1207–1229; Michael Rochlitz, "Corporate Raiding and the Role of the State in Russia," *Post-Soviet Affairs* 30, nos. 2–3 (2014): 90;

Vadim Volkov, "Hostile Enterprise Takeovers: Russia's Economy in 1998–2002," *Review of Central and East European Law* 29, no. 4 (2004): 527–548.

74. See Evan Osnos, *Age of Ambition: Chasing Fortune, Truth, and Faith in New China* (New York: Farrar, Straus and Giroux, 2014); Tom Milliken and Jo Shaw, *The South Africa–Vietnam Rhino Horn Trade Nexus*, TRAFFIC, Johannesburg, 2012, 135–136, http://www.npr.org/documents/2013/may/traffic_species_mammals.pdf, accessed June 11, 2017.

75. "Statement for the Record: Worldwide Threat Assessment of the US Intelligence Community," Office of the Director of National Intelligence (DNI), February 13, 2018, https://www.dni.gov/index.php/newsroom/congressional-testimonies/item/1845-statement-for-the-record-worldwide-threat-assessment-of-the-us-intelligence-community, accessed February 20, 2018.

76. Ray Godson, ed., *Menace to Society: Political-Criminal Collaborations around the World* (New Brunswick, NJ: Transaction Publishers, 2004).

77. Peter B. Maggs, Olga Schwartz, and William Burnham, *Law and Legal System of the Russian Federation*, 6th ed. (Huntington, NY: Juris Publishing, 2015), 275–276.

78. Enrique Desmond Arias, *Criminal Enterprises and Governance in Latin America and the Caribbean* (Cambridge: Cambridge University Press, 2017).

79. Louise Shelley, "Crime and the Collapse of the Soviet State," in *Social Legacy of Communism*, ed. James R. Millar and Sharon L. Wolchik (Washington, DC, and New York: Woodrow Wilson Center Press and Cambridge University Press, 1994), 130–148; Louise Shelley, "Is the Russian State Coping with Organized Crime and Corruption?," in *Building the Russian State: Institutional Crisis and the Quest for Democratic Governance*, ed. Valerie Sperling (Boulder, CO: Westview Press, 2000), 91–112.

80. Gretchen Peters, "How Opium Profits the Taliban," Peaceworks 60, US Institute of Peace, August 2009, www.usip.org/sites/default/files/resources/taliban_opium_1.pdf, accessed June 11, 2017; Emil Giatzidas, "The Challenge of Organized Crime in the Balkans and the Political and Economic Implications," *Journal of Communist Studies and Transition Politics* 23, no. 3 (2007): 37–51; Juan Carlos Garzón, *Mafia & Co.: La Red criminal en México, Brasil, y Colombia* (Bogotá: Editorial Planeta Colombiana, 2008); Arias, *Criminal Enterprises and Governance in Latin America and the Caribbean*.

81. Michael Dziedzic, *Criminalized Power Structures: The Overlooked Enemies of Peace* (Lanham, MD: Rowman and Littlefield, 2016).

82. Joshua Partlow, *A Kingdom of Their Own: The Family Karzai and the Afghan Disaster* (New York: Alfred A. Knopf, 2016).

83. Doris Buddenberg and William A. Byrd, eds., *Afghanistan's Drug Industry: Structure, Functioning, Dynamics, and Implications for Counter-Narcotics Policy*, Report 38931, World Bank, 2006, 1, http://documents.worldbank.org/curated/en/151161467996726308/Afghanistans-drug-industry-structure-functioning-dynamics-and-implications-for-counter-narcotics-policy, accessed June 11, 2017.

84. Author's discussions with members of the Serious Organized Crime Agency (SOCA), London, 2012.

85. David Kushner, "Drug-Sub Culture," *New York Times*, April 23, 2009, http://www.nytimes.com/2009/04/26/magazine/26drugs-t.html, accessed June 11, 2017; author's discussions with American law enforcement officers; Robert I. Friedman, *Red Mafiya: How the Russian Mob Has Invaded America* (Boston: Little, Brown, 2000), 155–159, 166–168. I have visited this club and discussed the case with the federal investigators.

86. Bruce Hoffman, *Inside Terrorism*, rev. ed. (New York: Columbia University Press, 2006); Walter Laqueur, *The New Terrorism: Fanaticism and the Arms of Mass Destruction* (Oxford: Oxford University Press, 1999).

87. Shelley, *Dirty Entanglements*; David Keen, "Incentives and Disincentives for Violence," in Berdal and Malone, *Greed and Grievance*, 19–42; Michael L. Ross, "Oil, Drugs, and Diamonds: The Varying Roles of Natural Resources in Civil War," in *The Political Economy of Armed Conflicts: Beyond Greed and Grievance*, ed. Karen Ballentine and Jake Sherman (Boulder, CO: Lynne Rienner Publishers, 2003), 47–70; "The Global Illicit Tobacco Trade: A Threat to National Security," US Department of State, December 2015, https://2009-2017.state.gov /documents/organization/250513.pdf, accessed February 20, 2018.

88. Mazhar Farooqi, "Online Fake Degrees: XPRESS Investigates," *Gulf News*, June 4, 2014, http://gulfnews.com/news/uae/education/online-fake -degrees-xpress-investigates-1.1342936, accessed June 15, 2017; "Algerian Arrested in Italy in Connection with Probe into Paris, Brussels Attacks," *Associated Press*, March 27, 2016, http://www.france24.com/en/20160327-italy-algerian -arrested-paris-brussels-attacks-probe, accessed June 15, 2017.

89. Steven Lee Myers and Nicholas Kulish, "'Broken System' Allows ISIS to Profit from Looted Antiquities," *New York Times*, January 9, 2016, http://www .nytimes.com/2016/01/10/world/europe/iraq-syria-antiquities-islamic-state .html, accessed June 15, 2017; Amr Al-Azm, Salam Al-Kuntar, and Brian I. Daniels, "ISIS Antiquities Sideline," *New York Times*, September 2, 2014, http://www .nytimes.com/2014/09/03/opinion/isis-antiquities-sideline.html, accessed June 15, 2017; Louise Shelley, "Following the Money: Examining Current Terrorist Financing Trends and the Threat to the Homeland," testimony before the US House of Representatives Committee on Homeland Security, May 12, 2016, https:// homeland.house.gov/hearing/following-money-examining-current-terrorist -financing-trends-threat-homeland/, accessed June 15, 2017; Tania Rakhmanova, *Art Trafficking* (film no longer available online), *Al-Jazeera*, March 17, 2017, http://www.aljazeera.com/programmes/specialseries/2017/02/art-trafficking -170228090044987.html, accessed April 14, 2017; Neil Brodie, "The Internet Market in Antiquities," in Desmarais, *Countering Illicit Traffic in Cultural Goods*, 11–20.

90. Retired Jordanian general, remarks at George C. Marshall European Center for Security Studies seminar on "21st-Century Converging Threats: Nexus of Terrorism, Drugs, and Illicit Trafficking," September 2015.

91. International Center for the Study of Radicalisation, King's College, London, presentation at the conference "Eurasia and Armed Radicalism Spaces: Flows and Finances of an Evolving Terrorism," NATO Foundation Defense College Foundation, Berlin, January 27, 2016.

92. Fazel Hawramy, "Islamic State Turns to Cigarette Smuggling to Fund Itself," Center for International Relations and Sustainable Development, November 30, 2016, https://www.cirsd.org/en/cirsd-recommends/islamic-state-turns-to-cigarette-smuggling-to-fund-itself; Ryan Gingeras, "Corruption, Crime, and Scandal in Turkey," OUPblog (Oxford University Press blog), November 4, 2014, http://blog.oup.com/2014/11/corruption-smuggling-turkey-government/, accessed June 15, 2017.

93. Thomas M. Sanderson, "The Challenge of Deterring ISIS," in *Global Flashpoints 2015: Crisis and Opportunity*, ed. Craig Cohen and Josiane Gabel (Lanham, MD: Rowman and Littlefield, 2015), 22; Phillippe de Koster, "Session II: Financing of Foreign Terrorist Fighters (FTFs), FTF Returnees, and Dormant Cells," presentation at joint special meeting of the Counter-Terrorism Committee and the ISIL and Al-Qaida Sanctions Committee, UN headquarters, New York, December 12–13, 2016, https://www.un.org/sc/ctc/wp-content/uploads/2016/12/2016-12-12-Session-II-1130-1300-Philippe-de-Koster-CTIF-FI.pdf, accessed June 15, 2017; Rajan Basra, Peter R. Neumann, and Claudia Brunner, *Criminal Pasts, Terrorist Futures: European Jihadists and the New Crime-Terror Nexus* (London: International Centre for the Study of Radicalisation and Political Violence (ICSR), 2016); Magnus Normark and Magnus Ranstorp, *Understanding Terrorist Finance: Modus Operandi and National CTF Regimes*, Swedish Defence University, Stockholm, 2015, http://www.fi.se/contentassets/733cb77e383d49a98aa060a16d011392/understanding_terrorist_finance_160315.pdf, accessed June 15, 2017.

94. Author's interview with senior Europol official, May 2016.

95. Daniel H. Heinke, "German Foreign Fighters in Syria and Iraq: The Updated Data and Its Implications," *CTC Sentinel* 10, no. 3 (March 10, 2017), https://ctc.usma.edu/posts/german-foreign-fighters-in-syria-and-iraq-the-updated-data-and-its-implications, accessed September 22, 2017.

96. Anton W. Weenink, "Behavioral Problems and Disorders among Radicals in Police Files," *Perspectives on Terrorism* 9, no. 2 (2015): 17–33.

97. DNI, "Statement for the Record."

98. "New UNODC Campaign Highlights Transnational Organized Crime as a US$870 Billion a Year Business," UNODC, July 16, 2012, https://www.unodc.org/unodc/en/frontpage/2012/July/new-unodc-campaign-highlights-transnational-organized-crime-as-an-us-870-billion-a-year-business.html, accessed August 22, 2017; May, *Transnational Crime and the Developing World*, xi.

99. "Economic and Social Consequences of Drug Abuse and Illicit Trafficking," UNODC, 3–4, https://www.unodc.org/pdf/technical_series_1998-01-01_1.pdf, accessed July 28, 2017.

100. *World Drug Report 2017: Booklet 1*, UNODC, May 2017, 9, https://www.unodc.org/wdr2017/field/Booklet_1_EXSUM.pdf, accessed August 1, 2017.

101. The RAND Corporation estimated American annual expenditures for illegal drugs (excluding abused prescription drugs) between 2000 and 2010 at $100 billion; see "How Big Is the US Market for Illegal Drugs?," RAND Corporation, 2014, https://www.rand.org/pubs/research_briefs/RB9770.readonline

.html. Europe, a distant second to US markets, estimated its sales at between $26 billion and $31 billion annually; see *EU Drug Markets Report 2016*, Europol, European Monitoring Center for Drugs and Drug Addiction, 7–8, https://www .europol.europa.eu/publications-documents/eu-drug-markets-report-2016, accessed August 22, 2017.

102. "Global Estimates of Modern Slavery: Forced Labour and Forced Marriage," International Labour Organization (ILO) and Walk Free Foundation, September 19, 2017, http://www.ilo.org/wcmsp5/groups/public/---dgreports ---/dcomm/documents/publication/wcms_575479.pdf, accessed May 14, 2018.

103. ILO and Walk Free Foundation, "Global Estimates of Modern Slavery."

104. May, *Transnational Crime and the Developing World*, xi.

105. May Bulman, "People Smuggling in Europe Comparable to the Illegal Drugs Market, Warns Report," *Independent*, March 9, 2017, http://www .independent.co.uk/news/world/europe/people-trafficking-smuggling-refugees -migrants-europol-a7621586.html, accessed July 27, 2017; Arthur Neslen, "Number of Criminal Gangs Operating in Europe Surges to 5,000, Says Europol," *Guardian*, March 9, 2017, https://www.theguardian.com/uk-news/2017/mar/09 /more-than-5000-crimnal-gangs-operating-in-europe-warns-europol, accessed August 4, 2017.

106. May, *Transnational Crime and the Developing World*, xi, 14.

107. Isa Blumi, "Thwarting the Ottoman Empire: Smuggling through the Empire's New Frontiers in Yemen and Albania, 1878–1910," *International Journal of Turkish Studies* 9, nos.1 and 2 (Summer 2003): 251–270.

108. Lindita Arapi, "The Balkan Route to Western Europe for Yugoslavia Guns," DW, December 5, 2015, http://www.dw.com/en/the-balkan-route-to -western-europe-for-yugoslavia-guns/a-18896280, accessed August 3, 2017; author's interview with Belgian law enforcement official, 2016; Nils Duquet, "Paris Attacks: Is Belgium Europe's Favourite Gun Shop?," *BBC News*, November 19, 2015, http://www.bbc.com/news/world-europe-34871872, accessed June 26, 2016; Christian Oliver and Duncan Robinson, "Paris Attacks: Belgium's Arms Bazaar," *Financial Times*, November 19, 2015, https://next.ft.com/content /33a2d592-8dde-11e5-a549-b89a1dfede9b, accessed June 26, 2016.

109. Mitch Prothero, "Why Europe Can't Find the Jihadis in Its Midst," *BuzzFeed News*, August 21, 2016, https://www.buzzfeed.com/mitchprothero /why-europe-cant-find-the-jihadis-in-its-midst, accessed August 3, 2017.

110. Naina Bajekal and Vivienne Walt, "How Europe's Terrorists Get Their Guns," *Time*, December 7, 2015, http://time.com/how-europes-terrorists-get -their-guns/, accessed August 20, 2017.

111. OECD, *Trade in Counterfeit and Pirated Goods*. The author was present at the events in Paris connected to the presentation of this report and had a chance to discuss the work with the research team.

112. Gerard McLinden and Amer Zafar Durani, "Corruption in Customs," *World Customs Journal* 7, no. 2 (September 2013): 3–10.

113. Sharon Melzer and Chris Martin, "A Brief Overview of Illicit Trade in Tobacco Products," in OECD, *Illicit Trade*, 124, 128.

114. "Drones Fly Smuggled Smokes into the EU," *RadioFreeEurope*, January 31, 2018, https://www.rferl.org/a/ukraine-slovakia-smuggling/29009982.html, accessed February 20, 2018.

115. Nellemann et al., *The Rise of Environmental Crime*, 7.

116. Hanson et al., "Warfare in Biodiversity Hotspots."

117. "Over 90% of the major armed conflicts between 1950 and 2000 occurred within countries containing biodiversity hotspots, and more than 80% took place directly within hotspot areas. Less than one-third of the 34 recognized hotspots escaped significant conflict during this period, and most suffered repeated episodes of violence. This pattern was remarkably consistent over these five decades." Hanson et al., "Warfare in Biodiversity Hotspots," 578.

118. Christian Nellemann et al., *The Environmental Crime Crisis: Threats to Sustainable Development from Illegal Exploitation and Trade in Wildlife and Forest Resources: A UNEP Rapid Response Assessment*, UNEP and GRID-Arendal, Nairobi, 2014, 15, http://pfbc-cbfp.org/news_en/items/Environnmental-Crime-en .html; Nellemann et al., *The Rise of Environmental Crime*, 7.

119. Jason Bittel, "Borneo Has Lost Half of Its Orangutans in Recent Years—but There's Still Hope," Natural Resources Defense Council (NRDC), February 20, 2018, https://www.nrdc.org/onearth/borneo-has-lost-half-its-orangutans -recent-years-theres-still-hope.

120. Nellemann et al., *The Environmental Crime Crisis*, 15.

121. Jeremy McDermott, "Gold Overtakes Drugs as Source of Colombia Rebel Funds," *BBC News*, June 17, 2012, http://www.bbc.com/news/world-latin -america-18396920, accessed June 15, 2017.

122. "Conflict Gold Sold on International Markets Despite Sector Clean Up Says New UN Report," Global Witness, January 20, 2015, https://www .globalwitness.org/en/archive/conflict-gold-sold-international-markets-despite -sector-clean-says-new-un-report/, accessed June 15, 2017; "UN Experts Unearth Gold Smuggling Network That Funds Conflict in DRC," *East African*, July 2, 2016, http://www.theeastafrican.co.ke/business/UN-experts-unearth-gold-smuggling -network-in-DR-Congo/2560-3277488-suwp6qz/index.html, accessed August 7, 2017.

123. Ian Smillie, *Diamonds* (Cambridge: Polity Press, 2014); Ian Smillie, *Blood on the Stone: Greed, Corruption, and War in the Global Diamond Trade* (London and Ottawa: Anthem Press and International Development Research Centre, 2010).

124. "KP Basics," Kimberley Process, https://www.kimberleyprocess.com /en/about, accessed June 15, 2017.

125. David Rhode, "The Kimberley Process Is a 'Perfect Cover Story' for Blood Diamonds," *Guardian*, March 24, 2014, https://www.theguardian.com /sustainable-business/diamonds-blood-kimberley-process-mines-ethical, accessed August 7, 2017.

126. George Monbiot, "My Search for a Cell Phone Not Soaked in Blood," *Guardian*, March 11, 2013, https://www.theguardian.com/commentisfree/2013 /mar/11/search-smartphone-soaked-blood, accessed June 13, 2017.

127. "Incautan a las FARC más de 3,5 toneladas de coltán que se dirigían a Venezuela," *El Estímulo*, March 24, 2016, http://elestimulo.com/blog/incautan-a-las-farc-mas-de-35-toneladas-de-coltan-que-se-dirigian-a-venezuela/, accessed June 16, 2017; Dena Montague, "Coltan and Conflict in the Democratic Republic of the Congo," *SAIS Review* 22, no. 1 (Winter/Spring 2002): 103–118; Marco Simoncelli, "Congo, bambini in miniera ad estrarre cobalto per cellulari, tablet, computer, e auto," *La Repubblica*, January 27, 2016, http://www.repubblica.it/solidarieta/diritti-umani/2016/01/27/news/miniere_di_cobalto-132142114/, accessed June 15, 2017.

128. Carl Zimmer, "Pushing Primates to the Edge," *New York Times*, January 24, 2017; Brianna, "Coltan Commotion," March 10, 2015, http://blogs.sandiegozoo.org/2015/03/10/the-coltan-commotion/, accessed May 14, 2018.

129. Nellemann et al., *The Environmental Crime Crisis*, 19; David Tilman et al., "Future Threats to Biodiversity and Pathways to Their Prevention," *Nature* 546 (June 1, 2017): 73–81.

130. "Illegal Fishing: Which Fish Species Are at Highest Risk from Illegal and Unreported Fishing?," World Wildlife Fund (WWF), October 29, 2015, https://www.worldwildlife.org/publications/illegal-fishing-which-fish-species-are-at-highest-risk-from-illegal-and-unreported-fishing.

131. Christian Nellemann et al., *Waste Crime, Waste Risks: Gaps in Meeting the Global Risk Challenge: A UNEP Rapid Response Assessment*, UNEP and GRID-Arendal, Nairobi, 2015, 4, https://wedocs.unep.org/bitstream/handle/20.500.11822/9648/-Waste_Crime_-_Waste_Risks_Gaps_in_Meeting_the_Global_Waste_Challenge_a_Rapid_Response_As.pdf?sequence=2&isAllowed=y.

132. Jacquelynn Doyon-Martin, "Cybercrime in West Africa as a Result of Transboundary E-Waste," *Journal of Applied Social Research* 10, no. 2 (2015): 207–220.

133. "Remarks by Assistant Secretary for Terrorist Financing Daniel Glaser at Chatham House," US Department of the Treasury, February 8, 2016, https://www.treasury.gov/press-center/press-releases/Pages/jl0341.aspx, accessed October 3, 2017.

134. Wim Zwijnenburg and Annica Waleij, "Fire and Oil: The Collateral Environmental Damage of Airstrikes on ISIS Oil Facilities," New Security Beat, Wilson Center and Environmental Change and Security Program, January 13, 2016, https://www.newsecuritybeat.org/2016/01/fire-oil-collateral-damage-airstrikes-isis-oil-facilities/, accessed June 15, 2017.

135. Guadalupe Correa-Cabrera, *Los Zetas Inc.: Criminal Corporations, Energy, and Civil War in Mexico* (Austin: University of Texas Press, 2017), 157–244.

136. "Oil Theft Lubricates Corruption in West Africa," UNODC, July 10, 2009, https://www.unodc.org/unodc/en/frontpage/2009/July/illegal-oil-trade-in-nigeria-worsens-rule-of-law-in-west-africa.html, accessed January 3, 2018; Elisha Bala Gbogbo and Angelina Rascouet, "Nigeria Deploys Troops to Protect Oil Facilities from Sabotage," *Business Day*, March 3, 2016, http://www.businessdayonline.com/nigeria-deploys-troops-to-protect-oil-facilities-from-attack/, accessed June 15, 2017.

137. "Thousands of Barrels of Oil Seeping into Nigerian Waterways after Pipelines Bombed," *Associated Press*, February 1, 2016, http://www.cp24.com/world /thousands-of-barrels-of-oil-seeping-into-nigerian-waterways-after-pipelines -bombed-1.2759798, accessed June 15, 2017.

138. Jack Losh, "War in Ukraine Helps Smugglers in the Black Market Get Richer," *Washington Post*, October 11, 2016, https://www.washingtonpost.com /news/worldviews/wp/2016/10/11/rebel-ukraine-turns-to-smuggling-for -income/?utm_term=.ae382eb3179e, accessed September 1, 2017; Mark Galeotti, "How the Invasion of Ukraine Is Shaking Up the Global Crime Scene, *Vice*, November 6, 2014, http://www.vice.com/read/how-the-invasion-of-ukraine-is -shaking-up-the-global-crime-scene-1106, accessed June 15, 2017.

139. Correa-Cabrera, *Los Zetas Inc.*, 157–244.

140. Mark Shaw and Tuesday Reitano, "Instability and Opportunities: The Political Economy of Trafficking and Trade in the Sahara," Global Initiative against Transnational Organized Crime, 2014, http://globalinitiative.net/instability -and-opportunities-illicit-trafficking-and-trade-in-the-sahara/; Benoît Faucon, "Smuggled Libya Gas Fuels Conflict," *Wall Street Journal*, March 22, 2015, https:// www.wsj.com/articles/smuggled-libya-gas-fuels-conflict-1427064365, accessed June 15, 2017.

141. Kate Hodal, "Aung San Suu Kyi Moves to Clean Up Myanmar's Murky Jade Trade," *Guardian*, August 9, 2016, https://www.theguardian.com/global -development/2016/aug/09/aung-sun-suu-kyi-clean-up-myanmar-murky-jade -trade, accessed June 15, 2017; "Jade: 'Myanmar's Big State Secret,'" Global Witness, October 25, 2016, https://www.globalwitness.org/en/campaigns/oil-gas -and-mining/myanmarjade/, accessed June 15, 2017.

142. Guilbert Gates, Jack Ewing, Karl Russell, and Derek Watkins, "Explaining Volkswagen's Emissions Scandal," *New York Times*, September 12, 2016, http://www.nytimes.com/interactive/2015/business/international/vw-diesel -emissions-scandal-explained.html, accessed June 17, 2017; Aruna Viswanatha and Christina Rogers, "VW Engineer Pleads Guilty in Emissions-Cheating Scandal," *Wall Street Journal*, September 9, 2016, http://www.wsj.com/articles/former -vw-engineer-to-plead-guilty-in-emissions-cheating-scandal-1473433341, accessed June 16, 2017; Jack Ewing, "Ex-Volkswagen CEO Charged with Fraud over Diesel Emissions," *New York Times*, May 3, 2018, https://www.nytimes.com/2018 /05/03/business/volkswagen-ceo-diesel-fraud.html, accessed May 9, 2018.

143. Geoff Colvin, "Why Volkswagen's Emission Scandal Has No End," *Fortune*, January 11, 2017, http://fortune.com/2017/01/11/volkswagen-emissions -scandal-2/, accessed February 8, 2017; Steph Yin, "Volkswagen's Emission Fraud May Affect Mortality Rate in Europe," *New York Times*, March 6, 2017, https://www.nytimes.com/2017/03/06/science/volkswagen-emissions-scandal -air-pollution-deaths.html, accessed March 7, 2017; Bill Vlasic, "Volkswagen Executive Pleads Guilty in Diesel Emissions Case," *New York Times*, August 4, 2017, https://www.nytimes.com/2017/08/04/business/volkswagen-diesel-oliver -schmidt.html?emc=edit_mbe_20170807&nl=morning-briefing-europe&nlid= 47439486&te=1&_r=0.

144. Gates et al., "Explaining Volkswagen's Emissions Scandal."

145. Tom Krisher and Eric Tucker, "Second VW Official Arrested over Emissions Scheme," *Associated Press*, January 10, 2017, http://bigstory.ap.org/article/85a02541e4f2418aafd593a38b23f422; accessed June 16, 2017; Vlasic, "Volkswagen Executive Pleads Guilty in Emissions Case." The fact that European investigators have also begun investigating Mercedes-Benz for falsifying emission standards suggests that it is an industrywide problem; see Jack Ewing, "An Emissions Scandal Widens: Diesel's Future in Europe Looks Shaky," *New York Times*, July 25, 2017, https://www.nytimes.com/2017/07/25/business/diesel-emissions-volkswagen-bmw-mercedes.html, accessed August 8, 2017.

146. "Security Council, Adopting Resolution 2195 (2014), Urges International Action to Break Links between Terrorists, Transnational Organized Crime," United Nations, December 19, 2014, https://www.un.org/press/en/2014/sc11717.doc.htm.

147. Neil Brodie, "Syria and Its Regional Neighbors: A Case of Cultural Property Protection Policy Failure?," *International Journal of Cultural Property* 22 (2015): 317–335.

148. Donna Yates, "Illicit Cultural Property from Latin America: Looting, Trafficking, and Sale," in Desmarais, *Countering Illicit Traffic in Cultural Goods*, 33–45; Jessica Gelt, "Getty Agrees to Return 1st Century BC Sculpture to Italy," *Los Angeles Times*, June 13, 2017, http://www.latimes.com/entertainment/arts/la-et-cm-getty-repatriation-20170613-story.html, accessed August 22, 2017; Tom Mashberg and Max Bearak, "The Ultimate Temple Raider? Inside an Antiquities-Smuggling Operation," *New York Times*, July 23, 2015, https://www.nytimes.com/2015/07/26/arts/design/the-ultimate-temple-raider-inside-an-antiquities-smuggling-operation.html?mcubz=1, accessed August 22, 2017. I was in Kapoor's gallery with someone very knowledgeable about Indian art who recognized a piece in the gallery similar to one he had seen in an Indian temple. He said, "I hope this piece has a good provenance." Kapoor replied, "Only the best."

149. May, *Transnational Crime and the Developing World*, xii.

150. Derek Fincham, "What Fools the Curator Also Fools the Collector," Illicit Cultural Property, April 21, 2009, http://illicit-cultural-property.blogspot.com/2009/04/what-fools-curator-also-fools-collector.html, accessed August 20, 2017.

151. Lyubov Grigorova Mincheva and Ted Robert Gurr, *Crime-Terror Alliances and the State: Ethnonationalist and Islamist Challenges to Regional Security* (London: Routledge, 2013), 15–16.

Chapter 4. The Tragic Trajectory of the Rhino Horn Trade

1. John M. Sellar, "Extinction through Profitable Crime: The Rhinoceros," *FBI: Law Enforcement Bulletin*, January 11, 2017, https://leb.fbi.gov/2017/january/extinction-through-profitable-crime-the-rhinoceros, accessed May 18, 2017.

2. "Poaching Statistics," Save the Rhino, https://www.savetherhino.org/rhino_info/poaching_statistics, accessed June 14, 2017.

3. *DNews*, "Poachers Kill 1,175 Rhinos in South Africa in 2015," Seeker, January 21, 2016, https://www.seeker.com/poachers-kill-1175-rhinos-in-south-africa -in-2015-1770751042.html.

4. "Reading beyond the Statistics: Why South Africa's Poaching Crisis Isn't Over," Save the Rhino, July 2017, https://www.savetherhino.org/latest_news /news/1711_reading_beyond_the_statistics_why_south_africa_s_poaching_crisis _isn_t_over, accessed January 14, 2018.

5. Christopher Torchia, "South African Group Reports Rhino Poaching Drop in 2015; Others Say Picture Still Dire," *Star*, January 2, 2016, http://www.thestar .com/news/world/2016/01/02/south-african-group-reports-rhino-poaching -drop-in-2015-others-say-picture-still-dire.html, accessed June 14, 2017.

6. Louise Shelley, "The Geography of Soviet Criminality," *American Sociological Review* 45 (February 1980): 111–122.

7. John R. Platt, "How the Western Black Rhino Went Extinct," *Scientific American*, November 13, 2013, http://blogs.scientificamerican.com/extinction -countdown/how-the-western-black-rhino-went-extinct/, accessed June 14, 2017.

8. Milliken and Shaw, *The South Africa–Vietnam Rhino Horn Trade Nexus*, 24.

9. Julie Ayling, "What Sustains Wildlife Crime? Rhino Horn Trading and the Resilience of Criminal Networks," *Journal of International Wildlife Law and Policy* (2013): 1, 4; "Rhino Population Figures," Save the Rhino, https://www .savetherhino.org/rhino_info/rhino_population_figures, accessed June 14, 2017; Milliken and Shaw, *The South Africa–Vietnam Rhino Horn Trade Nexus*, 4, 24.

10. Nellemann et al., *The Environmental Crime Crisis*, 8.

11. Author's meeting with General Jooste, Pretoria, South Africa, May 2016.

12. "Estimating the Value of Illicit Drug Markets," *World Drug Report 2005*, UNODC, 2005, 127, https://www.unodc.org/pdf/WDR_2005/volume_1_chap2 .pdf, accessed May 9, 2017.

13. Varun Vira, Thomas Ewing, and Jackson Miller, "Out of Africa: Mapping the Global Trade in Illicit Ivory," Born Free USA and C4ADS, August 2014, https://static1.squarespace.com/static/566ef8b4d8af107232d5358a/t /56af83ee1f40390e88337743/1454343151910/Out+of+Africa.pdf, accessed May 9, 2017.

14. "Gold Market News: Latest Price and Chart for CBOT Gold 100 Oz.," NASDAQ, http://www.nasdaq.com/markets/gold.aspx, accessed May 9, 2017; "UNODC Statistics Online—Cocaine-Type," UNODC, https://data.unodc.org/ #state:1, accessed 9, 2017.

15. Hübschle, "A Game of Horns," 19; Annette Hübschle, "Study of Transnational Flows of Rhino Horn," PhysOrg, February 24, 2017, https://phys.org/news /2017-02-transnational-rhino-horn.html#jCp, accessed May 17, 2017.

16. Hübschle, "A Game of Horns," 19.

17. Rupert Neate, "Recession Bypasses Market for Luxury Goods," *Guardian*, February 15, 2013, http://www.theguardian.com/business/2013/feb/15 /recession-bypasses-luxury-goods-market, accessed May 9, 2017.

18. Norimtsu Onishi, "China's Woes Deflate Hopes for Economic Rise in Africa," *International New York Times*, January 26, 2016, 1.

19. "Africa-China Exports Fall by 40% after China Slowdown," *BBC News*, January 13, 2016, http://www.bbc.com/news/world-africa-35303981, accessed May 9, 2017.

20. Van Noorden, "Worst Year Ever for Rhino Poaching in Africa."

21. Author's meetings with South African specialists, South Africa, May 2016.

22. Sam M. Ferreira et al., "Disruption of Rhino Demography by Poachers May Lead to Population Declines in Kruger National Park, South Africa," *PLoS ONE* 10, no. 6 (June 29, 2015): e0127783, http://journals.plos.org/plosone/article?id=10.1371/journal.pone.0127783. However, the white rhino population has been better able to survive on private South African game ranges, where owners spend a fortune to promote their survival and better-paid staff are not as susceptible to corruption as in the national parks.

23. Louise Shelley, "Time to Take Action: Working Globally to Identify and Counter the TOC Networks behind Rhino Poaching," author's TraCCC research under a US State Department grant, October 1, 2014–September 30, 2015.

24. Regional conference on wildlife trafficking, CSIR International Conventional Centre, Pretoria, South Africa, May 24–25, 2016.

25. Bartholomäus Grill, "Kidnapped in Mozambique: In the Clutches of Rhino Poachers," *Spiegel*, March 12, 2015, http://www.spiegel.de/international/world/investigation-into-rhino-poaching-turns-into-kidnapping-a-1022611.html, accessed May 17, 2017.

26. Author's interviews in South Africa, May 2016.

27. Alec Russell, "Rhino Poaching: Inside the Brutal Trade," *Financial Times*, October 2, 2015, http://www.ft.com/cms/s/2/f71d53ea-67b3-11e5-97d0-1456a776a4f5.html, accessed June 15, 2017; Scott C. Johnson, "Where the Wild Things Die," *Foreign Policy*, July 22, 2014, http://foreignpolicy.com/2014/07/22/where-the-wild-things-die-2/, accessed June 15, 2017.

28. Discussion with specialists in the field at author's Capetown lecture.

29. "Mozambique Country Profile," *BBC News*, November 2, 2017, http://www.bbc.com/news/world-africa-13890416, accessed May 10, 2017.

30. Gilbert A. Lewthwaite, "Creating a Park for All S. Africans Preserve," *Baltimore Sun*, April 30, 1998, http://articles.baltimoresun.com/1998-04-30/news/1998120138_1_apartheid-kruger-national-park-south-africa, accessed June 14, 2017.

31. Duffy, *Nature Crime*, 117.

32. Regional conference on wildlife trafficking, South Africa, May 2016.

33. Author's interviews in South Africa based on research conducted there, May 2016.

34. Maano Ramutsindela, *Parks and People in Postcolonial Societies: Experiences in Southern Africa* (New York: Kluwer Academic Publishers, 2005), 112–116; regional conference on wildlife trafficking, South Africa, May 2016; Kenichi Serion, "The Human Victims in the Fight over Rhino Poaching in Africa," *Al-Jazeera America*, January 7, 2015, http://america.aljazeera.com/multimedia/2015/1/the-human-cost-ofrhinopoaching.html, accessed May 16, 2017; Rademeyer, *Beyond Borders*.

35. Kevin Sieff, "It's Still Apartheid," *Washington Post*, February 13, 2016, A1 and A8.

36. Shelley, "The Geography of Soviet Criminality," 111–122; Martin Schönteich and Antoinette Louw, "Crime in South Africa: A Country and Cities Profile," Occasional Paper 49-2001, Institute for Security Studies, https://www.issafrica.org/uploads/paper49.pdf, accessed June 15, 2017.

37. This recalls the famous novel of Alan Paton, *Cry the Beloved Country*, about a burglary committed to acquire a grub stake going terribly wrong and ending in murder. The novel was set sixty-five years ago, but unfortunately little has changed for many black South Africans.

38. Grill, "Kidnapped in Mozambique."

39. Kenichi Serino, "The Human Victims in the Fight over Rhino Poaching in South Africa," *Al-Jazeera America*, January 7, 2015, http://america.aljazeera.com/multimedia/2015/1/the-human-cost-ofrhinopoaching.html, accessed June 15, 2017; author's meetings in South Africa, May 2016.

40. TraCCC teams' telephone interviews, Skukuza, South Africa, April 2014, January 2015; Shelley, "Time to Take Action."

41. "OC-Scan Policy Brief: Involvement of an Irish Mobile OCG," File 2521-86, Europol Public Information, July 11, 2011, https://www.europol.europa.eu/content/publication/oc-scan-policy-brief-involvement-irish-mobile-ocg-illegal-trade-rhino-horn-1485, accessed June 14, 2017; see also Charles Homans, "The Dead Zoo Gang," *The Atavist* 35, https://read.atavist.com/dead-zoo-gang, accessed June 14, 2017; Martin Bailey, "Criminal Gang Convicted of Stealing Antiquities and Rhino Horn from UK Museums," March 1, 2016, https://www.culturalheritagelaw.org/widget/culturalheritagenews/3853069, accessed May 14, 2018.

42. For a discussion of the origin of Chinese and Vietnamese networks in the Czech Republic, see Miroslav Nožina, "The Czech Republic: A Crossroads for Organised Crime," in *Organised Crime in Europe: Concepts, Patterns, and Control Policies in the European Union and Beyond*, ed. Cyrille Fijnaut and Letizia Paoli (Dordrecht: Springer, 2004), 455–456; Miroslav Nožina, "Crime Networks in Vietnamese Diasporas: The Czech Republic Case," *Crime Law and Social Change* 53, no. 10 (2010): 229–258.

43. Michael Parsons, "The Market for Rhino Horn Gives Auction Houses a Dilemma," *Irish Times*, February 15, 2014, http://www.irishtimes.com/life-and-style/homes-and-property/fine-art-antiques/the-market-for-rhino-horn-gives-auction-houses-a-dilemma-1.1691991, accessed June 14, 2017.

44. Thomas T. Allsen, *The Royal Hunt in Eurasian History* (Philadelphia: University of Pennsylvania Press, 2006), 23, 144, 234.

45. Sellar, *The UN's Lone Ranger Combating International Wildlife Crime*, 168.

46. Ayling, "What Sustains Wildlife Crime?," 61; Save the Rhino, "Rhino Population Figures."

47. Joanna Waley-Cohen, *The Sextants of Beijing: Global Currents in Chinese History* (New York: W. W. Norton & Co., 2000), 11–53.

48. Chen Hui-hsia, "The Historical Significance of Rhinoceros Horn Raft Carvings during Late Ming and Early Ch'ing Period," *National Palace Museum Journal* 25, no. 2 (Winter 2007), http://www.npm.gov.tw/en/Article.aspx?sNo= 05003074, accessed June 14, 2017.

49. TRAFFIC International, "What's Driving the Wildlife Trade? A Review of Expert Opinion on Economic and Social Drivers of the Wildlife Trade and Trade Control Efforts in Cambodia, Indonesia, Lao PDR, and Vietnam," East Asian and Pacific Region Sustainable Development, World Bank, October 2008, www .trafficj.org/publication/08_what's_driving_the_wildlife_trade.pdf, accessed May 16, 2017.

50. Duffy, *Nature Crime*, 223.

51. See Evan Osnos, *Age of Ambition: Chasing Fortune, Truth, and Faith in New China* (New York: Farrar, Straus and Giroux, 2014); Milliken and Shaw, *The South Africa–Vietnam Rhino Horn Trade Nexus*.

52. Author's interview with a Vietnamese individual who advised top-level government officials, 2016.

53. See "Demand for Rhino Horns in Viet Nam Decreases as a Result of Humane Society International and Viet Nam CITES Management Authority Partnership Campaign, Poll Says," October 16, 2014, http://www.hsi.org/assets/pdfs /vietnam-rhino-horn-campaign-poll-results.pdf, accessed May 17, 2017.

54. Sellar, *The UN's Lone Ranger*, 167–168.

55. Presentation by Campbell Fraser at George Mason University, TraCCC, January 21, 2016, http://traccc.gmu.edu/events/events-2014-2017/, accessed June 14, 2017.

56. Gwyn Guilford, "Why Does a Rhino Horn Cost $300,000? Because Vietnam Thinks It Cures Cancer and Hangovers," *Atlantic*, May 15, 2013, http://www .theatlantic.com/business/archive/2013/05/why-does-a-rhino-horn-cost-300 -000-because-vietnam-thinks-it-cures-cancer-and-hangovers/275881/, accessed June 14, 2017.

57. Sellar, *The UN's Lone Ranger*, 170.

58. "Map Exposes the Scale and the Nature of the Rhino Horn Trade," EIA, June 9, 2016, https://eia-international.org/map-exposes-the-scale-and-nature-of -rhino-horn-trade, accessed May 16, 2017.

59. Yufang Gao et al., "Rhino Horn Trade in China: An Analysis of the Arts and Antiquities Market," *Biological Conservation* 201 (September 2016): 343–347.

60. "South Africa," Observatory of Economic Complexity (OEC), https:// atlas.media.mit.edu/en/profile/country/zaf/, accessed January 14, 2018.

61. Ross Anthony, "South Africa and China: Behind the Smoke and Mirrors," *Mail & Guardian*, January 11, 2016, http://mg.co.za/article/2016-01-11-south -africa-and-china-behind-the-smoke-and-mirrors, accessed June 14, 2017.

62. Author's discussions with Kathi Austin, who is working on the arms trade and the rhino horn trade, and with Fundisile Mketeni, Executive Office, South African National Parks.

63. Author's interview with a cigarette official working against illicit trade, Doha, February 2015. President Zuma was ousted in February 2018 for this corruption.

64. Hongxiang Huang, a Chinese journalist who interned in South Africa (http://www.chinafile.com/contributors/huang-hongxiang), wrote in *Southern Weekly*, October 10, 2013; for a report on his work, see University of the Witwatersrand, Africa-China Reporting Project, Johannesburg, http://africachinareporting.co.za/?s=Hongxiang. http://www.infzm.com/content/94643, accessed June 14, 2017; discussion at author's lecture at Capetown University, May 2016.

65. Kimon De Greef and Serge Raemaekers, "Africa's Illicit Abalone Trade: An Updated Overview and Knowledge Gap Analysis," TRAFFIC International, 2014, 6, http://static1.1.sqspcdn.com/static/f/157301/25583011/1414148973007/W-TRAPS-Abalone-report.pdf?token=J2JdwIqK8xi4GhZdtu6V7fHRAIw%3D, accessed June 14, 2017.

66. Milliken and Shaw, *The South Africa–Vietnam Rhino Horn Trade Nexus*, 76.

67. "Trade in Rhino Horns in the Territory of the Czech Republic, Report of Czech Enforcement Authorities," https://cites.org/sites/default/files/eng/com/sc/66/E-SC66-51-01-A6.pdf, accessed June 14, 2017. The customs agents, having received a tip-off from their colleagues investigating Vietnamese cigarette smuggling, seized the package in transit; analysis done by a Czech researcher for the author's TraCCC research project on the rhino trade.

68. Rademeyer, *Beyond Borders*, 22.

69. Cassara, *Trade-Based Money Laundering*, 85.

70. Hübschle, "A Status Symbol to Die For," 74; Hübschle, "A Game of Horns."

71. Hübschle, "A Status Symbol to Die For," 74. For further analysis of this idea, see Duffy, *Nature Crime*, 55.

72. Hübschle, "A Status Symbol to Die For," 74; Gao et al., "Rhino Horn Trade in China."

73. "Godfather of Cocaine," PBS, *Frontline*, broadcast March 25, 1997, http://www.pbs.org/wgbh/pages/frontline/shows/drugs/archive/godfather cocaine.html, accessed June 15, 2017.

74. See, for example, "Plains Game Hunting South Africa," Ash Adventures, http://www.africanskyhunting.co.za/trophies/white-rhiino-hunting.html, accessed June 15, 2017.

75. See "The Poaching Crisis in South Africa," Save the Rhino, 2012, https://www.savetherhino.org/rhino_info/thorny_issues/poaching_crisis_in_south_africa, accessed May 10, 2017.

76. Jo Shaw, quoted in Save the Rhino, "Poaching Crisis in South Africa."

77. Further understanding of pseudo-hunts can be gained by reading the research of Julian Rademeyer, *Killing for Profit*; Rademeyer, "Tipping Point: Transnational Organised Crime and the "War" on Poaching," part 1, Global Initiative Against Transnational Organized Crime, July 11, 2016, 35–47, http://globalinitiative.net/wp-content/uploads/2016/07/TGIATOC-Tipping-Point_-Transnational

-organised-crime-and-the-%E2%80%98war%E2%80%99-on-poaching-web.pdf. See also author's interview with founder of Oxpeckers in South Africa, 2015; "Business as Usual for Rhinos," Oxpeckers, October 5, 2016, http://oxpeckers.org/2016 /10/business-as-usual-for-rhinos/, accessed June 15, 2017.

78. W. D. Moreto and A. M. Lemieux, "From CRAVED to CAPTURED: Introducing a Product-Based Framework to Examine Illegal Wildlife Markets," *European Journal on Criminal Policy and Research* 21, no. 3 (2015): 312; Mic Smith, "Amid Rhinoceros Poaching Frenzy, Dark Days for South African Society," Mongabay, June 6, 2015, https://news.mongabay.com/2015/06/amid-rhinoceros -poaching-frenzy-dark-days-for-south-african-society/, accessed June 15, 2017.

79. Hannah Osborne, "Poaching and Prostitutes: Thai Man Sentenced to 40 Years for Smuggling Rhino Horns in South Africa," *International Business Times*, November 9, 2012, http://www.ibtimes.co.uk/rhino-poaching-longest-sentence -wwf-south-africa-403466, accessed August 10, 2017; Rademeyer, *Killing for Profit*, 176–182.

80. "South Africa Safari Operator Dawie Groenewald Convicted of Felony," *Hunting Report*, June 10, 2010, http://huntingreport.redpointresolutions.com/?s =South+Africa+Safari+Operator+Dawie+Groenewald+; see also Rademeyer, *Killing for Profit*, 142–143.

81. US Government vs. Dawie Jacobus Groenewald, Janneman George Groenewald, and Valinor Trading Company CC, d/b/a Out of Africa Adventurous Safaris, indictment filed October 16, 2014, in US District Court, Middle of Alabama Northern Division, http://killingforprofit.com/wp-content/uploads/2014/10 /Rhino-Indictment.pdf, accessed June 15, 2017.

82. "Owners of Safari Company Indicted for Illegal Rhino Hunts," US Department of Justice, Office of Public Affairs, October 23, 2014, http://www.justice .gov/opa/pr/owners-safari-company-indicted-illegal-rhino-hunts, accessed June 15, 2017.

83. Miroslav Nožina, research for TraCCC, 2015.

84. Miroslav Nožina, research for TraCCC, 2015; see also "Lovec pozemků," *Silvarium*, May 12, 2012, http://www.silvarium.cz/zpravy-z-oboru-myslivost /lovec-pozemku-reflex-cz, accessed June 15, 2017.

85. The Czech-language website that advertised the hunts can be accessed through Internet Archive at http://web.archive.org/web/20111217093303/http: /www.limpona-safari.com/co-se-lovi/, accessed June 15, 2017.

86. "Triads" are a Chinese organized crime group that operate in mainland China, Hong Kong, and elsewhere in Asia.

87. Hübschle, "A Game of Horns."

88. Nick Davies and Oliver Holmes, "The Crime Family at the Centre of Asia's Animal Trafficking Network," *Guardian*, September 26, 2016, https://www .theguardian.com/environment/2016/sep/26/bach-brothers-elephant-ivory -asias-animal-trafficking-network, accessed January 13, 2018.

89. Davies and Holmes, "The Crime Family at the Centre of Asia's Animal Trafficking Network."

90. TraCCC research team's interviews, Pretoria and Skukuza, January 2015.

91. "The Shuidong Connection: Exposing the Global Hub of the Illegal Ivory Trade," EIA, July 2017, https://eia-international.org/wp-content/uploads/EIA -The-Shuidong-Connection-FINAL-1.pdf, accessed July 31, 2017.

92. TraCCC research team's telephone interviews, Skukuza, April 2014, January 2015; see also Grill, "Kidnapped in Mozambique."

93. TraCCC research team's interviews, Pretoria, January 2015.

94. Hübschle, "A Status Symbol to Die For," 74.

95. "Major South African Politician Allegedly Exposed in Undercover Poaching Documentary," *SA People News*, November 13, 2016, http://www.sapeople .com/2016/11/13/investigative-doc-the-poachers-pipeline-exposes-major-south -african-politician/, accessed May 18, 2017.

96. Author's interviews, South Africa, Washington, DC, 2016–2017.

97. Rademeyer, *Beyond Borders*, 22–27.

98. **EIA**, "Call for Trade Sanctions to Halt Vietnam's Vast Illegal Rhino Horn Trade: Vietnamese Diplomats and Criminal Syndicates Driving Poaching," *Cision PR Newswire*, March 11, 2013, http://www.prnewswire.com/news-releases/call -for-trade-sanctions-to-halt-vietnams-vast-illegal-rhino-horn-trade-vietnamese -diplomats-and-criminal-syndicates-driving-poaching-196962831.html, accessed June 15, 2017; see also Rademeyer, *Killing for Profit*, 257–259; "Vietnam's Illegal Rhino Horn Trade: Undermining the Effectiveness of CITES," EIA, March 5, 2013, https://eia-international.org/report/vietnams-illegal-rhino-horn-trade -undermining-the-effectiveness-of-cites-report.

99. Julian Rademeyer, "North Korean Diplomat Expelled from SA for Rhino Horn Trafficking," *News24*, December 23, 2015, http://www.news24.com /SouthAfrica/News/exclusive-north-korean-diplomat-expelled-from-sa-for -rhino-horn-trafficking-20151223, accessed May 17, 2017.

100. US Senate Committee on Homeland Security and Governmental Affairs, Federal Financial Management, Government Information, and International Security Subcommittee, "North Korea: Illicit Activity Funding the Regime," Senate Hearing 109-887, 109th Cong., 2nd sess., April 25, 2006; author's interview with Suzanne Hayden, 2015. Hayden is mentioned on p. 17 of this hearing as a key investigator.

101. "Combating Wildlife Trafficking: Executive Order 13648," The White House, Office of the Press Secretary, July 1, 2013, *Federal Register* 78, no. 129, https://obamawhitehouse.archives.gov/the-press-office/2013/07/01/executive -order-combating-wildlife-trafficking, accessed June 13, 2017.

102. Stanley Johnson, "Prince William and Charles: 'We Will Combat the Illegal Wildlife Trade,'" *Guardian*, February 12, 2014, http://www.theguardian.com /environment/blog/2014/feb/12/prince-william-charles-illegal-wildlife-trade, accessed June 13, 2017.

103. "Prayer for Lions with Archbishop Emeritus Desmond Tutu," March 14, 2014, https://www.youtube.com/watch?v=5DJMKbfvcCA, accessed June 13, 2017.

104. International NGOs such as the World Wildlife Fund (WWF), TRAFFIC International, the African Wildlife Foundation, and the International Fund for Animal Welfare (IFAW) operate in Africa against the rhino horn trade.

105. Shaw, "Poaching Crisis in South Africa."

106. Alisha Falberg, "The Living Are Getting Rarer: The Causes and Consequences of the International Trade in White Rhinoceros Horns under the Convention on International Trade in Endangered Species," *Penn State Journal of Law and International Affairs* 2, no. 1 (April 2013): 182–236.

107. Mark Shaw and Julian Rademeyer, "A Flawed War: Rethinking 'Green Militarisation' in the Kruger National Park," *Politikon* 43, no. 2 (2016): 816–832.

108. Hübschle, "Study of Transnational Flows of Rhino Horn."

109. Rachel Nuwer, "High Above, Drones Keep Watchful Eyes on Wildlife in Africa," *New York Times*, March 13, 2017, https://www.nytimes.com /2017/03/13/science/drones-africa-poachers-wildlife.html, accessed May 18, 2017; Thomas Snitch, "Drones Help Rangers Fight Poachers," *Slate*, January 28, 2015, http://www.slate.com/blogs/wild_things/2015/01/28/drones _for_wildlife_conservation_rangers_uavs_and_math_protect_elephants .html discussions with Professor Thomas Snitch, accessed May 18, 2017.

110. Hübschle, "A Status Symbol to Die For," 73–75.

111. Serino, "The Human Victims in the Fight over Rhino Poaching in South Africa."

112. Laurel Nome, "For Rangers on the Front Lines of Anti-Poaching Wars, Daily Trauma," *National Geographic*, June 27, 2014, http://news.nationalgeographic .com/news/2014/06/140627-congo-virunga-wildlife-rangers-elephants-rhinos -poaching/, accessed June 15, 2017.

113. Kelly Starzak, "New Study: Infusing Rhino Horns with Poison Does Not Work," Earth Touch News Network, May 30, 2014, https://www.earthtouchnews .com/environmental-crime/poaching/new-study-infusing-rhino-horns-with -poison-doesnot-work/, accessed May 18, 2017 (page no longer exists).

114. Jessica Aldred, "Richard Branson Fronts Nail-Biting Campaign against Rhino Poaching," *Guardian*, January 13, 2016, https://www.theguardian.com /environment/2016/jan/13/richard-branson-fronts-nail-biting-campaign -against-rhino-poaching, accessed May 18, 2017.

115. Alex Mitchley, "US Add to 'Groenewald Gang' Charge Sheet," *Citizen*, October 25, 2014, http://citizen.co.za/263495/us-add-to-groenewald-gang -charge-sheet/, accessed June 14, 2017; "The Case against Dawie Groenewald," uploaded by Julian Rademeyer, Scribd, http://www.scribd.com/doc/234546421 /The-case-against-Dawie-Groenewald. Groenewald was charged with 1,872 counts in South Africa ranging from illegal rhino hunting to racketeering, permit violations, illegal trade in rhino horn, money laundering, and violating the Biodiversity Act and the Act on the Prevention of Organized Crime.

116. Author's discussions with South African law enforcement officials, May 2016; Ilse de Lange, "Rhino Poaching Trial Delayed," *Citizen*, July 27, 2016, http://citizen.co.za/news/1225805/rhino-poaching-trial-delayed/, accessed

May 10, 2017; Rademeyer, "The Tipping Point," part 1; Simon Bloch, "Alleged Rhino Poaching Brothers Win Bail, Vow to Fight US Extradition," *News24*, June 23, 2017, https://www.news24.com/SouthAfrica/News/alleged-rhino -poaching-brothers-win-bail-vow-to-fight-us-extradition-20170623, accessed January 14, 2018.

117. Osborne, "Poaching and Prostitutes"; see also Rademeyer, *Killing for Profit*, 178–194. Chumlong Lemtongthai is currently serving a thirteen-year sentence for bringing Thai trafficked women to South Africa to pose as hunters and take part in white rhino trophy hunts on game farms in the North West Province; see "Chumlong Lemtongthai Supreme Court of Appeal Judgment," 2014, uploaded by Julian Rademeyer, Scribd, http://www.scribd.com/doc/241035369 /Chumlong-Lemtongthai-Supreme-Court-of-Appeal-judgment, accessed May 18, 2017.

118. Czech Environmental Inspectorate, "Operation RHINO—Case of 'Pseudo-Hunting'—Seizure of 22 Rhino Horns," *CITES News: Czech Republic* 105 (2013), www.cizp.cz/file/wh3/CITESnews-Prague105-Operation-RHINO.pdf, accessed May 18, 2017.

119. Simon Bloch, "Two Arrested for Rhino Horn Smuggling at Hong Kong Airport," *News24*, June 11, 2017, http://m.news24.com/news24/SouthAfrica /News/two-arrested-for-rhino-poaching-at-hong-kong-airport-20170611, accessed July 31, 2017.

120. Khristine Phillips, "A Kingpin Smuggled Ivory Tusks and Rhino Horns for Years, Police Say. The Suspect Was Finally Caught," *Washington Post*, January 20, 2018, https://www.washingtonpost.com/news/worldviews/wp/2018 /01/20/a-kingpin-smuggled-ivory-tusks-and-rhino-horns-for-years-police-say -the-suspect-was-finally-caught/?hpid=hp_no-name_hp-in-the-news%3Apage %2Fin-the-news&utm_term=.2a1477af672f, accessed February 10, 2018.

121. Russell Goldman, "South African Court Ends Ban on Sale of Rhinoceros Horns," *New York Times*, April 5, 2017, https://www.nytimes.com/2017/04/05 /world/africa/south-africa-rhinoceros-horns-rhinos.html, accessed May 18, 2017.

122. Sellar, *The UN's Lone Ranger*, 7–9; see also "How CITES Works," CITES, https://www.cites.org/eng/disc/how.php, accessed May 17, 2017, and "White Rhinos," CITES, https://cites.org/eng/gallery/species/mammal/white_rhino .html. The greatest CITES protections for wildlife are listed in appendix I of the CITES Convention, which currently includes all rhinos except the white rhino found in South Africa and Swaziland, which are in appendix II with regard to trophy hunting and the export of live animals to appropriate and acceptable destinations (which require CITES export permits). In correspondence with the author, John Sellar, former head of CITES enforcement, explains that all other forms of trade require that rhinos be treated as if they were in appendix I.

123. Selene Brophy, "Domestic Trade in Rhino Horn Could See 'Medical' Tourism Spike in South Africa," Traveller24, January 21, 2016, http://traveller24 .news24.com/Explore/Bush/domestic-trade-in-rhino-horn-could-see-medical -tourism-spike-in-sa-20160121, accessed June 15, 2017.

124. "Rhinoceros Horn Carvings from The Edward," Sotheby's, April 8, 2011, http://www.sothebys.com/en/auctions/2011/rhinoceros-horn-carvings-from-the-edward-and-franklin-chow-collection-hk0370.html, accessed July 31, 2017; Sellar, *The UN's Lone Ranger*, 177.

125. "Operation Crash," US Fish and Wildlife Service, February 21, 2017, https://www.fws.gov/le/pdf/Operation-Crash-Fact-Sheet.pdf, accessed July 31, 2017; "Black Market Trade in Rhinoceros Horn," US Department of Justice, updated April 15, 2015, https://www.justice.gov/enrd/black-market-trade-rhinoceros-horn, accessed July 31, 2017.

126. M. L. R. Smith and Jasper Humphreys, "The Poaching Paradox: Why South Africa's 'Rhino Wars' Shine a Harsh Spotlight on Security and Conservation," in Brisman, South, and White, *Environmental Crime and Social Conflict*, 197–220.

127. *World Drug Report 2014*, UNODC, 2014, xl, https://www.unodc.org/documents/wdr2014/World_Drug_Report_2014_exsum.pdf, accessed June 13, 2017.

128. Sellar, *The UN's Lone Ranger*, 61–63. Ivory, however, is available on the web; Jessica Phelan, "You Can Buy Ivory Necklaces through Yahoo Japan for Pennies," *Global Post/PRI*, February 11, 2016, http://www.globalpost.com/article/6731678/2016/02/11/japan-ivory-online-trade, accessed February 13, 2016.

129. Kenneth D. Rose et al., "Early Eocene Fossils Suggest That the Mammalian Order Perissodactyla Originated in India," *Nature Communications* 5 (2014): 5570, http://doi.org/10.1038/ncomms6570.

130. Stephen Montgomery, "Natural Selection," Charles Darwin & Evolution, http://darwin200.christs.cam.ac.uk/node/76, accessed February 22, 2016.

131. Charles Darwin, "VIII. Instinct: Summary," in *The Origin of Species* (Harvard Classics, 1909–1914), http://www.bartleby.com/11/8005.html, accessed January 25, 2017.

132. The criminal assailants are discussed in John M. Sellar, "Policing the Trafficking of Wildlife: Is There Anything to Learn from Law Enforcement Responses to Drug and Firearms Trafficking?," Global Initiative on Transnational Crime, February 2014, 1, http://globalinitiative.net/wildlifecrime/, accessed July 11, 2016; see also Sellar, *The UN's Lone Ranger*, 20.

133. "What Will Happen after the Rhinos Are Gone?," *Conservation*, February 19, 2014, http://conservationmagazine.org/2014/02/will-happen-rhinos-gone/, accessed February 16, 2016; see also P. G. M. Cromsigt and Mariska te Beest, "Restoration of a Megaherbivore: Landscape-Level Impacts White Rhinoceros in Kruger National Park, South Africa," *Journal of Ecology* 102, no. 3 (2014): 566, DOI:10.1111/1365-2745.12218.

134. Kathleen Garrigan, "Going Tuskless," African Wildlife Foundation, February 4, 2015, http://www.awf.org/blog/going-tuskless, accessed August 10, 2017; Amy Yee, "Poaching Leaving Elephant Daughters in Charge," *New York Times*, July 4, 2016, https://www.nytimes.com/2016/07/05/science/female-elephants-follow-in-their-mothers-footsteps.html, accessed August 10, 2017.

Chapter 5. Business Models: Historical Transformation of Illicit Entrepreneurship and Trade

1. Raj Samami, "The Evolution of Traditional Crime," in *Beyond Convergence: World without Order*, ed. Hilary Matfess and Michael Miklaucic (Washington, DC: Center for Complex Operations, 2016), 275–294, http://cco.ndu.edu/Portals/96/Documents/books/Beyond%20Convergence/BEYOND%20CONVERGENCE%20%20World%20Without%20Order%20.pdf?ver=2016-10-25-125406-170, accessed July 15, 2017.

2. Thomas S. Kuhn, *The Structure of Scientific Revolutions* (Chicago: University of Chicago Press, 1962).

3. David S. Wall, *Cybercrime: The Tranformation of Crime in the Information Age* (Cambridge: Polity, 2007), 93–94.

4. Gergana Bulanova-Hristova et al., "Introduction," in Bulanova-Hristova et al., *Cyber-OC—Scope and Manifestations in Selected EU Member States*. These sellers and buyers are trading on what are sometimes referred to as cryptomarkets.

5. "Operation Dual Identity: Cuban VIN Cloning King-Pin Pablo Barrio Still on the Run after Tampa Fl Take Down," February 6, 2010, https://pibillwarner.wordpress.com/2010/02/06/update-operation-dual-identity-cuban-vin-cloning-king-pin-pablo-barrio-still-on-the-run-after-tampa-fl-take-down/, accessed July 21, 2017 (site now deleted).

6. "Tracking Illicit Networks with the FBI: An Interview with Special Agent Bijan Hunter," George Mason University, TraCCC, 2013, http://traccc.gmu.edu/inside-traccc-issue-4/#7, accessed July 7, 2017; author's discussions with Bijan Hunter.

7. "Operation Dual Identity: Cuban VIN Cloning King-Pin Pablo Barrio."

8. "Car Clone Subjects Being Sought—Operation Dual Identity," FBI, Tampa Division, March 25, 2009, https://www.fbi.gov/tampa/press-releases/2009/ta032509.htm; Rich Phillips, "FBI Breaks up $25 Million 'Car Cloning' Ring," *CNN*, March 24, 2009, http://www.cnn.com/2009/CRIME/03/24/cloned.cars/index.html, accessed July 7, 2017.

9. Alison Holt, "Victims Trafficked from Vietnam to Work on Illegal UK Cannabis Farms," *BBC News*, March 14, 2014, http://www.bbc.com/news/26443575, accessed July 7, 2017; Annie Kelley and Mei-Ling McNamara, "3,000 Children Enslaved in Britain after Being Trafficked from Vietnam," *Guardian*, May 23, 2015, http://www.theguardian.com/global-development/2015/may/23/vietnam-children-trafficking-nail-bar-cannabis, accessed July 7, 2017; author's interviews with British law enforcement.

10. Thomas J. Holt, "Identifying Gaps in the Research Literature on Illicit Markets On-line," *Global Crime* 18, no. 1 (2017): 1–10.

11. Damon McCoy et al., "PharmaLeaks: Understanding the Business of Online Pharmaceutical Affiliate Programs," 2013, 1, http://damonmccoy.com/papers/pharmaleaks.pdf, accessed July 1, 2017; author's conversations with Damon McCoy. A conflict between the online pharmaceutical companies—the

equivalent of a cyber gang war—made the work of the analysts who took apart the business model of the online pharmaceutical companies easier. To understand this online business, see also Brian Krebs, *Spam Nation: The Inside Story of Organized Cybercrime—from Global Epidemic to Your Front Door* (Naperville, IL: Sourcebooks, 2014). The computer scientists who analyzed the business are some of the leading researchers in the United States. The conflict provided data on 800,000 purchasers using the online pharmacies as well as on the managers of the online pharmacies and their business practices.

12. "Episode 430: "Black Market Pharmacies and the Spam Empire behind Them," interview with Brian Krebs and computer scientist Stefan Savage, *Planet Money*, January 15, 2013, http://www.npr.org/sections/money/2013/01/15/169424047/episode-430-black-market-pharmacies-and-the-spam-empire-behind-them, accessed August 12, 2017.

13. "Distributor of Counterfeit Pharmaceutical Drugs Sentenced," US Food and Drug Administration (FDA), January 15, 2009, http://wayback.archive-it.org/7993/20180126100008/https://www.fda.gov/ICECI/CriminalInvestigations/ucm261012.htm.

14. McCoy et al., "PharmaLeaks"; Krebs, *Spam Nation*.

15. Musumeci, Cortemiglia, and D'Angelo, *Counterfeiting as an Activity Managed by Transnational Organised Crime*, 13.

16. "Situation Report on Counterfeiting in the European Union," Europol, 2015, 17, https://www.europol.europa.eu/publications-documents/2015-situation-report-counterfeiting-in-european-union, accessed July 14, 2017. This figure includes diverted pharmaceuticals, parallel trade, and substandard pharmaceuticals.

17. Damon McCoy, "Payment Processing and Advertising Based E-Crime," talk presented at George Mason University in the illicit trade class, 2012.

18. "Countering the Growing Intellectual Property Theft Threat," FBI, January 22, 2016, https://www.fbi.gov/news/stories/countering-the-growing-intellectual-property-theft-threat, accessed July 18, 2017.

19. Goodman, *Future Crimes*, 181.

20. McCoy, "Payment Processing and Advertising Based E-Crime."

21. Greg Williams, "The Digital Detective: Mikko Hypponen's War on Malware Is Escalating," *Wired*, March 19, 2012, http://www.wired.co.uk/article/the-digital-detective, accessed July 10, 2017.

22. *Planet Money*, "Black Market Pharmacies and the Spam Empire behind Them."

23. McCoy, "Payment Processing and Advertising Based E-Crime."

24. Krebs, *Spam Nation*; McCoy et al., "PharmaLeaks"; author's conversations with Damon McCoy.

25. Darren Pauli, "Spammer Sprung to Run Russian National Payment System," The Register, June 4, 2014, http://www.theregister.co.uk/2014/06/04/hacker_hired_to_build_russias_national_payment_system_report, accessed July 1, 2017; see also the muckraking Russian website that discusses Vrublevsky's

fake antivirus software, "Chernye proekty Chronoplay Vrublevskogo (Black Projects of Vrublevsky's Chronoplay)," http://www.compromat.ru/page_30941 .htm, accessed July 1, 2017.

26. Author's discussion with a computer crime specialist providing these insights, mid-2017.

27. Greg Gordon, Kevin G. Hall, and David Goldstein, "Russia's Pension Money for Its Veterans Escapes Scrutiny as It Flows into the US," *McClatchy*, February 21, 2017, http://www.mcclatchydc.com/news/nation-world/national /article133879684.html, accessed July 14, 2017.

28. For a discussion of Vrublevsky's two sides, see this article in the leading Russian investigative newspaper: Irek Murtazin, "Kiberprestupnik No. 1 Pavel Vrublevskii: Superagent ili zhertva FSB?" (Cybercriminal No. 1 Pavel Vrublevski: Superagent or Victim of the FSB?), *Novaya Gazeta*, November 29, 2012, https:// www.novayagazeta.ru/articles/2012/11/30/52573-kiberprestupnik-8470-1-pavel -vrublevskiy-superagent-ili-zhertva-fsb, accessed July 1, 2017.

29. United States of America vs. flux and flux 2, complaint, November 28, 2016.

30. Robert Wainwright and Frank J. Ciluffo, "Responding to Cybercrime at Scale: Operation Avalanche—A Case Study Issue," Brief 2017-3, George Washington University, Center for Cyber and Homeland Security, March 2017, 6, https:// cchs.gwu.edu/sites/cchs.gwu.edu/files/Responding%20to%20Cybercrime%20at %20Scale%20FINAL.pdf, accessed July 15, 2017.

31. One furniture business in California had $737,000 transferred from its bank accounts. Two Pennsylvania companies had $630,000 transferred out of their accounts at major banks. Matt Fair, "Bulgarian Faces Indictment in Pa. over Malware Attacks," Law360, December 12, 2016, https://www.law360.com /articles/872160/bulgarian-faces-indictment-in-pa-over-malware-attacks, accessed July 15, 2017; "Bulgarian Charged with GozNym Malware Attacks in the US," US Department of Justice, US Attorney's Office, Western District of Pennsylvania, December 12, 2016, https://www.justice.gov/usao-wdpa/pr/bulgarian -charged-goznym-malware-attacks-us, accessed July 15, 2017; US Government vs. Krasimir Nikolov, indictment filed October 4, 2016, in US District Court, Western District of Pennsylvania, https://assets.documentcloud.org/documents /3251405/Nikolovindict-1.pdf, accessed July 15, 2017.

32. "'Avalanche' Crime Leader Eludes Justice," Krebson Security, December 8, 2016, https://krebsonsecurity.com/2016/12/avalanche-crime-ring-leader -eludes-justice/, accessed July 14, 2017; "The Poltava Court Arrested a Cyber-criminal That Was Sought for 4 Years by Europol and the FBI" (translation), *Prestupnosti.net*, December 2, 2016, https://news.pn/ru/criminal/173397, accessed July 23, 2017. The website has a video of the prosecutor.

33. US Department of Justice, "Avalanche Network Dismantled in International Cyber Operation."

34. Europol, "'Avalanche' Network Disrupted in Cyber Operation."

35. United States of America vs. flux and flux 2, complaint, November 28, 2016.

36. Patrick Vibert, "The Ransomware Industry's Rapid Evolution," *Cyber Security Review*, May 2016, http://www.cybersecurity-review.com/articles/the-rapid-evolution-of-the-ransomware-industry/; Glenny, *DarkMarket*; US Department of Justice, "Avalanche Network Dismantled in International Cyber Operation."

37. Mandak, "Prosecutor's Office Paid Bitcoin Ransom in Cyberattack." The case documents refer to "many" victims in western Pennsylvania because federal law enforcement's greatest effort against computer crime is based in Pittsburgh in partnership with Carnegie Mellon University.

38. Jay S. Albanese, *Transnational Crime and the 21st Century: Criminal Enterprise, Corruption, and Opportunity* (Oxford: Oxford University Press, 2011).

39. Marie-Helen Maras, *Cybercriminology* (New York: Oxford University Press, 2017), 334.

40. "Pharmaceutical Crime and Organized Crime Groups: An Analysis of the Involvement of Organized Criminal Groups in Pharmaceutical Crime since 2008," Interpol, July 17, 2014, https://illicittrade.com/reports/downloads/PUBLIC%20VERSION%20Pharmaceutical%20Crime%20and%20Organised%20Criminal%20Groups.pdf; "Pharmaceutical Crime on the Darknet: A Study of Online Marketplaces," Interpol, February 24, 2015, https://www.gwern.net/docs/sr/2015-interpol-pharmaceuticals.pdf, accessed August 12, 2017. The latter Interpol report looks at the role of Silk Road 2.0 in online pharmaceutical sales. On intimidation associated with Pharmaleaks, see Yuliya Zabyelina, "Can Criminals Create Opportunities for Crime? Malvertising and Illegal Online Medicine Trade," *Global Crime* 18, no. 1 (2017): 31–48.

41. Goodman, *Future Crimes*, 196; Andy Greenberg, "Silk Road Boss' First Murder-for-Hire Was His Mentor's Idea," *Wired*, April 1, 2015, https://www.wired.com/2015/04/silk-road-boss-first-murder-attempt-mentors-idea/, accessed October 29, 2016. The founder of Silk Road paid for hit men in five attempted homicides to take out those who had bilked him or threatened him. Krebson Security, "'Avalanche' Crime Leader Eludes Justice."

42. Andreas, *Smuggler Nation*, 291–329.

43. Curtin, *Cross-Cultural Trade in World History*.

44. Matthew Levitt, *Hezbollah: The Global Footprint of Lebanon's Party of God* (Washington, DC: Georgetown University Press, 2013).

45. Gingeras, *Heroin, Organized Crime, and the Making of Modern Turkey*.

46. David S. Wall, "Internet Mafias? The Di-Organisation of Crime on the Internet," in *Organized Crime, Corruption, and Crime Prevention: Essays in Honor of Ernesto U. Savona*, ed. Stefano Caneppele and Francesco Calderoni (Cham, Switzerland: Springer, 2014), 227–238; Werner and Korsell, "Cyber-OC in Sweden," 116.

47. Peter Andreas, *Border Games: Policing the US-Mexico Divide* (Ithaca, NY: Cornell University Press, 2009); see also Andreas, *Smuggler Nation*; Angelique Chrisafis, "All over for Tomcat and Gremlin as New Breed of Gangsters Take Hold in Marseille," *Guardian*, February 12, 2009, https://www.theguardian.com/world/2009/feb/13/marseille-crime, accessed February 9, 2017; Maria Pia

Pedani, "Ottoman Merchants in the Adriatic Trade and Smuggling," *Acta Histriae* 16 (2008): 1–2, 163–164; Gingeras, *Heroin, Organized Crime, and the Making of Modern Turkey*.

48. Shelley, *Human Trafficking*, 122–123.

49. Musumeci, Cortemiglia, and D'Angelo, *Counterfeiting as an Activity Managed by Transnational Organised Crime*, 83.

50. Nožina, "Crime Networks in Vietnamese Diasporas," 229–258.

51. Steve McGough, "Ultimate Community Organizing—Somali Pirates Launch Community Stock Exchange," *RadioVice Online*, December 2, 2009, http://radioviceonline.com/ultimate-community-organizing-somali-pirates-launch-community-stock-exchange/, accessed July 15, 2017; author's discussions about this market during a visit to Africom in 2012.

52. Goodman, *Future Crimes*, 189–193.

53. Brian Krebs, "Hacker Who Sent Me Heroin Faces Charges in the US," Krebson Security, October 15, 2015, http://krebsonsecurity.com/2015/10/hacker-who-sent-me-heroin-faces-charges-in-u-s/, accessed July 14, 2017.

54. Author's discussions with former law enforcement official who engaged in undercover work.

55. Goodman, *Future Crimes*, 182–183.

56. Shelley, *Human Trafficking*, 107–108; Stephen Ellis, *This Present Darkness: A History of Nigerian Organised Crime* (Oxford: Oxford University Press, 2016), 180–187.

57. Goodman, *Future Crimes*, 182, 209–211.

58. Brian O'Keefe, "Inside Big Chocolate's Child Labor Problems," *Fortune*, March 1, 2016, http://fortune.com/big-chocolate-child-labor/, accessed July 14, 2017.

59. Cole Stangler, "Apple Supplier in China's Poor Labor Practices Clash with US Tech Giant's Promises to Lift Supply Chain Standards: Report," *International Business Times*, February 23, 2016, http://www.ibtimes.com/apple-supplier-chinas-poor-labor-practices-clash-us-tech-giants-promises-lift-supply-2320357, accessed July 14, 2017.

60. Kevin Short, "5 Reasons American Companies Refused to Sign Bangladesh Safety Accord," *Huffington Post*, July 11, 2013, http://www.huffingtonpost.com/2013/07/11/rival-bangladesh-factory-safety-plans_n_3574260.html, accessed July 14, 2017.

61. For differences between licit and illicit commerce, see Edward R. Kleemans, "Criminal Organization and Transnational Crime," in *Histories of Transnational Crime*, ed. Gerben Bruinsma (New York: Springer, 2015), 175.

62. Francisco E. Thoumi, "Organized Crime in Colombia: The Actors Running the Illegal Drug Industry," in *The Oxford Handbook of Organized Crime*, ed. Letizia Paoli (New York: Oxford University Press, 2014), 177–183.

63. *Demand: A Comparative Examination of Sex Tourism and Trafficking in Jamaica, Japan, the Netherlands, and the United States*, Shared Hope International, 2012, 89, http://sharedhope.org/wp-content/uploads/2012/09/DEMAND.pdf, accessed July 14, 2017.

64. Author's analysis presented at the eighth annual "Interdisciplinary Human Trafficking" conference, University of Nebraska, October 6–8, 2016.

65. Meredith Dank et al., "Estimating the Size and Structure of the Underground Commercial Sex Economy in Eight Major US Cities," Urban Institute, March 11, 2014, http://www.urban.org/research/publication/estimating-size -and-structure-underground-commercial-sex-economy-eight-major-us-cities /view/full_report, accessed July 14, 2017; Snejana Farberov, "Pimp My Instagram: How Suspected Sex Trafficker Used Social Media to Document His Luxury Lifestyle with Louis Vuitton Bags and Lobster Dinners," *Daily Mail*, August 22, 2014, http://www.dailymail.co.uk/news/article-2732179/Pimp-Instagram-How -suspected-sex-trafficker-used-social-media-document-luxe-lifestyle-Louis -Vuitton-lobster-dinners.html, accessed July 14, 2017.

66. "Attorneys General Call for Craigslist to Get Rid of Adult Services Ads," *CNN*, August 26, 2010, http://www.cnn.com/2010/CRIME/08/25/craigslist .adult.content/index.html, accessed July 13, 2017.

67. Tom Jackman and Jonathan O'Connell, "Backpage Has Always Claimed It Doesn't Control Sex-Related Ads. New Documents Show Otherwise," *Washington Post*, July 11, 2017, https://www.washingtonpost.com/local /public-safety/backpage-has-always-claimed-it-doesnt-control-sex-related-ads -new-documents-show-otherwise/2017/07/10/b3158ef6-553c-11e7-b38e -35fd8e0c288f_story.html?utm_term=.e4df360dde77.

68. Jackman and O'Connell, "Backpage Has Always Claimed It Doesn't Control Sex-Related Ads."

69. *CNN*, "Attorneys General Call for Craigslist to Get Rid of Adult Services Ads."

70. US Senate, Permanent Subcommittee on Investigations "Backpage.com's Knowing Facilitation of Online Sex Trafficking," 46–47, https://www.mccaskill .senate.gov/imo/media/doc/2017.01.10%20Backpage%20Report.pdf.

71. Christopher Mele, "CEO of Backpage, Known for Escort Ads, Is Charged with Pimping a Minor," *New York Times*, October 6, 2016, http://www.nytimes .com/2016/10/07/us/carl-ferrer-backpage-ceo-is-arrested.html, accessed October 7, 2016.

72. Charlie Savage and Timothy Williams, "US Seizes Backpage.com, a Site Accused of Enabling Prostitution," *New York Times*, April 7, 2018, https://www .nytimes.com/2018/04/07/us/politics/backpage-prostitution-classified.html, accessed April 28, 2018.

73. Tom Jackman and Mark Berman, "Top Officials at Backpage.com Indicted after Classifieds Site Taken Offline," *Washington Post*, April 9, 2018, https:// www.washingtonpost.com/local/public-safety/top-officials-at-backpagecom -indicted-after-classifieds-site-taken-offline/2018/04/09/0b646f36-39db-11e8 -9c0a-85d477d9a226_story.html?utm_term=.937f81eb3d6f, accessed April 29, 2018.

74. Musumeci, Cortemiglia, and D'Angelo, *Counterfeiting as an Activity Managed by Transnational Organised Crime*, 70–71.

75. Goodman, *Future Crimes*, 183–184.

76. "Shedding Light on the Dark Web," *Economist*, July 16, 2016, https://www
.economist.com/news/international/21702176-drug-trade-moving-street-online
-cryptomarkets-forced-compete, accessed July 16, 2017.

77. Miklaucic and Brewer, *Convergence*.

78. Correa-Cabrera, *Los Zetas Inc.*; Gerardo Reyes of Univision, presentation on the panel "Corruption, Security, and Organized Crime," International
Anti-Corruption Conference (IACC), Panama City, Panama, December 3, 2016,
https://17iacc.sched.com/event/8SD7/corruption-security-and-organized
-crime, accessed July 9, 2017.

79. Arthur Neslen, "Number of Criminal Gangs Operating in Europe Surges
to 5,000, Says Europol," *Guardian*, March 9, 2017, https://www.theguardian.com
/uk-news/2017/mar/09/more-than-5000-crimnal-gangs-operating-in-europe
-warns-europol, accessed August 4, 2017; Karl Lallerstedt, "The Neglected Mega-
Problem: Illicit Trade in 'Normally Licit' Goods," in Matfess and Miklaucic, *Beyond Convergence*, 257.

80. "Tracking Illicit Networks with the FBI: An Interview with Special Agent
Bijan Hunter"; author's discussions with Bijan Hunter.

81. James Bargent, "Colombia's Informal Gold Miners Feel the Heat from All
Sides," *World Politics Review*, January 26, 2016, http://www.worldpoliticsreview
.com/articles/17770/colombia-s-informal-gold-miners-feel-the-heat-from-all
-sides, accessed July 15, 2017.

82. "Organized Crime and Illegally Mined Gold in Latin America," Global
Initiative against Transnational Organized Crime, March 30, 2016, http://
globalinitiative.net/organized-crime-and-illegally-mined-gold-in-latin-america/.

83. Basra, Neumann, and Brunner, *Criminal Pasts, Terrorist Futures*, 44.

84. Nellemann et al., *The Rise of Environmental Crime*, 22.

85. Krebs, *Spam Nation*.

86. Jamie Bartlett, *The Dark Net: Inside the Digital Underworld* (Brooklyn,
NY: Melville House, 2015), 144–146.

87. Pino Arlacchi, *Mafia Business: The Mafia Ethic and the Spirit of Capitalism* (London: Verso, 1986); Letizia Paoli, *Mafia Brotherhoods: Organized Crime,
Italian Style* (Oxford: Oxford University Press, 2003); Isaia Sales, *Storia dell'Italia
Mafiosa: Perché le mafie hanno avuto successo* (Soveria Mannelli: Rubbettino,
2015).

88. Diego Gambetta, *The Sicilian Mafia: The Business of Private Protection*
(Cambridge, MA: Harvard University Press, 1993).

89. S. K. Wasser et al., "Genetic Assignment of Large Seizures of Elephant
Ivory Reveals Africa's Major Poaching Hotspots," *Science* 349, no. 6243 (2015):
84–87, published online June 18, 2015, DOI:10.1126/science.aaa2457.

90. Wainwright and Ciluffo, "Responding to Cybercrime at Scale," 3, 5.

91. Based on author's fieldwork and interviews.

92. Author's interview with Indonesian law enforcement, summer 2015, and
Taiwanese law enforcement, February 2018.

93. Xavier Raufder, *Cyber-criminologie* (Paris: CNRS Éditions, 2015), 85–115.

94. "Cyber Criminal Pleads Guilty to Developing and Distributing Notorious Spyeye Malware," US Department of Justice, Office of Public Affairs, January 28, 2014, https://www.justice.gov/opa/pr/cyber-criminal-pleads-guilty-developing -and-distributing-notorious-spyeye-malware, accessed July 15, 2017.

95. Goodman, *Future Crimes*, 204.

96. Werner and Korsell, "Cyber-OC in Sweden," 105–106.

97. UNODC, *World Drug Report 2017: Booklet 1*, 14.

98. "Federal Designer Drug Manufacturers and Dealers Sentenced to Imprisonment," US Department of Justice, US Attorney's Office, District of Arizona, April 7, 2014, https://www.justice.gov/usao-az/pr/federal-designer-drug -manufacturers-and-dealers-sentenced-imprisonment, accessed August 13, 2017.

99. "Captured by Captagon: A New Drug of Choice in the Middle East," *Economist*, July 22, 2017, https://www.economist.com/news/middle-east-and-africa /21725167-dangerous-arrival-dangerous-region-new-drug-choice-gulf, accessed January 20, 2018.

100. "Myanmar Police Seize '$100m Worth of Methamphetamines,'" *BBC News*, July 28, 2015, http://www.bbc.com/news/world-asia-33695748, accessed July 2, 2017.

101. Peggy E. Chaudhry, "The Looming Shadow of Illicit Trade on the Internet: Botnets, Malware, and Malvertising," in *Handbook of Research on Counterfeiting and Illicit Trade*, ed. Peggy E. Chaudhry (Cheltenham, UK: Edward Elgar, 2017), 366–383.

102. See, for example, "Are You and Your Loved Ones in Danger?," Law Offices of David H. Greenberg, http://www.greenbergaccidentlawyer.com/toyota -defective-seatbelt-problems/, accessed July 17, 2017.

103. Interpol, *Against Organized Crime: Interpol Trafficking and Counterfeit Casebook 2014* (Lyon: Interpol, 2014).

104. "Toxic Metals in Children's Products: An Insight into the Market in Eastern Europe, the Caucasus, and Central Asia," IPEN and GRID-Arendal, 2013, https://gridarendal-website.s3.amazonaws.com/production/documents/: s_document/124/original/toxicrep_eng_scr.pdf?1483646620, accessed July 17, 2017.

105. Donald W. Scott, "Policing Corporate Collusion," *Criminology* 27, no. 3 (August 1989): 559–587; Edwin H. Sutherland, "White Collar Criminality," *American Sociological Review* 5, no. 1 (February 1940): 1–12.

106. Kyle Soska and Nicolas Christin, "Measuring the Longitudinal Evolution of the Online Anonymous Marketplace Ecosystem," in "Proceedings of the Twenty-Fourth USENIX Security Symposium," Washington, DC, August 12–14, 2015, https://www.usenix.org/system/files/conference/usenixsecurity15/sec15 -paper-soska-updated.pdf, accessed August 12, 2017.

107. Thomas Firestone, "Criminal Corporate Raiding in Russia," *International Lawyer* 42, no. 4 (Winter 2008): 1207–1229; Michael Rochlitz, "Corporate Raiding and the Role of the State in Russia," *Post-Soviet Affairs* 30, nos. 2–3 (2014): 90;

Vadim Volkov, "Hostile Enterprise Takeovers: Russia's Economy in 1998–2002," *Review of Central and East European Law* 29, no. 4 (2004): 527–548.

108. Lauren Gensler, "The World's Largest Retailers 2016: Wal-Mart Dominates but Amazon Is Catching Up," *Forbes*, May 27, 2016, http://www.forbes .com/sites/laurengensler/2016/05/27/global-2000-worlds-largest-retailers/ #4b2ac3b29a9e, accessed October 27, 2016.

109. Musumeci, Cortemiglia, and D'Angelo, *Counterfeiting as an Activity Managed by Transnational Organised Crime*, 91–92.

110. Shelley, *Dirty Entanglements*, 224–227.

111. *2015 Situation Report on Counterfeiting in the European Union*, Europol and Office for Harmonization in the Internal Market, April 2015, 15–16, https:// euipo.europa.eu/ohimportal/documents/11370/80606/2015+Situation+Report +on+Counterfeiting+in+the+EU, accessed June 29, 2017; Musumeci, Cortemiglia, and D'Angelo, *Counterfeiting as an Activity Managed by Transnational Organised Crime*, 91–92.

112. Mathew, *Margins of the Market*; Vira, Ewing, and Miller, "Out of Africa."

113. Odinot et al., "Cyber-OC in the Netherlands," 37; Jordan Robinson and Michael Riley, "The Mob's IT Department: How Two Technology Consultants Helped Drug Traffickers Hack the Port of Antwerp," *Bloomberg*, July 7, 2015, https://www.bloomberg.com/graphics/2015-mob-technology-consultants-help -drug-traffickers/.

114. Dylan Scott, "Bipartisan Bill Aims to Crack Down on Illicit Opioid Shipments into US," STAT, February 14, 2017, https://www.statnews.com/2017/02 /14/opioid-shipment-crackdown/, accessed August 13, 2017.

115. *Illicit Trade Environment Index*, *Economist* Intelligence Unit, 2016, 12, http://illicittradeindex.eiu.com/ECC%20Illicit%20trade%20paper%20V9 _Oct12.pdf, accessed July 17, 2017.

116. *Controlling the Zone: Balancing Facilitation and Control to Combat Illicit Trade in the World's Free Trade Zones*, International Chamber of Commerce and BASCAP, May 2013, https://iccwbo.org/publication/controlling-the-zone -balancing-facilitation-and-control-to-combat-illicit-trade-in-the-worlds-free -trade-zones-2013/, accessed July 16, 2017; *Economist* Intelligence Unit, *Illicit Trade Environment Index*.

117. International Chamber of Commerce and BASCAP, *Controlling the Zone*, 6.

118. International Chamber of Commerce and BASCAP, *Controlling the Zone*, 6–7.

119. International Tax and Investment Center (ITIC), "Toolkit to Reduce the Use of Free Trade Zones for Illicit Trade in Tobacco Products," presentation at the Fifth OECD Task Force Meeting on Countering Illicit Trade, OECD Conference Center, March 16, 2017, http://www.oecd.org/officialdocuments /publicdisplaydocumentpdf/?cote=GOV/PGC/HLRF/TFCIT/RD(2017)4& docLanguage=En, accessed July 23, 2017.

120. "Corruption Perception Index: Singapore," Transparency International, https://www.transparency.org/news/feature/corruption_perceptions_index

_2017?gclid=CjwKCAjwt5DXBRAtEiwAa3vyEpdDF5cKMqwAJf5cLHOFo6lXw5 _arFl1TEMwyvpxmnJbn77f-BmArhoC2kMQAvD_BwE, accessed April 28, 2018.

121. *Economist* Intelligence Unit, *Illicit Trade Environment Index*, 12.

122. John Marzulli, "Feds Bust Frozen Fish Filled with Cocaine in Brooklyn," *New York Daily News*, May 9, 2016, http://www.nydailynews.com/new-york /brooklyn/feds-bust-frozen-fish-filled-cocaine-brooklyn-article-1.2630867, accessed October 19, 2016; "Spanish and Portuguese Police Find Cocaine in Pineapples," OCCRP, January 19, 2018, https://www.occrp.org/en/daily/7529 -spanish-and-portuguese-police-find-cocaine-in-pineapples, accessed January 24, 2018.

123. James Edgar, "Drugs in Rugs: Heroin Worth £5 Million Found Woven into Carpets," *Telegraph*, June 10, 2014, http://www.telegraph.co.uk/news /uknews/crime/10889639/Drugs-in-rugs-heroin-worth-5-million-found-woven -into-carpets.html, accessed October 19, 2016.

124. OECD, *Illicit Trade*, 127.

125. Musumeci, Cortemiglia, and D'Angelo, *Counterfeiting as an Activity Managed by Transnational Organised Crime*, 90.

126. Author's conversation with head of Thai Interpol, summer 2015.

127. Lectures by National Park Service personnel on illicit trade in park resources at Shenandoah National Park, September 11, 2016; "Looters Steal Civil War History at Petersburg National Battlefield," National Park Service, Office of Communications, https://www.nps.gov/orgs/1207/05-27-2016b.htm, accessed July 18, 2017.

128. Vira, Ewing and Miller, "Out of Africa," 18.

129. "Nuclear Materials Smugglers Arrested," *UPI*, March 11, 2013, https:// www.upi.com/Nuclear-materials-smugglers-arrested/80861362997303/; information provided by Leonard Spector.

130. "Illicit Trade," Institute for Science and International Security, http://isis -online.org/studies/category/illicit-trade, accessed January 21, 2018.

131. Goodman, *Future Crimes*, 201.

132. Ellen Gabler and Rich Harris, "On Reddit, Intimate Glimpses of Addicts in Thrall to Opioids," *New York Times*, July 20, 2017, https://www.nytimes.com /2017/07/20/us/opioid-reddit.html, accessed July 21, 2017; Jo Hastie and Tania McCrea-Steele, *Wanted Dead or Alive: Exposing Online Wildlife Trade* (London: IFAW, 2014); Interpol and IFAW, *Project Web: An Investigation into the Ivory Trade over the Internet within the European Union* (Lyon: Interpol, 2013).

133. Dan Levin, "In China Illegal Drugs Are Sold Online in an Unbridled Market," *New York Times*, June 21, 2015, http://www.nytimes.com/2015/06/22 /world/asia/in-china-illegal-drugs-are-sold-online-in-an-unbridled-market .html, accessed August 2, 2017.

134. C. J. Chivers, "Facebook Groups Act as Weapons Bazaars for Militias," *New York Times*, April 6, 2016, https://www.nytimes.com/2016/04/07/world /middleeast/facebook-weapons-syria-libya-iraq.html, accessed August 10, 2017.

135. Andy Greenberg, "Over Eighty Percent of Dark-Web Visits Relate to Pedophilia, Study Finds," *Wired*, December 30, 2014, https://www.wired.com/2014

/12/80-percent-dark-web-visits-relate-pedophilia-study-finds/, accessed July 10, 2017.

136. FBI, "Countering the Growing Intellectual Property Theft Threat."

137. E. Rutger Leukfeldt, Edward R. Kleemans, and Wouter P. Stol, "Cyber-criminal Networks, Social Ties, and Online Forums: Social Ties versus Digital Ties within Phishing and Malware Networks," *British Journal of Criminology* 57, no. 3 (May 2017): 704–722.

138. Dark Net Conference, George Mason University, January 11–13, 2017.

139. "Definition of Corporate Social Responsibility," *Financial Times* Lexicon, http://lexicon.ft.com/Term?term=corporate-social-responsibility-(CSR), accessed July 24, 2017.

140. Enrique Desmond Arias, "Gang Politics in Rio de Janeiro, Brazil," in *Global Gangs: Street Violence across the World*, ed. Jennifer M. Hazen and Dennis Rodgers (Minneapolis: University of Minnesota Press, 2014), 250.

141. Shelley, *Dirty Entanglements*, 82–83.

142. Dev Kar and Brian Le Blanc, *Illicit Financial Flows from Developing Countries: 2002–2011*, GFI, December 2013, vii, http://iff.gfintegrity.org/iff2013/Illicit_Financial_Flows_from_Developing_Countries_2002-2011-HighRes.pdf, accessed June 11, 2017.

143. The author heard discussions of the case by one of the investigators at the International Anti-Corruption Forum in Malaysia on September 2–4, 2015; see also "1MDB: The Case That Has Riveted Malaysia," *BBC News*, July 22, 2016, http://www.bbc.co.uk/news/world-asia-33447456, accessed September 1, 2017.

144. On Turkmenistan and Equatorial Guinea, see "Undue Diligence: How Banks Do Business with Corrupt Regimes," Global Witness, March 2009, https://www.globalwitness.org/en/campaigns/corruption-and-money-laundering/banks/undue-diligence/, accessed June 11, 2017. On Ukraine, see Shaun Walker and Oksana Grytsenko, "Ukraine's New Leaders Begin Search for Missing Billions," *Guardian*, February 27, 2014, https://www.theguardian.com/world/2014/feb/27/ukraine-search-missing-billions-yanukovych-russia, accessed June 11, 2017.

145. "Panama Papers," International Consortium of Investigative Journalists (ICIJ), https://panamapapers.icij.org/, accessed June 11, 2017. The head of the ICIJ investigative team, Marina Walker Guevara, spoke at TraCCC on the Panama Papers on May 11, 2016.

146. Michael Levi, "Money Laundering," in Paoli, *The Oxford Handbook of Organized Crime*, 418–443; Friedrich Schneider, "The Hidden Flows of Organized Crime: A Literature Review and Some Preliminary Empirical Results," in *Illicit Trade and the Global Economy*, ed. Cláudia Costa Storti and Paul de Grauwe (Cambridge, MA: MIT Press, 2012), 31–48; "Fifth Report of the Secretary-General on the Threat Posed by ISIL (Da'esh) to International Peace and Security and the Range of United Nations Efforts in Support of Member States in Countering the Threat," S/2017/467, UN Security Council, May 31, 2017, https://reliefweb.int/report/world/fifth-report-secretary-general-threat-posed-isil-da-esh-international-peace-and; "UNODC Launches Training to Tackle

Cryptocurrency-Enabled Organized Crime," UNODC, May 8, 2017, https://www.unodc.org/unodc/en/frontpage/2017/May/unodc-launches-training-to-tackle-money-laundering-and-bitcoin-banking-fraud.html, accessed June 15, 2017; Scott W. Duxbury and Dana L. Haynie, "The Network Structure of Opioid Distribution on a Darknet Cryptomarket," *Journal of Quantitative Criminology* (June 2017), DOI 10.1007/s10940-017-9359-4.

147. Brigitte Unger and Joras Ferwerda, *Money Laundering in the Real Estate Sector: Suspicious Properties* (Cheltenham, UK: Edward Elgar, 2011).

148. Author's interview with the Dutch prosecutor of this case at the Organization for Security and Cooperation in Europe (OSCE).

149. "FinCEN Renews Real Estate 'Geographic Targeting Orders' to Identify High-End Cash Buyers in Six Major Metropolitan Areas," US Department of the Treasury, Financial Crimes Enforcement Network, February 23, 2017, https://www.fincen.gov/news/news-releases/fincen-renews-real-estate-geographic-targeting-orders-identify-high-end-cash; "FinCEN Takes Aim at Real Estate Secrecy in Manhattan and Miami: 'Geographic Targeting Orders' Require Identification for High-End Cash Buyers," US Department of the Treasury, FinCEN, January 13, 2016, https://www.fincen.gov/news/news-releases/fincen-takes-aim-real-estate-secrecy-manhattan-and-miami, accessed August 5, 2017; Safak Herdem, "Turkey: Money Laundering Report of Turkey," Mondaq, September 9, 2013, http://www.mondaq.com/turkey/x/261560/Money+Laundering/Money+Laundering+Report+Of+Turkey2012, accessed June 25, 2016; Mahmut Cengiz, *Turkish Organized Crime: From Local to Global* (Saarbrücken: Verlag Dr. Müller, 2011); Mitchell Roth and Murat Sever, "The Kurdish Workers Party (PKK) as Criminal Syndicate: Funding Terrorism through Organized Crime: A Case Study," *Studies in Conflict and Terrorism* 30, no. 10 (2007): 901–920, http://dx.doi.org/10.1080/10576100701558620.

150. Simon Little, "'It's a Crisis': BC Attorney General Responds to Report Linking Drugs, Money Laundering, Real Estate," April 19, 2018, https://globalnews.ca/news/4155822/vancouver-model-david-eby-money-laundering/, accessed April 28, 2018.

151. R. T. Naylor, *Wages of Crime: Black Markets, Illegal Finance, and the Underworld Economy* (Ithaca, NY: Cornell University Press, 2002), 133–196; Jason C. Sharman, *The Money Laundry: Regulating Criminal Finance in the Global Economy* (Ithaca, NY: Cornell University Press, 2011).

152. Alan Katz and Dakin Campbell, "Inside the Money Laundering Scheme That Citi Overlooked for Years: How Citigroup's Banamex USA Unit Turned a Blind Eye on the Mexican Border," *Bloomberg Markets*, November 20, 2015, http://www.bloomberg.com/news/articles/2015-11-20/inside-the-money-laundering-scheme-that-citi-overlooked-for-years, accessed August 4, 2017; Ed Vulliamy, "HSBC Has Form: Remember Mexico and Laundered Drug Money," *Guardian*, February 15, 2015, https://www.theguardian.com/commentisfree/2015/feb/15/hsbc-has-form-mexico-laundered-drug-money, accessed June 25, 2016; Curt Anderson, "Wachovia to Settle Drug-Money Laundering Case," *NBC News*,

March 17, 2010, http://www.nbcnews.com/id/35914759/ns/business-world_business/t/wachovia-settle-drug-money-laundering-case/#.WYXwKCuQzZs, accessed August 4, 2017; Jean-François Gayraud, *Le Nouveau capitalisme criminel* (Paris: Odile Jacob, 2014), 94–108.

153. "Colombian Black Market Peso Exchange," US Department of the Treasury, FinCEN, *FinCEN Advisory*, November 1997, https://www.fincen.gov/sites/default/files/shared/advisu9.pdf, accessed August 6, 2017.

154. Lowell Bergman, "US Companies Tangled in Web of Drug Dollars," *New York Times*, October 10, 2000, http://www.nytimes.com/2000/10/10/us/us-companies-tangled-in-web-of-drug-dollars.html, accessed August 6, 2017.

155. "Stairway to Tax Heaven," ICIJ, https://panamapapers.icij.org/stairway_tax_heaven_game/, accessed August 6, 2017.

156. Ryan Chittum, Jake Bernstein, and Michael Hudson, "The Malefactors of Mossack Fonseca," ICIJ, May 9, 2016, https://panamapapers.icij.org/20160509-malefactors-criminals-offshore.html, accessed August 6, 2017; "Giant Leak of Offshore Financial Records Exposes Global Array of Crime and Corruption: Millions of Documents Show Heads of State, Criminals, and Celebrities Using Secret Hideaways in Tax Havens," ICIJ, April 3, 2016, https://panamapapers.icij.org/20160403-panama-papers-global-overview.html, accessed August 6, 2017.

157. "Les Documents d'Information de L'Assemblée Nationale," *L'esclavage, en France, aujourd'hui*, vol. 2; *Auditions*, vol. 1, no. 3459 (2001), 33.

158. State of Arizona vs. Western Union Financial Services, settlement agreement, February 11, 2010, https://www.azag.gov/sites/default/files/sites/all/docs/swbamla/State%20of%20Arizona%20v.%20Western%20Union%20Settlement%20Agreement%20compact.pdf, accessed August 6, 2017; Aaron Vehling, "Investor Sues Western Union over Drug Cartel Transfers," Law360, February 21, 2014, http://www.law360.com/articles/512052/investor-sues-western-union-over-drug-cartel-transfers, accessed August 6, 2017; author's interview with former Arizona state attorney general Terry Goddard; author's interview with a former monitor of Western Union. Goddard testified against Western Union.

159. Lauren Gensler, "Western Union Slammed for Aiding Crooks, Agrees to Pay $586 Million," *Forbes*, January 19, 2017, https://www.forbes.com/sites/laurengensler/2017/01/19/western-union-anti-money-laundering-consumer-fraud-violations/#496ebe0a7238, accessed August 6, 2017.

160. Odinot et al., "Cyber-OC in the Netherlands," 82.

161. "The Panama Papers Panel: Tax Havens—Who, Why, & Impacts," George Mason University, TraCCC, May 11, 2016, http://traccc.gmu.edu/wp-content/uploads/2016/04/Panama-Papers-flyer.pdf. This event featured Marina Walker Guevara, manager of the ICIJ Panama Papers investigation, and Juan Ricardo Ortega, former commissioner of tax and customs in Colombia.

162. Cassara, *Trade-Based Money Laundering*.

163. Odinot et al., "Cyber-OC in the Netherlands," 82–83, 86.

164. Russell Brandom, "Feds Have Taken Down Two Dark Web Marketplaces," *Verge*, July 20, 2017, https://www.theverge.com/2017/7/20/16003046/alphabay-takedown-hansa-marketplace-fbi-europol-sessions, accessed July 24, 2017.

165. "Russian National and Bitcoin Exchange Charged in 21-Count Indictment for Operating Alleged International Money Laundering Scheme and Allegedly Laundering Funds from Hack of Mt. Gox," US Department of Justice, US Attorney's Office, Northern District of California, July 26, 2017, https://www.justice.gov/usao-ndca/pr/russian-national-and-bitcoin-exchange-charged-21-count-indictment-operating-alleged, accessed August 6, 2017. The recent indictment of Russian hackers for their role in the US election features their use of bitcoin; see U.S. vs. Viktor Borisovich Netyksho et al. (18 U.S.C. §§ 2, 371, 1030, 1028A, 1956, Viktor Borisovich Netyksho, * and 3551 et seq.), https://www.justice.gov/file/1080281/, accessed July 26, 2018.

166. Xiaojing Liao et al., "Lurking Malice in the Cloud: Understanding and Detecting Cloud Repository as a Malicious Service," paper presented at the twenty-third ACM conference "Computer and Communications Security," Vienna, October 24–28, 2016, 1541–1552, http://dx.doi.org/10.1145/2976749.2978349.

167. Goodman, *Future Crimes*, 209–211; ANSER, *Risks and Threats of Virtual Currencies*.

Chapter 6. Destroyers of Human Life

1. "Up to Two Years Behind Bars for a Cigarette-Trafficking Network," European Observatory on Illicit Trade, December 4, 2017, https://www.eurobsit.eu/article/up-to-two-years-behind-the-bars-for-a-cigarette-trafficking-network_2-2, accessed January 31, 2017.

2. Sheena Chestnut Greitens, "Illicit: North Korea's Evolving Operations to Earn Hard Currency," Committee for Human Rights in North Korea, April 15, 2014, 15, https://www.hrnk.org/uploads/pdfs/SCG-FINAL-FINAL(1).pdf, accessed June 17, 2017; "North Korea 'Ramps up Manufacture of Illicit Drugs' amid Sanctions," DW, August 21, 2017, http://www.dw.com/en/north-korea-ramps-up-manufacture-of-illegal-drugs-amid-sanctions/a-40169753, accessed January 31, 2018.

3. James Queally and Richard Winston, "Flight Attendant Accused of Smuggling 70 Pounds of Cocaine at LAX Due in Court," *Los Angeles Times*, March 24, 2016, http://www.latimes.com/local/lanow/la-me-ln-flight-attendant-smuggling-cocaine-lax-20160324-story.html, accessed June 17, 2017.

4. David Widdowson, "Bordering on Corruption: An Analysis of Corrupt Customs Practices That Impact the Trading Community," *World Customs Journal* 7, no. 2 (2013): 11–20; Gerard McLinden and Miles McKenna, "Eliminating Customs of Corruption: New Approaches in Cameroon and Afghanistan," World Bank, April 6, 2014, http://blogs.worldbank.org/trade/eliminating-customs-corruption-new-approaches-cameroon-afghanistan, accessed July 2, 2017.

5. Godson, *Menace to Society*.

6. Ivan Briscoe, Catalina Perdomo, and Catalina Uribe Burcher, *Illicit Networks and Politics in Latin America* (Stockholm and The Hague: International IDEA, NIMD, and Clingendael, 2014).

7. Randal C. Archibald, "Manuel Noriega, Dictator Ousted by US in Panama, Dies at 83," *New York Times*, May 30, 2017, https://www.nytimes.com/2017/05/30/world/americas/manuel-antonio-noriega-dead-panama.html?mcubz=1, accessed July 1, 2017.

8. Jon Boone, "WikiLeaks Cables Portray Hamid Karzai as Corrupt and Erratic," *Guardian*, December 2, 2010, https://www.theguardian.com/world/2010/dec/02/wikileaks-cables-hamid-karzai-erratic, accessed July 1, 2017.

9. "2016 Man of the Year in Organized Crime and Corruption," OCCRP, 2016, https://www.occrp.org/personoftheyear/2016/, accessed July 1, 2017.

10. Mark Shaw, "'We Pay, You Pay': Protection Economies, Financial Flows, and Violence," in Matfess and Miklaucic, *Beyond Convergence*, 241–245.

11. Bertil Lintner, *Blood Brothers: The Criminal Underworld of Asia* (New York: Palgrave Macmillan, 2003), 238–243.

12. Nyein, "Report Links Increased Militarization and Drug Trade in Eastern Shan State," *Irrawaddy*, October 27, 2016, http://www.irrawaddy.com/news/report-links-increased-militarization-and-drug-trade-in-eastern-shan-state.html, accessed October 29, 2016. I visited the Thai-Myanmar border area in the early 1990s.

13. Ko-Lin Chin, *Chinatown Gangs: Extortion, Enterprise, and Ethnicity Triads* (New York: Oxford University Press, 2000); Lintner, *Blood Brothers*; Peter B. E. Hill, *The Japanese Mafia: Law and the State* (New York: Oxford University Press, 2003); Jean-François Gayraud, *Le Monde des mafias: Géopolitique du crime organisé* (Paris: Odile Jacob, 2008), 96–105; Ko-Lin Chin, "Chinese Organized Crime," in Paoli, *The Oxford Handbook of Organized Crime*, 219–233.

14. Paul Gootenberg, *Andean Cocaine: The Making of a Global Drug* (Chapel Hill: University of North Carolina Press, 2008); "Drug Trades in Latin America," in *The Oxford Bibliography of Latin American History*, ed. Ben Vinson III, 2014, DOI:10.1093/OBO/9780199766581-0176.

15. David A. Shirk, *The Drug War in Mexico: Confronting a Shared Threat* (Washington, DC: Council on Foreign Relations, 2011); Garzón, *Mafia & Co.*; Bruce M. Bagley and Jonathan D. Rosen, *Drug Trafficking, Organized Crime, and Violence in the Americas Today* (Gainesville: University Press of Florida, 2015); Luis Jorge Garay Salamanca and Eduardo Salcedo-Albarán, *Narcotráfico, corrupción, y Estados: Cómo las redes ilícitas han reconfigurado las instituciones en Colombia, Guatemala, y México* (Barcelona: Ediciones Grijalbo, 2012).

16. *Frontline*, "Godfather of Cocaine"; Peter S. Green, Mack Gelber, Fara Warner, and Christine Sanders, "Cocainenomics," WSJ Custom Studios, https://www.wsj.com/ad/cocainenomics, accessed August 3, 2017; Francisco E. Thoumi, *Illegal Drugs, Economy, and Society in the Andes* (Washington, DC: Woodrow Wilson Center Press, 2003), 141–231.

17. Andreas, *Border Games*.

18. Topher McDougal, David A. Shirk, Robert Muggah, and John H. Patterson, "The Way of the Gun: Estimating Firearms Traffic Across the US-Mexico Border," Igarapé Institute and University of California–San Diego, March 2013,

http://catcher.sandiego.edu/items/peacestudies/way_of_the_gun.pdf, accessed July 31, 2017.

19. For a challenge to this high number, see David Gagne, "2000 Illegal Weapons Cross US-Mexico Border per Day: Report," InSight Crime, January 22, 2015, http://www.insightcrime.org/news-analysis/2000-illegal-weapons-cross-us -mexico-border-every-day, accessed July 31, 2017.

20. Correa-Cabrera, *Los Zetas Inc.*; Jeremy Slack and Howard John Campbell, "On Narco-Coyotaje: Illicit Regimes and Their Impacts on the US-Mexico Border," *Antipode* 48, no. 5 (2016): 1380–1399; Jeremy Slack and Scott Whiteford, "Caught in the Middle: Undocumented Migrants' Experiences with Drug Violence," in *A War That Can't Be Won: Binational Perspectives on the War on Drugs*, ed. Tony Payán, Kathleen Staudt, and Z. Anthony Kruszewski (Tucson: Arizona University Press, 2013), 193–213; *Organized Crime Involvement in Trafficking in Persons and Smuggling of Migrants*, UNODC, 2010, http://www.unodc.org/documents/human -trafficking/FINAL_REPORT_06052010_1.pdf, accessed on August 10, 2017.

21. Arias, *Criminal Enterprises and Governance in Latin America and the Caribbean*.

22. Thoumi, *Illegal Drugs, Economy, and Society in the Andes*, 159–180; James Cockayne, *Hidden Power: The Strategic Logic of Organized Crime* (New York: Oxford University Press, 2016), 16–19; Garay Salamanca and Salcedo-Albarán, *Narcotráfico, corrupción, y estados*; Kayonne Marston, "In Pursuit of Illicit Goals: Structure, Dynamics, and Disruption of Crime Facilitating Networks in Jamaica," PhD diss., George Mason University, School of Policy, Government and International Affairs, 2016; Briscoe, Perdomo and Burcher, *Illicit Networks and Politics in Latin America*.

23. Paoli, *Mafia Brotherhoods*; Arlacchi, *Mafia Business*.

24. "Not Just in Transit: Drugs, the State, and Society in West Africa," West African Commission on Drugs, June 2014, 16, www.wacommissionondrugs.org /report/, accessed July 2, 2017.

25. Yeşılgöz and Bovenkerk, "Urban Knights and Rebels in the Ottoman Empire," 181–224; Gingeras, *Heroin, Organized Crime, and the Making of Modern Turkey*, 19–52.

26. Mark Galeotti, "Narcotics and Nationalism: Russian Drug Policies and Futures," Brookings Institution, 2016, https://www.brookings.edu/wp-content /uploads/2016/07/Galeotti-Russia-final.pdf, accessed July 1, 2017.

27. Gretchen Peters, *Seeds of Terror: How Heroin Is Bankrolling the Taliban and Al Qaeda* (New York: St. Martin's Press, 2009).

28. Stephen Tankel, *Storming the World Stage: The Story of Lashkar-e-Taiba* (New York: Columbia University Press, 2011), 90; Ryan Clarke, *Crime-Terror Nexus in South Asia: States, Security, and Non-State Actors* (Abingdon, UK: Routledge, 2011), 48–55.

29. Dana Ford, "Fortune Drops Drug Lord Joaquin 'El Chapo' Guzman from Billionaires' List," *CNN*, March 5, 2013, http://edition.cnn.com/2013/03/04 /business/forbes-el-chapo/, accessed July 2, 2017.

30. Erin Carlyle, "Billionaire Druglords: El Chapo Guzman, Pablo Escobar, the Ochoa Brothers," *Forbes*, March 13, 2012, https://www.forbes.com/sites/erincarlyle/2012/03/13/billionaire-druglords-el-chapo-guzman-pablo-escobar-the-ochoa-brothers/#76c251d5ef45, accessed August 8, 2017.

31. Loretta Napoleoni, *Terror Incorporated: Tracing the Dollars behind the Terror Networks* (New York: Seven Stories Press, 2005), 65–80.

32. "Drug Trafficking and the Financing of Terrorism," UNODC, http://www.unodc.org/unodc/en/frontpage/drug-trafficking-and-the-financing-of-terrorism.html, accessed July 1, 2017; "UN Security Council, Adopting Resolution 2195 (2014), Urges International Action Break Links between Terrorists, Transnational Organized Crime," UN Office of Counter-Terrorism, December 19, 2014, https://www.un.org/counterterrorism/ctitf/en/security-council-adopting-resolution-2195-2014-urges-international-action-break-links-between, accessed July 1, 2017.

33. "Foreign Terrorist Organizations," US State Department, September 28, 2012, http://www.state.gov/j/ct/rls/other/des/123085.htm, accessed January 8, 2013; Michael Braun, "Drug Trafficking and Middle Eastern Terrorist Groups: A Growing Nexus?," Washington Institute, July 25, 2008, http://www.washingtoninstitute.org/policy-analysis/view/drug-trafficking-and-middle-eastern-terrorist-groups-a-growing-nexus, accessed July 1, 2017.

34. John Rollins and Liana Sun Wyler, "Terrorism and Transnational Crime: Foreign Policy Issues for Congress," Congressional Research Service, June 11, 2013, 3, https://fas.org/sgp/crs/terror/R41004.pdf, accessed July 1, 2017.

35. Jennifer L. Hesterman, *The Terrorist-Criminal Nexus: An Alliance of International Drug Cartels, Organized Crime, and Terror Groups* (Boca Raton, FL: CRC Press, 2013), 85–86; Peters, "How Opium Profits the Taliban"; Michael Kenney, *From Pablo to Osama: Trafficking and Terrorist Networks, Government Bureaucracies, and Competitive Adaptation* (University Park: Pennsylvania State University Press, 2006).

36. Gabriel Koehler-Derrick, ed., *A False Foundation? AQAP, Tribes, and Ungoverned Spaces in Yemen*, Combating Terrorism Center at West Point, October 3, 2011, 104, https://ctc.usma.edu/posts/a-false-foundation-aqap-tribes-and-ungoverned-spaces-in-yemen, accessed July 1, 2017; Rollins and Wyler, "Terrorism and Transnational Crime," 3.

37. Ahmed AL-Imam et al., "Captagon: Use and Trade in the Middle East," *Human Psychopharmacology: Clinical and Experimental* 32, no. 3 (2016): e2548, DOI10.1002/hup.2548.

38. "Chinese Chemical Engineer Sentenced for Conspiracy and Importation of Synthetic Drugs and Controlled Substances," US Department of Justice, US Attorney's Office, Middle District of Florida, April 27, 2016, https://www.justice.gov/usao-mdfl/pr/chinese-chemical-engineer-sentenced-conspiracy-and-importation-synthetic-drugs-and, accessed August 4, 2017; "Treasury Sanctions Members of a Chinese Synthetic Drug Trafficking Organization," US Department of the Treasury, July 29, 2014, https://www.treasury.gov/press-center/press-releases/Pages/jl2593.aspx, accessed August 4, 2017; "Zhang Lei: A Story

of Synthetic Drugs, International Drug Trafficking, and OFAC SDN Designations," OFAC Sanctions Attorney Price Benowitz LLP, https://ofaclawyer.net /blog/zhang-lei-story-synthetic-drugs-international-drug-trafficking-ofac-sdn -designations/, accessed January 25, 2018.

39. Goodman, *Future Crimes*, 194–198; Bilton, *American Kingpin*. Gergana Bulanova-Hristova identifies the same phenomenon occurring in Europe on a significant scale (about 50 percent of participants depending on the country analyzed); Bulanova-Hristova et al., *Cyber-OC—Scope and Manifestations in Selected EU Member States*.

40. The Sackler family members who own the company are largely uninvolved in the day-to-day management of Purdue and have never been charged; Chase Peterson-Withorn, "Fortune of Family behind OxyContin Drops amid Declining Prescriptions," *Forbes*, June 29, 2016, https://www.forbes.com/sites /chasewithorn/2016/06/29/fortune-of-family-behind-oxycontin-drops-amid -declining-prescriptions/#765a91d26341, accessed October 1, 2017.

41. Nadia Kounang, "41 State Attorneys General Subpoena Opioid Manufacturers," *CNN*, September 20, 2016, http://www.cnn.com/2017/09/19/health /state-ag-investigation-opioids-subpoenas/index.html, accessed October 1, 2017.

42. Monique Tello, "A Primary Care Doctor Delves into the Opioid Epidemic," Harvard Health Publishing, February 20, 2017, http://www.health .harvard.edu/blog/a-primary-care-doctor-delves-into-the-opioid-epidemic -2017022011199, accessed July 1, 2017; Nora D. Volkow, "America's Addiction to Opioids: Heroin and Prescription Drug Abuse," presentation to Senate Caucus on International Narcotics Control, May 14, 2014, https://www.drugabuse .gov/about-nida/legislative-activities/testimony-to-congress/2016/americas -addiction-to-opioids-heroin-prescription-drug-abuse/, accessed July 1, 2017; Dan Sullivan, "Accountant for Drug Trafficking Organization Gets Four Years in Prison," *Tampa Bay Times*, June 14, 2017, http://www.tampabay.com/news /courts/criminal/accountant-for-plant-city-drug-trafficking-group-gets-four -years-in-prison/2327271, accessed July 1, 2017; "Ex-Prosecutor-Turned Drug Cartel Lawyer Gets Prison," *Los Angeles Times*, June 12, 1999, http://articles .latimes.com/1999/jun/12/news/mn-45739, accessed July 1, 2017.

43. Ed Vulliamy," How a Big US Bank Laundered Billions from Mexico's Murderous Drug Gangs," *Guardian*, April 3, 2011, https://www.theguardian .com/world/2011/apr/03/us-bank-mexico-drug-gangs, accessed July 1, 2011; Jill Treanor and Dominic Rushe, "HSBC Pays Record $1.9bn Fine to Settle US Money-Laundering Accusations," *Guardian*, December 11, 2012, https://www .theguardian.com/business/2012/dec/11/hsbc-bank-us-money-laundering, accessed July 1, 2017; Michael Corkery and Ben Protess, "Citigroup Agrees to $97.4 Million Settlement in Money Laundering Inquiry," *New York Times*, May 22, 2017, https://www.nytimes.com/2017/05/22/business/dealbook/citigroup -settlement-banamex-usa-inquiry.html, accessed July 1, 2017.

44. "New York Rabbis Convicted of Laundering Cash for Drug Dealers," Campaign for Radical Truth in History, December 23, 1997, www.revisionisthistory .org/essay13.html, accessed July 1, 2017.

45. Tom Howell Jr., "Postal Service Unwittingly Fuels Opioid Epidemic by Delivering Foreign Drugs Right to US Doorsteps," *Washington Times*, September 26, 2016, http://www.washingtontimes.com/news/2016/sep/26/postal-service-fuels-opioid-epidemic-by-delivering/, accessed July 2, 2017; author's discussions with Dave Williams, former inspector general of the US Postal Service.

46. US Senate Permanent Subcommittee on Investigations, Committee on Homeland Security and Governmental Affairs, *Combating the Opioid Crisis: Exploiting Vulnerabilities in International Mail: Staff Report*, https://www.portman.senate.gov/public/index.cfm/files/serve?File_id=12F93202-C8EC-4AF1-8A66-181EE6716F37, accessed January 25, 2018.

47. "Human Trafficking and Smuggling," US Immigration and Customs Enforcement (ICE), January 16, 2013, https://www.ice.gov/factsheets/human-trafficking, accessed July 3, 2017. See "Chapter XVIII: Penal Matters: 12b: Protocol against the Smuggling of Migrants by Land, Sea, and Air, Supplementing the United Nations Convention against Transnational Organized Crime," Doc. A/55/383, *UN Treaty Series* 2241, November 15, 2000, https://treaties.un.org/Pages/ShowMTDSGDetails.aspx?src=UNTSONLINE&tabid=3&mtdsg_no=XVIII-12-b&chapter=18&lang=en, accessed July 3, 2017; "Protocol to Prevent, Suppress, and Punish Trafficking in Persons Especially Women and Children, Supplementing the United Nations Convention against Transnational Organized Crime," UN Office of the High Commissioner, November 15, 2000, http://www.ohchr.org/EN/ProfessionalInterest/Pages/ProtocolTraffickingInPersons.aspx, accessed July 3, 2017.

48. John Pomfret, "Bribery at Border Worries Officials," *Washington Post*, July 15, 2006, www.washingtonpost.com/wp-dyn/content/article/2006/07/14/AR2006071401525.html, accessed July 2, 2017; "Corruption and Human Trafficking," Working Paper 3/2011, Transparency International, June 27, 2011, https://www.transparency.org/whatwedo/publication/working_paper_corruption_and_human_trafficking, accessed July 2, 2017.

49. "Invisible Victims: Migrants on the Move in Mexico," Amnesty International, 2010, https://www.amnestyusa.org/wp-content/uploads/2017/04/amr410142010eng.pdf, accessed August 10, 2017; Jorge Ramos, *Dying to Cross: The Worst Immigrant Tragedy in American History* (New York: HarperCollins, 2006); Wendy A. Vogt, "Crossing Mexico: Structural Violence and the Commodification of Undocumented Central American Migrants," *American Ethnologist* 40, no. 4 (2013): 764–780.

50. "Mexico: Trafficking in Persons Report 2016," US Department of State, Office to Monitor and Combat Trafficking in Persons, https://www.state.gov/j/tip/rls/tiprpt/countries/2016/258821.htm, accessed August 8, 2017; Michael Evans, "Mexico's Recurring Nightmare," *Nation*, January 29, 2015, http://www.thenation.com/article/mexicos-recurring-nightmare/, accessed August 8, 2017; author's discussions with Guadalupe Correa-Cabrera on her research on this topic.

51. Oliver Holmes, "Thailand Convicts Traffickers after 2015 Mass Graves Discovery," *Guardian*, July 19, 2017, https://www.theguardian.com/world/2017/jul

/19/thailand-convicts-dozens-of-traffickers-after-mass-graves-discovery, accessed July 21, 2017; author's interview with high-level Thai law enforcement official, summer 2015; "Guilty Verdicts for Rohingya Trafficking Deaths," *Al-Jazeera*, July 19, 2017, http://www.aljazeera.com/news/2017/07/thai-court-deliver-verdict-people-smuggling-case-170719024750630.html, accessed August 2, 2017.

52. For a discussion of North Koreans in forced labor in Russia, see "Trafficking in Persons Report 2017," US Department of State, Office to Monitor and Combat Trafficking in Persons, 336, https://www.state.gov/j/tip/rls/tiprpt/2017/.

53. "Thailand: Trafficking in Persons Report 2016," US Department of State, Office to Monitor and Combat Trafficking in Persons, http://www.state.gov/j/tip/rls/tiprpt/countries/2016/258876.htm, accessed July 9, 2017.

54. "Vietnam: Trafficking in Persons Report 2016," US Department of State, Office to Monitor and Combat Trafficking in Persons, https://www.state.gov/j/tip/rls/tiprpt/countries/2016/258892.htm.

55. "Uzbekistan: Trafficking in Persons Report 2016," US Department of State, Office to Monitor and Combat Trafficking in Persons, https://www.state.gov/j/tip/rls/tiprpt/countries/2016/258890.htm, accessed July 13, 2017.

56. Dave Lee, "Exploring the World of Japan's Yakuza Mafia," *BBC News*, October 5, 2010, http://www.bbc.com/news/world-asia-pacific-11446716, accessed July 2, 2017; Shiro Okubo and Louise Shelley, eds., *Human Security, Transnational Crime, and Human Trafficking: Asian and Western Perspectives* (London: Routledge, 2011).

57. Annie Kelly and Lorenzo Kondo, "Trafficking of Nigerian Women into Prostitution in Europe 'at Crisis Level,'" *Guardian*, August 8, 2016, https://www.theguardian.com/global-development/2016/aug/08/trafficking-of-nigerian-women-into-prostitution-in-europe-at-crisis-level, accessed July 3, 2017; Walter Kemp, *Crooked Kaleidoscope: Organized Crime in the Balkans* (Geneva: Global Initiative against Transnational Organized Crime, 2017), 10. See also US Department of State, "Trafficking in Persons Report 2017," 304.

58. Correa-Cabrera, *Los Zetas Inc.*; Gerardo Reyes of Univision, presentation on the panel "Corruption, Security, and Organized Crime," IACC, Panama City, Panama, December 3, 2016, https://17iacc.sched.com/event/8SD7/corruption-security-and-organized-crime, accessed July 9, 2017.

59. Correa-Cabrera, *Los Zetas Inc.*, 96.

60. "Situation Report Trafficking in Human Beings in the EU 2016," Europol, February 2016, 19, https://www.europol.europa.eu/publications-documents/trafficking-in-human-beings-in-eu, accessed July 2, 2017.

61. Europol, "Situation Report Trafficking in Human Beings in the EU 2016," 17.

62. Ottilia Anna Maunganidze, "Beyond Anecdotes: Getting to the Heart of Human Smuggling," Council on African Security and Development, January 4, 2017, http://www.casade.org/beyond-anecdotes-getting-to-the-heart-of-human-smuggling/.

63. *Transnational Organized Crime in East Asia and the Pacific*, UNODC, 2013, v, http://www.unodc.org/documents/data-and-analysis/Studies/TOCTA_EAP_web.pdf, accessed August 3, 2017.

64. Sheldon X. Zhang, *Chinese Human Smuggling Organizations: Families, Social Networks, and Cultural Imperatives* (Stanford, CA: Stanford University Press, 2008).

65. Chantal Da Silva, "Inside the 'Free Market' of People Smuggling," *Independent*, October 24, 2017, http://www.independent.co.uk/news/long_reads /people-smuggling-libya-syria-facebook-social-media-free-market-a8011686 .html, accessed January 31, 2017.

66. Arthur Neslen, "Number of Criminal Gangs Operating in Europe Surges to 5,000, Says Europol," *Guardian*, March 9, 2017, https://www.theguardian.com /uk-news/2017/mar/09/more-than-5000-crimnal-gangs-operating-in-europe -warns-europol, accessed August 4, 2017.

67. "Migrant Smuggling in the EU," Europol, February 2016, 7, https://www .europol.europa.eu/publications-documents/migrant-smuggling-in-eu, accessed July 13, 2017.

68. Europol, "Situation Report: Trafficking in Human Beings in the EU 2016," 14.

69. Jana Arsovska and Stef Janssens, "Human Trafficking and Policing: Good and Bad Practices," in *Strategies against Human Trafficking: The Role of the Security Sector*, ed. Cornelius Friesendorf (Vienna: National Defence Academy and Austrian Ministry of Defence and Sport, 2009), 213.

70. William Lacy Swing, "The World Needs a New Strategy to Tackle the Migration Crisis," *Guardian*, January 14, 2017, https://www.theguardian.com /commentisfree/2017/jan/15/migration-deaths-europe-davos-strategy?CMP= Share_iOSApp_Other, accessed January 17, 2017.

71. Swing, "The World Needs a New Strategy to Tackle the Migration Crisis."

72. David Spener, *Clandestine Crossings: Migrants and Coyotes on the Texas-Mexico Border* (Ithaca, NY: Cornell University Press, 2009).

73. Author's discussions with Guadalupe Correa-Cabrera, a specialist in Mexican organized crime and border issues.

74. Adam Isaacson, Maureen Meyer, and Hannah Smith, "WOLA Report: Mexico's Southern Border—Security, Central American Migration, and US Policy," June 29, 2017, https://www.wola.org/analysis/wola-report-mexicos -southern-border-security-central-american-migration-u-s-policy/, accessed August 9, 2017.

75. Holly Yan and Aaron Kessler, "By the Numbers: Migrant Deaths and Human Trafficking in the US," *CNN*, July 28, 2017, http://www.cnn.com/2017 /07/28/us/migrant-deaths-and-human-trafficking-by-the-numbers/index.html, accessed October 1, 2017.

76. Shelley, *Human Trafficking.*

77. Dina Siegel and Sylvia de Blank, "Women Who Traffic Women: The Role of Women in Human Trafficking Networks—Dutch Cases," *Global Crime* 11, no. 4 (2010), 436–447; Alexis Aronowitz, *Human Trafficking, Human Misery: The Global Trade in Human Beings* (Westport, CT: Praeger, 2009), 52–55.

78. Patrick Radden, *The Snakehead: An Epic Tale of the China Underworld and the American Dream* (New York: Doubleday, 2009).

79. Cathy Otten, "Slaves of ISIS: The Long Walk of the Yazidi Women," *Guardian*, July 25, 2017, https://www.theguardian.com/world/2017/jul/25/slaves-of-isis-the-long-walk-of-the-yazidi-women, accessed August 1, 2017.

80. Shelley, *Dirty Entanglements*, 178–179.

81. Warren Strobel, Jonathan Landay, and Phil Stewart, "Exclusive: Islamic State Sanctioned Organ Harvesting in Document Taken in US Raid," *Reuters*, December 25, 2014, http://www.reuters.com/article/us-usa-islamic-state-documents-idUSKBN0U805R20151225, accessed July 5, 2017.

82. An illicit kidney trade also functions in the Indian subcontinent and in China for profit.

83. Nancy Scheper-Hughes, "Organ Trafficking during Times of War and Political Conflict," *International Affairs Forum* 7, no. 2 (Fall 2016): 123–136.

84. Arnold Ahlert, "ISIS Trafficking Human Organs?," *Frontpage*, February 19, 2015, http://www.frontpagemag.com/fpm/251753/isis-trafficking-human-organs-arnold-ahlert, accessed July 5, 2017; "Human Organ Trafficking with Dr. Campbell Fraser," Mason Schar School, 2016, https://vimeo.com/156708248, accessed July 5, 2017.

85. Cyrus R. Vance Jr., statement at the US House of Representatives, Financial Services Committee hearing "Following the Money: How Human Traffickers Exploit US Financial Markets," January 30, 2018, https://financialservices.house .gov/calendar/eventsingle.aspx?EventID=402952, accessed January 31, 2018.

86. US Senate, Permanent Subcommittee on Investigations, "Backpage.com's Knowing Facilitation of Online Sex Trafficking: Staff Report," 7, https://www .mccaskill.senate.gov/imo/media/doc/2017.01.10%20Backpage%20Report.pdf, accessed July 11, 2017.

87. Greenemeier, "Human Traffickers Caught on Hidden Internet"; see also "*Scientific American* Exclusive: DARPA Memex Data Maps," especially map 4.

88. "Leveraging Anti–Money Laundering Regimes to Combat Trafficking in Human Beings," OSCE, 2014, http://www.osce.org/secretariat/121125 ?download=true, accessed July 3, 2017; House Financial Services Committee, "Following the Money."

89. Bulgaria is another such country; see "A Hazy Crisis: Illicit Cigarette Smuggling in the OSCE Region" (hearing), US Helsinki Commission, July 19, 2017, https://www.csce.gov/international-impact/events/hazy-crisis-illicit-cigarette-smuggling-osce-region, accessed July 23, 2017. For a fuller discussion of state-sponsored illicit trade, see Shelley, *Dirty Entanglements*, 265, 267; see also US Senate Committee on Homeland Security and Governmental Affairs, "North Korea: Illicit Activity Funding the Regime"; Zarate, *Treasury's War*, 232–237.

90. "The Global Illicit Trade in Tobacco: A Threat to National Security," US Department of State, 2015, 12, https://2009-2017.state.gov/documents /organization/250513.pdf, accessed July 1, 2015; Greitens, "Illicit: North Korea's Evolving Operations to Earn Hard Currency"; Julian Rademeyer, "Diplomats and Deceit: North Korea's Criminal Activities in Africa," Global Initiative against Transnational Organized Crime, September 22, 2017, vi, 4, http://globalinitiative .net/diplomats-and-deceit-north-koreas-criminal-activities-in-africa/.

91. "2015 Man of the Year in Organized Crime," OCCRP, 2015, https://www .occrp.org/personoftheyear/2015/, accessed June 17, 2017.

92. OCCRP, "2015 Man of the Year in Organized Crime."

93. Leo Sisti, "The Montenegro Connection: Love, Tobacco, and the Mafia," OCCRP, July 9, 2009, https://www.reportingproject.net/underground/index .php?option=com_content&view=article&id=7&Itemid=20, accessed June 17, 2017; Francesco Calderoni, "A New Method for Estimating the Illicit Cigarette Market at the Subnational Level and Its Application to Italy," *Global Crime* 15, nos. 1–2 (2014): 51–76. Calderoni cites the February 2, 2005, report on the Italian investigation conducted by Italy's Direzione Investigativa Antimafia (DIA), available at: https://www.reportingproject.net/unholyalliances/docs/Smuggling_2 .pdf, accessed May 16, 2018; Kemp, *Crooked Kaleidoscope*, 13–14, 19–22.

94. Andrew Martin and Juan Pablo Spinetto, "Can Paraguay Escape Decades of Despotism, Ineptitude, and Corruption?," *Bloomberg*, March 22, 2016, http:// www.bloomberg.com/features/2016-paraguay-president-horacio-cartes/, accessed June 17, 2017.

95. Benoît Gomis and Natalia Carrillo Botero, "Paraguay's Tobacco Business Fuels Latin America's Black Market," *Foreign Affairs*, February 5, 2016, https:// www.foreignaffairs.com/articles/paraguay/2016-02-05/sneaking-smoke, accessed July 1, 2017.

96. Martin and Spinetto, "Can Paraguay Escape Decades of Despotism, Ineptitude, and Corruption?"

97. Kyra Gurney, "Brazil Cigarette Seizures Highlight Paraguay Contraband Trade," InSight Crime, May 2014, http://www.insightcrime.org/news-briefs /brazil-cigarette-seizures-highlight-paraguay-contraband-trade, accessed July 1, 2017; Gomis and Botero, "Paraguay's Tobacco Business Fuels Latin America's Black Market."

98. *Project SUN: A Study of the Illicit Cigarette Market in the European Union, Norway, and Switzerland: 2016 Results*, KPMG, 2017, https://assets.kpmg.com /content/dam/kpmg/uk/pdf/2017/07/project-sun-2017-report.pdf, accessed July 13, 2017.

99. Klaus von Lampe, "The Trafficking in Untaxed Cigarettes in Germany: A Case Study of the Social Embeddedness of Illegal Markets," in *Upperworld and Underworld in Cross-Border Crime*, ed. Petrus van Duyne, Klaus von Lampe, and Nikos Passas (Nijmegen: Wolf Legal Publishers, 2002), 141–161; Miroslav Nožina, "Crime Networks in Vietnamese Diasporas: The Czech Republic Case," *Crime Law and Social Change* 53 (2010): 229–258; Miroslav Nožina, "The Czech Republic: A Crossroads for Organised Crime," in *Organised Crime in Europe: Concepts, Patterns, and Control Policies in the European Union and Beyond*, ed. Cyrille Fijnaut and Letizia Paoli (Dordrecht: Springer, 2004), 435–466; Miroslav Nožina and Filip Kraus, "Bosses, Soldiers, and Rice Grains: Vietnamese Criminal Networks and Criminal Activities in the Czech Republic," *Europe-Asia Studies* 68, no. 3 (2016): 508–528; Laurent Martinet, "La France, championne d'Europe des cigarettes de contrebande," *l'Express*, June 8, 2016, http://lexpansion.lexpress

.fr/actualite-economique/la-france-championne-deurope-des-cigarettes-de
-contrebande_1800103.html; accessed June 16, 2017; Bill Wirtz, "Why Counterfeit Tobacco Is Plaguing France," Foundation for Economic Education, April 17,
2017, https://fee.org/articles/why-counterfeit-tobacco-is-plaguing-france/, accessed June 16, 2017.

100. Isaia Sales, "Droga e contrabbando, stesso affare di Camora," *Il Mattino*,
August 1, 2016; Calderoni, "A New Method for Estimating the Illicit Cigarette
Market at the Subnational Level."

101. "Spanish Customs," in Interpol, *Against Organized Crime*, 36; Martinet,
"La France, championne d'Europe des cigarettes de contrebande."

102. Mincheva and Gurr, *Crime-Terror Alliances and the State*, 95.

103. Anne Vidalie, "Contrebande: Le boom des marques clandestines de
cigarettes," *l'Express*, July 12, 2016, http://www.lexpress.fr/actualite/societe
/contrebande-le-boom-des-marques-clandestines-de-cigarettes_1811389
.html, accessed June 15, 2017; Francesco Calderoni et al., "The Factbook on
Illicit Trade in Tobacco Products—8 France," Transcrime, June 1, 2016, http://
www.transcrime.it/pubblicazioni/the-factbook-on-the-illicit-trade-in-tobacco
-products-8-france/, accessed June 15, 2017; see also Nordstrom, *Global Outlaws*, 23.

104. Gingeras, *Heroin, Organized Crime, and the Making of Modern Turkey*,
122–123; Jonathan V. Marshall, *The Lebanese Connection: Corruption, Civil War,
and the International Drug Traffic*, Stanford Studies in Middle Eastern and Islamic
Societies and Cultures Series (Stanford, CA: Stanford University Press, 2012),
33–48.

105. Nacer Lalam, "France from Local Elites to National Leaders," in *Corruption and Organized Crime in Europe: Illegal Partnership*, ed. Philip Gounev and
Vincenzo Ruggiero (Abingdon, UK: Routledge, 2012), 109–110.

106. Martinet, "La France, championne d'Europe des cigarettes de contrebande"; *Project SUN: A Study of the Illicit Cigarette Market: 2015 Results*, KPMG,
June 8, 2016, https://home.kpmg.com/uk/en/home/insights/2015/05/project
-sun-a-study-of-the-illicit-cigarette-market.html, accessed June 16, 2017. Project
SUN is a project of KPMG as part of the agreements concluded among Philip
Morris International, the European Commission, the European Anti-Fraud Office (OLAF), and the EU member states to tackle the illicit trade. Project SUN
involves all four major multinational tobacco manufacturers: Philip Morris International, British American Tobacco, Imperial Tobacco, and Japan Tobacco
International.

107. Basra, Neumann, and Brunner, *Criminal Pasts, Terrorist Futures*, 44; Ka-
trin Bennhold and Eric Schmitt, "Gaps in France's Surveillance Are Clear; Solutions Aren't," *New York Times*, February 17, 2015, https://www.nytimes.com
/2015/02/18/world/gaps-in-surveillance-are-clear-solutions-arent.html, accessed June 16, 2017.

108. Mincheva and Gurr, *Crime-Terror Alliances and the State*, 95–96; Shelley,
Dirty Entanglements, 1–4.

109. Mincheva and Gurr, *Crime-Terror Alliances and the State*, 95–96; Shelley, *Dirty Entanglements*, 1–4; Matthew Levitt, *Hamas: Politics, Charity, and Terrorism in the Service of Jihad* (New Haven, CT: Yale University Press, 2006); Levitt, *Hezbollah.*

110. Hawramy, "Islamic State Turns to Cigarette Smuggling to Fund Itself."

111. Gomis and Botero, "Paraguay's Tobacco Business Fuels Latin America's Black Market"; Alma Keshavarz, "Iran and Hezbollah in the Tri-border Areas of Latin America: A Look at the 'Old TBA' and the 'New TBA,'" *Small Wars Journal*, November 12, 2015, http://smallwarsjournal.com/jrnl/art/iran-and-hezbollah-in-the-tri-border-areas-of-latin-america-a-look-at-the-%E2%80%9Cold-tba%E2%80%9D-and-the, accessed July 1, 2017.

112. "The Global Illicit Trade in Tobacco: A Threat to National Security," US Department of State, 2015, 21, https://2009-2017.state.gov/documents/organization/250513.pdf, accessed June 15, 2017; Hawramy, "Islamic State Turns to Cigarette Smuggling to Fund Itself."

113. US Department of State, "The Global Illicit Trade in Tobacco: A Threat to National Security"; Jim Cusack, "Suez Canal Attack by al-Qaida Blew Irish Cigarette Smuggling Ring," *Belfast Telegraph*, November 4, 2013, https://www.belfasttelegraph.co.uk/news/republic-of-ireland/suez-canal-attack-by-alqaida-blew-irish-cigarette-smuggling-ring-29723681.html, accessed April 28, 2018.

114. KPMG, *Project SUN: A Study of the Illicit Cigarette Market: 2016 Results*, 10, https://assets.kpmg.com/content/dam/kpmg/uk/pdf/2017/07/project-sun-2017-report.pdf, accessed April 28, 2018.

115. Author's interview with a PMI official in France in 2015.

116. C. Ben Lakhdar, "Quantitative and Qualitative Estimates of Cross-Border Tobacco Shopping and Tobacco Smuggling in France," *Tobacco Control* 17, no. 1 (February 1, 2008): 12–16.

117. "Imperial Tobacco Targets Facebook Fraudsters," Scottish Local Retailer, July 14, 2016, http://www.slrmag.co.uk/imperial-tobacco-targets-facebook-fraudsters/, accessed June 17, 2017.

118. Jonathan Stempel, "FedEx Fails to End New York Lawsuit over Illegal Cigarettes," *Reuters*, April 1, 2016, http://www.reuters.com/article/us-fedex-lawsuit-cigarettes-idUSKCN0WY4XR, accessed July 21, 2017; "US Court Fines UPS $247 Million over Illegal Cigarette Shipments," *Reuters*, May 25, 2017, https://www.reuters.com/article/us-united-parcel-lawsuit/u-s-court-fines-ups-247-million-over-illegal-cigarette-shipments-idUSKBN18M09O, accessed January 30, 2018.

119. "What Is Food Security?," World Food Program (WFP), https://www.wfp.org/node/359289, accessed July 21, 2017.

120. "Record Seizures in Worldwide 'Food Fraud' Operation," OCCRP, March 31, 2016, https://www.occrp.org/en/daily/5107-record-seizures-in-worldwide-food-fraud-operation, accessed June 29, 2017; "Largest-Ever Seizures of Fake Food and Drink in INTERPOL-Europol Operation," Europol, March 30, 2016, https://www.europol.europa.eu/newsroom/news/largest-ever-seizures-of-fake-food-and-drink-in-interpol-europol-operation, accessed August 9, 2017.

121. Interpol, *Against Organized Crime Trafficking and Counterfeiting Casebook 2014*, 45.

122. Dana Goodyear, "Mezcal Sunrise Searching for the Ultimate Artisanal Distillate," *New Yorker*, April 4, 2016, 46.

123. Kathryn Senior and Alfredo Mazza, "Italian 'Triangle of Death' Linked to Waste Crisis," *Lancet Oncology* 5, no. 9 (2004): 525–527. The dumping of toxic waste in the "Triangle of Death" did not cease after this case came to light; see Neil Connor, "China Busts 50 Factories Making Fake Branded Seasoning with 'Dangerous' Ingredients in Latest Food Scandal," *Telegraph*, January 17, 2017, http://www.telegraph.co.uk/news/2017/01/17/china-busts-50-factories-making-fake-branded-seasoning-dangerous/, accessed June 18, 2017.

124. Eurispes, *Agromafie I° rapporto sui crimini agroalimentari in Italia* (Rome: Eurispes, 2011); Eurispes, *Agromafie 3° rapporto sui crimini agroalimentari in Italia* (Rome: Eurispes, 2015).

125. Monica Rubino, "Agromafie, il business del cibo supera i 16 miliardi," *La Repubblica*, February 17, 2016, http://www.repubblica.it/economia/2016/02/17/news/agromafie_il_business_del_cibo_supera_il_16_miliardi-133591052/, accessed June 17, 2017; Eurispes, *Agromafie 4° rapporto sui crimini agroalimentari in Italia* (Rome: Minerva, 2016).

126. Interpol, *Against Organized Crime Trafficking and Counterfeiting Casebook*, 46; Eurispes, *Agromafie I° rapporto sui crimini agroalimentari in Italia*, 43–45; Laurence Cockcroft and Anne Christine Wegener, *Unmasked: Corruption in the West* (London: I. B. Tauris and Co., 2017), 151.

127. "Il Generale della Forestale: Ho sequestrato tonnellate di verdura piena di veleni," *Corriere del Mezzogiorno*, September 24, 2013, http://corrieredelmezzogiorno.corriere.it/napoli/notizie/cronaca/2013/24-settembre-2013/generale-forestale-ho-sequestratotonnellate-verdura-piena-veleni-2223269409275.shtml, accessed June 18, 2017.

128. Eurispes, *Agromafie I° rapporto sui crimini agroalimentari in Italia*, 41.

129. Eurispes, *Agromafie 4° rapporto sui crimini agroalimentari in Italia*, 63.

130. Author's discussion with Chris Beyrer, director of the Center for Public Health and Human Rights, Johns Hopkins University, Bellagio, Italy, October 15, 2016.

131. Interpol, *Against Organized Crime Trafficking and Counterfeiting Casebook 2014*, 45.

132. "Six Arrested in Fake 'Similac' Baby Formula in China," *New Straits Times*, April 5, 2016, http://www.nst.com.my/news/2016/04/137486/six-arrested-fake-similac-baby-formula-china, accessed September 13, 2016; Alice Yan, "Suspect in China's 'Biggest Baby Milk Scandal in Decade' to Go on Trial," *South China Morning Post*, March 27, 2017, http://www.scmp.com/news/china/policies-politics/article/2082409/suspects-chinas-biggest-baby-milk-scandal-decade-go, accessed July 20, 2017.

133. Yanzhong Huang, "The 2008 Tainted Milk Scandal Revisited," *Forbes*, July 16, 2014, http://www.forbes.com/sites/yanzhonghuang/2014/07/16/the-2008-milk-scandal-revisited/#53261f944428, accessed June 18, 2017.

134. Interpol, *Against Organized Crime Trafficking and Counterfeiting Casebook 2014*, 50; Chris Buckley, "Rat Meat Sold as Lamb Highlights Fear in China," *New York Times*, May 3, 2013, http://www.nytimes.com/2013/05/04/world/asia/rat-meat-sold-as-lamb-in-china-highlights-fears.html, accessed June 18, 2017; Jonathan Kaiman, "China Fake Meat Scandal; Telling Your Rat from Your Mutton," *Guardian*, May 3, 2013, https://www.theguardian.com/world/2013/may/03/china-fake-meat-rat-mutton, accessed July 20, 2017.

135. Buckley, "Rat Meat Sold as Lamb Highlights Fear in China"; "Rat Meat Sold as Lamb in China," Food Quality & Safety, May 14, 2013, http://www.foodqualityandsafety.com/article/rat-meat-sold-as-lamb-in-china/, accessed March 25, 2016; Linhai Wu and Dian Zhu, *Food Safety in China: A Comprehensive Review* (Boca Raton, FL: CRC Press, 2014).

136. He Na, "14 Gangs Busted for Smuggling Frozen Meat," *China Daily*, June 24, 2015, 4.

137. Ivan Necepurenko, "Deaths Push Russia to Restrict Products with Alcohol," *New York Times*, December 23, 2016.

138. Tasha Eichenseher, "'Water Mafias' Put Stranglehold on Public Water Supply," *National Geographic News*, August 21, 2008, http://news.nationalgeographic.com/news/2008/08/080821-water-mafias.html, accessed June 29, 2017; Louise Shelley and Nazia Hussain, "Karachi: Organized Crime in a Key Megacity," *Connections: The Quarterly Journal* 15, no. 3 (2016): 5–15; *Organized Crime: A Cross-Cutting Threat to Sustainable Development,* Global Initiative against Transnational Crime, 2015, 38, http://globalinitiative.net/wp-content/uploads/2015/04/global-initiative-organized-crime-as-a-cross-cutting-threat-to-development-january-2015.pdf.

139. Aman Sethi, "At the Mercy of the Water Mafia," *Foreign Policy*, July 17, 2015, http://foreignpolicy.com/2015/07/17/at-the-mercy-of-the-water-mafia-india-delhi-tanker-gang-scarcity/, accessed June 29, 2017; Hussain, "Tracing Order in Seeming Chaos," 127–131.

140. "Substandard" refers to the production of drugs of inferior quality rather than deliberately falsified drugs; see "Substandard and Falsified and Medical Products," Fact sheet 275, World Health Organization (WHO), January 2018, http://www.who.int/mediacentre/factsheets/fs275/en/, accessed May 16, 2018. See also the editorial "Vaccine Scandal and Confidence Crisis in China," *Lancet*, vol. 392, issue 10145, P360, August 4, 2018, https://www.thelancet.com/journals/lancet/article/PIIS0140-6736(18)31695-7/fulltext, DOI:10.1016/S0140-6736(18)31695-7.

141. "Growing Threat from Counterfeit Medicines," *Bulletin of the World Health Organization* 88, no. 4 (April 2010): 241–320, http://www.who.int/bulletin/volumes/88/4/10-020410/en/, accessed January 29, 2017.

142. Peggy E. Chaudhry, "The Challenge of Curtailing the Escalation of Counterfeit Pharmaceuticals," in Chaudhry, *Handbook of Research on Counterfeiting and Illicit Trade*, 158.

143. "Total Number of Incidents, CY2012–CY2016," Pharmaceutical Security Institute (PSI), 2018, http://www.psi-inc.org/incidentTrends.cfm.

144. "How to Buy Medicines Safely from an Online Pharmacy," Food and Drug Administration (FDA), updated January 25, 2018, http://www.fda.gov /ForConsumers/ConsumerUpdates/ucm048396.htm.

145. Diana Camerini, Serena Favarin, and Marco Dugato, "Estimating the Counterfeit Markets in Europe," *Transcrime Research in Brief*, no. 3 (October 2015): chap. 7, http://www.transcrime.it/wp-content/uploads/2015/10 /Estimating-the-counterfeit-markets-in-Europe.pdf, accessed June 29, 2017.

146. Europol and Office for Harmonization in the Internal Market, *2015 Situation Report on Counterfeiting in the European Union*, 13.

147. Tim K. Mackey, Bryan A. Liang, Peter York, and Thomas Kubic, "Counterfeit Drug Penetration into Global Legitimate Medicine Supply Chains: A Global Assessment," *American Journal of Tropical Medicine and Hygiene* 5 no. 92, suppl. 6 (June 3, 2015): 59–67.

148. Erwin A. Blackstone, Joseph P. Fuhr Jr., and Steve Pociask, "The Health and Economic Effects of Counterfeit Drugs," *American Health and Drug Benefits* 7, no. 4 (June 2014): 216–224.

149. Alexander McCall Smith, *Blue Shoes and Happiness* (New York: Anchor Books, 2006), 199–204.

150. "Illicit Medicine Manufacturers Shut Down in INTERPOL Operation against Pharmaceutical Crime," Interpol, September 18, 2015, http://www .interpol.int/News-and-media/News/2015/N2015-134, accessed July 1, 2017.

151. "Tracking Black Market Malaria Drugs," Malaria.com, November 11, 2013, http://www.malaria.com/news/black-market-malaria-drugs, accessed July 1, 2017; Benoît Faucon, Nicholas Bariyo, and Jeanne Whalen, "Thieves Hijacking Malaria Drugs in Africa: US Investigating How Important Medicine Ends Up on the Black Market," *Wall Street Journal*, November 11, 2013, http://www.wsj.com /news/articles/SB10001424052702304672404579181632935636414, accessed July 1, 2017; author's interviews with corporate officials of the drug company producing antimalarial drugs, 2012.

152. "Russian Federation," Institute for Health Metrics and Evaluation, 2015, http://www.healthdata.org/russia, accessed December 27, 2016; Daria Litvinova, "Why Is Russia's Growth in Life Expectancy Slowing?," *Moscow Times*, August 30, 2015, https://themoscowtimes.com/news/why-is-russias-growth-in -life-expectancy-slowing-49224, accessed July 1, 2017.

153. N. F. Fayzrakhmanov, "Fighting Trafficking of Falsified and Substandard Medicinal Products in Russia," *International Journal of Risk and Safety in Medicine* 27, suppl. 1 (2015): S37–40.

154. "Operazione Pharmalab—Ricettavano farmaci provenienti da furti, 9 gli arresti," *Guardia di Finanza*, June 2015, http://www.gdf.gov.it/stampa/ultime-notizie /anno-2015/giugno-2015/operazione-pharmalab-ricettavano-farmaci-provenienti -da-furti-9-gli-arresti, accessed June 29, 2017; see also Michele Riccardi and Gabriele Proietto, "Illicit Trade of Pharmaceutical Products," paper presented at "High Level Meeting of Experts on Illicit Trade and Related Crimes," Siracusa International Institute for Criminal Justice and Human Rights, Siracusa, Italy, March 1–3, 2017; Michele Riccardi, Marco Dugato, Marcello Polizzotti, and Veronica Pecile,

"The Theft of Medicines from Italian Hospitals," *Transcrime Research in Brief*, no. 2 (March 2015): 4, http://www.transcrime.it/wp-content/uploads/2015/03 /Research-in-Brief-theft-of-medicines.pdf, accessed June 29, 2017.

155. US Attorney's Office, Southern District of California, "Internet Pharmacy Operator Sentenced to Two Years in Prison," FBI, September 12, 2013, https:// archives.fbi.gov/archives/sandiego/press-releases/2013/internet-pharmacy -operator-sentenced-to-two-years-in-prison, accessed June 29, 2017; Atholl John-ston and David W. Holt, "Substandard Drugs: A Potential Crisis for Public Health," *British Journal of Clinical Pharmacology* 78, no. 2 (August 2014): 218–243.

156. "Distributor of Counterfeit Pharmaceutical Drugs Sentenced," FDA, Jan-uary 15, 2009, https://www.fda.gov/ICECI/CriminalInvestigations/ucm261012 .htm (page no longer available); author's interview with retired investigator of pharmaceutical crimes, September 2017.

157. Author's discussions with personnel employed in private shipping com-panies and also with personnel of the Inspector General's Office of the US Postal Service, 2016.

158. Tim K. Mackey, Janani Kalyanam, Takeo Katsuki, and Gert Lanckriet, "Twitter-Based Detection of Illegal Online Sale of Prescription Opioid," *Ameri-can Journal of Public Health*, November 8, 2017, http://ajph.aphapublications.org /doi/abs/10.2105/AJPH.2017.303994, accessed February 11, 2018.

159. Mackey et al., "Twitter-Based Detection of Illegal Online Sale of Pre-scription Opioid," 13.

160. Author's interview with a pharmaceutical industry investigator, London, September 2017.

161. Niyanah Siva, "How Investigators Unravelled Europe's Biggest Ever Fake-Medicine Scam," *Wired*, November 29, 2011, accessed June 29, 2017, http://www .wired.co.uk/article/fake-pills.

162. US Attorney's Office, Southern District of California, "Internet Pharmacy Operator Sentenced to Two Years in Prison," FBI, San Diego Division, September 12, 2013, https://archives.fbi.gov/archives/sandiego/press-releases/2013/internet -pharmacy-operator-sentenced-to-two-years-in-prison, accessed June 29, 2017; "Pittsburgh Oncology Practice Pleads Guilty to Buying Unapproved Foreign Drugs," FBI, San Diego Division, September 19, 2013, https://archives.fbi.gov /archives/sandiego/press-releases/2013/pittsburgh-oncology-practice-pleads -guilty-to-buying-unapproved-foreign-drugs, accessed June 29, 2017; "Iowa Doc-tor Settles Allegations That He Recklessly Billed for Cancer Drugs and Visits That Never Happened," NIT, November 29, 2016, http://northiowatoday.com/2016 /11/29/iowa-doctor-settles-allegations-that-he-recklessly-billed-for-cancer-drugs -and-visits-that-never-happened/, accessed June 29, 2017; "President of Pharma-ceutical Companies Sentenced to 60 Months in Prison for Long-Running Scheme to Sell Misbranded and Unapproved Chemotherapy and Other Prescription Drugs," US Attorney's Office, Eastern District of New York, June 2, 2016, https:// www.justice.gov/usao-edny/pr/president-pharmaceutical-companies-sentenced -60-months-prison-long-running-scheme-sell, accessed July 1, 2017.

163. United States of America, Plaintiff, v. Martin Paul Bean, III, Defendant, US District Court, Southern District of California, Case 12cr3734-WQH, March 7, 2013, http://www.leagle.com/decision/In%20FDCO%2020130312773 /U.S.%20v.%20BEAN, accessed June 27, 2017.

164. Hepeng Jia, "China's Battle with Fake Drugs," *Chemistry World*, May 24, 2007, https://www.chemistryworld.com/news/chinas-battle-with-fake-drugs /1013594.article, accessed July 13, 2017; "China Detains 1,300 People Suspected of Making, Selling Fake Drugs: Media," *Reuters*, December 15, 2013, http://www .reuters.com/article/us-china-crime-fake-idUSBRE9BE01P20131215, accessed July 13, 2017; "Two Pakistani Nationals Extradited to District of Columbia to Face Charges Involving Illegal Pharmaceutical Shipments: Defendants Allegedly Shipped Nearly $780,000 of Drugs into US," US Department of Justice, US Attorney's Office, District of Columbia, May 20, 2013, https://www.justice.gov /usao-dc/pr/two-pakistani-nationals-extradited-district-columbia-face-charges -involving-illegal, accessed June 29, 2017; "Two Pakistani Nationals Sentenced for Conspiring to Illegally Ship Pharmaceuticals into the United States," US Department of Justice, Office of Public Affairs, November 4, 2016, https://www .justice.gov/opa/pr/two-pakistani-nationals-sentenced-conspiring-illegally -ship-pharmaceuticals-united-states, accessed June 29, 2017; Lev Kubiak, Director, National Intellectual Property Rights Coordination Center, and Howard Sklamberg, Food and Drug Administration, statement at hearing on "Counterfeit Drugs: Fighting Illegal Supply Chains," February 27, 2014, https://www.hsdl.org /?view&did=750762, accessed February 14, 2018.

165. "La Jolla Oncologist and Medical Practice Plead Guilty to Dispensing Unapproved Drugs," US Department of Justice, US Attorney's Office, Southern District of California, January 24, 2013, https://www.justice.gov/usao-sdca/pr /la-jolla-oncologist-and-medical-practice-plead-guilty-dispensing-unapproved -drugs.

166. "Excursion to Tindari," *Inspector Montalbano*, BBC, http://www.bbc.co .uk/programmes/b00g3lqt, accessed July 1, 2017.

167. Scheper-Hughes, "Organ Trafficking during Times of War and Political Conflict"; Susanne Lindin, *Organs for Sale: An Ethnographic Examination of the International Organ Trade* (New York: Palgrave Pivot, 2015); author's interview with Professor Susanne Lindin, *International Affairs Forum* 7, no. 2 (Fall 2016): 117–122.

168. ILO, "Global Estimates of Modern Slavery: Forced Labour and Forced Marriage"; Adam Taylor, "There Are an Estimated 40 Million Slaves in the World. Where Do They Live and What Do They Do?," *Washington Post*, September 19, 2017, https://www.washingtonpost.com/news/worldviews/wp/2017 /09/19/there-are-an-estimated-40-million-slaves-in-the-world-where-do-they -live-and-what-do-they-do/?utm_term=.04e2133631ec, accessed January 30, 2017.

169. Chaudhry, "The Challenge of Curtailing the Escalation of Counterfeit Pharmaceuticals."

Chapter 7. Destroyers of the Planet

1. "Environmental Risks of Mining," http://web.mit.edu/12.000/www/m2016/finalwebsite/problems/mining.html, accessed June 17, 2017; Suzanne Daley, "Peru Scrambles to Drive out Illegal Gold Mining and Save Precious Land," *New York Times*, July 26, 2016, http://www.nytimes.com/2016/07/26/world/americas/peru-illegal-gold-mining-latin-america.html, accessed June 17, 2017; Office of DNI, "Statement for the Record: Worldwide Threat Assessment of the US Intelligence Community," 14.

2. Amanda Shaver and Sally Yozell, "Casting a Wider Net: The Security Implications of Illegal, Unreported, and Unregulated Fishing," Stimson Center, January 2018, https://www.stimson.org/sites/default/files/file-attachments/Casting%20a%20Wider%20Net%20Report.pdf, accessed February 10, 2018; Rob White, *Transnational Environmental Crime: Toward an Eco-global Criminology* (London: Routledge, 2011), 88–104.

3. Aksel Sundström and Tanya Wyatt, "Corruption and Organized Crime in Conservation," in *Conservation Criminology*, ed. Meredith Gore (Chichester, UK: John Wiley & Sons, 2017), 97–110.

4. Gore, *Conservation Criminology*, 11.

5. I saw *The Borneo Case* on December 2, 2016, at the 17th IACC Film Festival, Panama City, Panama, where the producers discussed the film; "Films 4 Transparency," IACC, https://iaccseries.org/films-for-transparency/, accessed June 17, 2017. On the film, see "*The Borneo Case* (2017)," Swedish Film Institute, Swedish Film Database, http://www.sfi.se/en-GB/Swedish-film-database/Item/?type=MOVIE&itemid=73828, accessed June 17, 2017.

6. Gore, *Conservation Criminology*, 11.

7. Gore, *Conservation Criminology*, 101.

8. Lukas Straumann, *Money Logging on the Trail of the Asian Timber Mafia* (Basel: Bergli Books, 2014), 16.

9. Straumann, *Money Logging on the Trail of the Asian Timber Mafia*, 302.

10. Straumann, *Money Logging on the Trail of the Asian Timber Mafia*, 303.

11. Straumann, *Money Logging on the Trail of the Asian Timber Mafia*, 303.

12. Straumann, *Money Logging on the Trail of the Asian Timber Mafia*, 22–41, 244.

13. Sophie Tatum and Pamela Brown, "First on CNN: Report Finds National Security Agencies at Risk in Foreign-Owned Building," *CNN*, January 30, 2017, http://edition.cnn.com/2017/01/30/politics/gao-report-foreign-ownership/index.html, accessed June 17, 2017. The property in Seattle is named in the GAO report, but not the owner who benefits; see "Federal Real Property GSA: GSA Should Inform Tenant Agencies When Leasing High Security Space from Foreign Owners," GAO-17-195, GAO, January 2017, 15, http://www.gao.gov/assets/690/681883.pdf, accessed June 17, 2017.

14. Alex Shoumatoff, "In Borneo's Ruined Forests, Nomads Have Nowhere Else to Go," *Smithsonian*, March 2016, http://www.smithsonianmag.com/science-nature/borneos-ruined-forests-nomads-have-nowhere-to-go

-180958107/, accessed July 10, 2017; Alex Shoumatoff, *The Rivers Amazon* (San Francisco: Sierra Club Books, 1986), 13–25; Oliver Balch, "Indonesia's Forest Fires: Everything You Need to Know," *Guardian*, November 11, 2015, https://www.theguardian.com/sustainable-business/2015/nov/11/indonesia-forest-fires-explained-haze-palm-oil-timber-burning, accessed June 17, 2017.

15. "The Paris Agreement," UN Climate Change, updated January 18, 2018, http://unfccc.int/paris_agreement/items/9485.php.

16. On this concept, see Calderoni, "The Analysis and Containment of Organized Crime and Transnational Organized Crime."

17. Brian Deese, "Paris Isn't Burning: Why the Climate Agreement Will Survive Trump," *Foreign Affairs* 94, no. 4 (July/August 2017): 83–92.

18. Donald R. Liddick, *Crimes against Nature: Illegal Industry and the Global Environment* (Santa Barbara, CA: ABC-CLIO, 2011); Jennifer Clapp, "Illicit Trade in Hazardous Waste and CFCs: International Responses to Environmental 'Bads,'" *Trends in Organized Crime* 3, no. 2 (1997): 14–18; Naím, *Illicit*, 169–171. CFCs are any of several gaseous compounds of carbon, hydrogen, chlorine, and fluorine and are typically used in refrigerants and aerosol propellants. They are harmful to the ozone layer in the earth's atmosphere owing to the release of chlorine atoms upon exposure to ultraviolet radiation; "Update on the Illegal Trade in Ozone-Depleting Substances," EIA Briefing to the 38th Meeting of the Open-Ended Working Group of the Parties to the Montreal Protocol, July 18–21, 2016, 1, 3, http://conf.montreal-protocol.org/meeting/oewg/oewg-38/publications/Observer%20Publications/EIA%20OEWG38%20ODS%20Illegal%20Trade%20briefing%20July%202016.pdf, accessed June 17, 2017.

19. Lorraine Elliott, "Smuggling Networks and the Black Market in Ozone Depleting Substances," in *Hazardous Waste and Pollution: Preventing Green Crimes*, ed. Tanya Wyatt (Cham, Switzerland: Springer, 2016), 51; Ning Liu, Vira Somboon, and Carl Middleton, "Illicit Trade in Ozone Depleting Substances," in *Handbook of Transnational Environmental Crime*, ed. Lorraine Elliott and William H. Schaedla (Cheltenham, UK: Edward Elgar, 2016), 228–229.

20. *Transnational Organized Crime in East Asia and Pacific: A Threat Assessment*, UNODC, April 2013, 119, https://www.unodc.org/documents/data-and-analysis/Studies/TOCTA_EAP_web.pdf.

21. Eric Hand, "Ozone Layer on the Mend, Thanks to Chemical Ban," *Science*, June 30, 2016, http://www.sciencemag.org/news/2016/06/ozone-layer-mend-thanks-chemical-ban, accessed June 17, 2017; "CFCs," The Ozone Hole, http://www.theozonehole.com/cfc.htm, accessed June 17, 2017; Chris Buckley and Henry Fountain, "In a High-Stakes Environmental Whodunit, Many Clues Point to China," June 24, 2018, https://www.nytimes.com/2018/06/24/world/asia/china-ozone-cfc.html, accessed June 25, 2018.

22. Coral Davenport, "Nations, Fighting Powerful Refrigerant That Warms Planet, Reach Landmark Deal," *New York Times*, October 15, 2016, http://www.nytimes.com/2016/10/15/world/africa/kigali-deal-hfc-air-conditioners.html, accessed June 17, 2017.

23. UNODC, *Transnational Organized Crime in East Asia and Pacific*, 115–119.

24. EIA, "Update on the Illegal Trade in Ozone-Depleting Substances."

25. UNODC, *Transnational Organized Crime in East Asia and Pacific*, 119.

26. Stefano Caneppele, Michele Riccardi, and Patricia Standridge, "Green Energy and Black Economy: Mafia Investments in the Wind Power Sector in Italy," *Crime, Law, and Social Change* 59, no. 3 (April 2013): 319–339.

27. Anthony Faiola, "Sting Operations Reveal Mafia Involvement in Renewable Energy," January 22, 2013, https://www.washingtonpost.com/world/europe/sting-operations-reveal-mafia-involvement-in-renewable-energy/2013/01/22/67388504-5f39-11e2-9dc9-bca76dd777b8_story.html?utm_term=.6a4d6e50b236.

28. Guy Dunmore, "Mafia Link to Sicily Wind Farms Probed," *Financial Times*, May 5, 2009, https://www.ft.com/content/b69fdf3a-38d1-11de-8cfe-00144feabdc0?mhq5j=e3, accessed June 22, 2017.

29. Lizzy Davies, "Assets Worth €1.3bn Seized from Italian Businessman 'with Mafia Links,'" *Guardian*, April 3, 2013, https://www.theguardian.com/world/2013/apr/03/vito-nicastri-assets-seized-mafia, accessed June 17, 2017; Emilio Randacio, "Scandalo Eolico: Confermata in appello condanna per Vito Nicastri," *La Repubblica*, March 18, 2016, http://www.repubblica.it/economia/finanza/2016/03/18/news/scandalo_eolico_confermata_in_appello_condanna_per_vito_nicastri-135768817/, accessed June 17, 2017.

30. Sarah Dowdey, "How Carbon Trading Works," Science: How Stuff Works, http://science.howstuffworks.com/environmental/green-science/carbon-trading.htm, accessed June 23, 2017.

31. "Definition of Carbon Market," *Financial Times* Lexicon, http://lexicon.ft.com/Term?term=carbon-market, accessed June 23, 2017.

32. Interpol, *Guide to Carbon Trading Crime*, Global Initiative against Transnational Organized Crime, June 18, 2013, 1, http://globalinitiative.net/interpol-guide-to-carbon-trading-crime/.

33. Christian Egenhofer, "The Making of the EU Emissions Trading Scheme: Status, Prospects, and Implications for Business," *European Management Journal* 25, no. 6 (December 2007): 453–463.

34. "Multi-billion Euro Carbon-Trading Fraud Trial Opens in Paris," *France24*, May 4, 2016, http://www.france24.com/en/20160503-france-trial-multi-billion-carbon-emissions-trading-fraud-opens-paris, accessed December 29, 2016; Marius-Cristian Frunza, *Fraud and Carbon Markets* (Abingdon, UK: Routledge, 2013); Interpol, *Guide to Carbon Trading Crime*.

35. McKenzie Funk, "The Hack That Warmed the World," *Foreign Policy*, January 30, 2015, http://foreignpolicy.com/2015/01/30/climate-change-hack-carbon-credit-black-dragon/, accessed June 17, 2017.

36. Interpol, *Guide to Carbon Trading Crime*.

37. Interpol, *Guide to Carbon Trading Crime*.

38. Chris Lang, "Three Carbon Credit Fraud Suspects Wanted in Germany for Tax Fraud and Money Laundering," REDD, April 27, 2016, http://www.redd-monitor.org/2016/04/27/three-carbon-credit-fraud-suspects-wanted-in-germany-for-tax-evasion-and-money-laundering/, accessed June 17, 2017.

39. Lang, "Three Carbon Credit Fraud Suspects Wanted in Germany."

40. Robert Tie, "Tax Fraud Crisis: Innovators Needed," *Fraud* (November/December 2013), http://www.fraud-magazine.com/article.aspx?id=4294980282, accessed June 17, 2017.

41. Karin Matussek, "Seven Ex–Deutsche Bank Managers Guilty in CO2 Tax Fraud Case," *Bloomberg*, June 13, 2016, https://www.bloomberg.com/news/articles/2016-06-13/seven-ex-deutsche-bank-managers-convicted-in-c02-tax-fraud-case, accessed June 17, 2017.

42. Hannah Roberts, "Briton Wanted for £1 Billion Fraud Used to 'Finance Terrorism' by Ripping off Italian Government through Scheme Designed to Combat Global Warming," *Daily Mail*, September 24, 2014, http://www.dailymail.co.uk/news/article-2768348/Briton-wanted-1-billion-fraud-used-finance-terror-ripping-Italian-government-scheme-designed-combat-global-warming.html, accessed June 17, 2017; Luigi Ferrarella and Giuseppe Guastella, "La Grande truffa dell'Iva in Italia per finanziare i gruppi islamici," *Correire Della Sera*, September 24, 2014, http://www.corriere.it/cronache/14_settembre_24/grande-truffa-dell-iva-italia-finanziare-gruppi-islamici-ec394336-43a5-11e4-bbc2-282fa2f68a02.shtml?refresh_ce-cp, accessed March 7, 2017; author's interviews with European law enforcement officers who investigated and prosecuted these cases.

43. The author has discussed the case with French academic crime specialists and investigative journalists.

44. Patrick Swirc, "Arrête-moi si tu peux: Cyril Astruc, le suspect numéro 1 de l'escroquerie du siècle, raconte tout," *Vanity Fair*, August 2015, http://www.vanityfair.fr/actualites/france/articles/cyril-astruc-lescroc-du-siecle/27006, accessed June 17, 2017.

45. AFP, "Escroquerie à la 'taxe carbone': Fin de cavale de Marco Mouly," *Ladepeche*, November 11, 2016, http://www.ladepeche.fr/article/2016/11/16/2459793-escroquerie-a-la-taxe-carbone-un-des-protagonistes-arrete.html, accessed June 17, 2017.

46. Funk, "The Hack That Warmed the World."

47. "Hacker Jailed for Bid to Steal Carbon Credits from UN," *Telegraph*, March 19, 2013, http://www.telegraph.co.uk/news/uknews/crime/9939718/Hacker-jailed-for-bid-to-steal-carbon-credits-from-UN.html, accessed June 17, 2017.

48. Aline Robert, "EU Carbon Market Fraudsters Face Heavy Jail Sentences," *Euractiv*, May 26, 2016, https://www.euractiv.com/section/euro-finance/news/eu-carbon-market-fraudsters-face-heavy-jail-sentences/, accessed June 17, 2016. Klapucki was sentenced in France to seven years' imprisonment and a fine of 1 million euros; Chris Lang, "Jail Sentences for 11 in France's Carbon Scam of the Century," REDD, July 8, 2016, http://www.redd-monitor.org/2016/07/08/jail-sentences-for-11-in-frances-carbon-scam-of-the-century/, accessed December 30, 2016.

49. "Three Jailed for Servicing Cyprus-Based Boiler Room That Made Millions," City of London Police, March 23, 2016, https://www.cityoflondon.police.uk/advice-and-support/fraud-and-economic-crime/fraudsquads/fraudsquad

-News/Pages/Three-jailed-for-servicing-Cyprus-based-boiler-room-that-made
-millions.aspx, accessed June 17, 2017.

50. "Goletta Verde salpa domani da Genova, Legambiente presenta il suo
dossier Mare Monstrum," Legambiente, June 17, 2016, http://www.legambiente
.it/contenuti/comunicati/goletta-verde-salpa-domani-da-genova-legambiente
-presenta-il-suo-dossier-mare-m, accessed June 17, 2017.

51. David D'Ippolito, "Rifiuti tossici in Calabria: Sempre più pentiti ne parlano
ma la verità è ancora sotterrata insieme alle scorie radioattive," *Calabrianotizie*,
August 13, 2015, http://www.calabrianotizie.it/rifiuti-tossici-in-calabria-sempre
-piu-pentiti-ne-parlano-ma-la-verita-e-ancora-sotterrata-insieme-alle-scorie
-radioattive/, accessed June 17, 2017; author's interviews on visits to Naples in
2015 and 2016.

52. Simonetta Falasca-Zamponi, *Waste and Consumption: Capitalism, the Environment, and the Life of Things* (Abingdon, UK: Routledge, 2012), 28.

53. Shelley, *Dirty Entanglements*, 301.

54. Joan Tiloine, "Nigera Maiduguri tient tête à Boko Haram," *Le Monde*, July
2–3, 2017, 16.

55. Jonathan Russell and David Harrison, "Dolphins Are Slaughtered as Cocaine
Smugglers Take to Tuna Fishing," *Telegraph*, March 31, 2002, http://www.telegraph
.co.uk/news/worldnews/northamerica/usa/1389415/Dolphins-slaughtered-as
-cocaine-smugglers-take-to-tuna-fishing.html, accessed June 17, 2017.

56. "Mafias capatan a pescadores para llevar droga," *El Comercio*, February
23, 2016, http://www.elcomercio.com/actualidad/mafias-captan-pescadores
-llevar-droga.html, accessed June 17, 2017.

57. Gavin du Venage, "Chinese Tastes Push Lethal Abalone Trade," *Asia
Times*, November 20, 2012, http://www.atimes.com/atimes/China_Business
/NK10Cb02.html, accessed June 17, 2017.

58. Ganapathiraju Pramod, Katrina Nakamura, Tony J. Pitcher, and Leslie
Delagran, "Estimates of Illegal and Unreported Fish in Seafood Imports to the
USA," *Marine Policy* 48 (September 2014): 102–113.

59. Alistair Couper, Hance D. Smith, and Bruno Ciceri, *Fishers and Plunderers: Theft, Slavery, and Violence at Sea* (London: Pluto Press, 2015); Barton
Seaver, "Can Technology End Pirate Fishing?," *National Geographic*, August
26, 2013, http://voices.nationalgeographic.com/2013/08/26/can-technology
-end-pirate-fishing/, accessed June 17, 2017; Shaver and Yozell, "Casting a
Wider Net," 8.

60. Nellemann et al., *The Rise of Environmental Crime*, 57.

61. Teale N. Phelps Bondaroff, "The Illegal Fishing and Organized Crime
Nexus: Illegal Fishing as Transnational Organized Crime," Global Initiative
against Transnational Organized Crime, April 2015, 48, http://theblackfish.org
/Fishing_Crime.pdf, accessed January 17, 2017; "Seven Chinese Vessels Detained
Off West Africa for Illegal Fishing," *Reuters*, May 3, 2017, https://www.reuters
.com/article/us-westafrica-china-fishing/seven-chinese-vessels-detained-off
-west-africa-for-illegal-fishing-idUSKBN17Z1GS, accessed October 4, 2017.

62. Pramod et al., "Estimates of Illegal and Unreported Fish in Seafood Imports to the USA."

63. Nellemann et al., *The Rise of Environmental Crime*, 57.

64. Andrew Jacobs, "China's Appetite Pushing Fisheries to the Brink," *New York Times*, April 30, 2017, https://www.nytimes.com/2017/04/30/world/asia/chinas-appetite-pushes-fisheries-to-the-brink.html, accessed October 4, 2017; author's discussions with a top official of a multinational security organization, September 2017.

65. "Indonesian Navy Fires on Chinese Fishing Boat, Injuring One, Beijing Claims," *Guardian*, June 19, 2016, https://www.theguardian.com/world/2016/jun/20/indonesian-navy-fires-on-chinese-fishing-boat-injuring-one-beijing-claims, accessed August 4, 2017.

66. Hong Soon-do, "Chinese Illegal Fishing Threatens World's Waters," *Asia Today*, June 12, 2016, http://www.huffingtonpost.com/asiatoday/chinese-illegal-fishing-t_b_10425236.html, accessed January 2, 2016.

67. "Illegal Migration to Europe Consequence of Illegal Fishing and Overfishing in West Africa," Global Initiative against Transnational Organized Crime, May 8, 2015, http://globalinitiative.net/illicit-migration-to-europe-consequences-of-illegal-fishing-and-overfishing-in-west-africa/, accessed February 20, 2017.

68. Couper, Smith, and Ciceri, *Fishers and Plunderers*, 140–141.

69. Couper, Smith, and Ciceri, *Fishers and Plunderers*, 134–140; discussion at 2015 International Workshop on Strategies for Combating Human Trafficking, Taipei, Taiwan, July 29, 2015.

70. Couper, Smith, and Ciceri, *Fishers and Plunderers*, 154; Supang Chantavanich, Samarn Laodumrongchai, and Christina Stringer, "Under the Shadow: Forced Labour among Sea Fishers in Thailand," *Marin Policy* 68 (June 2016): 1–7.

71. *Transnational Organized Crime in the Fishing Industry: Focus on Trafficking in Persons, Smuggling of Migrants, Illicit Drugs Trafficking*, UNODC, 2011, 21–26, http://www.unodc.org/documents/human-trafficking/Issue_Paper_-_TOC_in_the_Fishing_Industry.pdf, accessed June 17, 2017.

72. Emanuel Stoakes, Chris Kelly, and Annie Kelly, "Revealed: How the Thai Trafficking Fishing Industry Trafficks, Imprisons, and Enslaves," *Guardian*, July 20, 2015, https://www.theguardian.com/global-development/2015/jul/20/thai-fishing-industry-implicated-enslavement-deaths-rohingya, accessed June 16, 2017.

73. Jewel Topsfield, "Modern-Day Slavery: Indonesia Cracks Down on Brutal Conditions on Foreign Fishing Boats," *Sydney Morning Herald*, January 24, 2017, http://www.smh.com.au/world/modernday-slavery-indonesia-cracks-down-on-brutal-conditions-on-foreign-fishing-boats-20170124-gtxseo.html, accessed June 15, 2017; *Report on Human Trafficking, Forced Labour, and Fisheries Crime in the Indonesian Fishing Industry—IOM*, International Organization for Migration (IOM), http://indonesia.iom.int/human-trafficking-forced-labour-and-fisheries-crime-indonesian-fishing-industry-iom, accessed June 16, 2017.

74. IOM, *Report on Human Trafficking, Forced Labour, and Fisheries Crime*, 127.

75. Rollo Romig, "How to Steal a River," *New York Times*, March 1, 2017, https://www.nytimes.com/2017/03/01/magazine/sand-mining-india-how-to-steal-a-river.html, accessed February 10, 2018.

76. E. O. Wilson, *Half-Earth: Our Planet's Fight for Life* (New York: W. W. Norton & Co., 2016).

77. Author's interviews with Tanzanian officials working to counter wildlife poaching, September 2016.

78. Nellemann et al., *The Rise of Environmental Crime*, 51.

79. Aaron Beitman, "Russia's Far East under the Ax," George Mason University, TraCCC, October 10, 2013, http://traccc.gmu.edu/2013/10/10/russias-far-east-under-the-ax/, accessed June 17, 2017.

80. Beitman, "Russia's Far East under the Ax," 20; Christian Nellemann, ed., *Green Carbon Black Trade: Illegal Logging Tax Fraud and Laundering in the World's Tropical Forests: A Rapid Response Assessment*, UNEP and GRID-Arendal, 2012, https://www.grida.no/publications/126, accessed June 17, 2017.

81. "Forests," Global Witness, https://www.globalwitness.org/fr/campaigns/forests/, accessed June 17, 2017; "US Government Confirms Imports of Illegal Timber from Peru," EIA, August 18, 2016, https://eia-global.org/press-releases/us-government-report-confirms-imports-of-illegal-timber-from-peru, accessed June 17, 2017.

82. Jani Actman, "From Trees to Tigers: Case Shows Costs of Illegal Logging," *National Geographic*, November 10, 2015, http://news.nationalgeographic.com/2015/11/151110-timber-russian-far-east-illegal-logging-siberia/, accessed June 17, 2017; Romana Puiulet and Anna Babinets, "Clear Cut Crimes," OCCRP, September 20, 2016, https://www.occrp.org/en/investigations/5655-clear-cut-crimes, accessed July 17, 2016; "EIA Report Shows Holzindustrie Schweighofer's Illegal Activities, WWF Submits EUTR Complaint," EIA, October 21, 2015, https://eia-global.org/press-releases/eia-report-shows-holzindustrie-schweighofers-illegal-activities-wwf-submits, accessed June 17, 2017.

83. Nithin Coca, "Indonesia's Anti-corruption Fight," *Diplomat*, February 8, 2016, http://thediplomat.com/2016/02/indonesias-anti-corruption-fight/, accessed June 17, 2017.

84. UNODC, *Transnational Organized Crime in East Asia and the Pacific*, 93.

85. Pahala Nainggolan, Deputy for Prevention, Corruption Eradication Commission, Indonesia, presentation to the panel "Corruption, Climate Change, and Illegal Timber Trade," Paris, April 20, 2016, at the 2016 OECD Integrity Forum (attended by the author) entitled "Fighting the Hidden Tariff: Global Trade without Corruption"; see also "Permitting Crime: How Palm Oil Expansion Drives Illegal Logging in Indonesia," EIA, 9, https://eia-international.org/wp-content/uploads/Permitting-Crime.pdf, accessed June 17, 2017.

86. Report at Transparency International (TI) meeting (attended by the author), Malaysia, September 2015; Sarah Schonhardt, "Indonesia Seeks to Resolve Timber Reporting Issues," *Wall Street Journal*, February 24, 2016, http://www.wsj.com/articles/indonesia-seeks-to-resolve-timber-reporting-issues-1456325915, accessed June 17, 2017.

87. Wahyudi Soeriaatmadja, "Indonesia Arrests Seven Company Executives for Illegal Forest Fires," *Straits Times*, September 17, 2015, http://www.straitstimes.com/asia/se-asia/indonesia-arrests-seven-company-executives-for-illegal-forest-fires, accessed January 11, 2017.

88. Oliver Balch, "Indonesia's Forest Fires: Everything You Need to Know," *Guardian*, November 11, 2015, https://www.theguardian.com/sustainable-business/2015/nov/11/indonesia-forest-fires-explained-haze-palm-oil-timber-burning, accessed June 17, 2017.

89. "The Last Frontier: Illegal Logging in Papua and China's Massive Timber Theft," Telapak and EIA, February 2005, 17–19, www.eia-international.org/wp-content/uploads/The-Last-Frontier.pdf, accessed June 17, 2017.

90. Nainggolan, panel presentation at the 2016 OECD Integrity Forum.

91. UNODC, *Transnational Organized Crime in East Asia and the Pacific*, 93.

92. Said Ismail, "Charcoal Trade Stripping Somalia of Trees," Somalia Report, August 23, 2011, http://piracyreport.com/index.php/post/1426/Charcoal_Trade_Stripping_Somalia_of_Trees, accessed June 17, 2017.

93. Nellemann et al., *The Environmental Crime Crisis*, 71, 75.

94. "The Charcoal Conundrum: Ending the Somali Illegal Charcoal Trade," Global Initiative against Transnational Organized Crime, June 10, 2014, http://globalinitiative.net/somalia-charcoal/, accessed September 28, 2016.

95. Nellemann et al., *The Environmental Crime Crisis*, 80–81.

96. Puiulet and Babinets, "Clear Cut Crimes"; "Stealing the Last Forest," EIA, October 21, 2015, https://eia-global.org/reports/st, accessed February 10, 2018; Lumm Schlingemann et al., "Combating Wildlife and Forest Crime in the Danube-Carpathian Region," UNEP, Eurac Research, and WWF, 2017, https://docs.wixstatic.com/ugd/655326_8b228497edc64f8e8fe64353400dfdce.pdf, accessed February 10, 2018.

97. "Austrian Timber Giant Ransacking Romania's Forests," *Ecologist*, October 21, 2015, http://www.theecologist.org/News/news_round_up/2985976/austrian_timber_giant_ransacking_romanias_forests.html, accessed June 23, 2017.

98. Puiulet and Babinets, "Clear Cut Crimes."

99. Puiulet and Babinets, "Clear Cut Crimes."

100. Ida Karlsson, "IKEA under Fire for Ancient Tree Logging," *Guardian*, May 29, 2012, https://www.theguardian.com/environment/2012/may/29/ikea-ancient-tree-logging, accessed June 17, 2017.

101. Actman, "From Trees to Tigers"; "Lumber Liquidators Inc. Sentenced for Illegal Importation of Hardwood and Related Environmental Crimes," US Department of Justice, Office of Public Affairs, February 1, 2016, https://www.justice.gov/opa/pr/lumber-liquidators-inc-sentenced-illegal-importation-hardwood-and-related-environmental, accessed March 7, 2016.

102. "Inside the Plywood: Material of the Modern World Exhibition," Victoria & Albert Museum, London, July 19–November 12, 2017, https://www.vam.ac.uk/articles/inside-the-plywood-material-of-the-modern-world-exhibition, accessed November 3, 2017. The online illustration shows the section of the exhibition that the author visited in September 2017.

103. Thomas Lovejoy, "A Tsunami of Extinction," *Scientific American* 308, no. 1 (January 2013): 33–34.

104. Elizabeth Kolbert, *The Sixth Extinction: An Unnatural History* (New York: Picador, 2014), 125–147.

105. Rodolfo Dirzo et al., "Defaunation in the Anthropocene," *Science* 345, no. 6195 (July 25, 2014): 401–406.

106. Richard Monastersky, "Anthropocene: The Human Age," *Nature*, March 11, 2015, http://www.nature.com/news/anthropocene-the-human-age-1.17085, accessed January 25, 2017; Damian Carrington, "The Anthropocene Epoch: Scientists Declare Dawn of Human-Influenced Age," *Guardian*, August 29, 2016, https://www.theguardian.com/environment/2016/aug/29/declare-anthropocene-epoch-experts-urge-geological-congress-human-impact-earth, accessed January 25, 2017.

107. Ledio Cakaj, "Tusk Wars inside the LRA and the Bloody Business of Ivory," Enough, October 2015, http://www.enoughproject.org/files/Tusk_Wars_10262015.pdf, accessed June 15, 2017; Bryan Christy, "How Killing Elephants Finances Terror in Africa," *National Geographic*, August 12, 2015, http://www.nationalgeographic.com/tracking-ivory/article.html, accessed June 15, 2017.

108. *World Wildlife Crime Report 2016*, UNODC, 13, http://www.unodc.org/documents/data-and-analysis/wildlife/Exsum_Wildlife_report_2016.pdf, accessed October 5, 2017.

109. Tania Wyatt, *Wildlife Trafficking: A Deconstruction of the Crime, the Victims, and the Offenders* (New York: Palgrave Macmillan, 2013).

110. UNODC, *Transnational Organized Crime in East Asia and the Pacific*, 78–80; Nellemann et al., *The Rise of Environmental Crime*, 41.

111. UNODC, *Transnational Organized Crime in East Asia and the Pacific*, viii; UNODC, *World Wildlife Crime Report 2016*, 17.

112. "Joint Undercover Operation Links International Black Market to Virginia Mountains," National Park Service, January 7, 2004, https://www.nps.gov/aboutus/news/release.htm?id=451, accessed October 5, 2017; author's discussions with investigators for the National Park Service, September 2016.

113. Nellemann et al., *The Rise of Environmental Crime*, 41; *Stolen Apes: The Illicit Trade in Chimpanzees, Gorillas, Bonobos, and Orangutans: A Rapid Response Assessment*, UNEP and UNESCO, 2013, http://www.un-grasp.org/stolen-apes-counts-illegal-trade-toll/, accessed October 5, 2017.

114. UNODC, *Transnational Organized Crime in East Asia and the Pacific*, 82.

115. *Killing with Keystrokes: An Investigation of the Illegal Wildlife Trade on the World Wide Web*, IFAW, 2008, 3, https://s3.amazonaws.com/ifaw-pantheon/sites/default/files/legacy/Killing%20with%20Keystrokes.pdf.

116. UNODC, *Transnational Organized Crime in East Asia and the Pacific*, 82; *Killing with Keystrokes 2.0: IFAW's Investigation into the European Online Ivory Trade*, IFAW, July 26, 2012, 8–15, https://s3.amazonaws.com/ifaw-pantheon/sites/default/files/legacy/FINAL%20Killing%20with%20Keystrokes%202.0%20report%202011.pdf.

117. Rob Denny, "Fake Pesticides . . . A Growing Problem," Tenants of the Land, January 13, 2015, https://tenantsoftheland.wordpress.com/2015/01/13/fake-pesticides-a-growing-problem/, accessed June 19, 2017.

118. "Counterfeit and Illegal Pesticides," European Crop Protection Association (ECPA), http://www.ecpa.eu/regulatory-policy-topics/counterfeit-illegal-pesticides and http://www.ecpa.eu/stewardship/counterfeit-illegal-pesticides#section4073, accessed June 19, 2017; "2016 Special 301 Report," Office of the US Trade Representative, April 2016, 33, https://ustr.gov/sites/default/files/USTR-2016-Special-301-Report.pdf, accessed June 17, 2017.

119. "Illegal or Counterfeit Pesticides," National Pesticide Information Center, updated December 15, 2015, http://www.npic.orst.edu/ingred/ptype/illegal/index.html, accessed June 19, 2017.

120. R. J. Whitehead, "FICCI Report: One-Third of Indian Pesticides Are Dangerous Fakes," Food Navigator, October 6, 2015, http://www.foodnavigator-asia.com/Policy/Ficci-report-One-third-of-Indian-pesticides-are-dangerous-fakes, accessed June 17, 2017; FICCI, *Study on Sub-standard Spurious/Counterfeit Pesticides in India*, Tata Strategic Management Group, 2015, 17, 22, https://croplife.org/wp-content/uploads/2015/10/Study-on-sub-standard-spurious-counterfeit-pesticides-in-India.pdf, accessed June 17, 2017.

121. "The Bad Earth: Contaminated Soil Is the Biggest Neglected Threat to Public Health in China," *Economist*, June 10–17, 2017, 20–22.

122. Li Yang, "Ban on Highly Toxic Pesticides Should Be the First Step," *China Daily*, April 23, 2015, http://www.chinadaily.com.cn/opinion/2015-04/23/content_20515155.htm, accessed June 17, 2017.

123. Linda L. Leake, "Food Safety in Asia," Food Quality & Safety, June 15, 2015, http://www.foodqualityandsafety.com/article/food-safety-in-asia/3/, accessed June 17, 2017.

124. "Counterfeiting Cases Investigated by China in First 7 Months of 2013," Havocscope, http://www.havocscope.com/counterfeiting-cases-investigated-by-china-in-first-7-months-of-2013/.

125. Yu. O. Karpysheva, "Problems in Combating the Illegal Use of Pesticides and Agrochemicals in Agricultural Cultivation in Eastern Siberia," George Mason University, TraCCC, 2012, http://traccc.gmu.edu/about-us/international-centers/study-centers-in-eurasia/eurasia-publications/summary-of-research-problems-in-combating-the-illegal-use-of-pesticides-and-agrochemicals-in-agricultural-cultivation-in-eastern-siberia-2011/, accessed June 19, 2017.

126. Frederick M. Fishel, "The Global Increase in Counterfeit Pesticides," PI 174, University of Florida, Institute of Food and Agricultural Sciences (IFAS) Extension, Agronomy Department, originally published January 2009, revised February 2018, http://edis.ifas.ufl.edu/pi210.

127. "Europol Warns of Growing Trade in Counterfeit Pesticides Worth Billions of Euros a Year," Europol, January 13, 2012, https://www.europol.europa.eu/newsroom/news/europol-warns-of-growing-trade-in-counterfeit-pesticides-worth-billions-of-euros-yea, accessed June 19, 2017.

128. "Huge Seizures of 190 Tonnes of Counterfeit Pesticides," Europol, December 18, 2015, https://www.europol.europa.eu/content/huge-seizures-190-tonnes-counterfeit-pesticides, accessed June 19, 2017; Robert Mace et al., "Illicit Pesticides, Organized Crime, and Supply Chain Integrity," UNICRI, 2016, 52, http://www.unicri.it/in_focus/files/The_problem_of_illicit_pesticides_low_res1.pdf, accessed June 19, 2017.

129. Glenn Hess, "Counterfeit Pesticides Damage EU Economy," *Chemical and Engineering News* 95, no. 8 (February 2017): 16; "EU Sweeps on Counterfeit Pesticides That Cost European Countries More Than $2 Billion Euros," *EU Reporter*, July 6, 2017, https://www.eureporter.co/frontpage/2017/07/06/europol-122-tonnes-of-illegal-or-counterfeit-pesticides-seized-during-operation-silver-axe-ii/, accessed August 3, 2017.

130. "Fake Pesticides Are a Real Threat," Growing Georgia, October 23, 2011, http://growinggeorgia.com/news/2011/10/fake-pesticides-are-real-threat/, accessed June 19, 2017.

131. Zhou Siyu, "Sowing the Seeds of Doubt," *China Daily*, August 3, 2011, http://www.chinadaily.com.cn/cndy/2011-08/03/content_13037586.htm.

132. Kathleen Brophy, "Working Together to Stop Fake Agricultural Products in Uganda," Transparency International, March 28, 2014, https://blog.transparency.org/2014/08/28/working-together-to-stop-fake-agricultural-products-in-uganda/, accessed March 24, 2016.

133. Francisco Toro, "Fake Seeds Force Ugandan Farmers to Resort to 'Bronze Age' Agriculture," *Guardian*, April 8, 2014, https://www.theguardian.com/sustainable-business/counterfeit-fake-seeds-uganda-farmers-crop-failure.

134. Senior and Mazza, "Italian 'Triangle of Death' Linked to Waste Crisis."

135. Ian Birrell, "How the Mafia Is Causing Cancer," Mosaic, June 24, 2016, https://mosaicscience.com/story/how-mafia-causing-cancer, accessed June 17, 2017.

136. For more on the land of fires, see Isaia Sales, *Storia dell'Italia Mafiosa: Perché le mafie hanno avuto successo* (Soveria Mannelli: Rubbetino, 2015), 352–359; Roberto Saviano, *Gomorrah: A Personal Journey into the Violent International Empire of Naples' Organized Crime System* (New York: Picador, 2007), 282–301; Antonio Michele Moccia, *La Terra dei Fuochi: Il popolo campano ucciso dalle istituzioni* (Cosenza: Falco Editore, 2014); Eurispes, *Agromafie 4° rapporto sui crimini agroalimentari in Italia*, 171–179.

137. "European Court Fines Italy over 'Land of Fires,'" ANSA, July 16, 2015, http://www.ansa.it/english/news/2015/07/16/eu-court-fines-italy-over-land-of-fires_dd65650c-5065-4c6a-a8b9-dc91c288c811.html, accessed June 17, 2017.

138. "A Caivano veleni in un'area cento volte più grande dell'Ilva," *Corriere del Mezzogiorno*, May 29, 2013, http://corrieredelmezzogiorno.corriere.it/napoli/notizie/cronaca/2013/29-maggio-2013/a-caivano-veleni-un-area-cento-volte-piu-grande-ilva-2221385413054.shtml, accessed June 17, 2017; Margherita De Bac, "Emergenza bambini nella Terra dei Fuochi: 'I tumori già a 1 anno,'"

Corriere della Sera, January 12, 2016, http://www.corriere.it/salute/16_gennaio
_12/emergenza-bambini-terra-fuochi-tumori-gia-1-anno-6f051a2a-b906-11e5
-85a5-46ffd263e960.shtml, accessed June 17, 2017.

139. Paolo Tripodi, *The Colonial Legacy in Somalia: Rome and Mogadishu: From Colonial Administration to Operation Restore Hope* (Basingstoke, UK: Macmillan, 1999).

140. "Russia Loses 6% of GDP to Ecological Problems—Putin," *Moscow Times*, December 27, 2016, https://themoscowtimes.com/news/damages-from
-ecology-problems-amount-to-6-of-russias-gdp-putin-56661, accessed June 17, 2017.

141. UNODC, *Transnational Organized Crime in East Asia and the Pacific*, viii.

142. Nellemann et al., "Waste Crime, Waste Risks," 4; UNODC, *Transnational Organized Crime in East Asia and the Pacific*, viii; "Electronic Waste and Organized Crime: Assessing the Links: Phase II Report for the Interpol Pollution Crime Working Group," Interpol, May 2009, http://www.ifap.ru/pr/2009
/n090714a.pdf.

143. Jacopo Ottaviani, "E-Waste Republic," *Al-Jazeera*, https://interactive
.aljazeera.com/aje/2015/ewaste/index.html.

144. Zhaohua Wang, Bin Zhang, and Dabo Guan, "Take Responsibility for Electronic Waste Disposal," *Nature* 536 (August 3, 2016): 23–25, http://www
.nature.com/news/take-responsibility-for-electronic-waste-disposal-1.20345,
accessed June 17, 2017.

145. Sharman, *The Money Laundry*.

146. Matthew Bunn, "Corruption and Nuclear Proliferation," in Rotberg, *Corruption, Global Security, and World Order*, 139.

147. Bunn, "Corruption and Nuclear Proliferation," 139.

148. Javier Serrat, "Financial Interdictions to Curb Proliferation," Arms Control Association, July–August 2012, https://www.armscontrol.org/2012_07-08
/Financial_Interdictions_To_Curb_Proliferation, accessed June 17, 2017; Sonia Ben Ouagrham-Gormley, "Banking on Nonproliferation: Improving the Efficiency of Counter-Proliferation Financing Policies," *Nonproliferation Review* 19, no. 2 (2012): 241–265. Ouagrham-Gormley suggests that some banks were not cognizant of being a party to these transactions and needed more training to identify patterns of proliferation finance.

149. Kevin McCoy, "HSBC Will Pay $1.9 Billion for Money Laundering," *USA Today*, December 11, 2012, http://www.usatoday.com/story/money
/business/2012/12/11/hsbc-laundering-probe/1760351/, accessed July 17, 2017;
Paul Farrell et al., "The HSBC Files." *Guardian*, February 8, 2015, http://www
.theguardian.com/news/2015/feb/09/hsbc-swiss-files-leading-australian-figures
-held-offshore-bank-accounts, accessed June 17, 2017.

150. "European Union Serious Organised Crime Theft Assessment 2017:
Crime in the Age of Technology," Europol, 2017, 7, https://www.europol.europa
.eu/activities-services/main-reports/european-union-serious-and-organised
-crime-threat-assessment-2017, accessed June 17, 2017.

151. Ashfaq Yusufzai, "Pakistan's Forests Fall Victim to the Taliban," *Guardian*, January 17, 2012, https://www.theguardian.com/environment/2012/jan/17/pakistan-forests-taliban, accessed June 17, 2017.

152. Geoff Colvin, "Why Volkswagen's Emission Scandal Has No End," *Fortune*, January 11, 2017, http://fortune.com/2017/01/11/volkswagen-emissions-scandal-2/, accessed February 8, 2017; Steph Yin, "Volkswagen's Emission Fraud May Affect Mortality Rate in Europe," *New York Times*, March 6, 2017, https://www.nytimes.com/2017/03/06/science/volkswagen-emissions-scandal-air-pollution-deaths.html, accessed March 7, 2017; Bill Vlasic, "Volkswagen Executive Pleads Guilty in Diesel Emissions Case," *New York Times*, August 4, 2017, https://www.nytimes.com/2017/08/04/business/volkswagen-diesel-oliver-schmidt.html?emc=edit_mbe_20170807&nl=morning-briefing-europe&nlid=47439486&te=1&_r=0.

Chapter 8. Summing Up

1. Charles Tilly, "War Making and State Making as Organized Crime," in *Bringing the State Back In*, ed. Peter Evans, Dietrich Rueschemeyer, and Theda Skocpol (Cambridge: Cambridge University Press, 1985), 169–186.

2. James Martin, *Drugs on the Dark Net: How Cryptomarkets Are Transforming the Global Trade in Illicit Drugs* (Houndsmills, UK: Palgrave Macmillan, 2014).

3. *Fourth National Climate Assessment*, US Global Change Research Program, to be released in late 2018, http://www.globalchange.gov/nca4, accessed November 11, 2017.

4. Itty Abraham and Willem van Schendel, "Introduction: The Making of Illicitness," in *Illicit Flows and Criminal Things: States, Borders, and the Other Side of Globalization*, ed. Willem van Schendel and Itty Abraham (Bloomington: Indiana University Press, 2005), 1–37.

5. Tilly, "War Making and State Making as Organized Crime."

6. Thomas Y. Allsen, *The Royal Hunt in Eurasian History* (Philadelphia: University of Pennsylvania Press, 2006).

7. William Beinart and Lotte Hughes, *Environment and Empire* (Oxford: Oxford University Press, 2007).

8. Edwards, "Global Forced Displacement Hits Record High"; Joe Somerlad, "World Refugee Day 2018: How Many Displaced People Are There around the Globe and What Is Being Done to Help?," June 20, 2018, https://www.independent.co.uk/news/world/world-refugee-day-2018-un-conflict-war-famine-syria-myanmar-displaced-stateless-people-a8407401.html, accessed July 25, 2018.

9. Associated Press, "Morocco Protests after Fisherman Crushed to Death in a Garbage Truck," *Guardian*, October 31, 2016, https://www.theguardian.com/world/2016/oct/31/morocco-protests-after-fisherman-crushed-to-death-in-a-garbage-truck, accessed September 1, 2016.

10. "Morocco's Refusal to Listen" (editorial), *New York Times*, September 1, 2017, https://www.nytimes.com/2017/09/01/opinion/morocco-protests.html, accessed September 1, 2017.

11. Jens Beckert and Matias Dewey, eds., *Architecture of Illegal Markets: To-wards an Economic Sociology of Illegal Markets* (New York: Oxford University Press, 2017), 80.

12. Shelley, *Human Trafficking.*

13. Kathleen McLaughlin, "Underground Labs in China Are Devising Potent New Opiates Faster Than Authorities Can Respond," *Science*, March 29, 2017, http://www.sciencemag.org/news/2017/03/underground-labs-china-are-devising-potent-new-opiates-faster-authorities-can-respond, accessed November 11, 2017; Jeremy Berg, "Modeling the Growth of Opioid Overdose Deaths," *Science*, June 5, 2017, http://blogs.sciencemag.org/sciencehound/2017/06/05/modeling-the-growth-of-opioid-overdose-deaths/, accessed November 11, 2017; "Overdose Death Rates," National Institute on Drug Abuse, updated September 2017, https://www.drugabuse.gov/related-topics/trends-statistics/overdose-death-rates, accessed February 11, 2018.

14. Kan, Bechtol, and Collins, "Criminal Sovereignty"; Peter A. Prahar, "Prepared Statement: North Korea: Illicit Activity Funding the Regime," US Senate Homeland Security and Government Affairs Committee, Subcommittee on Financial Management, Government Information, and International Security, Senate Hearing 109-887, April 25, 2006, https://www.gpo.gov/fdsys/pkg/CHRG-109shrg28241/html/CHRG-109shrg28241.htm, accessed November 3, 2017.

15. United States of America vs. Reza Zarab, Camelia Zamshidy, and Hossein Zajafzadeh, indictment filed in US District Court, Southern District of New York, https://www.justice.gov/opa/file/834146/download, accessed November 4, 2017.

16. Robert Orttung and Christopher Walker, "Putin's Frozen Conflicts," *Foreign Policy*, February 13, 2015, http://foreignpolicy.com/2015/02/13/putins-frozen-conflicts/, accessed November 4, 2017; "UN Panel of Experts Reveals Gold Smuggling and Cluster Bombs in Darfur," Enough, April 12, 2016, https://enoughproject.org/blog/un-panel-experts-reveals-gold-smuggling-and-cluster-bombs-darfur, accessed October 9, 2017.

17. Naím (*Illicit*, 20) discusses the important role of states in counterfeiting generally.

18. OECD/EUIPO, *Trade in Counterfeit and Pirated Goods.*

19. Mujib Mashal, "An Afghan Insurgency Morphs into a Drug Cartel," *New York Times*, October 30, 2017.

20. Luis Jorge Garay Salamanca, Eduardo Salcedo-Albarán, Isaac de León, and Bernardo Guerrero, *La Captura y reconfiguración cooptada del estado en Colombia* (Bogotá: Fundación Método, Fundación Avina y Transparencia por Colombia, 2008); Luis Jorge Garay Salamanca and Eduardo Salcedo-Albarán, "Institutional Impact of Criminal Networks in Colombia and Mexico," *Crime Law and Social Change* 57 (2012): 177–194.

21. Gambetta, *The Sicilian Mafia.*

22. Michael Moyer, "Manipulation of the Crowd: How Trustworthy Are Online Ratings?," *Scientific American*, July 1, 2010, https://www.scientificamerican.com/article/manipulation-of-the-crowd/, accessed November 26, 2017.

23. James Martin and Nicolas Christin, "Ethics in Cryptomarket Research," *International Journal of Drug Policy* 35 (2016): 84–91.

24. Michael Dziedzic, *Criminalized Power Structures: The Overlooked Enemies of Peace* (Lanham, MD: Rowman & Littlefield, 2016).

25. Jeffrey Gettleman, "Smuggled, Beaten, and Drugged: The Illicit Global Ape Trade," *New York Times*, November 4, 2017, https://www.nytimes.com/2017 /11/04/world/africa/ape-trafficking-bonobos-orangutans.html?_r=0, accessed November 11, 2017.

26. Phillip Connor and Jens Manuel Krogstad, "About Six-in-Ten Syrians Are Now Displaced from Their Homes," Pew Research Center, June 13, 2016, http:// www.pewresearch.org/fact-tank/2016/06/13/about-six-in-ten-syrians-are-now -displaced-from-their-homes/, accessed October 9, 2017.

27. Paul Collier and Anke Hoffler, "Greed and Grievance in Civil War," *Oxford Economic Papers* 56 (2004): 563–595.

28. "Security Council, Adopting Resolution 2195 (2014), Urges International Action to Break Links between Terrorists, Transnational Organized Crime," UN, December 19, 2014, https://www.un.org/press/en/2014/sc11717.doc.htm, accessed November 11, 2017; "Unanimously Adopting Resolution 2199 (2015), Security Council Condemns Trade with Al-Qaida Associated Groups, Threatens Further Targeted Sanctions," UN, February 12, 2015, https://www.un.org/press /en/2015/sc11775.doc.htm, accessed November 11, 2017.

29. Jean-François Gayraud, *Théorie des hybride terrorisme et crime organisé* (Paris: CNRS Editions, 2017).

30. Hübschle, "A Game of Horns."

31. Bilton, *American Kingpin.*

32. *Forbes* named Pablo Escobar seven times to its list of billionaires; "Pablo Escobar in *Forbes*' Billionaire Issues," *Forbes*, https://www.forbes.com/pictures /eehd45ekgjj/1987/#a08cf3b9d7d1, accessed November 11, 2017; Alex Morrell, "The OxyContin Clan: The $14 Billion Newcomer to *Forbes* 2015 List of Richest US Families," *Forbes*, July 1, 2015, https://www.forbes.com/sites/alexmorrell /2015/07/01/the-oxycontin-clan-the-14-billion-newcomer-to-forbes-2015-list -of-richest-u-s-families/#543bd71c75e0.

33. Jonathan Dienst, "Man Shipped Viagra and Fake Oxycodone from NYC Apartment, Gave Buyers Tracking Numbers: Feds," *NBC 4 New York*, October 24, 2017, http://www.nbcnewyork.com/news/local/Fake-Oxycodone-New -York-City-Bronx-Arrest-Feds-452869913.html, accessed October 30, 2017; author's communication with a pharmaceutical executive addressing the issue of counterfeits.

34. Associated Press, "Volkswagen Executive Pleads Guilty in Emissions Scandal," *Los Angeles Times*, August 4, 2017, http://www.latimes.com/business /la-fi-hy-volkswagen-emissions-guilty-20170804-story.html; accessed October 30, 2017; "US vs. Volkswagen, 16-CR-20394," US Department of Justice, US Attorney's Office, Eastern District of Michigan, July 26, 2017, https://www.justice .gov/usao-edmi/us-v-volkswagen-16-cr-20394, accessed February 11, 2018; "EU Anti-Fraud Office Send Volkswagen Probe Findings to German Prosecutors,"

Reuters, August 1, 2017, https://www.reuters.com/article/us-volkswagen-emissions-eu-fraud/eu-anti-fraud-office-send-volkswagen-probe-findings-to-german-prosecutors-idUSKBN1AH46S, accessed February 11, 2018.

35. See, for example, Patrick Radden Keefe, "The Family That Built an Empire of Pain," *New Yorker*, October 30, 2017, https://www.newyorker.com/magazine/2017/10/30/the-family-that-built-an-empire-of-pain, accessed October 30, 2017.

36. "Raid of Online Firm in Philippines Yields Sex-Trade Data," *Philippine Star*, July 3, 2017, http://www.philstar.com/headlines/2017/07/03/1715829/raid-online-firm-philippines-yields-sex-trade-data, accessed October 30, 2017.

37. Cesare Beccaria, *On Crimes and Punishment*, trans. David Young (Indianapolis: Hackett Publishing, 1986), 14–16.

38. Guiseppe Tomasi di Lampedusa, *The Leopard* (New York: Pantheon, 2007).

39. See, for example, Keefe, "The Family That Built an Empire of Pain."

40. Sean O'Neill, "Accused Oligarch Donated £6m to Cambridge," *Times*, February 25, 2017, https://www.thetimes.co.uk/article/wanted-oligarch-donated-6m-to-cambridge-3dqnpcmzl, accessed November 11, 2017.

41. See the French Pamphlet Collections at the Newberry Library website, http://publications.newberry.org/frenchpamphlets/?tag=louis-mandrin, accessed November 11, 2017.

42. See Ilya Zaslavsky, "How Non-State Actors Export Kleptocratic Norms to the West," Hudson Institute, September 2017, https://s3.amazonaws.com/media.hudson.org/files/publications/Kleptocratic_Norms.pdf, accessed November 11, 2017.

43. "Pimps n Hoes," Playlists.net, http://playlists.net/pimps-n-hoes, accessed October 11, 2017.

44. "10 Most Memorable Pimps in Movies," IFC, http://www.ifc.com/2013/10/10-most-memorable-pimps-in-movies, accessed October 11, 2017.

45. For this point on human trafficking, see Shelley, *Human Trafficking*, 324.

Conclusion: Countering the Challenges Posed by Illicit Trade

1. Such steps have been taken at the level of the UN Security Council; see UN, "Security Council, Adopting Resolution 2195 (2014), Urges International Action."

2. Susan Strange, *Mad Money: When Markets Outgrow Governments* (Ann Arbor: University of Michigan Press, 1998).

3. Peter Baker, "Trump Abandons Trans-Pacific Partnership, Obama's Signature Trade Deal," *New York Times*, January 23, 2017, https://www.nytimes.com/2017/01/23/us/politics/tpp-trump-trade-nafta.html, accessed January 23, 2017.

4. "TPP: What Is It and Why Does It Matter?," *BBC News*, November 22, 2016, http://www.bbc.com/news/business-32498715, accessed January 20, 2017.

5. Cass Sunstein and Richard Thaler, *Nudge: Improving Decisions about Health, Wealth, and Happiness* (New Haven, CT: Yale University Press, 2008).

6. Susan Strange referred to continuing impact of nonstate actors as the *Retreat of the State: Diffusion of Power in the World Economy* (Cambridge: Cambridge University Press, 1996).

7. Jarrett Blaustein, Nathan W. Pino, Kate Fitz-Gibbon, and Rob White, "Criminology and the UN Sustainable Development Goals: The Need for Support and Critique," *British Journal of Criminology*, DOI:10.1093/bjc/azx061.

8. Linnéa Engström, "Laws Are Signals: Europe Could Learn from Sweden on Human Trafficking Prevention," *Euractiv*, May 10, 2016, https://www.euractiv.com/section/social-europe-jobs/opinion/laws-are-signals-europe-could-learn-from-sweden-on-human-trafficking-prevention/, accessed November 21, 2016; "Netherlands—3. Implementation of Anti-Trafficking Policy," European Commission, https://ec.europa.eu/anti-trafficking/member-states/netherlands-3-implementation-anti-trafficking-policy_en, accessed November 21, 2017.

9. Engström, "Laws Are Signals."

10. Foreign Narcotics Kingpin Designation Act, H.R. 3164, 106th Cong., 1st sess., https://www.gpo.gov/fdsys/pkg/BILLS-106hr3164ih/pdf/BILLS-106hr3164ih.pdf, accessed November 4, 2017; Correa-Cabrera, *Los Zetas Inc.*, 15–55.

11. Carlo Morselli, *Inside Criminal Networks* (New York: Springer Science and Business Media, 2009).

12. Van Schendel and Abraham, *Illicit Flows and Criminal Things*.

13. Judge Mark L. Wolf, "The Case for an Anti-Corruption Court," Brookings, July 23, 2014, https://www.brookings.edu/research/the-case-for-an-international-anti-corruption-court/, accessed February 14, 2018.

14. John Picarelli, *Trafficking, Slavery, and Peacekeeping* (Turin: UNICRI, 2002); see also the film *The Whistleblowers* (2011).

15. Peter Andreas and Ethan Nadelmann, *Policing the Globe* (New York: Oxford University Press, 2006); Ethan A. Nadelmann, "Global Prohibition Regimes: The Evolution of Norms in International Society," *International Organization* 44, no. 4 (October 1990): 479–526.

16. Mathew, *Margins of the Market*, 175; Friman and Andreas, *Illicit Global Economy and State Power*.

17. US Department of State, "The Global Illicit Trade in Tobacco."

18. Douglass North, paper for one of the workshops of Joan M. Nelson, Charles Tilly, and Lee Walker, eds., *Transforming Post-Communist Political Economies* (Washington, DC: National Academy Press, 1997).

19. "Public Service Announcements (PSA)," WWF, https://www.worldwildlife.org/pages/public-service-advertisements-psa, accessed November 24, 2017; "Wildlife Crime: Don't Be Part of It! UNODC Launches New Public Service Announcement to Raise Awareness of Criminal Trade in Wildlife Products," UNODC, November 19, 2013, https://www.unodc.org/unodc/en/press/releases/2013/November/unodc-launches-new-public-service-announcement-to-raise-awareness-of-criminal-trade-in-wildlife-products.html, accessed November 24, 2017.

20. EU-OECD High Level Seminar on Countering Illicit Trade, "Countering Illicit Trade."

21. Santiago Díaz-Cediel, Hyomin Pak, and Erwin Prasetyo, "Illicit Trade and the World Trade Organization: Raising Awareness, Identifying Limitations,

and Building Strategies," TradeLab, June 15, 2017, https://tradelab.legal.io /guide/5942ae1fe93c1b021a000f89/Illicit+Trade+and+the+World+Trade +Organizaion+Raising+awareness+identifying+limitations+and+building +strategies.

22. For some of the best, see Peter Kurie, "7 Films to Watch during National Slavery and Human Trafficking Prevention Month," Sundance Institute, January 26, 2016, https://www.sundance.org/blogs/special-edition/7-films-to-watch -during-national-slavery-and-human-trafficking-prevention-month, accessed November 24, 2017.

23. I visited this program in Sicily in 2003.

24. Tim Golden, "Cardinal in Mexico Killed in a Shooting Tied to Drug Battle," *New York Times*, May 25, 1993, http://www.nytimes.com/1993/05/25/world /cardinal-in-mexico-killed-in-a-shooting-tied-to-drug-battle.html, accessed November 24, 2017; Lorenzo Tondo, "Meet the Priests Who Risk Their Lives Defying the Mafia," *Time*, April 19, 2016, http://time.com/4291976/meet-the-priests -who-risk-their-lives-defying-the-mafia/.

25. "Kailash Satyarthi—Facts," NobelPrize.org, https://www.nobelprize.org /nobel_prizes/peace/laureates/2014/satyarthi-facts.html, accessed August 3, 2017; author's discussions with Satyarthi at the World Economic Forum Global Agenda Council in 2012.

26. "Child Labor and Slavery in the Chocolate Industry," Food Empowerment Project, http://www.foodispower.org/slavery-chocolate/, accessed November 24, 2017.

27. Author's conversation with Vijay Mahajan of the BASIX Social Enterprise Group while in residence at Bellagio of the Rockefeller Foundation, October 2016.

28. Yepoka Yeebo, "The African Startup Using Phones to Spot Counterfeit Drugs," *Bloomberg*, July 31, 2015, https://www.bloomberg.com/news/features /2015-07-31/the-african-startup-using-phones-to-spot-counterfeit-drugs. Yeebo discusses the work of Bright Simon, whom I met at World Economic Forum events and with whom I discussed this project.

29. Victoria & Albert Museum, "Inside the Plywood."

30. "Art/Afrique, Le Nouvel Atelier," Fondation Louis Vuitton, April 26–September 4, 2017, http://www.fondationlouisvuitton.fr/en/expositions /art_afrique_le_nouvel_atelier.html. I visited the show in July 2017; the website pictures one of the decorated orange containers. An exhibition at the New Tate had a photo by the artist Taryn Simon of contraband seized at JFK airport; see "Taryn Simon," Tate, http://www.tate.org.uk/art/artists/taryn-simon-11458, accessed November 26, 2017.

31. Jon Henley, Stephanie Kirchgaessner, and Jamie Grierson, "Ten Arrested over Murder of Maltese Journalist Daphne Caruana Galizia," *Guardian*, December 4, 2017, https://www.theguardian.com/world/2017/dec/04/daphne -caruana-galizia-malta-journalist-eight-arrested-murder-inquiry?utm_source= esp&utm_medium=Email&utm_campaign=GU+Today+USA+-+Collections

+2017&utm_term=255186&subid=21762379&CMP=GT_US_collection, accessed February 14, 2018.

32. For updates, see Committee to Protect Journalists, https://cpj.org/data/killed/2017/?status=Killed&motiveConfirmed%5B%5D=Confirmed&type%5B%5D=Journalist&end_year=2017&group_by=location, accessed May 5, 2018.

33. GJIN Staff, "Today's the Day: End Impunity for Crimes against Journalists," Global Investigative Journalism Network, November 2, 2017, https://gijn.org/2017/11/02/todays-the-day-end-impunity-for-crimes-against-journalists/, accessed November 3, 2017.

34. See the ICIJ website at https://www.icij.org/, the GIJN website at https://gijn.org/, and the OCCRP website at https://www.occrp.org/en, all accessed November 3, 2017.

35. "Preventing Illegal Tobacco Sales: Fighting Illicit Trade," PMI, https://www.pmi.com/sustainability/fighting-illicit-cigarette-trade, accessed November 3, 2017; see also PMI Impact, www.pmi-impact.com, accessed February 14, 2018.

36. "Pharmaceutical Security Institute (PSI)," Fight the Fakes, http://fightthefakes.org/partners/psi/, accessed November 2, 2017.

37. "OECD Task Force on Countering Illicit Trade (TF-CIT)," OECD, http://www.oecd.org/gov/risk/oecdtaskforceoncounteringillicittrade.htm, accessed February 14, 2018.

38. "Bristol and Transatlantic Slavery," Port Cities: Bristol, http://www.discoveringbristol.org.uk/slavery/, accessed November 20, 2017. The author visited the cathedral in August 2017.

39. Michele Ford and Lenore Lyons, "Smuggling Cultures in the Indonesia-Singapore Borderlands," in *Transnational Flows and Permissive Polities: Ethnographies of Human Mobilities in Asia*, ed. Barak Kalir and Malini Sur (Amsterdam: Amsterdam University Press, 2012), 91–108.

40. Tagliacozzo, *Secret Trades, Porous Borders.*

41. Andrea Viski and Quentin Michel, "Free Zones and Strategic Trade Controls," *Strategic Trade Review* 3 (Autumn 2016): 27–41.

42. "United States Files Civil Action to Forfeit Thousands of Ancient Iraqi Artifacts Imported by Hobby Lobby," US Department of Justice, US Attorney's Office, Eastern District of New York, July 5, 2017, https://www.justice.gov/usao-edny/pr/united-states-files-civil-action-forfeit-thousands-ancient-iraqi-artifacts-imported, accessed November 24, 2017; Julie Zauzmer and Sarah Pulliam Pailey, "Hobby Lobby's $3 Million Smuggling Case Casts a Cloud over the Museum of the Bible," *Washington Post,* July 6, 2017, https://www.washingtonpost.com/news/acts-of-faith/wp/2017/07/06/hobby-lobbys-3-million-smuggling-case-casts-a-cloud-over-the-museum-of-the-bible/?utm_term=.46f79bfb1083, accessed November 24, 2017.

43. Sunstein and Thaler, *Nudge.*

44. Eric Hand, "Ozone Layer on the Mend, Thanks to Chemical Ban," *Science,* June 30, 2016, http://www.sciencemag.org/news/2016/06/ozone-layer-mend-thanks-chemical-ban, accessed November 21, 2017.

45. Daniel Nepstad, David McGrath, Claudia Stickler, Ane Alencar, Andrea Azevedo, Briana Swette, Tathiana Bezerra, et al., "Slowing Amazon Deforestation through Public Policy and Interventions in Beef and Soy Supply Chains," *Science* 344, no. 6188 (2014): 1118–1123; Nellemann et al., *The Rise of Environmental Crime*, 76.

46. I have followed KPK's work and heard its presentation at Transparency International's International Anti-Corruption Conference (IACC) in Malaysia, September 2–4, 2015; I also met and had discussions with KPK members. See also Sara Schonhardt, "Indonesia Seeks to Resolve Timber-Reporting Issues: Country Potentially Lost as Much as $9 Billion from Companies Underreporting Production," *Wall Street Journal*, February 14, 2016, http://www.wsj.com/articles/indonesia-seeks-to-resolve-timber-reporting-issues-1456325915, accessed November 21, 2017.

47. "Community Development," African Parks, https://www.african-parks .org/our-work/community-development, accessed November 20, 2017; author's interview with the African Parks director in South Africa, May 2016.

48. *Travel and Tourism Economic Impact*, World Travel & Tourism Council, 2017, 1, https://www.wttc.org/-/media/files/reports/economic-impact-research /regions-2017/subsaharanafrica2017.pdf, accessed November 22, 2017.

49. Patrick Love, "A Lesson in Resources Management from Elinor Ostrom," OECD Insights, July 1, 2011, http://oecdinsights.org/2011/07/01/a-lesson-in -resources-management-from-elinor-ostrom/, accessed November 22, 2017.

50. Author's discussion with top NATO official, Washington, DC, September 2017.

51. Author's discussions with Frances Beinecke, retired director of the NRDC, January 2018.

52. "Agreement on Port State Measures to Prevent, Deter, and Eliminate Illegal, Unreported, and Unregulated Fishing," approved November 22, 2009, FAO Conference, 36th sess., http://www.fao.org/fileadmin/user_upload/legal/docs /037t-e.pdf, accessed February 14, 2018.

53. "'Beginning of End for Rogue Fishing,' Says UN Agency as More States Back Landmark Treaty," *UN News*, June 1, 2017, http://www.un.org/apps/news /story.asp?NewsID=56879#.WhV4N2QrLZs, accessed November 22, 2017.

54. "Sustainable Management of External Fishing Fleets," European Parliament, http://www.europarl.europa.eu/legislative-train/theme-fisheries/file -sustainable-management-of-external-fishing-fleets, accessed November 22, 2017.

55. Linnéa Engström, "China Continues to Violate Sustainable Fishing Practices in Africa," *Euractiv*, June 1, 2017, https://www.euractiv.com/section/energy -environment/opinion/china-continues-to-violate-sustainable-fishing-practices -in-africa/, accessed November 22, 2017.

56. Author's discussions with Peter Eigen, chair of the FiTI board, Boston, June 2017; see Fisheries Transparency Initiative, http://fisheriestransparency.org/.

57. "Sustainable Fisheries," NRDC, https://www.nrdc.org/issues/sustainable -fishing, accessed November 22, 2017; author's discussions with the former

long-term director of NRDC while in residence at Bellagio of the Rockefeller Foundation, October 2016.

58. "What We Do," Oceana, http://usa.oceana.org/what-we-do, accessed November 22, 2017; "Protecting Our Oceans," Greenpeace, http://www.greenpeace.org/usa/oceans/, accessed November 22, 2017; "Seafood Watch," Monterey Bay Aquarium, https://www.montereybayaquarium.org/conservation-and-science/our-programs/seafood-watch, accessed November 22, 2017.

59. When I visited the police academy in Hangzhou, China, the corporate headquarters of Alibaba, in 2015, many academy personnel reported on their former coworkers who had gone to work for Alibaba to weed out the illegitimate sales on that platform; see also Cao Li, "Alibaba Faces Growing Pressure over Counterfeit Goods," *New York Times*, December 22, 2016, http://www.nytimes.com/2016/12/22/business/alibaba-ustr-taobao-counterfeit.html, accessed November 24, 2017.

60. Mark Latonero, "Private-Sector Initiatives," University of Southern California, Technology & Human Trafficking Project, https://technologyandtrafficking.usc.edu/private-sector-initiatives/, accessed November 24, 2017.

61. Jonathan Freedland, "From Peppa Pig to Donald Trump, the Web Is Shaping Us. It's Time We Fought Back," *Guardian*, November 17, 2017, https://www.theguardian.com/commentisfree/2017/nov/17/peppa-pig-donald-trump-internet-social-media-algorithms, accessed November 24, 2017.

62. Kelly Sheridan, "A Call for Greater Regulation of Digital Currencies," DarkReading, November 21, 2017, https://www.darkreading.com/vulnerabilities-threats/a-call-for-greater-regulation-of-digital-currencies/d/d-id/1330478, accessed November 21, 2017.

63. "Remarks by the President to the Clinton Global Initiative," The White House, Office of the Press Secretary, September 25, 2012, https://www.whitehouse.gov/the-press-office/2012/09/25/remarks-president-clinton-global-initiative, accessed November 24, 2017.

64. Mark Latonero, "How Mobile Communication Helps Refugees . . . and Smugglers" (interview with Mark Latonero), *CBC Radio*, January 31, 2016, https://datasociety.net/output/how-mobile-communication-helps-refugees-and-smugglers/, accessed November 22, 2017.

65. Nicole Fisher, "Human Trafficking Is in Plain Sight. Are You Supporting It without Knowing," *Forbes*, April 24, 2017, https://www.forbes.com/sites/nicolefisher/2017/04/24/human-trafficking-in-plain-sight/2/#4df241d67c92, accessed November 24, 2017.

66. "About TraffickCam," TraffickCam, https://traffickcam.com/about, accessed November 24, 2017.

67. LaborVoices, https://www.laborvoices.com/, accessed November 24, 2017.

68. Global Fishing Watch, http://globalfishingwatch.org/, accessed November 22, 2017.

69. Kate Shepperd, "Check out Google's New Tool for Monitoring Global Fishing," *Huffington Post*, June 5, 2015, https://www.huffingtonpost.com/2015

/06/05/google-global-fishing-tool_n_7519440.html, accessed November 24, 2017.

70. "Timber Traceability and Legality," SGS SA, http://www.sgs.com/en/public-sector/monitoring-services/timber-traceability-and-legality, accessed November 24, 2017.

71. Alan Bersin, "Lines, Flows, and Transnational Crime: Toward a Revised Approach to Countering the Underworld of Globalization," George Mason University, TraCCC, February 6, 2018, http://traccc.gmu.edu/events/events-2014-2017/, accessed February 15, 2018.

72. "US Financial Coalition Against Child Pornography," International Centre for Missing & Exploited Children (ICMEC), https://www.icmec.org/fcacp/, accessed November 24, 2017.

73. Eric Olson and Jonathan Tomek, "Cryptocurrency and the BlockChain: Technical Overview and Potential Impact on Commercial Child Sexual Exploitation," report prepared for the FCACP and ICMEC, May 2017, https://www.icmec.org/wp-content/uploads/2017/05/ICMEC-FCACPCryptocurrencyPaperFINAL517.pdf, accessed November 24, 2017.

74. European Financial Coalition against Commercial Sexual Exploitation of Children Online, http://www.europeanfinancialcoalition.eu/, accessed November 24, 2017.

75. Thorn, https://www.wearethorn.org/deterrence-prevent-child-sexual-abuse-imagery/, accessed February 14, 2018; "Who We Are," Thorn, https://www.wearethorn.org/about-our-fight-against-sexual-exploitation-of-children/.

76. Christina Bain and Louise Shelley, "Hedging Risk by Combating Human Trafficking," World Economic Forum, February 18, 2015, https://www.weforum.org/reports/hedging-risk-combating-human-trafficking-insights-private-sector, accessed November 24, 2017.

77. Author's interview with a banking official who led Super Bowl–related data-mining efforts in Minneapolis in February 2018.

78. Latonero, "Private-Sector Initiatives."

79. "California Transparency in Supply Chains Act," California Department of Justice, Office of the Attorney General, https://oag.ca.gov/SB657, accessed November 24, 2017.

80. "Moroccan Authorities Sentence Two in Zotob Computer Worm Attack," FBI, September 13, 2006, https://archives.fbi.gov/archives/news/pressrel/press-releases/moroccan-authorities-sentence-two-in-zotob-computer-worm-attack, accessed November 24, 2016.

81. "Avalanche Malware Network Hit with Law Enforcement Takedown," Symantec Security Response, December 1, 2016, https://www.symantec.com/connect/blogs/avalanche-malware-network-hit-law-enforcement-takedown, accessed November 24, 2017.

82. Jide Idowu, "FarmaTrust Review: Facing out Fake Drugs with Blockchain Technology," Use The Bitcoin (UTB), February 16, 2018, https://usethebitcoin.com/farmatrust-review-facing-fake-drugs-blockchain-technology/, accessed February 23, 2018.

83. Harish Natarjan et al., "Distributed Ledger Technology (DLT) and Blockchain," Fin Tech Note 1, International Bank for Reconstruction and Development/World Bank, 2017, ix, http://documents.worldbank.org /curated/en/177911513714062215/pdf/122140-WP-PUBLIC-Distributed-Ledger -Technology-and-Blockchain-Fintech-Notes.pdf, accessed February 24, 2018.

84. Author's private correspondence with Solvej Krause; Everledger, https:// www.everledger.io/; Jeff John Roberts, "The Diamond Industry Is Obsessed with Blockchain," *Fortune*, September 12, 2017, http://fortune.com/2017/09/12 /diamond-blockchain-everledger/, accessed February 23, 2018.

85. Natarjan et al., "Distributed Ledger Technology (DLT) and Blockchain."

86. I thank John Sellar, initial head of CITES enforcement, for this insight; personal correspondence, late 2017.

87. Joseph Spanjers and Matthew Salomon, "Illicit Financial Flows to and from Developing Countries: 2005–2014," Global Financial Integrity, May 1, 2017, http://www.gfintegrity.org/report/illicit-financial-flows-to-and-from -developing-countries-2005-2014/.

88. ICIJ, "Offshore Leaks Database," https://offshoreleaks.icij.org/, accessed May 16, 2018.

89. The Panama Papers exposed the major Guatemalan drug trafficker and money launderer Marllory Chacón Rossell; see Michael Lohmuller, "Panama Papers Reveal Offshore Account of Guatemala Drug 'Queen,'" InSight Crime, April 5, 2016, https://www.insightcrime.org/news/brief/panama-papers-reveal -offshore-account-guatemala-drug-queen/, accessed November 25, 2017.

90. Bracking, *The Financialisation of Power*, 111–113; Cassara, *Trade-Based Money Laundering*, 13–31, 111–124.

91. Louise Shelley, "Money Laundering into Real Estate," in Miklaucic and Brewer, *Convergence*, 131–146.

92. Boris Kachka, "Annie Proulx Gave One of the Best National Book Award Speeches in Recent Memory," Vulture, November 16, 2017, http://www.vulture .com/2017/11/annie-proulx-national-book-award-speech.html, accessed November 25, 2017.

93. John Evans, "There Are No Jobs on a Dead Planet," *OECD Observer*, no. 304, November 2015, http://www.oecdobserver.org/news/fullstory.php/aid /5294/There_are_no_jobs_on_a_dead_planet.html, accessed November 26, 2017.

INDEX

abalone trafficking, 73, 98, 196
access to capital, 121, 124–25
advertisements, 2, 67–68, 100, 157, 162, 176, 243
advertising strategies, 117, 119, 120, 128, 132, 163
Afghanistan, 46, 47, 55, 76, 137, 152, 154, 211, 215
Africa, 31, 39–40, 43–45, 53–54, 55, 65, 72, 135, 190–91, 238–39; conflict diamonds in, 82, 124–25; counterfeit medicine in, 172–73, 233; deforestation in, 191, 193. *See also* elephant tusk trafficking; rhino horn trafficking; *and individual countries*
African Parks, 238–39
Ahmed, Yakub, 185–86
Algeria, 133, 165–67
Alibaba, 241, 346n59
Al-Nusra Front. *See* terrorist groups
AlphaBay Market, 67, 70, 146, 290n32, 291n48
Al-Qaeda. *See* terrorist groups
Al-Shabaab. *See* terrorist groups
Amazon.com, 8, 117, 129, 136–37, 147, 241
American Revolution, 28–29, 37, 46, 213
American Samoa, 74
Andreas, Peter, 28, 35, 48–49
Angola, 54, 82, 173
anonymity and anonomizing, 2–4, 17, 68–69, 88, 113, 126, 133, 157, 162, 197, 205, 227, 242–43, 245
antiquities trade, 9, 10, 35, 38, 40, 77–78, 84–85, 107, 219, 224; Civil War relics, 140; Hobby Lobby and, 236; UNESCO Convention on, 40
Apple, 126, 162, 247
apps, 243, 246
Arabian Peninsula, 19, 21, 134
Arab Spring, 6, 62–64, 208, 213
Archimedes, 20
Argentina, 29–30, 189

Aristotle, 21, 41
Armenians, 133
arms trafficking, 38, 50–51, 52, 79–80, 141, 153; nuclear weapons (WMD) components, 53, 67, 75, 140, 164, 202, 235, 236–37; 3-D printing and, 220
art trafficking, 53, 267n55
Assad, Bashar al-, 62–64, 214
Assad, Hafez al-, 62–63
Assyria, 34
asymmetric advantage, 123, 162, 206, 242
asymmetric threat, 71, 78, 147
Audubon Society, 50
Australia, 80, 112, 134, 155, 169, 179, 217; Sydney, 180
Austria, 49, 155, 194, 197, 218
Avalanche case, 112–13, 118–19, 122, 126, 132, 246, 248
Azerbaijan, 117, 133

Babinets, Anna, 194
Bach brothers, 102, 106
Backpage, 127–29, 163, 176, 216–17
Balkans, 10, 39, 76, 80, 118, 123–24, 154, 158–60, 213–14, 228
Bangladesh, 35, 65, 126, 139, 171
banks and bankers, 3, 7, 10, 23, 71, 117, 119–22, 143–46, 149, 151, 156, 165, 180–81, 185, 193, 210, 217, 220, 244, 249
bear bile, 196
Beccaria, Cesare, 217
Beddoes, Matthew, 186
Bedouins, 22, 133
Belaúnde Terry, Fernando, 55
Belgium, 80, 137, 169, 199, 215
beneficial ownership, 144, 248
biodiversity hotspots and armed conflict, 5–6, 54–55, 81, 282n117
Bitcoin. *See* cryptocurrencies
black markets, 10, 52, 56, 74
Black Sea, 10

A NOTE ON THE TYPE

This book has been composed in Adobe Text and Gotham.
Adobe Text, designed by Robert Slimbach for Adobe,
bridges the gap between fifteenth- and sixteenth-century
calligraphic and eighteenth-century Modern styles.
Gotham, inspired by New York street signs, was designed
by Tobias Frere-Jones for Hoefler & Co.